Mary's Bodily Assumption

Mary's Bodily Assumption

MATTHEW LEVERING

UNIVERSITY OF NOTRE DAME PRESS
NOTRE DAME, INDIANA

University of Notre Dame Press
Notre Dame, Indiana 46556
undpress.nd.edu
All Rights Reserved

Published in the United States of America

Library of Congress Cataloging-in-Publication Data

Levering, Matthew, 1971–
Mary's bodily Assumption / Matthew Levering.
pages   cm
Includes bibliographical references and index.
ISBN 978-0-268-03390-3 (pbk. : alk. paper) —
ISBN 0-268-03390-0 (pbk. : alk. paper)
1. Mary, Blessed Virgin, Saint—Assumption.
2. Catholic church—Doctrines.   I. Title.
BT630.L48   2014
232.91'4—dc23
2014033014

Contents

Acknowledgments

This book had its origin in a book review by Michael Allen of my *Christ and the Catholic Priesthood*. Michael gave a sympathetic survey of my arguments in that book, but he pointed out that in my defense of hierarchical order in the Church, I had not accounted for such things as the Marian dogmas. The challenge he gave me was to explain how the Catholic Church can teach dogmatically that Mary was assumed body and soul into heaven. Whether or not I have succeeded in the present book, I owe a large debt to Michael for his generous ecumenical question.

Jörgen Vijgen, on whose key eye and friendship I have relied for many years, read an early version of this manuscript and offered numerous helpful corrections, as did Sean Fagan, who brought to bear his Lutheran and Orthodox theological training. Hans Boersma read an early draft and, without being persuaded by the arguments, was both encouraging and critical in ways that improved the manuscript. Andrew Hofer, O.P., prompted me to add chapter 6 and to rewrite the introduction, among other crucial contributions. This book could not have gone forward without Fr. Hofer's generous help. Matthew Olver, an Episcopalian priest who is now undertaking a doctorate at Marquette University, provided me with a lengthy and rich set of corrections and suggestions. I fear to think how much poorer this book would have been without his careful work. He and I first spoke about this topic (and this manuscript) at a meeting of the Wilken Colloquium at Baylor University, and I am grateful to Thomas Hibbs for hosting the Wilken Colloquium and thereby making such conversations possible. Thanks also to three superb doctoral students: Elizabeth Farnsworth for preparing the bibliography and Alan Mostrom and Jason Heron for assisting me in obtaining articles.

Chuck Van Hof shepherded this manuscript through the University of Notre Dame Press. I thank him for his friendship and encouragement. The two readers for the Press offered very helpful suggestions; one remained anonymous and the other was John Betz. With gratitude, let me observe that John is a theologian who cares about the souls of his students and colleagues, and this book benefited from his spiritual sensitivity. During the copyediting phase, Elizabeth Sain improved the manuscript in a large number of ways, for which I am thankful.

Part of chapter 3 appeared as "Mary in the Theology of Joseph Ratzinger/Pope Benedict XVI," in *Explorations in the Theology of Benedict XVI*, edited by John C. Cavadini (Notre Dame: University of Notre Dame Press, 2012): 276–97. I gratefully acknowledge John Cavadini's invitation to speak at a conference of the same name. His friendship is one of the real fruits of this book. Part of chapter 4 appeared as "Readings on the Rock: Typological Exegesis in Contemporary Scholarship," *Modern Theology* 28 (2012): 707–31. An excerpt from this chapter was originally delivered at a conference at Regent College co-organized by Hans Boersma and me, and funded by a grant from the Association of Theological Schools. One of the conference attendees was Jim Fodor, and he graciously helped to get my article and other conference papers published in a special issue of *Modern Theology* that Hans and I coedited.

Further debts during the period of this manuscript's preparation are too numerous to name, but let me at least acknowledge the friendship and encouragement given to me during this period by, among others, Lewis Ayres, Todd Billings, Michael Carter, Romanus Cessario, O.P., Reinhard Hütter, Guy Mansini, O.S.B., Bruce Marshall, David Meconi, S.J., Francesca Murphy, François Rossier, S.M., Michele Schumacher, Jared Staudt, Michael Vanderburgh, Thomas Joseph White, O.P., and Bill Wright.

Right before this book was accepted for publication by the University of Notre Dame Press, I received a job offer from Fr. Robert Barron, rector of Mundelein Seminary and an extraordinary evangelist, scholar, and friend. I owe the privilege of working at Mundelein Seminary also to Francis Cardinal George and to Jim and Molly Perry. Many thanks, too, to Fr. Thomas Baima, academic dean of the seminary, and to Melanie Barrett, Fr. Emery de Gaál, Denis McNamara, the late (and greatly missed) Edward Oakes, S.J., and numerous other faculty and staff who welcomed me and my family so generously.

My wife and dearest friend, Joy Levering, is the center and star of our family. Her strong and mature faith, hard work, and love of our children and her friends are extraordinary. Thank you, dearly beloved Joy!

I dedicate this book to Hans and Gerald Boersma. Beginning in 2009, Hans and I have undertaken a number of joint projects whose main purpose is Catholic-Evangelical dialogue. Hans has been a wonderful friend, and I was able to teach Gerald during his master's degree, prior to his PhD under Lewis Ayres. Gerald is now established as a professor of theology and inspires all who meet him with the joy that he, like Hans, takes in being a Christian theologian.

Introduction

Since the seventh and eighth centuries A.D., when belief in Mary's Assumption took firm root in the Eastern and Western churches, Catholic and Orthodox Christians have borne witness to the reality that Mary, the mother of Jesus, was assumed body and soul into heaven after her death.[1] According to Catholic and Orthodox faith, Mary's body did not corrupt in the grave but was assumed into heaven, which explains why the Church never possessed relics of Mary's body. Beginning in the fifth century with such works as Jacob of Serug's *Homily on the Dormition*— and earlier still with the *Liber Requiei*, a Gnostic Christian narrative— legends existed about the miraculous transition of Mary's body to heaven. Although liturgical celebrations of Mary's Assumption employed imagery taken from these legends, however, the Church's faith in Mary's Assumption is not based on the legends. Rather, the Church's faith generated the legends, which were always a secondary element in the Church's meditation upon the Mother of God under the guidance of the Holy Spirit.[2] Thus, as René Laurentin explains, "the Assumption is not the object of a *historical* tradition of *apostolic origin,* but of a dogmatic explicitation rooted in reflection on the whole of revelation."[3] This point is also made in Pope Pius XII's *Munificentissimus Deus* (1950), which defined Mary's Assumption as a dogma of faith. Rather than being manifested publicly in a manner accessible to historians, Mary's

Assumption was an event whose historical reality the Holy Spirit taught the Church over time.[4]

For this reason, the testimony proper to Mary's Assumption is to be found *in Scripture* and no new public testimony is required. Metropolitan Kallistos Ware has rightly observed that Mary's Assumption "is not to be regarded as a further truth added to the truths already found in Scripture. Rather, it is the fruit of the assimilation of those Scriptural truths under the inspiration of the Holy Spirit."[5] In this process of assimilation, once Mary was proclaimed "Theotokos" at the Council of Ephesus in 431, the doctrine of Mary's bodily Assumption soon entered into Christian consciousness.[6]

Today, faith in Mary's Assumption rests upon three scriptural pillars: the role of typological reasoning in the New Testament's portrait of the mother of Jesus Christ and in our understanding of her mission; the Church's authority as interpreter of divine revelation under the guidance of the Holy Spirit; and the fittingness of the Assumption of Mary within God's carefully orchestrated plan for salvation.[7] Rather than focusing on the historical development of the doctrine, the present book examines each of these pillars of the doctrine of Mary's Assumption.[8] My goal is to set forth the rationale for belief in Mary's Assumption, with a particular eye to those who do not understand how contemporary Christians could believe such a thing. As a work of systematic and ecumenical theology, this study contributes to a discussion that has somewhat lapsed in recent years; the last book published in English on Mary's Assumption appeared over thirty years ago.[9] During this same time period, however, Protestant (and especially Evangelical) interest in Mary has increased significantly, and so I am hoping that the time is ripe for an introductory book such as this one. Many Catholics today also do not understand the rationale for this doctrine.

I have structured the book in two parts of three chapters each. The first, historical part introduces the vibrant twentieth-century Catholic discussions of Mary's Assumption, as found respectively in the Church's Magisterial teaching, neoscholastic theology, and the *nouvelle théologie*. These three chapters are largely expository, although I indicate what I consider to be the more fruitful approaches. The writings examined in these chapters provide a helpful introduction to the patristic, medieval, neoscholastic, and twentieth-century background of the doctrine of

Mary's Assumption. Most importantly, this first part displays the three pillars at work: as we will see, neoscholastic theology and preconciliar Magisterial teaching tend to emphasize the authority of the Church and doctrinal fittingness (although biblical typology is certainly present as well), whereas the *nouvelle théologie* and postconciliar Magisterial teaching tend to emphasize biblical typology, indeed sometimes to the neglect of the other two pillars.[10] The second, constructive part investigates and defends each of the three pillars of the doctrine of Mary's Assumption. In this second part, each chapter begins with a consideration of Blessed John Henry Newman's teaching on Mary, both because of his appreciation for the three pillars and because belief in Mary's Assumption involves what Newman calls "converging" or "accumulated" probabilities.[11] I hope to show that when taken together, the three pillars provide sound scriptural and theological foundations for Christian belief in Mary's Assumption.

I should note at the outset that although this book is about Mary's Assumption, the book also discusses other Marian doctrines in passing, such as Mary's Immaculate Conception, perpetual virginity, and sinlessness, as well as Marian titles such as Co-Redemptrix. The theological writings and Church documents that I survey in the first three chapters speak of these topics, and so they inevitably make their way into my book. But rather than entering into the debate about each of the Marian doctrines, I focus on articulating the rationale for Mary's Assumption, both because it is one of the most controversial Marian doctrines (especially in Protestant-Catholic dialogue) and because I wish to understand it better myself.

Catholics, Orthodox, and Mary's Assumption

The proclamation of Mary's Assumption came first from the East. Indeed, Brian Daley points out that the "major elements of classical Catholic Mariology are all, in their liturgical celebration and central role in the religious consciousness of the Christian community, originally Eastern, rather than Western themes."[12] Admittedly, Catholics and Orthodox disagree about whether Mary's Assumption should be considered a dogma. For the Orthodox, only those doctrines defined by the first seven ecumenical councils count as dogma. Regarding public preaching (as opposed to inner Tradition), the Orthodox hold only one Marian doctrine—namely, that Mary is *Theotokos*, God-bearer. The further doctrines about Mary are known and proclaimed indirectly, largely through the liturgy and iconography. This does not mean that these Marian doctrines are less true. As Metropolitan Kallistos observes, it means simply that Mary's Assumption "is accessible only to 'those who are within.'"[13] Summarizing the Orthodox Church's theology of Mary, Metropolitan Kallistos teaches with faith's certitude that after Mary's "death she was assumed into heaven, where she now dwells—with her body as well as her soul—in eternal glory with her Son."[14]

Catholics and Orthodox agree that the reasoning on which the doctrine of Mary's Assumption relies is best learned within the Church, not least through the liturgy and iconography.[15] But in the Catholic view, it is also appropriate that the truth of the Assumption of the Mother of God receive the status of dogma in the Church. The dogmatic status of Mary's Assumption illumines the salvation wrought by the new Adam, Mary's Son. Nikos Nissiotis, who as an Orthodox theologian holds that Mary's Assumption is a truth of faith but not a dogma, explains why study of Christ's saving work should include reflection on Mary: "Reference to Mary makes theology take seriously into consideration the biblical and kerygmatic witness of the Church regarding the interpenetration of the divine and human elements in full reciprocity and unbroken cobelongingness."[16] The dogma of Mary's Assumption affirms the marvelous extent to which God invites and enables the cooperation of human persons in the history of salvation.

Avery Dulles points out that Pope Pius XII defined the dogma "in an atmosphere of great Marian enthusiasm and magisterial self-confidence."[17] Since the Church had for centuries proclaimed the truth of Mary's Assumption, the influence of this atmosphere on the proclamation of this truth's dogmatic status should not be exaggerated. Whatever the prevailing atmosphere in 1950, the Church had already liturgically celebrated and taught Mary's Assumption for more than a millennium. As Bernard Lonergan stated two years before the dogmatic definition, "Were the Assumption not truth but error, then one would have to admit what no Catholic can admit, namely, that God has not promised preservation from error to the Church."[18] Yet the "great Marian enthusiasm" waned quickly after 1950. Less than twenty years later, Joseph Ratzinger commented: "Since that day in 1950 a great deal has changed, and the dogma that caused such exultation then is rather a hindrance now. . . . We instinctively ask whether it is not really nonsensical, foolish, and a provocation to claim that a human being can be taken bodily into heaven."[19] For many Europeans of the late twentieth century (though certainly not for Ratzinger), a secular worldview seemed the only reasonable position.

In his fall 1997 McGinley Lecture, Dulles underscored that the Church's Marian "teaching, constructed laboriously over long centuries, belongs inalienably to the patrimony of the Church and can scarcely be contested from within the Catholic tradition."[20] Even so, some contemporary Catholic theologians have called for the abandonment of the doctrine of Mary's Assumption, while others have tried to reinterpret it so as to remove Mary's uniqueness. In 1996, for example, the Assumptionist priest George Tavard published "a sober assessment of the situation in which the Christian world has been thrown by the solemn proclamation of these doctrines [Mary's Immaculate Conception and Assumption] in the context of the papal infallibility that was defined at Vatican I."[21] Tavard reached the conclusion that "the ethereal figure of a woman elevated to heaven," as imagined "in the Orthodox and Catholic traditions," has been an unfortunate and false illusion, quite far from "the modest and discreet Mary of the New Testament."[22]

Protestantism and Mary's Assumption

Catholic criticisms such as Tavard's provide an ecumenical opportunity for the theology of Mary's Assumption.[23] As is well known, strong objections to the doctrine of Mary's Assumption have been advanced by Protestant theologians since the Reformation. These objections first and foremost reflect the concern that neither Mary's Assumption nor certain other Marian doctrines are supported by Scripture's explicit teaching. The argument that the New Testament treats Mary typologically, thus justifying the Church's liturgical/typological conclusions about Mary, has not persuaded many Protestants.[24] In addition, Protestant objections to the doctrine of Mary's Assumption also have roots in the doctrine of justification. Thus Karl Barth argues that Mary's Assumption and other Marian doctrines disclose "the one heresy of the Roman Catholic Church which explains all the rest. The 'mother of God' of Roman Catholic Marian dogma is quite simply the principle, type and essence of the human creature co-operating servantlike (*ministerialiter*) in its own redemption on the basis of prevenient grace, and to that extent the principle, type and essence of the Church."[25] Furthermore, even if one were to grant that redemption involved such cooperation, there still would seem to be no need for Marian dogma, since Christ alone is the Redeemer. In Barth's view, therefore, "the more this strangely contrived and decorated figure became the object of 'dulia' or 'hyperdulia' . . . and the more the teaching office of the Church, as in 1854 and 1950, could appeal to the 'consensus of the Church' as a form of divine revelation, the more complicated, unnatural, and difficult it became for theologians to make the best of it."[26] This appears to be Tavard's position as well.

Catholic theologians, however, have generally thought that much more can be said for the doctrine of Mary's Assumption than either Tavard or Barth think possible. To see why this is so, it may be helpful to consider the biblical scholar Scot McKnight's recent *The Real Mary: Why Evangelical Christians Can Embrace the Mother of Jesus*, which rejects most Marian doctrines but urges evangelicals to pay more attention to Mary. With regard to Mary, McKnight expresses the difference between Protestant and Catholic believers quite starkly: "No Roman Catholic is bothered by the routine Protestant accusation that what they believe about Mary can't be found in the New Testament. They already know that, and it doesn't faze them."[27] For McKnight, the key question is therefore inevitably the role of Tradition, because "Protestants limit their theology as much as possible to the Bible," whereas "Roman Catholics anchor their beliefs in both the Bible and the ongoing, developing sacred Tradition."[28]

From the Catholic (and Orthodox) perspective, however, to speak of Tradition is to acknowledge that Scripture has been written and handed down in the Church alongside its legitimate interpretation and in the whole context of the apostolic teaching.[29] As Ratzinger says, "There is a priority of scriptures as witness and a priority of the Church as the vital environment for such witness, but both are linked together in constantly alternating relationships, so that neither can be imagined without the other."[30] Furthermore, the biblical witness involves not only historical expressions of the kind that modern historians can recognize, but also typological reasoning that conveys historical realities. The doctrine of Mary's Assumption is anchored in the New Testament's typological portraits of Mary—portraits that become especially apparent as the Church, charged with the task of interpreting divine revelation, proclaims Scripture in the liturgy. The key questions, then, have to do not so much with Tradition per se but rather with the ways in which the Bible can be legitimately interpreted, what counts as biblical evidence, and the role of the Holy Spirit in the Church. As Ratzinger puts it: "How is scripture recognised in the Church? Who decides whether what you say is in accord with scripture or not?"[31]

McKnight is aware of some of the typological arguments that bolster Catholic and Orthodox Marian doctrine, but he treats them summarily. For example, he explains the traditional Catholic interpretation of Genesis 3:15 as follows: "As Eve disobeyed, so Mary obeyed. As Eve's sin led to the unmaking of others, so Mary's choice not to sin led to the remaking of others. Accordingly, as Adam disobeyed, so Jesus obeyed. Thus: if there is a Second Adam (Christ), there is also a Second Eve (Mary)."[32] Regarding this Catholic interpretation, he comments only that some evangelicals find it to be "tantamount to blasphemy, for it virtually places Mary alongside Jesus in the redemptive work of God."[33] This seems to be his own concern as well, even if he does not press the blasphemy charge. But his presentation of Mary as the second Eve solely in her obedient fiat does not adequately describe the Catholic position—even though his concerns that Mary enters too closely into Christ's redemptive work might not be assuaged by a more adequate description. For Catholics (and Orthodox), as I will explain further in the chapters that follow, Mary is the new Eve and Daughter Zion (Israel/Church) who is now fittingly united with her Son in his Resurrection, just as she was united with him in the mysteries of his Incarnation and Cross by which he conquered "that ancient serpent, who is called the Devil and Satan, the deceiver of the whole world" (Rev 12:9).[34] By intimately associating himself with a mere creature (Mary), Jesus Christ—the sole Redeemer and Mediator—reveals how tightly he has chosen to unite himself to his elect people.[35]

When McKnight turns to the dogma of the bodily Assumption of Mary, he explains it simply as a logical deduction from the doctrine of the Immaculate Conception. The consequence of sin is death, and Mary was sinless; therefore, "[i]nstead of dying and decaying as other humans, Mary 'died' in the presence of others, yet when they checked on her tomb she was gone."[36] This story of Mary's empty tomb is taken by McKnight from a homily by John of Damascus, which includes legendary elements. The implication is that Catholic and Orthodox theology of Mary's Assumption is simply a mixture of logical deduction (from Mary's sinlessness) and mere legend.[37] McKnight adds that in Genesis and 2 Kings, the Bible suggests that Enoch and Elijah were in some sense "assumed" into heaven. Jesus, too, is taken up into heaven (Acts 1:9). It follows that, as McKnight says, "Such things can happen."[38] Did it happen to Mary? McKnight concludes: "As Protestants we go to the Bible first, but we find nothing about Mary's death or her assumption in the Bible. Does that mean Mary wasn't 'assumed' into heaven? Obviously not. None of us believes that everything was recorded in the Bible, so we are left to examine the evidence and make up our own minds."[39]

The evidence that McKnight might consider, however, can only become apparent if one allows for the New Testament's typological portraits of Mary and for the Holy Spirit's guidance of the Church. Paul Griffiths defines typology as follows: "One event or utterance figures another when, while remaining unalterably what it is, it announces or communicates something other than itself. . . . The second event—the figured—encompasses and includes the first, without removing its reality. The first—the figuring—has its reality, however, by way of participation in the second."[40] Griffiths gives the example of Eve's disobedience and Mary's obedience. Regarding the New Testament's typological portraits of Mary, Trent Pomplun remarks, "Matthew and Luke make it crystal clear that the early Church saw Mary as the typological fulfillment of earlier prophecies."[41] Indeed, as I will argue, typological reasoning suggests the truth of Mary's Assumption, and this truth has received liturgical and doctrinal confirmation from the Church as authoritative interpreter of revelation under the guidance of the Spirit.

Admittedly, the presence of specific typologies in the New Testament's portraits of Mary will always be a matter of debate, in part because seeing the typologies (with the eyes of faith) is aided by anticipating their presence. This is, I think, what Metropolitan Kallistos means by stating, "The mystery of the Mother of God is *par excellence* a liturgical mystery."[42] I should observe that a number of Protestant theologians are aware that Catholics (and Orthodox) consider the doctrine of Mary's Assumption to be biblically rooted. The Reformed theologian Hans Boersma speaks for such Protestant scholars when he states, "In discussing Mariology, we need to remember (1) that Catholics accept the evangelical point that all doctrine is a matter of biblical interpretation, and (2) that evangelicals (at least those like [Kevin] Vanhoozer and me) accept the Catholic point that all doctrine is a matter of development."[43] Boersma recognizes that Catholics ground the doctrine of Mary's Assumption in Scripture's typological portraits of Mary. As he states, "This means that our disagreements on Marian teaching are disagreements on what constitutes the correct interpretation of Scripture."[44]

Boersma nonetheless considers that Marian doctrines such as that of Mary's Assumption are not "legitimate expositions of the christological anchor."[45] Since Christ Jesus is our Redeemer, Boersma does not see why Christians need to believe, or to make a big deal out of, the Assumption of Mary. In the chapters that follow, therefore, I explore why Catholics consider the Assumption of Mary to be biblically legitimate, true, and important.

The Plan of the Work

Let me review in more detail the structure of the book. Chapter 1 surveys the key twentieth-century Magisterial documents that treat Mary's Assumption, including Pope Pius XII's *Munificentissimus Deus*, the Second Vatican Council's *Lumen Gentium*, and Pope John Paul II's encyclical *Redemptoris Mater*. We will find that the Church's authority as interpreter of revelation and the speculative unity of the truths of faith are most emphasized in *Munificentissimus Deus*, and that biblical typology is most emphasized in *Lumen Gentium* and *Redemptoris Mater*. Yet all three elements are present in each of the documents, and together they will help us to understand the basis on which the Church has taught

Mary's bodily Assumption. Chapter 2 treats the period leading up to the definition of the dogma in 1950, with a particular focus on the work of Réginald Garrigou-Lagrange. This period was marked by extensive historical research into the development of the doctrine of Mary's Assumption, and it was also shaped by theological argumentation that highlighted the unity of the truths of faith and that proposed theological demonstrations of the truth of Mary's Assumption. The role of biblical typology appears most fully in the work of the *nouvelle théologie* (from the 1940s to the present), and so chapter 3 examines the Marian teaching of Karl Rahner, Hans Urs von Balthasar, Louis Bouyer, and Joseph Ratzinger (Pope Benedict XVI). In this chapter, eschatology is also a significant theme, since Rahner and Balthasar suggest that Mary's Assumption may simply exemplify what happens to all of us when we die.

Chapter 4 examines biblical typology and inquires into how this mode of biblical exegesis works. My interlocutors in this chapter are three Protestant scholars: the New Testament scholar Richard B. Hays, the Old Testament scholar Peter Enns, and the theologian Peter Leithart. These scholars would not accept the doctrine of Mary's Assumption, but they all—to different degrees and in different ways—defend the value of typological reasoning both in Scripture itself *and* for the Church today. My conclusion is that, on biblical grounds, typological reasoning remains a viable option for the Church's doctrinal development, rooted in the typologies of Scripture. Chapter 5 engages the authority of the Church as interpreter of divine revelation, with attention to papal infallibility in the context of the Church's infallibility under the guidance of the Holy Spirit.[46] I argue on the basis of Scripture that the Church, gathered in Eucharistic worship, is sustained by the Holy Spirit in the faithful interpretation of divine revelation. Chapter 6 explores how Mary's Assumption fits with and sheds important light upon other doctrines of Christian faith, specifically the mysteries of creation and fall, the election of Israel, and the Incarnation of the Word. What is at stake here is the role of the "analogy of faith" in perceiving the unity and fullness of God's plan of salvation.

In this book, admittedly introductory though it is, I hope to contribute to a renewed appreciation for the biblically rooted truth and significance of Mary's Assumption. The basic insight has been well put by Adrienne von Speyr:

Adam and Eve form a pair, but Eve comes after Adam. Yet she is of equal birth to him, and she commits sin together with him. Christ and Mary also form a pair; but Mary comes to the world before her Son. She is not of equal birth to him, insofar as he is God from eternity, nor does she think in terms of equality, but rather of service. When, however, the Son elevates her so that despite everything they form a pair in the same way that Christ as Bridegroom and the Church as bride form a pair, the Mother lets this happen in the knowledge that everything he does is done well.[47]

This is the mystery of Mary: the Father, Son, and Holy Spirit, in choosing to save humankind by healing us and elevating us into the Trinitarian life through the Son, Jesus Christ, in the unity of the Holy Spirit, drew a mere creature—Mary—into this saving plan to be Christ's mother. The intimacy between Christ and his bride the Church is therefore already embodied in Mary. The new Adam is the sole Savior, but he does not thereby lack the cooperation of the new Eve, whether at the Incarnation, at the Cross, or at the right hand of the Father. Mary's Assumption means that we can say of Mary: "My soul magnifies the Lord, and my spirit rejoices in God my Savior, for he has regarded the low estate of his handmaiden. For behold, henceforth all generations will call me blessed; for he who is mighty has done great things for me, and holy is his name" (Lk 1:46–49). In the Assumption of Mary, God has indeed "exalted those of low degree" (Lk 1:52).[48]

PART I

Twentieth-Century Magisterial Teaching on Mary and Her Assumption

In part due to the dogmatic definition of Mary's Immaculate Conception in 1854, the early decades of the twentieth century witnessed a widespread popular movement in Catholicism to define Mary's Assumption as a dogma of faith. When Pope Pius XII did this in 1950, he did so using the fruits of historical research combined with neoscholastic theological arguments. Historical and dogmatic studies of Mary's Assumption proliferated in the two decades before the definition. These studies generally agreed that the Church's reasoning need not rest upon a quest for historical evidence from the earliest centuries in favor of the doctrine's truth. Certainly, in order to be dogmatically defined, the doctrine of Mary's Assumption must belong to Christ Jesus' communication of the "deposit of faith" to the apostles. Yet the doctrine of Mary's Assumption could be implicitly rather than explicitly present in this apostolic deposit (Scripture and the early witnesses to Tradition). Furthermore, almost all Catholic theologians considered the consistent affirmation of this doctrine by the ordinary magisterium of the Church since the late patristic period to provide secure evidence that the Assumption of Mary belongs to the faith that Jesus Christ wills to communicate to us. For most Catholic theologians of the period, then, the main purpose of the dogmatic definition was simply to underscore the importance of Mary's Assumption for our understanding of salvation. Namely, the way in which Christ Jesus involves a mere creature, Mary, in the mysteries of the new creation reveals to us the power of Christ's love, which operates through and rewards human cooperation with God in prayer and suffering.

Beginning with Pope Pius XII's *Munificentissiumus Deus* and ending with the Magisterial teaching on Mary of Pope John Paul II, the present chapter traces developments in the second half of the twentieth century with respect to how the Church should account for the truth and significance of the doctrine of Mary's Assumption. After the dogmatic definition of 1950, Marian devotion remained a significant part of Catholic life—witness the Marian Year celebrated by Pius XII in 1954—but theological currents soon began to shift quickly. The debate at the Second Vatican Council over whether to include a separate document on Mary produced the closest vote of the Council. The result was the decision to integrate the discussion of Mary into the Dogmatic Constitution on the Church, *Lumen Gentium*. By the early 1960s, the leading young theologians were persuaded that the articulation of the Marian dogmas needed to be done in the context of ecclesiology and needed to be more explicitly biblical and typological in approach. As we will see, the treatment in *Lumen Gentium* of Mary's motherhood and her mission as the new Eve is nonetheless, in many respects, much like what one finds in theological writings on Mary from the 1940s. Yet unlike *Munificentissimus Deus*, whose purpose is simply to proclaim and define the doctrine of Mary's Assumption to which centuries of Catholic piety and theology bear witness, *Lumen Gentium* places Mary's Assumption fully within the context of the Church's other teachings about Mary and refers more directly to the concrete biblical portraits of Mary's life.

This effort to exposit Marian doctrine by following the order of the New Testament's references to Mary's life appears even more prominently in Pope John Paul II's 1987 encyclical on Mary, *Redemptoris Mater*.[1] By 1987, the Catholic Church was undergoing significant turmoil among both priests and laity with respect to a variety of doctrinal and moral teachings, including Marian doctrine. A major purpose of *Redemptoris Mater* is to reintroduce the Church's Marian doctrine in a persuasive way, drawing heavily upon *Lumen Gentium*. *Redemptoris*

Mater proceeds upon the supposition that the best way to reignite the Church's faith in the Marian doctrines, including the doctrine of Mary's Assumption, is to root them ever more clearly and deeply in Scripture. At the same time, the basic claims of *Munificentissimus Deus* are fully retained, not least because *Munificentissimus Deus*, too, is deeply cognizant of biblical typology and of the typological reasoning at work among the saints and doctors who over the centuries defended the doctrine of Mary's Assumption.

The present chapter is the first of three chapters in which I survey the extraordinarily vibrant twentieth-century Catholic discussion of Mary. This twentieth-century discussion involved not only the highest levels of the Magisterium but also the greatest Catholic theologians of the period. As will be clear, the insights of this fertile period both situate and ground my own ecumenical effort to engage Mary's Assumption in the second part of this book. Looking forward, I should note that the arguments of *Munificentissimus Deus* should largely be paired with my second chapter, which focuses on studies of Mary's Assumption published in the years leading up to the 1950 definition. The arguments of *Lumen Gentium* and *Redemptoris Mater* should be paired more closely with chapter three, which presents the Marian teaching of four eminent Catholic theologians broadly associated with the *nouvelle théologie*.

Munificentissimus Deus: Mary's Privilege of Bodily Assumption

At the outset of *Munificentissimus Deus*, Pope Pius XII speaks of the sorrows and joys of his time.[2] Having recently emerged from World War II and the Holocaust, Pius XII clearly has reason to speak of sorrows. Among the joys, he names the increase of devotion to the Virgin Mary, in accord with the "harmony of graces" that God gave her (§ 3). Affirming the development of doctrine, he points out that "it is in our own age that the privilege of the bodily Assumption into heaven of Mary, the Virgin Mother of God, has certainly shone forth more clearly" (§ 3). While the deposit of faith does not change, nonetheless the Holy Spirit guides the Church in perceiving more fully the content of faith. In particular, Pius XII suggests, the definition of the dogma of Mary's Immaculate Conception has stimulated reflection on Mary's Assumption. Since

God's plan of salvation forms a wise and harmonious whole, certain consequences follow from Mary's Immaculate Conception. God's perfect redemption of Mary from sin meant that "she was not subject to the law of remaining in the corruption of the grave, and she did not have to wait until the end of time for the redemption of her body" (§ 5).[3] It was fitting for her to be assumed bodily into heaven prior to the general resurrection.

Pius XII goes on to mention the many bishops, theologians, and groups of laity that, ever since the definition of Mary's Immaculate Conception, urged the pope to define Mary's Assumption. In 1946, in his *Deiparae Virginis Mariae*, Pius XII asked the bishops whether they, with their dioceses, desired Mary's Assumption to be defined. With almost complete unanimity, the bishops answered in the affirmative. Pius XII had thereby been able to perceive "the concordant teaching of the Church's ordinary doctrinal authority and the concordant faith of the Christian people which the same doctrinal authority sustains and directs" (§ 12).[4] After emphasizing that this teaching belongs to the deposit of faith that Christ delivered to the Church, Pius XII turns briefly to the biblical portrait of Mary. He focuses upon her participation in Christ's Cross, as foretold by Simeon: "[A] sword will pass through your own soul also" (Lk 2:35). Her unique participation in Christ's Cross makes fitting her unique participation in his Resurrection.

Although Mary certainly "passed from this life" (§ 14), Christians over the centuries understood with increasing clarity that her body did not corrupt in the grave. Pius XII notes in this regard the many ancient churches dedicated to Mary's Assumption, the icons depicting the Assumption, the religious institutes dedicated to the Assumption, the rosary's inclusion of the Assumption, and above all the liturgical feast commemorating the Assumption. Both the Roman liturgy and the Byzantine liturgy have included such a feast for more than a millennium, and the popes have gradually increased the solemnity of this feast.[5] Pius XII also mentions the testimony of late-patristic theologians, especially John of Damascus and Germanus of Constantinople.

Examining the ways in which scholastic theologians defended Mary's Assumption, Pius XII observes that they began with the doctrine's accordance with the other truths of God's salvific economy. The scholastic theologians especially focused on her divine motherhood, from which follows her holiness, her intimate union with Christ, and the love that Christ particularly owes to his mother. In addition to these arguments, they also employed biblical texts to shed light on the truth of Mary's Assumption. As Pius XII puts it, they were "rather free in their use of events and expressions taken from Sacred Scripture to explain their belief in the Assumption" (§ 26). Among the biblical passages that they interpreted typologically in favor of Mary's Assumption, he cites Psalm 132:8, "Arise, O Lord, and go to thy resting place, thou and the ark of thy might"; Exodus 25:10–16 (about the ark of the covenant); Psalm 45:13–15, "The princess is decked in her chamber with gold-woven robes; in many-colored robes she is led to the king. . . . With joy and gladness they are led along as they enter the palace of the king"; Isaiah 60:13–14, "I will make the place of my feet glorious. . . . All who despised you shall bow down at your feet; they shall call you the City of the Lord, the Zion of the Holy One of Israel"; and Song of Solomon 3:6, 11, "What is that coming up from the wilderness, like a column of smoke, perfumed with myrrh and frankincense, with all the fragrant powders of the merchant? . . . Go forth, O daughters of Zion, and behold King Solomon, with the crown with which his mother crowned him on the day of his wedding, on the day of the gladness of his heart." Mary is the typological fulfillment of these texts: she is the true ark of the covenant and the true Queen Mother, now enthroned by the side of her Son.

Pius XII also notes that scholastic theologians considered Revelation 12 to be a typological depiction of Mary's Assumption, especially its presentation of "a woman clothed with the sun, with the moon under her feet, and on her head a crown of twelve stars" (Rev 12:1).[6] In the angel Gabriel's greeting to Mary as "full of grace" and in Elizabeth's testimony that Mary is blessed among women, scholastic theologians likewise saw indications that Mary, as the new Eve, had been rewarded with a share in Christ's victory. Pius XII quotes Amadeus of Lausanne, Anthony of Padua, Thomas Aquinas, Bonaventure, and Bernadino of Siena. Among baroque theologians, he cites Robert Bellarmine, Francis de Sales, Peter Canisius, and Francisco Suárez. These theologians, he says, based their arguments in favor of Mary's Assumption "upon the Sacred Scriptures as their ultimate foundation" (§ 38).[7]

Pius XII continues by remarking that, in the Scriptures, these theologians found that Mary was always associated with her Son, "always sharing his lot" (§ 38). They therefore found it to be supremely fitting that her Son would take his mother to dwell, body and soul, in heaven with him. Indeed, at a human level, "it seems impossible to think of her, the one who conceived Christ, brought him forth, nursed him with her milk, held him in her arms, and clasped him to her breast, as being apart from him in body, even though not in soul, after this life" (§ 38). When viewed from this angle, the Assumption of Mary shows Jesus honoring his parents, in obedience to the commandment. In this way *Munificentissimus Deus* makes room for the broadly sentimental arguments of fittingness that, while of lesser theological weight, have a notable late-patristic and medieval pedigree as exemplifications of Mary's extraordinary intimacy with Jesus.[8]

Pius XII emphasizes that since the second century, on the basis of numerous biblical texts, theologians have understood Mary as the new Eve, associated with Christ the new Adam. As he recalls, in Genesis 3:15 (the "protoevangelium") God prophesies, "I will put enmity between you [the serpent] and the woman, and between your seed and her seed; he shall bruise your head, and you shall bruise his heel." This passage is not a "just-so" story about the conflict between snakes and humans.[9] Rather, it prophesies the struggle that "would finally result in that most complete victory over the sin and death which are always mentioned together in the writings of the Apostle of the Gentiles" (§ 39), for example in Romans 5–6 and 1 Corinthians 15. Through his Cross, the new Adam won the victory and was glorified in the flesh. At the foot of the Cross, Mary participates in his sufferings, and the glorification of her body means that she shares uniquely in his victory too. In this regard Pius XII applies 1 Corinthians 15:54 to Mary: "When the perishable puts on the imperishable, and the mortal puts on immortality, then shall come to pass the saying that is written: 'Death is swallowed up in victory'" (§ 39). As the mother of her Son and the new Eve, "the noble associate of the divine Redeemer who has won a complete triumph over sin and its consequences," Mary now "sits in splendor at the right hand of her Son, the immortal King of the Ages" (§ 40).

In addition to these arguments from doctrinal fittingness and from biblical typology, Pius XII appeals to the authority of the Church. Prior to its definition as a dogma of faith, Mary's Assumption was taught by the ordinary magisterium "over the course of centuries" (§ 41). Although the dogma was not clear in the earliest Church, nonetheless "[v]arious testimonies, indications and signs of this common belief of the Church are evident from remote times down through the course of centuries" (§ 13). Indicating the diverse foundations of the dogma, he states that it is a "truth which is based on the Sacred Scriptures, which is thoroughly rooted in the minds of the faithful, which has been approved in ecclesiastical worship from the most remote times, which is completely in harmony with other revealed truths, and which has been expounded and explained magnificently in the work, the science, and the wisdom of the theologians" (§ 41). He concludes with the hope that the definition of the dogma will strengthen believers' willingness to follow Christ, by helping us to "see clearly to what a lofty goal our bodies and souls are destined" and by strengthening our faith in bodily resurrection (§ 42). He likewise hopes that the dogma will undermine materialist worldviews such as those that produced the recent war.

There is a tendency today to depreciate theological arguments made in the period before the Second Vatican Council.[10] This is a mistake that we should not replicate here. The generally indirect way in which *Munificentissimus Deus* references the narrative of Scripture with regard to Mary and the more frequent appeals to ecclesiastical authority do indeed distinguish it from more recent Church documents on Mary. But it would be a mistake to conclude that this difference reflects poorly upon *Munificentissimus Deus*, which simply has different strengths. In setting forth the three pillars of biblical typology, Church authority, and doctrinal fittingness, *Munificentissimus Deus* devotes a good bit of attention to the defense of the doctrine by the saints and doctors of the Church, who very frequently employed typological interpretation of Scripture and whose profound faith encouraged them to rejoice in the wisdom and unity of God's plan. This welcome attention to the teaching of the saints recalls us to the truth that it is the Church as the *communio sanctorum*, filled with the Spirit, that across the centuries has received, contemplated, and handed down divine revelation. By this means, Pope Pius XII is able to show the Church's typological reasoning in action over the centuries as it builds upon and develops Scripture's own typological references to Mary.

Lumen Gentium: Motherhood and Mission

In 1961, in preparation for the Second Vatican Council, Joseph Ratzinger, then a young theologian at the University of Bonn, wrote a speech for Joseph Cardinal Frings, the archbishop of Cologne. In this speech, Ratzinger urges that Mariology be placed fully within the context of ecclesiology. He observes that Mary "is the living sign of the fact that Christian piety does not stand in isolation before God. . . . She is the sign that Christ does not intend to remain alone, but rather that redeemed, believing humankind has become one body with him, one single Christ, 'the whole Christ, head and members,' as St. Augustine said with unsurpassable beauty."[11] Ratzinger's plea that the doctrine of Mary be fully integrated into ecclesiology eventually met with the approval of the Council. Twenty-five years later, Ratzinger observed with appreciation that the inclusion of Mariology in *Lumen Gentium* shows that "the Church is not some piece of machinery, is not just an institution, is not even one of the usual sociological entities. It is a person. It is a woman. It is a mother. It is living. The Marian understanding of the Church is the most decisive contrast to a purely organizational or bureaucratic concept of the Church."[12]

How does *Lumen Gentium* articulate the basis for the Church's Marian doctrines, especially Mary's Assumption? It begins with Mary's motherhood: "The Virgin Mary, who at the message of an angel received the word of God in her heart and her body and brought forth life for the world, is recognised and honoured as the true mother of God and of the redeemer" (§ 53).[13] As mother of her Son, she receives certain privileges: "she is the specially loved daughter of the Father and the shrine of the Holy Spirit; and by this gift of pre-eminent grace she surpasses by far all other creatures in heaven and on earth" (§ 53).[14] The mother of the Redeemer is the greatest mere creature, specially loved by the divine Trinity. She is preeminent among those saved by Christ, and she is the greatest member of the Church. The Old Testament prefigures her in the prophecy of the enmity between the serpent and the woman and her seed (Gen 3:15). Daughter Zion is a type of Mary, from whom comes the Son of the promise (see § 55).[15] Mary is the new Eve, and therefore is "all holy and free from all stain of sin" (§ 56). She is "full of grace" and entirely obedient to God's Word (Lk 1:28, 38).

In accepting her motherhood, Mary takes on a *mission:* she "dedicated herself totally as the handmaid of the Lord to the person and work of her Son, under him and with him, by the grace of almighty God, at the service of the mystery of redemption" (§ 56). Her motherhood is not a merely physical or passive reality. Rather, it requires her whole being and her whole life. By her faith and obedience, she participates as the new Eve in the work of the new Adam. Quoting Irenaeus, *Lumen Gentium* contrasts her life-giving motherhood with Eve's bringing forth children bound to death. Mary's participation in Christ's work was recognized already by her cousin Elizabeth, who proclaimed Mary blessed among all women, and by Simeon, who foretold the destiny of her Son and Mary's own destiny. Mary interceded at the wedding feast at Cana, and her faith and love embodied Christ's insistence that the kingdom is based not on physical kinship but on spiritual kinship. At the foot of the Cross, she "associated herself with a mother's heart with his sacrifice" (§ 58).[16] Christ commanded his beloved disciple to take her as a mother, and Christ commanded her to take his disciple as a son. She devoted herself to prayer with the disciples in the upper room prior to Pentecost. Since she was free of sin, her participation in Christ's victorious Cross and Resurrection culminated in her Assumption into heaven, where Christ received her as queen. As the new Eve, she is fully conformed to the new Adam, who is "victor over sin and death" (§ 61).

Lumen Gentium takes care to affirm that Mary's participation in Christ's work does not undermine his uniqueness as the "one mediator" (1 Tim 2:5). Mary's role is made possible by Christ's work. Her graces flow from his merits, and everything that she does serves his redemptive work. In conceiving him in her womb, giving birth to him and nurturing him, and following him all the way to the Cross, she served both him and all those who are his members. Her motherhood is the basis of the intercessory role that she retains at Christ's side in heaven. Again, her intercession does not make her a second mediator on par with her Son. Rather, "the one mediation of the redeemer does not rule out, but rouses up among creatures, participated cooperation in the one unique source" (§ 62).[17]

Lumen Gentium also discusses Mary as a "type" of the Church (although she is at the same time a member of the Church). Like Mary, the Church is called to cooperate faithfully and obediently in the birth of the children of God by the grace of the Holy Spirit. In Mary, too, the Church "has already attained the perfection by which it is without stain or wrinkle (cf. Eph 5:27)" (§ 65). In history, the members of the Church strive to grow in holiness, learning from Mary's obedient devotion to her Son. The Word that took flesh in Mary's womb must "be born and grow in the hearts of the faithful" (§ 65). With regard to Mary as a type of the Church, Mary's Assumption manifests the reward received by the people of God who share in Christ's Cross through obedient love: "as already glorified in body and soul in heaven, she is the image and the beginning of the church which will receive fulfilment in the age that is to come" (§ 68).

Compared with *Munificentissimus Deus*, *Lumen Gentium* relies more on the biblical narrative of Mary's life and on biblical typology— which is certainly present in *Munificentissimus Deus* too—and somewhat less on the authority of the Church and on doctrinal fittingness. The latter two elements are not absent in *Lumen Gentium*, but they tend to be presumed rather than to be part of the explicit argument. The integration of Mary into the theology of the Church helps us to appreciate that, in Mary, the Church is already victorious with Christ in heaven even as the Church on earth endures suffering and sin. *Lumen Gentium*'s reference to Ephesians 5:27 is particularly significant for Mary's Assumption: "That he [Christ] might present the church to himself in splendor, without spot or wrinkle or any such thing, that she might be holy and without blemish."

Redemptoris Mater: Mary in the Old and New Testaments

The biblical-typological approach is exemplified even more by Pope John Paul II's *Redemptoris Mater*, which in many ways is a commentary on *Lumen Gentium*. John Paul II's encyclical integrates the Church's authority and doctrinal fittingness into its biblical argument.[18] Ratzinger had a role in this encyclical, just as he (with others) influenced *Lumen Gentium*. In his introduction to the encyclical, which he delivered as

Prefect of the Congregation for the Doctrine of the Faith, Ratzinger presents *Redemptoris Mater* as "a Marian encyclical whose entire purpose is to bring out what the Bible has to say."[19]

Redemptoris Mater begins with Mary's mission, which took place "when the time had fully come" for God to send "forth his Son, born of woman" (Gal 4:4).[20] In uttering her "fiat," her words of faith and obedience to God in acceptance of her mission of bearing Christ for the world, Mary "prefigures the Church's condition as spouse and mother" (§ 1). Mary's fiat was enabled by "the saving grace of Easter," already active in her Immaculate Conception (§ 1). Her fiat ultimately led her, in association with her Son, to the foot of the Cross. The Council of Ephesus in 431 taught definitively that Mary is the mother of God and not simply the mother of Christ's human nature. As the body of Christ, the Church extends the Incarnation over the course of history. It follows that the Church, too, is related to Mary. In faith and obedience, the Church brings forth children of God in the world. Mary's journey of faith "goes before" and guides the Church toward the eschatological fulfillment that Mary has attained by her Assumption (§ 5).[21]

The encyclical is divided into three chapters: "Mary in the Mystery of Christ," "The Mother of God at the Center of the Pilgrim Church," and "Maternal Mediation." In each of these chapters the biblical portrait is the starting point for doctrinal reflection. At the outset of the chapter on "Mary in the Mystery of Christ," John Paul II interprets Ephesians 1, which speaks about the predestination of Christ and of us in Christ. The predestination of Christ requires the predestination of his mother. By way of indicating the preparation in the Old Testament for Mary, John Paul II quotes *Lumen Gentium*'s typological interpretation of Genesis 3:15 as well as Isaiah 7:14/Matthew 1:23 on the virgin who will bear a son. In light of this depiction of Mary as the new Eve and mother of God, John Paul II explores the presentation of Mary in Luke 1.[22] Mary is "full of grace" and blessed among women (Lk 1:28, 38). She has been chosen or elected by God for her mission, so that God might come among us as Redeemer. This eternal election of Mary means that "together with the Father, the Son has chosen her, entrusting her eternally to the Spirit of holiness" (§ 8).[23] The Holy Spirit prepared Mary for her unique mission to be the one in whose womb the Incarnation takes place.

As such, Mary was made to be the greatest of mere creatures. She therefore received the greatest possible redemption, being utterly preserved from the wound of original sin. She received a radical incorporation into Christ from the first moment of her existence. John Paul II observes in this regard that "through the power of the Holy Spirit, in the order of grace, which is a participation in the divine nature, *Mary receives life from him to whom* she herself, in the order of earthly generation, *gave life* as a mother" (§ 10). The result is that in her fiat, Mary accepted her motherhood with a graced fullness of love that is commensurate "to the dignity of the divine motherhood" (§ 10).[24]

Here John Paul II returns again to Genesis 3:15, interpreted as a prophecy about the struggle against evil. He notes that the imagery of this prophecy is taken up again at the end of Scripture, in Revelation 12. As mother of the incarnate Word, Mary "is placed *at the very center of that enmity,* that struggle which accompanies the history of humanity on earth and the history of salvation itself" (§ 11). She was the one chosen to bear her Son, who crushed the "serpent" once and for all. By contrast to Eve, she believed the word of God; as her cousin Elizabeth proclaimed, "Blessed is she who believed that there would be a fulfilment of what was spoken to her from the Lord" (Lk 1:45). In response to God's gift, Mary believed God. Whereas Eve disobeyed God, Mary exemplified the "obedience of faith" (Rom 16:26), above all by her fiat in which she accepted the mission to be mother of the Lord.

Comparing Mary to Abraham, John Paul II states that Mary's faith and obedience inaugurated the New Covenant.[25] Like Abraham, she abandoned herself to the journey to which God called her. When Simeon told her that both she and her Son would suffer greatly on this path, she learned that she would "have to live her obedience of faith in suffering, at the side of the suffering Savior" (§ 16). She prepared for this during the years that she shared with Jesus (his "hidden life").[26] Even in the midst of this intimacy, she could know him properly only in faith; she had to learn to understand him (Lk 2:50; Mk 3:31–35). Her faith attained its full maturity at the foot of the Cross (Jn 19:25), where she joined herself in faith and love to Christ's self-emptying.[27] Citing *Lumen Gentium's* quotation of Irenaeus, John Paul II comments that "as a sharing in the sacrifice of Christ—the new Adam—it becomes in a certain sense *the counterpoise to the disobedience and disbelief* embodied in the sin of our first parents" (§ 19). By believing God's word, Mary showed herself to be the new Eve who uniquely participates in the redemption accomplished by the new Adam. Mary is blessed ultimately because she hears and keeps the word of God (Lk 8:21, 11:28).

In light of Mary's intercession with her Son at the wedding feast at Cana, John Paul II discusses Mary's mediation, a maternal role that, as *Lumen Gentium* says, flows from and depends upon Christ's unique mediation. The purpose of her maternal mediation in the order of grace is to serve "the revelation of his salvific power" (§ 22).[28] With respect to Mary's maternal mediation, John Paul II explores Jesus' command that his beloved disciple take Mary as mother and that Mary take the beloved disciple as son. Jesus' command shows that Mary is the mother of all Jesus' disciples and thus (since all humans are potentially Jesus' disciples) of the whole human race. Both at the wedding feast and in his command to Mary to take the beloved disciple as her son, Jesus addressed Mary as "woman," in a deliberate echo of Genesis 3:15—whose echo is found also in Revelation 12.[29] Mary's divine motherhood makes her the new Eve, sharing with her Son in his crushing of the "serpent" (Gen 3:15). As the new Eve, she is the mother of all who live in Christ (mother of the Church).[30]

In the second chapter, "The Mother of God at the Center of the Pilgrim Church," John Paul II focuses on Mary's presence to the people of God over the course of the Church's history. At Pentecost, she was in the upper room praying with the disciples. She was not an apostle, but she was the first to believe and her intimacy with Jesus was unparalleled. Neither the mystery of Christ, nor the mystery of the Church, can be contemplated without her. As Mary correctly prophesied, "All generations will call me blessed; for he who is mighty has done great things for me, and holy is his name" (Lk 1:48–49). By calling Mary blessed, we seek support for our faith in hers.[31] In this way John Paul II explains the history of Marian devotion around the globe. Catholics and Orthodox are to a large degree united regarding Mary, whereas Catholics and Protestants are generally divided regarding Mary. Calling for theological dialogue to clarify the relationship of Mary and the Church, he offers an extended meditation on the relationship of Mary's Magnificat (Lk 1:46–55) to the Church's mission.[32]

The final chapter on "Maternal Mediation" highlights Jesus Christ as the "one mediator" (1 Tim 2:5) and states that Mary's mediation, like that of other saints, is strictly "mediation in Christ" (§ 38). Mary's mediation of grace depends entirely on Christ's mediation and serves the direct union of believers with Christ. Her participated mediation is distinct from that of other saints because of her motherhood, which makes her uniquely Christ's companion in his work of redemption. In accepting her motherhood by her graced fiat, Mary gave herself entirely to the Lord. John Paul II notes that it is in this light that the Church understands Mary's virginity: her self-gift was absolute, so that she was completely focused on her Son and shared, in faith and love, in his journey to the Cross. From Mary's complete devotion to her Son comes her complete devotion to the members of his body, the Church. She continues even now to cooperate "in the saving work of her Son, the Redeemer of the world" (§ 40).

Mary's present role in the Church brings John Paul II to the topic of her Assumption into heaven. He argues that Mary bridges the earthly and heavenly Church, because Mary has already fully attained to the eschatological goal of salvation. John Paul II affirms that in defining the dogma of the Assumption, "Pius XII was in continuity with Tradition, which has found many different expressions in the history of the Church, both in the East and in the West" (§ 41). In Mary, the victory won by Christ (and depicted by Paul in 1 Corinthians 15) has been fully accomplished. The uniqueness of her bond with Christ in his first coming requires that "through her continued collaboration with him she will be united with him in expectation of the second" (§ 41). She is united to him in glory as one who serves. Her "royal exaltation" to the right hand of Christ is for the purpose of her ongoing "maternal mediation," whose goal is the eschatological perfection of the whole Church (§ 41).

John Paul II also takes up *Lumen Gentium*'s discussion of Mary as a type (or model) of the Church. In faith and obedience, the Church too brings forth children of God. In this vein he quotes Galatians 4:19, where Paul says, "My little children, with whom I am again in travail until Christ be formed in you!" The Church receives the grace of the Holy Spirit in order to generate children of God. The Church is "virgin" in the sense of preserving, in complete wholeness, fidelity to Christ as Christ's "bride" (Rev 21:9). Like Mary, the Church receives and ponders Christ's revelation. John Paul II adds that Mary is not only the type of the Church, but also cooperates by her maternal mediation in the Church's ongoing work. Mary is in this sense the mother of all disciples of her Son, in accord with Christ's command that she take the beloved disciple as her son. Her motherhood in the order of grace guides us to her Son, including to her Son as present in the holy Eucharist. As disciples of Christ, each of us receives a personal relationship with Mary as our mother. Within the mission given her by her Son, she cares for us with a maternal love and teaches us: "Do whatever he tells you" (Jn 2:5).

In this light, John Paul II returns once more to the "woman" whose enmity toward the "serpent" is depicted in Genesis 3:15 and Revelation 12. Showing how Mary's motherhood relates to her dignity as the new Eve, he observes that "Mary, present in the Church as the Mother of the Redeemer, takes part, as a mother, in that 'monumental struggle against the powers of darkness' [*Lumen Gentium* § 37] which continues throughout human history" (§ 47). Regarding the "woman" in Revelation 12, John Paul II wishes to affirm both the ecclesial referent (Israel/ Church) and the reference to Mary as the new Eve and type of the Church. The "woman clothed with the sun" (Rev 12:1) is the eschatological Church, and in Mary the Church has already attained this perfect state at the right hand of Christ, "without spot or wrinkle" (Eph 5:27). John Paul II points out that Catholics share this belief in Mary's Assumption with Orthodox Christians, and he hopes that it will serve to strengthen ecumenical bonds. He concludes by emphasizing the "*wonderment of faith* which accompanies the mystery of Mary's divine motherhood. . . . How wonderfully far God has gone, the Creator and Lord of all things, in the 'revelation of himself' to man!" (§ 51) Reflection on Mary as the mother of God must indeed provoke wonder at how far God has gone by becoming incarnate.

Even more than *Lumen Gentium*, this encyclical emphasizes Mary's faith in a way that shows how her entire mission is encapsulated in the biblical portrait of her fiat. Mary participates in the work of her Son, but does so always through her Son's merits and in obedience to her Son. Mary's faith and obedience make her a type of the Church; she is the new Eve who believes God rather than disobediently believing the "serpent." Indeed, her collaboration with Christ is so profound that Christ gives her, as "woman," to be the mother of all disciples. The eschatological perfection of the Church is already begun in Mary, assumed body and soul to the right hand of Christ so as to serve "the revelation of his salvific power" (§ 22) and to continue her maternal mediation in service to her Son.

The most striking thing about *Redemptoris Mater* is the profusion of biblical texts, especially in the first chapter but indeed throughout the encyclical. The use that John Paul II makes of Scripture enables him to interpret Mary in terms of an assemblage of Marian passages, and in light of the other mysteries of salvation (especially that of the Church). Not surprisingly, when we arrive at the third chapter of this book, we will find many similarities between *Redemptoris Mater* and Joseph Ratzinger's *Daughter Zion*. The encyclical also makes frequent reference to *Lumen Gentium*. In this context, the encyclical's approving citation of Pius XII and *Munificentissimus Deus* is even more significant. There is a strong continuity even while there is also a much greater use of Scripture, and even though the *Munificentisssimus Deus*'s appeal to a chain of authoritative saints and doctors of the Church is not present. This use of Scripture locates Mary's Assumption firmly within the context of her unique motherhood and her mission as the new Eve (Daughter Zion), whom God predestines to collaborate by faith and obedience with her Son. In addition to biblical texts specifically and clearly about Mary, *Redemptoris Mater* also makes use of typological texts such as Revelation 12 and Ephesians 5 to elucidate the Church's faith in Mary's Assumption.

Since the impetus for the definition of Mary's Assumption came in part from the logic of the Immaculate Conception, which had been formally defined in 1854, it was important for *Munificentissimus Deus* to underscore the fittingness of Mary's Assumption within the coherent whole of Catholic dogma. Similarly, since the proclamation of Mary's Assumption has a strong foundation in the Church's liturgical and theological tradition, it makes sense that the authority of the Church in the development of doctrine, as manifested by the teachings of saints, doctors, and popes, would be a central ground for the dogmatic definition of the doctrine. Not entirely supportively, Pius XII observes with respect to biblical typology and typological reasoning that theologians over the centuries "have been rather free in their use of events and expressions taken from Sacred Scripture to explain their belief in the Assumption" (§ 26). But *Munificentissimus Deus* makes clear that Scripture typologically reveals the truth of Mary's Assumption: Mary is the new Eve, the new ark of the covenant, the new Queen Mother elevated to the right hand of the Son of David. Pius XII affirms that "these proofs and considerations of the holy Fathers and the theologians are based upon the Sacred Scriptures as their ultimate foundation" (§ 38).

By comparison to *Munificentissimus Deus*, *Lumen Gentium* and *Redemptoris Mater* rely more heavily on the biblical portraits of the events of Mary's life. Unlike *Munificentissimus Deus*, of course, these documents do not focus on Mary's Assumption. Rather, *Lumen Gentium* and *Redemptoris Mater* set forth a biblical theology of Mary that aims to help believers understand why the Church teaches what it does about Mary. The goal is to show how the Church's teachings on Mary as the immaculately conceived mother of God, perpetual virgin, new Eve, intercessor, and "woman clothed with the sun" hold together. The Annunciation, the Visitation, the presentation of the infant Jesus at the Temple, the wedding at Cana, the Cross, and Pentecost provide the key landmarks for the documents' reflections, along with Genesis 3:15, Ephesians 5:27, and Revelation 12.

The Annunciation enables these documents to ground their Marian reflection in Mary's grace, faith, obedience, and divine motherhood. The Annunciation also provides a way of entering into the Fathers' presentation of Mary as the new Eve. The Visitation confirms Mary's blessedness among women, her extraordinary humility, and the suitability of Mary receiving praise from all generations of believers. The presentation at the Temple contains the prophecy that Mary will suffer greatly along with her Son. The wedding at Cana makes clear that Mary's intercession is always in service of her Son, and it also shows anew the intimate union of Christ's mission with hers. At the wedding at Cana and at the Cross, Christ calls his mother "woman," thus providing a link to Genesis 3:15's and Revelation 12's depiction of the struggle between the "serpent" and the woman and her Son. Mary's presence at the foot of the Cross displays her unique participation in the Cross of Christ, in accord not only with Simeon's prophecy, but also with the struggle prophesied in Genesis

3:15. By establishing Mary as the mother of all disciples, Jesus' words from the Cross show Mary's ongoing relationship to the Church: she is mother of Christ's members just as she is mother of Christ. Pentecost deepens this relationship of Mary to the Church, because she is among those praying at the outset of the Church's history.

This biblical narrative about Mary, found in the literal sense of Scripture, is rich in typological resonances, as we would expect. Indeed, the same is true about the biblical narrative of Christ, who is presented as the new Adam, the new Moses, the true temple, and so forth.[33] Even if biblical scholars often overlook the typological connections, the Magisterial documents are on solid ground in presenting Mary as the new Eve, whose mission is inextricably associated with the work of the new Adam in accomplishing our redemption.[34] Mary's sharing in his suffering is such that those attuned to the typology may expect her to share uniquely in his victory, his Resurrection. She is the new ark of the covenant who bears the Word of God: she is the one who, as Daughter Zion, "brought forth a male child, one who is to rule all the nations with a rod of iron" (Rev 12:5). She and her Son are the ones against whom "the ancient serpent, who is called the Devil and Satan" (Rev 12:9), fights. She is the queen of heaven, and she is triumphant through and with her Son.[35]

The biblical portrait in light of which Mary's Assumption makes sense is paramount in *Lumen Gentium* and *Redemptoris Mater*. These documents, however, also presuppose *Munificentissimus Deus*'s arguments for the authority of the Church (as expressed in the liturgical and theological tradition) and for the unity and harmony of the economy of salvation. Biblical-typological arguments cannot stand alone; they require an appreciation of doctrinal fittingness as well as a sense for the Church's role as "the pillar and bulwark of the truth" (1 Tim 2:15), guided by the Holy Spirit "into all the truth" (Jn 16:13).

CHAPTER 2

Early to Mid-Twentieth-Century Theologies
of Mary's Assumption

We now turn to representative theological arguments in favor of Mary's bodily Assumption that were made in the 1930s and 1940s, the period of preparation for the dogmatic definition. On the basis of a small selection of the vast literature devoted in these two decades to Mary's Assumption, I explore how historical and dogmatic theologians of this period approached the Church's belief that Mary's body did not corrupt in the tomb but instead was assumed into heaven.[1] The bulk of the chapter examines the theology of Mary set forth by the most eminent dogmatic theologian of the period, Réginald Garrigou-Lagrange. I describe the central elements of his doctrine of Mary's motherhood, grace, and Immaculate Conception before turning to his instructive treatment of Mary's Assumption. I also briefly survey two somewhat more historically oriented works on Mary's Assumption by Joseph Duhr and Aloïs Janssens. Their accounts of the historical development of the doctrine of Mary's Assumption, and their treatments of the doctrine's biblical and theological foundations, at times lack the speculative breadth of Garrigou-Lagrange's approach, which is able to ground Mary's Assumption in her predestination and in relation to the Incarnation. Yet their approaches have the merit of being more cautious and in certain ways more persuasive than Garrigou-Lagrange's, both because they avoid implausible historical reconstructions of how Mary's Assumption was revealed and because they argue for the truth of Mary's Assumption in a less syllogistic manner.

Joseph Duhr and Aloïs Janssens: Mary as the New Eve

Joseph Duhr

In the Jesuit theologian Joseph Duhr's 1948 book *The Glorious Assumption of the Mother of God*, he challenges Johann Ernst, a leading early twentieth-century critic of the dogmatic definability of Mary's Assumption.[2] Ernst had argued that Mary's Assumption is a pious belief but not one that belongs within the domain of the Church's dogmatic inheritance, because it cannot be found in the deposit of faith communicated to the apostles by Christ Jesus. For his part, Duhr grants that the deposit of faith includes only what the apostles received from Christ up to and including on the day of Pentecost. Since there is no explicit evidence from the apostles or the early Church regarding Mary's Assumption, how can her Assumption belong to the deposit of faith?

In response, Duhr begins by observing that only faith, not theological or historical research, can be the basis for knowing a truth of divine revelation. The Church's development of doctrine, therefore, cannot limit itself only to realities that are historically demonstrable. Neither Mary's Immaculate Conception nor her Assumption is historically demonstrable, but this does not mean that they are not realities that occurred in history. As Duhr says, then, "It can happen . . . that a fact implied in a dogma be imposed on our belief, even when all historical proof is impossible."[3] Given that doctrines can be defined without historical proof, the question is how the Church discerns what is truly implicit in divine revelation. Duhr argues that what is involved consists in "a real progress from the virtually implicit to the formally explicit," and he notes that such progress "supposes in the Church the power to discern and to define as dogma of divine faith truths whose formal existence in the revealed deposit is not obvious."[4] A truth that is "virtually implicit" lacks *intrinsic* theological or historical certitude, but it can be received as a "dogma of faith" once it has been made explicit by the

Church, guided by the illumination of the Holy Spirit.[5] A revealed truth can be defined as a dogma only if it has a central place within the economy of salvation. With regard to the Assumption, says Duhr, the key point is that "[t]he Son of God made man . . . wished to accomplish the work of our salvation only with the collaboration of the most holy Virgin, his Mother: the new Eve."[6] It is because of Mary's role as the new Eve that the Assumption of Mary could become a dogma of the Church, whereas (for example) the prophet Elijah's assumption into heaven could not be a dogma.

In tracing the development of the doctrine of Mary's Assumption, Duhr accepts that there is no evidence for it in the first four centuries, although he supposes that St. Epiphanius might be a late exception.[7] The liturgical feast of the Dormition/Assumption that began in the late fifth century is significant for Duhr, especially because it spread so quickly throughout the churches of the East and the West. He also gives attention to the apocryphal narratives of Mary's Assumption, especially early Coptic and Syriac versions and the later work of John of Thessalonica; the problem with these narratives, he argues, is that they sought to invent historical grounds for a belief that cannot in fact be demonstrated historically. He reviews medieval and baroque theological and artistic expositions of Mary's Assumption. In Duhr's view, the texts of Scripture that are widely cited, including Revelation 12:1, "do not serve to *establish* the Assumption but to *illustrate* the belief."[8] He adds, however, that there is one exception, Genesis 3:15, "not by itself but as clarified by the ordinary magisterium, which establishes a strict connection between the Redeemer and His Mother."[9] He finds significant the liturgical and ecclesiastical evidence that the Holy Spirit has been leading the Church increasingly toward an explicit knowledge of Mary's Assumption and toward an affirmation of its central role (because of Mary's motherhood) in the economy of salvation.

Expanding upon his remarks on Genesis 3:15, Duhr observes that Mary, as Christ's mother, was chosen by God not simply to give birth to Christ but to share in Christ's mission. Genesis 3:15 contains God's condemnation of the serpent, in which God promises, "I will put enmity between you [the serpent] and the woman, and between your seed and her seed." Here the "woman" retains an important role in salvation history. The Fathers and the liturgical tradition interpreted this passage as meaning that the new Adam, Christ, works together with the new Eve, Mary. Mary is "the 'new Eve' who has played a role in our restoration analogous to the one Eve played in our fall."[10] Mary is Christ's helper, and she succeeds where Eve (and Adam) failed. The Gospels show Mary's collaboration in the Incarnation at the Annunciation, and they show her collaboration in Christ's Passion when she prays at the foot of the Cross. Guided by the Holy Spirit and going beyond what could be evident to human exegetes without divine assistance, the Church affirms "that the role of the new Eve associated with the divine Saviour in His combat as in His victory, *is found to be contained* in Genesis, 3, 15."[11]

If Genesis 3:15 points to the future conflict with and victory over Satan by the new Adam and new Eve, then the descriptions of this victory found in 1 Corinthians 15 and elsewhere have relevance. Christ wins this victory through his Passion and Resurrection. Mary's participation in Christ's victory leads Duhr to ask: "If Mary is united to Jesus in His Incarnation and Passion, how will she be separated from Him in His Resurrection and victory?"[12] The new Eve can share uniquely in the new Adam's victory, as Genesis 3:15 promises will be the case, only by sharing uniquely in the new Adam's Resurrection. This typological argument of fittingness must be assessed in light of the Church's authority as interpreter of revelation, given the teaching of the Church's ordinary magisterium, which Duhr describes as "the habitual way in which she [the Church] transmits the received truth" and which is "endowed likewise with infallibility."[13]

Aloïs Janssens

In 1931, the eminent Mariological scholar Aloïs Janssens published a similar study whose reasoning also merits our attention. He begins by briefly treating early twentieth-century doubts about the doctrine, especially those of Ernst, and by setting forth the late patristic, medieval, and baroque witness to Mary's Assumption. He grants that there is no evidence, either pro or contra, in the first centuries. With regard to Scripture, he denies that it contains a clear prophecy or type of Mary's Assumption, and he also argues that "in theology the typical sense has no conclusive force unless its existence is first proven, either through other texts from the Sacred Scriptures, which is not the case for the assumption, or through a dogmatic tradition."[14] Furthermore, he denies that the late Fathers, medievals, or baroque theologians sought to demonstrate Mary's Assumption on the basis of Scripture. Certainly these theologians made mention of prototypes such as the ark of the covenant, but they did not see such prototypes as the theological grounding of the doctrine.

What about arguments for the truth of Mary's Assumption that are based upon such texts as Genesis 3:15 and 1 John 3:8 ("The reason the Son of God appeared was to destroy the works of the devil")? Janssens considers that "[f]rom a Catholic and theological point of view these arguments are unassailable. But the arguments should be presented as arguments based on the whole picture of Mary as the Mother of God and as the second Eve, as this picture flows from the sources of God's revelation, that is, from both the Sacred Scriptures and the dogmatic tradition."[15] At issue for Janssens is the ground of the doctrine of the Assumption, and he insists that the case for the doctrine cannot be made as though it depended *solely* on the typological interpretation of biblical texts. The traditional interpretation of these biblical texts has been strongly colored by "the traditional doctrine and pronouncements of the teaching authority of the Church."[16] Once this is understood, then one can return to the biblical texts and read them in light of the Fathers' "powerful parallel of Eve and Mary."[17] When Eve is seen as the type of Mary, the result is "the inseparability of Christ and Mary in the redemption of mankind and in the victory over the seed of the serpent."[18]

In later chapters, Janssens traces the liturgical feast of the Assumption from the seventh century onward, comments on the embarrassment and hesitation that the apocryphal writings caused baroque theologians, argues at length that Mary truly died (although her body did not decay), and denies that Enoch and Elijah enjoyed a "complete resurrection" along the lines that Mary received.[19] He treats private revelations, the arts, catechisms, and the like before turning in later chapters to the theological reasoning for Mary's Assumption. The theological principle that he relies upon is "Mary's singular dignity as Mother of God and the New Eve."[20] Mary's motherhood and her status as the new Eve have implications that include, for the eyes of faith, her Assumption. Just as Eve and Adam worked together in the Fall, so also the new Eve and the new Adam work together in redemption, although Mary works as Christ's helper and stands among the redeemed. Janssens explains: "As the first Eve had placed herself at the disposal of man's enemy and had voluntarily cooperated with him, in order to disinherit our first ancestor and his posterity, so Mary placed herself voluntarily in the service of God, in order to give to mankind the second ancestor, by whom redemption should come and with it divine life."[21] He concludes that Mary's motherhood necessarily contains within it the typological connection to Eve: "The concept of New Eve is contained in her voluntary motherhood."[22] The Holy Spirit has guided the Church to know the fullness of the new Eve's participation in the new Adam's victory; the portrait of Mary as mother of God and new Eve has rightly led the Church to make explicit the Assumption of Mary.[23]

I have focused on the way in which Duhr and Janssens, in treating the doctrine of Mary's Assumption, trace the doctrine's history and explore its biblical and theological foundations in light of the Church's teaching authority. I find their approaches to be generally balanced and helpful. They grant that there is no evidence of Mary's Assumption from the early patristic period, and they make clear that the doctrine of Mary's Assumption does not depend on the legends. They examine Mary's biblical-typological status as the new Eve (a status that flows from her unique motherhood) without claiming that biblical-typological arguments can be decisive absent the authority of the Church under the guidance of the Holy Spirit. They explain why the doctrine has soteriological importance in terms of the intimacy of Christ's association with those whom he redeems. In their books, Duhr and Janssens proceed in a historical and scholastic mode; they do not construct a defense of Mary's Assumption by tracing the various dimensions of the explicit biblical texts about Mary. Janssens in particular catalogues the positions of eminent theologians, and advances and defends various theses, in a scholastic manner; his chapter on whether and how Mary died is an especially noteworthy example of this method.

Réginald Garrigou-Lagrange: Mary's Motherhood, Faith, and Predestination

The most eminent theologian of this period was Réginald Garrigou-Lagrange. In his *The Mother of the Saviour and Our Interior Life*, originally published in 1941, he begins with two central truths about Mary: her motherhood and her fullness of grace. As he notes, theologians debate which truth is primary. Those who favor the primacy of her grace point to Jesus' words to the woman who praised his mother. Jesus corrects her: "Blessed rather are those who hear the word of God and keep it!" (Lk 11:28). This seems to mean that grace is more important than motherhood. Mary is foremost in the Gospel of Luke with respect to hearing and keeping the word of God. As we read, after the shepherds told what they had seen and heard, "Mary kept all these things, pondering them in her heart" (Lk 2:19); and after finding the twelve-year-old Jesus teaching in the Temple, Mary again "kept all these things in her heart" (Lk 2:51). Mary hears and keeps the word of God. She is "full of grace"; God is with her (Lk 1:28).

Yet most theologians conclude that Mary's motherhood is primary.[24] In this view, the woman whom Jesus corrected was speaking of natural motherhood rather than recognizing Mary's spiritual consent to be mother of the Redeemer. Mary became a mother when she heard and kept the word of God, by saying to the angel Gabriel, "Behold, I am the handmaid of the Lord; let it be to me according to your word" (Lk 1:38). Garrigou-Lagrange observes that Mary "said her fiat generously and with perfect conformity of will to God's good pleasure and all it involved for her, and she kept the divine words in her heart from the time of the Annunciation onwards."[25] Thus Elizabeth explicitly praised Mary's faith in the word of God: "Blessed is she who believed that there would be a fulfilment of what was spoken to her from the Lord" (Lk 1:45). By contrast, Garrigou-Lagrange points out, John the Baptist's father Zechariah was struck dumb because of his failure to believe the angel Gabriel's words (see Lk 1:20).

Mary's motherhood, then, was more than simply the rational consent of a human mother. Her consent to motherhood involved supernatural faith. As such, her consent to be the mother of the Redeemer was a consent in advance to the whole mystery of salvation, including the suffering that her Son would endure. From all eternity, God predestined her for this role (predestination being God's plan for his gifts of grace and glory).[26] By grace, God prepared her for her mission as mother of her Son. Garrigou-Lagrange finds that her motherhood has priority over her grace, on the grounds that the grace she received was for the purpose of her motherhood. God gave Mary grace "in view of the foreseen merits of her Son."[27] In predestining Jesus, God must predestine his mother. For this reason, says Garrigou-Lagrange, the Church sees Mary in Proverbs 8, where personified feminine wisdom says, "The Lord created me at the beginning of his work, the first of his acts of old" (Prov 8:22).[28] In God's eternal plan for the graced fulfillment of creation, God has Mary in view. Mary's predestination to be the mother of the Messiah is the reason for the many biblical images that typologically apply to her: "Mary had been promised as the woman who would triumph over the serpent (Gen. 3:15), as the Virgin who would bear Emmanuel (Is. 7:14); she had been prefigured by the ark of alliance, the house of gold, the tower of ivory."[29]

In addition to Mary's predestination to be the mother of her Son, Garrigou-Lagrange identifies another reason for the priority of her motherhood over her grace—namely, that Mary is related, in the flesh, to the divine Person Jesus Christ. Her relation to her Son is in what Garrigou-Lagrange calls "the hypostatic order," which requires us to think seriously about Mary's privileges as part of contemplating the Incarnation.[30] The hypostatic union of the divine and human natures is something that surpasses even the order of grace and glory. Mary's motherhood, insofar as it relates her to a divine Person, is greater in dignity even than her grace and glory. The point is not that Mary herself becomes divine, but rather that as the mother of her Son, she is not merely the mother of the human nature; she is the mother of Jesus Christ, who is one Person, the Son of God. As a result, her motherhood exceeds even adoptive sonship in dignity, because adoptive sonship is solely a spiritual relationship, whereas Mary enjoys both the spiritual relationship and the relationship constituted by physical motherhood. Only Mary has Jesus for her Son, and only to Mary does Jesus owe the particular debts that any child owes to his or her mother. That the only-begotten Son of the Father is also Son of Mary suffices to show the gloriousness of Mary's motherhood.

The unique grace that God bestows upon Mary enables her to give full and free assent to God's word announcing her mission. Because of her fullness of grace, she is able to "surround Him with the most motherly and most holy devotion" and "unite herself to Him in closest conformity of will," including her "second *fiat*" at the foot of the Cross.[31] The love with which she loves her Son is a supernatural charity that configures her to his supreme charity. Her grace, then, serves her motherhood. To express this, Garrigou-Lagrange cites the French poet Paul Claudel's "Corona benignitatis anni Dei." We venerate Mary as most blessed because she is mother of the Son of God, not because she is (as indeed she is) the greatest of the saints by her grace.

This does not take away from the dignity of her grace and glory, since of course her motherhood in itself, although it is "a real relation to the Incarnate Word," does not sanctify her. In predestining her to be the mother of her Son, God gives her the grace needed to undertake her mission—namely, the fullness of grace. In her motherhood, she is more blessed than any angel or any saint, and her mission is far more closely associated with that of Christ than is the mission of any apostle, martyr, or bishop. She is preeminently Christ's "associate and helper in the work of redemption."[32] In preparation for her mission, her Son "redeemed her," a supreme redemption because it was not a healing but a preserving from the stain of original sin.[33] This preservation made her prompt in obedience to every motion of the Holy Spirit, as her mission required. She was thus truly able to teach and raise her Son.

Having introduced Mary's motherhood and grace, Garrigou-Lagrange turns in his second chapter to Mary's Immaculate Conception. He first proposes that grace is a gift of God that exceeds any power of the order of created nature.[34] It lifts us up to union with God by sanctifying us. Indeed, as 2 Peter 1:4 suggests, it enables us to participate in the divine life itself, an extraordinary power indeed. Garrigou-Lagrange recognizes that in the original Greek, the phrase translated "full of grace" (Lk 1:28) means "well-beloved of God," but he notes that it is precisely sanctifying grace that makes us well-beloved of God.[35] What grace does is to make us "heirs of God and fellow heirs with Christ" (Rom 8:17) so as "to become children of God" (Jn 1:12). Grace prepares us for the life of glory. It does so by elevating and deifying the "essence" of the soul, and thereby transforming the soul's powers by infusing the virtues and the gifts of the Holy Spirit. By grace, therefore, we receive "a sort of second nature of such a kind as to enable us to perform con-naturally the supernatural and meritorious acts of the infused virtues and the seven gifts."[36] By grace the Father, Son, and Holy Spirit dwell in us "as in a temple where They are known and loved, even as it were experimentally," so that we know and love the distinct Persons of the one God.[37]

In support of this view Garrigou-Lagrange quotes Romans 8:15–16: "You have received the spirit of sonship. When we cry, 'Abba! Father!' it is the Spirit himself bearing witness with our spirit that we are children of God." In this way, grace enables us already to enter into eternal life (the kingdom of God), even if not yet fully. It should be clear that grace is so marvelous as to exceed, even in its least degree, the entirety of "all created natures" and the entirety of all miracles.[38]

Returning then to Mary, Garrigou-Lagrange supposes that the angel Gabriel recognized in her the gracious work by which God had prepared her to accept her motherhood. Her grace and charity, required for her mission, would have already been greater than that of a perfected angel. Jesus is the source of all grace after the Fall; in Jesus' predestination all others are predestined. Mary receives grace from her Son in a superabundant way pertaining to her motherhood, and thus in a greater way than any other saint. Her fullness of grace allowed for increase, however, and she grew in grace until her death.

Her initial fullness of grace comes from her Immaculate Conception. Because of the merits of her Son, she (and no other mere human) is preserved from "all stain of original sin," as Pope Pius IX states in his dogmatic definition.[39] What is original sin? Garrigou-Lagrange answers by enumerating the effects that the Church, at the Second Council of Orange and at the Council of Trent, associated with the Fall. To be preserved from these effects (e.g., "subjection to the law of concupiscence"), Mary had to be conceived in a state of sanctifying grace, of friendship with God.[40] Garrigiou-Lagrange specifies that Mary was not immaculately conceived in the sense of not needing redemption. Rather, her initial grace flowed from the foreknown merits of her Son. But if she was utterly free of sin at her conception, how is it that she can be said to need redemption? The answer is that redemption can be conceived in two ways: as a liberation from a stain already contracted, or as a liberation from contracting the stain. The latter is, indeed, the most perfect form of redemption. It is greater for a redeemer to ward off a wound than to heal a wound. Mary receives a "preservative redemption" because had she not received this grace, she would necessarily have been conceived in a state of sin, as the rest of us are.[41] Garrigou-Lagrange notes that the liturgy that Pope Sixtus VI approved in 1476 for the Feast of the Immaculate Conception makes this point (drawn from John Duns Scotus) about preservative redemption.[42]

On what basis does the Church say that Mary's Immaculate Conception belongs to the deposit of faith? Garrigou-Lagrange observes that in *Ineffabilis Deus*, which defined the dogma, Pope Pius IX quoted Genesis 3:15 and Luke 1:28, 42. Regarding Genesis 3:15, Garrigou-Lagrange recognizes that there is a difference between the Vulgate and the Hebrew: the Vulgate uses a feminine pronoun so that the words are "she shall crush [RSV: bruise] your head," whereas the Hebrew uses a masculine pronoun that stands for the "seed" or offspring of Eve. This difference, however, does not remove the main point, which is that "the woman is to be associated with the victory of Him Who will be the great representative of her posterity in their conflict with Satan throughout the ages."[43]

This association does not in itself demonstrate the truth that Mary was immaculately conceived. Rather, the significance of Genesis 3:15 for Pius IX appears in the typological connection between Eve and Mary drawn by the Fathers of the Church, a typological connection that associates Mary with the reversal of Eve's Fall. Garrigou-Lagrange is aware that to a historical-critical scholar, Genesis 3:15 will appear to be about the origins of the human antipathy toward snakes.[44] For the Fathers, however, it has a typological reference revealed in Christ. Furthermore, if Jesus were simply the "seed" or offspring of Eve, he too would be fallen. He is the offspring of Mary, and the "enmity" that the serpent (Satan) feels toward the "woman" is an enmity toward Mary. Garrigou-Lagrange comments appreciatively that "early Christianity never ceased to contrast Eve who shared in Adam's sin by yielding to the serpent's suggestion with Mary who shared in the redemptive work of Christ by believing the words of the angel on the morning of the Annunciation."[45] Since the Vulgate uses the word "crush" (*conterere*), Garrigou-Lagrange also appeals to the completeness of the victory over sin. In Genesis 3:15, he concludes, we find the Immaculate Conception of Mary, but only "as the oak is contained in the acorn."[46]

What about Luke 1:28 and 1:42, in which Mary is proclaimed "full of grace" and "blessed . . . among women"? By themselves, these texts are not sufficient to show Mary's Immaculate Conception; instead they must be read in the Church's exegetical tradition, beginning with St. Ephrem the Syrian and culminating in St. John of Damascus.[47] In their interpretation of Luke 1:28 and 1:42, these Fathers affirm that Mary is and always was utterly free from any stain of sin. Thus the Church, reading Scripture in the exegetical tradition and guided by the Holy Spirit, was justified in seeing in Luke 1:28 and 1:42 the implicit revelation of Mary's Immaculate Conception. The contrast between Eve as the cause of death and Mary as the cause of life was also made, as Garrigou-Lagrange notes, by St. Justin, St. Irenaeus, and Tertullian.

I will pass over Garrigou-Lagrange's treatment of Mary's perpetual virginity; he relies upon the biblical and patristic witness, as confirmed by councils and popes. He also treats Mary's participation in Christ's Cross, and he affirms the titles Mediatrix and Co-Redemptrix when properly understood as a uniquely graced sharing in the work of the one Mediator and Redeemer rather than as competition with her Son.[48] He imagines Mary's joy over Christ's Resurrection and her prayers with the apostles on the day of Pentecost. He envisions her uniting herself spiritually with Jesus in the Eucharistic sacrifice, and he imagines her hunger for the Eucharist and her reception of Jesus in the Eucharist from the apostle John, with whom she shared the contemplative life. He notes that "Mary became again the pure living tabernacle of the Lord when she communicated" in the Eucharist,[49] and he reflects on her increase in charity and faith as well as her possession of charisms such as discernment of spirits and even, perhaps, moments of beatific vision. He reviews her virtues and how they might have manifested themselves. He holds that Mary died, simply as a consequence of human nature which is subject to bodily decay unless upheld miraculously by God. Drawing on a homily by St. John of Damascus, he holds as a pious belief that her death was peaceful; she died of love, due to her readiness for heaven.[50]

Garrigou-Lagrange then turns to Mary's bodily Assumption. He first differentiates her Assumption from Jesus' Resurrection: Jesus, unlike Mary, rose by his own power. He defines the Assumption as "the taking up of Mary's body into heaven."[51] Even had witnesses seen her body transported from the grave, they could not have seen her arrival in heaven. For this reason, he thinks, there must have been a revelation (implicit or explicit) to the apostles, or at least to one apostle, regarding Mary's Assumption. This revelation must have been public, since a private revelation (such as certain saints have received with regard to Mary's Assumption) would not suffice for her Assumption to be included in the deposit of faith. Yet Scripture and the early Fathers do not bear explicit witness to a revelation of this kind. Can this impasse be overcome? Along lines that strike me as unpersuasive, Garrigou-Lagrange answers that "it can be proved indirectly from later documents that there was at least an implicit revelation since there are certain facts, dating from the 7th century, which are explicable in no other way."[52]

Preeminent among these facts is the celebration of the Feast of the Assumption by almost the whole Church beginning in the seventh century. In addition, especially from the seventh century onwards, numerous saints testify to Mary's Assumption. The celebration of the Feast of the Assumption exhibited the Church's faith, as confirmed by the successors of the apostles. Garrigou-Lagrange sees here the Church's ordinary magisterium at work, which in his view could not have happened so quickly unless the doctrine had been at least "implicitly revealed" to at least one of the apostles.[53] The agreement of the whole Church, furthermore, suggests that the revelation was not merely implicit but explicit. This is so, Garrigou-Lagrange thinks, because the whole Church would have confirmed a merely implicit revelation only after "much preliminary work and many preliminary councils," of which there are no records.[54] Why then is there no testimony before the fifth century to Mary's Assumption? Garrigou-Lagrange answers that, prior to this time, the mystery "was hidden behind a veil of silence, lest it be misunderstood through an unfortunate confusion with the fables concerning pagan goddesses."[55] He supposes that "the oral tradition of the Liturgy" must have transmitted the revelation about Mary's Assumption that had been made to the apostles (or to one of them), even though this liturgical tradition came into full view only in the seventh century.[56]

Garrigou-Lagrange also reviews properly theological or dogmatic arguments for affirming Mary's Assumption.[57] He provides two arguments that he considers to be fully demonstrative, rather than being arguments of fittingness. First, since Mary received the fullness of grace and was blessed among all women, she did not bear the curse of original sin—namely, to bear children in pain and to return to dust (see Gen 3:16–19). Her body therefore did not corrupt into dust in the tomb, as her body would have done if it had not been assumed into heaven.

Second, Christ won the victory over sin and death by his Passion, and Mary uniquely shared in his Passion through her supreme charity and compassion (that of his mother) at the foot of the Cross. Mary therefore also must have shared uniquely in Christ's victorious Resurrection, which she could only have done through her Assumption.

The premises of both arguments are revealed in Scripture, so long as one grants that Genesis 3:15 prefigures Mary, and so long as one interprets Simeon's prophecy to Mary that "a sword will pierce through your own soul also" (Lk 2:35) in light of Genesis 3:15. Regarding the second argument, some might suppose that it would suffice for Mary to be associated with Christ's victorious Resurrection by means of a resurrection on the last day. Garrigou-Lagrange argues, on the contrary, that because Mary shared more than anyone else in his victorious Cross—a victory that "included exemption from bodily corruption"—so Mary also must have shared in his exemption from bodily corruption.[58] The biblical texts that form the premises of these two arguments depict Mary as the new Eve, sharing with the new Adam in the reversal of the Fall. In Garrigou-Lagrange's view, the two arguments demonstrate that Mary's bodily Assumption is implicitly contained in divine revelation and is definable as a dogma of faith.

Garrigou-Lagrange also briefly notes four arguments of fittingness: Jesus would not have allowed his beloved mother's body to corrupt in the tomb; Mary's virginal purity, her lifelong freedom from all taint of sin, meant that the bonds of death (a consequence of sin) could not retain her body; Mary's Immaculate Conception would free her from death insofar as death is a consequence of sin; and, lastly, the fact that no relics of Mary's body exist implies that she was bodily assumed into heaven.

Even granted all these arguments for Mary's Assumption, however, why should the Church define it as a dogma of faith? (Recall that Garrigou-Lagrange's book was published in 1941.) He answers that, in combination with Jesus' Ascension, Mary's Assumption displays "the objective completion of the work of the Redemption, and gives our hope a new guarantee."[59] Its definition as a dogma would further strengthen the faithful against the representative errors of the day—specifically materialism, rationalism, and liberal Protestantism, all of which wish to minimize the content of faith "rather than to recognise that the gifts of God surpass our ideas of them."[60] The dogmatic definition of Mary's Assumption would spiritually nourish those who have faith and would thereby enhance their faith, hope, and charity. Regarding the impact that a dogmatic definition of Mary's Assumption would make on Protestants, he thinks that it would do them good by making "more manifest the power and goodness of Mary who has been given to men to lead them along the way of salvation."[61]

Garrigou-Lagrange's approach has strengths and weaknesses. Its greatest strength is perhaps its account of Mary's predestination and its insight that her motherhood has to do with the "hypostatic order." Its main weakness is its handling of historical arguments. Rather than admitting that the doctrine of Mary's Assumption cannot be based on surmises about historical evidence, Garrigou-Lagrange argues that in fact just such surmises are necessary in order to account for the Church's acceptance of the doctrine in the seventh and eighth centuries. In this regard, Duhr's strong warning against the appeal to history—a warning that he directs at both the authors of the legends and the skeptics—is preferable. Mary's Assumption was a hidden event, one that becomes knowable with the eyes of faith through the New Testament's typological portraits of Mary as interpreted by the Church under the guidance of the Holy Spirit. Garrigou-Lagrange appreciates these typological portraits of Mary, especially with regard to Luke 2:35. Nonetheless, in offering what he considers to be strict demonstrations of Mary's Assumption, he seems not to recognize how deeply his premises depend upon typological reasoning.

Recall Duhr's emphasis on the contribution of Genesis 3:15, as illumined by the Church's Tradition. He is aware that historical-critical readers of Scripture would not consider Genesis 3:15 to be a prophecy about Christ's and Mary's victory over Satan. Reading with the eyes of faith, however, he insists that the passage "establishes a strict connection between the Redeemer and His Mother" and "offers a scriptural basis for belief in the Assumption," unlike other biblical passages that are often quoted with regard to Mary's Assumption.[62] Duhr's book is largely devoted to surveying the history of the development and reception of the doctrine. His emphasis on Genesis 3:15 and on Mary as the new Eve, however, make clear the importance of determining what kind of biblical exegesis is at work in the Church's affirmation of Mary's Assumption.

Janssens follows a broadly similar path. While granting that there is no historical evidence from the early centuries, he holds that "the traditional idea of the most glorious and Blessed Mother is based, in a very considerable degree, on the data of the Sacred Scriptures."[63] In his view, however, the arguments from biblical texts will be forceful only in light of the "whole picture of Mary as the Mother of God and as the second Eve," a picture that flows not simply from Scripture but specifically from Scripture as read in light of the Church's authority as interpreter.[64] In this regard, he pays particular attention to the history of the liturgy and to the Fathers and doctors of the Church who favored the doctrine of the Assumption. In his theological reasoning, he begins with Mary's motherhood and then emphasizes that Mary is the new Eve, and his approach consists largely in arranging and evaluating texts from patristic, medieval, and baroque theologians.

Garrigou-Lagrange's approach is shaped speculatively or dogmatically by his argument in favor of the primacy of Mary's motherhood for understanding all Mariology. He views Mary's motherhood first in terms of her predestination. As mother of the divine Son of the Father, she is preeminently and uniquely Christ's associate and helper. On this basis, Garrigou-Lagrange makes manifest the important theological connections between the mysteries of Christ's life, Mary's Immaculate Conception, and Mary's Assumption, while carefully distinguishing Mary's Assumption from Christ's Resurrection. In my view, however, Garrigou-Lagrange errs when he argues that there must have been a public revelation of Mary's Assumption to at least one of the apostles, and when he claims to provide syllogistic demonstrations of the truth of Mary's Assumption. The fact that such a powerful thinker as Garrigou-Lagrange does not delve more deeply into the character of the biblical witness as a support for his views—instead presenting us with an alleged public revelation and two syllogisms—indicates the great need for the more focused engagement with biblical typology and with the biblical narrative that the *nouvelle théologie* provides.

The theologians of the 1930s and 1940s are at their strongest when linking Mary's Assumption with the other mysteries of faith, when highlighting the evidence from the Church's Tradition, and when speculatively extolling the greatness of Mary's motherhood. They also recognize, as does *Munificentissimus Deus*, the importance of biblical typology. We can find in these theologians, then, all the pillars of the doctrine of Mary's Assumption. As we will see in the next chapter, the theologians of the *nouvelle théologie* have their own distinctive strengths and weaknesses when it comes to articulating the doctrine of Mary's Assumption. What is needed, then, is to benefit from the strengths of both periods.

CHAPTER 3

The *Nouvelle Théologie* and Mary's Assumption

The year 1946 marked the beginning, in earnest, of the theological movement known as the *nouvelle théologie*. Other landmark events had occurred earlier: one thinks of the publication of Henri de Lubac's *Catholicisme* in 1938 and the founding by Jean Daniélou of the series *Sources chrétiennes* in 1941. Yet 1946 brought the debate between neoscholastic theologians and their younger colleagues into full view, notably through the publication of the first edition of de Lubac's *Surnaturel* and through the debate that took place in that same year between Daniélou, Marie-Michel Labourdette, and Réginald Garrigou-Lagrange.[1] In his "Les Orientations présentes de la pensée religieuse," Daniélou challenged the neoscholastic mode of theologizing as overly philosophical, propositional, and ahistorical. According to Daniélou, Catholic theology needed to reconnect with biblical exegesis, to be nourished by the Fathers (especially their typological exegesis and sense of history), and to learn from the liturgy rather than focusing on causality.[2] In a response titled "La Théologie et ses sources," Labourdette questioned whether theology, rooted as it is in supernatural faith, can rest upon historical research to the degree that Daniélou seemed to require.[3] For his part, in "La Théologie nouvelle, où va-t-elle?," Garrigou-Lagrange warned that a renewed modernism would be the result of the direction that Daniélou was taking.[4]

In retrospect, the debate between neoscholastic theology and the *nouvelle théologie* was short-lived. The main representatives of neoscholastic theology either died before the Second Vatican Council or had little influence upon the Council's documents. Furthermore, although the theologians of *nouvelle théologie* continued to write (voluminously in many cases) after the Council, post-conciliar theology went in a direction that surprised and dismayed many of them. Even so, the Magisterial writings of Pope John Paul II and Pope Benedict XVI were largely indebted to the *nouvelle théologie*, and Catholic and Protestant theologians today are more engaged than ever before with this movement of twentieth-century theology.[5]

In this chapter, I examine the contributions of the *nouvelle théologie* to the Church's understanding of the dogma of Mary's bodily Assumption. Pope Pius XII formally defined this dogma in the same year that he condemned, in his encyclical *Humani Generis*, certain strands of thought associated with the *nouvelle théologie*. How, then, did theologians associated with the *nouvelle théologie* interpret Mary's Assumption? I will suggest that they did so in two ways, one quite fruitful and the other less so. Fruitfully, many of them explored Mary's Assumption through typological exegesis of Scripture, guided by the Fathers and the liturgy. Less fruitfully, some of them explored the notion that the Church's traditional teaching on the intermediate state between death and bodily resurrection could be changed so as to hold that all humans, of whom Mary would be the exemplar, enter at the moment of death into resurrection life.

I will focus on four theologians. Three of them—Hans Urs von Balthasar, Louis Bouyer, and Joseph Ratzinger (Pope Benedict XVI)—clearly belong to the *nouvelle théologie*. The fourth, Karl Rahner, is generally not considered a *ressourcement* thinker, since he owes a great deal to classical Protestant liberalism and took part in founding *Concilium*, rather than *Communio*, after the Council. But in his recent book *Nouvelle Théologie—New Theology*, Jürgen Mettepenningen argues that Rahner, along with Edward Schillebeeckx, belonged at least in their original impulse to what Mettepenningen calls the "third phase of the *nouvelle théologie*."[6] As Mettepenningen shows, Rahner's complaints in the 1940s that neoscholastic theology was lifeless and cut off from Scripture echoed the concerns of Daniélou and de Lubac. Although in 1951

Rahner's superiors refused to allow his lengthy book on Mary's Assumption to be published, he was able to publish an influential article that showed the direction of his thought and whose basic thesis was taken up by Hans Urs von Balthasar.[7] Rahner and Balthasar suggest that Mary's Assumption is representative of what happens to all believers at the moment of death—a view that Ratzinger strongly contests. Bouyer and Ratzinger, joined by Balthasar, explore in detail the typological exegesis that supports the dogma of Mary's Assumption. Their biblical theology, which arises in part from desire to heal the Reformation divisions and which retrieves a central aspect of the patristic and medieval approach to this doctrine, enriches our ability to understand Mary's Assumption.

Karl Rahner: Mary the Exemplar of Resurrection-in-Death

From the early 1970s through the 1990s, Karl Rahner was the most influential voice in the Catholic theological academy. In his 1951 essay, "The Interpretation of the Dogma of the Assumption," Rahner sets out to interpret the meaning of the dogma that Pope Pius XII defined the previous year. In the text of *Munificentissimus Deus*, Pius XII notes that from John of Damascus through the great baroque theologians, theological expositions of Mary's Assumption were "based upon the Sacred Scriptures as their ultimate foundation," because Scripture presents Mary "as most intimately joined to her divine Son and as always sharing his lot" (§ 38). Rahner mentions this point in order to make clear that the purpose of his essay is not to show how Scripture provides the basis for the dogma; nor does he aim to show "how the dogma is contained explicitly or implicitly in the tradition of faith."[8] Instead, he wishes to investigate "the *content* of the new dogma," its "inner meaning," by asking what it means to say that a person has been glorified in the flesh in heaven.[9]

He first comments on Mary's role in salvation history. In her flesh and through her assent in faith, the divine Word became flesh, thus inaugurating eschatologically the salvation of the world. He is the sole Redeemer, but she cooperates with him by receiving him perfectly. She can do this because in her, "Christ's single and unique grace exhaustively surpassed man's sinfulness, even 'temporally' in a certain way, so that she can in no way (not even as to sin) call anything her own which is not the gift of the incomprehensible grace of the Father in the Son of her womb."[10] Rahner explains that this makes her the second Eve, who is the mother of all who live in Christ (and thereby the type of the Church).[11]

As a second step, he argues that human death is something more than mere biological cessation. It is instead "the furthest point of human existence," in which humans experience the "'hellish' depths" of alienation from God.[12] Having undergone such death, Jesus could be resurrected; there are no human depths that Jesus did not plumb, with the result that "man is saved through and through, and is capable of God's beatitude with his whole undivided being."[13] What Rahner calls "definitive salvation" is now available in Christ to each and every human person.[14] Christ descended into hell so as to lead others out of it; his Resurrection brought about in others (not only in himself) this victory over hell and death. Christ's bodiliness includes a relation to all other embodied persons, and his glorified body retains this relation to the community of human bodies. On this basis, Rahner challenges the notion that Christ's glorified body could remain alone, without other bodies, until the end of history. Such aloneness, Rahner insightfully points out, would deprive Christ's glorified body of something essential to bodiliness.

It follows that Matthew 27:52, which reports that after Christ's Crucifixion "many bodies of the saints who had fallen asleep were raised," is in Rahner's view "merely positive evidence from Scripture for what we would have expected anyway."[15] Given the social character of embodied human life, if Christ were alone in his glorified flesh, then he could hardly have "entered upon the fulfilment of his whole being."[16] Rahner adds that most of the theologians cited by *Munificentissimus Deus* in favor of Mary's Assumption also favored the view that Matthew 27:52 describes Old Testament saints who joined Christ in resurrection life. He cites and criticizes a 1950 article by Jean Daniélou, who argued that *Munificentissimus Deus* rules out interpreting Matthew 27:52 "in terms of a definitive, eschatological resurrection of these saints."[17]

What, however, is meant by a "glorified" body and by "heaven"? With respect to the glorified body, Rahner points out that its mode of existence can really only be known by those who are glorified. Even Jesus' manifestation to his disciples of his risen body did not answer the question. Nor can we understand to where Jesus ascended, given that his

Ascension cannot have been merely a spatial ascent (despite the ancient worldview that tended to assume this). We know only that we will be raised "imperishable," "in glory," "in power," and as "a spiritual body" bearing "the image of the man of heaven" (1 Cor 15:42–44, 49). Human bodiliness may require that heaven be a place, but heaven is not a place that we can locate. The event of Christ's Resurrection inaugurated a new space, incommensurable with the space that we know in this universe. Rahner states, "Beginning with Christ's body, this very world thus achieves even now a new mode of being by means of its history in Christ."[18] Christ's Resurrection established heaven as a new "order" that radically transforms this world, rather than replacing or refurbishing it; the bond between the old creation and the new must be emphasized, without neglecting the radical transformation of the present order into a new one.

What is the relationship of the new order, heaven, to God's eternity? Rahner states that "[t]he eternity in glory of the earthly and historical is not simply identical with God's eternity."[19] Our "eternity in glory" has a beginning, whereas God's eternity utterly transcends any temporal point of reference. As Rahner observes, "What is glorified retains a real connexion with the unglorified world, it belongs inseparably to a single, ultimately indivisible world; and that is why an occurrence of glorification possesses objectively its determinate place in this world's time, even if this point in time marks precisely the point at which a portion of this world ceases to endure time itself."[20] Christ's glorification takes place at a particular point in history, so that we cannot say that he has always already been glorified in the flesh. Our glorification and the glorification of "many of the dead" have not yet taken place.[21] There was also, then, a point in time when Mary was glorified in the flesh.

The "End of time" began when Christ rose from the dead. Humans enter into this End when they are raised and glorified in the flesh, and "thousands of years may still draw out this single End in Christ."[22] Rahner envisions people entering into this "single End" at various times along the course of history. We can say that some people have already entered into resurrection life with Christ, but we cannot say how many. Since Mary "is the ideal representation of exhaustive redemption" in her flesh and in her spiritual assent, she must now enjoy total salvation, "perfect communion with God in the glorified totality of her real being ('body and soul')."[23] Mary is with Christ in heaven, and to be in heaven means to have entered into the perfect redemption of one's whole being, spiritual and physical. Heaven is the realm established by Christ's Resurrection. Before Christ's Resurrection, no one could enter this realm, which explains why the "saints" (Mt 27:52) of the Old Covenant entered long after their deaths, whereas Mary experienced a much shorter "temporal interval between death and bodily glorification."[24] Rahner again emphasizes that Mary does not receive a privilege that others receive only at the end of history: "[S]ince the Resurrection it is completely 'normal' (which is not to say 'general') that there should be men in whom sin and death have already been definitively overcome."[25] In his glorified body, Christ is joined by a "bodily community" of glorified persons.[26]

Does this mean that many graves are empty, since many dead persons have entered into the total redemption won by Christ? Rahner does not say. He says simply that many of the dead have received the salvation of the body as part of the world's "transition to God's eternity."[27] Only those who have been completely redeemed in the totality of their being, like Mary, are in heaven. Rahner does not explain where the other dead are. Since Mary is the "perfect representation" of the Church, "the Church too is already redeemed totally, not in all her members certainly but already in reality in some of them."[28] Persons now alive on earth, for example, have still to go through death and have not yet been redeemed in their totality. According to Rahner, heaven is even now gradually extending itself, until eventually the whole world will have made the transition to the new realm of glory. The dogma of Mary's Assumption simply confirms that the total salvation born of Mary includes her.

Rahner develops his position significantly in an essay published in 1975 on "The Intermediate State." In this essay, Rahner addresses Pope Benedict XII's *Benedictus Deus* (1336), in which Benedict XII defines that the souls of the blessed are united to Jesus Christ in heaven, and enjoy the beatific vision, "even before the resumption of their bodies and the general judgment."[29] This doctrinal definition had been taken as a definition of, among other things, the existence of an intermediate state during which the separated soul awaits the resurrection of the body at the end of time. In Rahner's view, however, the definition simply affirms that death, for the faithful, leads to "the blessedness of their souls and the glorification of their bodies."[30] The intermediate state plays a role in the definition only as "an intellectual framework, or way of thinking"—in other words, as an "unconsidered assumption" that is not itself "a truth that is binding for faith."[31] For Rahner, the intermediate state itself does not form part of the teaching to which Catholics must assent; it is not heretical to reject the intermediate state.

Rahner then presents the theses that he wishes to defend in his essay: "that the single and total perfecting of man in 'body' and 'soul' takes place immediately after death; that the resurrection of the flesh and the general judgement take place 'parallel' to the temporal history of the world; and that both coincide with the sum of the particular judgements of individual men and women."[32] It should be clear that his theses generally fit with his 1951 position on the meaning of Mary's Assumption. In the earlier essay, he affirmed that many of the dead, including Mary, have already received the redemption of their whole being (spiritual and physical) and have thereby entered into heaven. The later essay adds that all humans at the moment of death enter into bodily resurrection and final judgment, so that all humans are in Mary's position of having received resurrection life at the moment of death. Although his earlier essay suggests that not all humans enter into resurrection life as Mary did, and that until Christ's Resurrection humans had to wait to be resurrected, the two essays are complementary. The 1951 essay holds that the dogma of Mary's Assumption confirms what we would expect to have happened to Mary and to many others as well. This perspective accords with the 1975 essay's argument that the moment of death ushers each human into "the resurrection of the flesh and the general judgement."

In "The Intermediate State," Rahner observes that his purpose is not to prove that the intermediate state does not exist, but simply to inquire into a topic about which theologians can legitimately have various opinions. He begins with the testimony of Scripture.[33] When Scripture speaks about "the resurrection of the flesh," it has in view, Rahner argues, the resurrection of the whole person. At the same time, Scripture contains assurances that at our death we will be with Christ, as for example when Christ tells the good thief, "Truly, I say to you, today you will be with me in Paradise" (Lk 23:43) and when Christ tells his disciples that "he who hears my word and believes him who sent me, has eternal life; he does not come into judgment, but has passed from death to life" (Jn 5:24). In the Old Testament, the doctrine of resurrection develops late; still later we find the doctrine that all humans, and not merely the blessed, will be raised. The Old Testament passages treat first the whole people of God, and only secondarily the individual as a member of the people. The salvation that the Old Testament envisions always involves the whole person, not simply the body or the soul. Insofar as Sheol is depicted as a disembodied state, it is depicted as a thoroughly unhappy one.[34] In the New Testament, Rahner asserts, to be "in Paradise" simply means to have escaped the powers of destruction. Thus the intermediate state "is not in itself New Testament doctrine."[35]

According to Rahner, patristic interpretation of Christ's descent into hell (Sheol) provides additional evidence against the intermediate state. Rahner claims that the Fathers considered the harrowing of hell to be "a *physical* resurrection" rather than "the freeing of the soul alone for the contemplation of God."[36] Certainly by the late medieval period, thanks partly to the impetus of Pope Benedict XII, theologians held that the soul receives its perfection prior to and independent of the future fate of the body, although some theologians argued that the resurrection of the body would enhance the perfection of the soul. The notion of the intermediate state, then, arose in the medieval period and, as "a stage in the history of theology," sought "to reconcile the collective and the individual view of eschatological perfection" by positing an intermediate period of time during which souls awaited the end of history.[37] A better way of reconciling collective and individual eschatology, Rahner suggests, would be to think of the individual's entrance into resurrection life as belonging to the "progressive transformation of world history and the cosmos in general."[38] Death ushers the individual beyond time, beyond any kind of free history.

This solution also handles the problem of the "separated soul." If the soul is the form of the body, so that soul and body constitute a substantial unity, then the soul itself is the act of informing the body. Take away this act, and one takes away the soul. Rahner notes that he had previously tried to resolve this problem by positing that the soul is primarily related to the unified matter of the whole cosmos, so that it is through this relation (which would not be destroyed by bodily death) that the soul is the form of the body. But he now thinks that the problem can be solved much easier by doing away with the notion of the separated soul.

One difficulty that arises from Rahner's solution, of course, is how to claim that the dead person's body has been raised when, at the very same time, the dead person's body is decomposing in the grave. In answer, Rahner argues that the identity between the person's glorified body and the person's dead body does not depend upon material continuity.[39] The matter in a person's living body changes constantly; none of us possesses the same matter that we had a decade ago. Since matter is not the principle of identity, there should be no difficulty in holding that a person's dead body can be decomposing in the grave even while that person's glorified body is alive in heaven. As Rahner says, "For us, identity consists, now and in the future, of the identity of the free, spiritual subject, which we call 'the soul'."[40] The dead body in the grave can be ignored, because death has ushered the person into the resurrection life of glorified bodiliness. This position, however, does seem to come at the cost of significantly downgrading the value of a human being's historical body.

Philosophically, Rahner thinks that the distinction between body and soul in the human person can be maintained, on the grounds that otherwise the person could not be the free "subject of what is transcendent without limit."[41] Yet he notes that precisely as such a subject, the human person is embodied. All intellectual acts bear the mark of our bodiliness, and so we truly can only conceive of the human being as a unity. It follows that the human person's free quest for transcendence "acquires finality before God" insofar as the whole person (body and soul) is transformed.[42] On these grounds, even philosophical reasoning can postulate the resurrection of the body. By contrast, neither philosophically nor on the basis of revelation can one conceive of a disembodied human existence of the kind required by an intermediate state.

For Rahner, then, the dogma of Mary's Assumption does not require us to hold that Mary received a special privilege, whatever its drafters might have supposed. The dogma sets Mary apart for the simple reason of her unique role in salvation history. We cannot say with theological certitude that all the blessed enter immediately into resurrection life, but we nonetheless can recognize that this is the most plausible way to expound and defend the dogma. Once the intermediate state has been ruled out, the dogma makes good sense of the transition that death involves, and does so in a way that should be acceptable not only to Catholics but also to Protestants.

Rahner takes up a final methodological objection—namely, that in the space of his short essay he has not treated certain texts from Scripture and Tradition that seem to favor an intermediate state. In answer, he observes that he need only show that the intermediate state is not a binding truth of faith; he need not answer texts that, given their cultural context, inevitably included Platonic accretions and presumed "a naively empirical view of the corpse in the grave."[43] He distinguishes here between "the binding content of a statement and temporally conditioned modes of expression based on an intellectual framework belonging to a particular period."[44] He is confident that these intellectual frameworks can be separated with relative ease from the "binding content," a confidence that flows from his optimism about his own intellectual framework as well as from his conviction that earlier intellectual frameworks entangled Christianity in a number of clearly false presumptions about physical being. Those who refuse to separate the binding doctrine from the ancient philosophical framework, he thinks, inevitably commit Christianity to such absurdities as "monogenism, a 'materialist' view of the resurrection body, hell-fire in the physical sense, and the idea of a unified 'substance' in the eucharistic bread."[45] The intermediate state is just such an absurdity, but, he thinks, a generally harmless one so long as it is not considered to be binding upon faith.

In short, Rahner considers that Mary's Assumption is a truth of theological anthropology: at the moment of death, Mary, like all the blessed, entered into resurrection life in her totality. She possesses her glorified body even though her earthly body remains in the grave. Since this position will be criticized ably by Ratzinger, I will not discuss it further here, other than to register my own disagreement with Rahner.[46]

Hans Urs von Balthasar: Giving Birth to Heaven through Self-Surrender

Although during his lifetime he never achieved the prominence of Rahner, Hans Urs von Balthasar was the leading light behind the international journal *Communio* and today his massive corpus of writings receives wider attention than does Rahner's. For Balthasar's approach to Mary's Assumption, we might begin with his *The Threefold Garland:*

The World's Salvation in Mary's Prayer, originally published in 1978. Regarding Mary's Assumption, Balthasar states, "Those who have wholly put themselves in the hands of God are also wholly accepted by God and wholly perfected by him. Mary's total submission was such that, along with her whole soul, she also offered up her whole body, and this is precisely what God needed in order to realize his plan of salvation."[47] Mary could not have fully assented to her motherhood as she did without offering herself totally to God in the holy action of her soul, a self-offering that included her body since she was called to be mother of the Christ, mother of God. From eternity, in God's plan, her spiritual assent is connected with the Son's redemptive assumption of flesh from her body. Balthasar argues that the bodily dimension of this assent, this union with her Son, cannot dissolve at her death: "[H]er word of assent will draw her back up into heaven in her totality."[48] He adds that Jesus "cannot be an isolated man without his fellow man, without a woman companion. An 'isolated man' is a contradiction in terms."[49] Drawing on Paul's identification of Jesus as the new Adam, Balthasar (like Rahner—and in my view quite rightly) holds that to posit that Jesus now experiences a solitary existence at the right hand of the Father would be to suggest that Jesus' risen existence, as regards his glorified flesh, is less than fully human because it lacks embodied sociality.

For Balthasar, Jesus "stands at the center" as the one in whom others find salvation.[50] In the Eucharist, Jesus shows that his body has "room enough" for the whole Church, so that "Jesus' body is everything but a private body."[51] In other words, all humans are social creatures, but the Son of God made man is even more so. In the flesh, he invites others to be united to him; he does not stand aloof. He is at the center not because he keeps others away, but because he draws others to himself. Now that he sits at the right hand of the Father, he draws all humans even more powerfully, by sharing his Spirit and his body eucharistically. Balthasar states that "the Church becomes one flesh with him through the Eucharist."[52] His flesh is from Mary. Mary, representative of the Church, "becomes one flesh with him" in heaven, just as he is one flesh with Mary.

Balthasar holds that Mary is the "immaculate Bride" that Christ prepares for himself, "that he might present the church to himself in splendor, without spot or wrinkle or any such thing, that she might be holy and without blemish" (Eph 5:27).[53] Yet Mary is also one of the members of this Bride. Because the Son takes flesh from her, her body too is not "a private body," although in a different way from her Son's. The individual body of Christ and the corporate body of Christ (the Church) correspond to Mary's dual status as an individual member of the Church and as the model of the Church. Mary "is the part and she is the whole, which is fashioned after her model and oriented toward her holiness,"[54] because all are called to share in her faithful response to her Son. Like her Son, Mary died. Because she was without sin, she freely surrendered her life to God. As Balthasar puts it with her whole life in view, "She lived continually in the transition from life in her own self to life in God."[55]

On what basis, however, does the Church know that Mary's life in God has indeed been perfected? Balthasar thinks that the answer consists in a form of typological exegesis, what he describes as "an in-depth meditation on the biblical texts if they are seen alongside each other and if their interior consequences are thought through."[56] He argues that it is unsurprising that it took the Church some time to understand the full "truth concerning Mary-the-Church," even though this truth was "very early" recognized "as an essential aspect of the truth about the Son of the Father and the conditions for his incarnation."[57] Balthasar also implies that death ushers *all* Christians into resurrection life, but he here leaves this aspect unclear. He says simply that if we die a Christian death, "It will be God's business that we reach him not as mere halves of ourselves, but as whole persons. With Christ and Mary the created world has already been taken up into transformation and transfiguration, and the Last Day has already begun. World history does indeed continue still, but in eternal life there is no time that corresponds to historical time."[58] The only way to reach God "not as mere halves of ourselves" would be to reach him as soul-body unities, just as the doctrine of Mary's Assumption testifies that she did.

In one of his last books, *Mary for Today* (originally published in 1987), Balthasar approaches the topic of Mary's Assumption in a different way. He begins by stating that by his Resurrection and Ascension, Christ established heaven for us. The heaven that Christ established is the same place that Paul has in mind when Paul states that he "would rather be away from the body and at home with the Lord" (2 Cor 5:8) and that "[m]y desire is to depart and be with Christ, for that is far better" (Phil 1:23). In heaven, Christ is with the "innumerable throng" of his saints.[59] This heaven is, in some sense, "the fullness of heaven."[60] Balthasar compares Christ's establishing heaven through his Resurrection and Ascension to "giving birth" to heaven, and he notes that each of us, by imitating Christ's self-surrendering love through the power of the Holy Spirit, gives birth to our own heaven "at the end of an earthly pregnancy."[61] He reasons that in light of the idea of giving birth to our heaven, "the proclamation of Mary's physical assumption into heaven will no longer seem so displeasing to us."[62]

Why would the idea of giving birth to our heaven render Mary's Assumption less difficult to understand? Balthasar connects Mary's giving birth to Christ with her "giving birth" to her heaven. Since "Mary as a whole," soul and body, was "the vessel for his [Christ's] entry" into earthly life, it makes sense that Mary's body-soul totality belongs to God's plan from eternity. Christ comes to redeem humankind and to give birth to heaven. Mary is present, body and soul, at the outset of this plan, and since the plan is for the sake of humankind, she should not be missing from the fulfillment of this plan. Balthasar states, "From this insight that Mary as a whole had her origin in God's heavenly plan, the Church understands that Mary also could only be taken up into the same total reality that has now been made real and where she had always had her place."[63] Furthermore, by suffering with Christ in the holy freedom of self-surrender, she was giving birth by the power of the Holy Spirit to her own heaven, and Balthasar considers that "there could be no accident, no miscarriage, in her earthly pregnancy that was bearing heaven."[64]

If her "earthly pregnancy" had as its denouement bodily Assumption into the heaven established by Christ, what about our own "giving birth"? Since her Son wills to come to us through Mary, Mary is mother of all who are in her Son, and she prays for us. While recognizing that Christ is the one Mediator and that Mary is never praying "over against" her Son but always in, with, and through him, Balthasar describes Mary as "the help we need that our birth into heaven may be successful."[65]

In the final volume of his *Theo-Drama*, originally published in 1983, Balthasar discusses Mary's Assumption and the intermediate state. He begins with the affirmation that "[t]he Bible, both Old and New Testaments, knows of only one Judgment, just as there is only one Day of Yahweh or of Christ."[66] This is important, because it means that there is no "particular judgment" that distinguishes, in an intermediate state prior to the general resurrection, those who have died. According to Balthasar, Scripture insists that the one general judgment is also the "personal and *particular* judgment."[67] In terms of historical time, there is one end of history and one judgment at the resurrection of the dead. The Resurrection of Jesus makes the eschatological future, the end-time, "a present reality."[68] This truth, Balthasar thinks, was depicted by the evangelist Matthew in his statement that "the tombs also were opened, and many bodies of the saints who had fallen asleep were raised" (Mt 27:52). Like Rahner, Balthasar states that "the majority of theologians assume that these saints were also received into heaven along with Jesus."[69]

If the end-time is a "present reality," established by Jesus' Resurrection and Ascension, then those who die in historical time enter directly, body and soul, into the judgment and eternal life. In Balthasar's view, there is a crucial sense in which "Jesus' Resurrection took place in all truth at the end of the world, since he has atoned for those who will come after him in time just as much as for those who were before him and contemporaneous with him."[70] This means that those who rose with him were also rising "at the end of the world"; it is not historical time that is definitive here, but rather it is Jesus' establishment of heaven and eternal life. Balthasar adds that with respect to the martyrs who are depicted as reigning with Christ in "the first resurrection" (Rev 20:5), "there is no suggestion here that this resurrection is a merely spiritual one."[71] The point is that Christ's Resurrection and Ascension establish heaven as a place where others dwell with him not merely as disembodied souls in an intermediate state, but rather in their body-soul totality.[72] The supposition of an intermediate state requires two judgments (a particular judgment and then the general judgment at the end of time), but as we have seen Balthasar has already ruled this out on biblical grounds.

What then is purgatory? Is it not descriptive of an intermediate state? Balthasar answers that it is simply "one aspect of the personal character of judgment," not an intermediate state.[73] Agreeing with Rahner, whose essay on the intermediate state he cites, Balthasar holds that the final judgment takes place immediately upon the death of the individual, so that the final judgment and eternal life do not await the end of historical time. There is no need, therefore, to speculate about a disembodied intermediate state or how the soul subsists without the body. Those who try to imagine a disembodied intermediate state are taking on a "difficult" task, and Balthasar urges that we not try to conceive of "a *communio sanctorum* made up of both embodied and disembodied souls."[74] Once we recognize that we die into body-soul eternal life, we can understand why Matthew reports the saints rising with Christ. Mary's Assumption into heaven is another example of this, and Balthasar reports that "many believe" that the apostle John was also assumed.[75] Is everyone then assumed into heaven, body and soul, at the moment of death? Balthasar says that we cannot know this with certainty, because "our ignorance of heavenly super-time (which does not even need to be internally affected by the end of chronological world-time) prevents us from coordinating the two levels satisfactorily."[76]

We can know, however, that when Jesus tells the Sadducees that the God of Abraham, Isaac, and Jacob is "not God of the dead, but of the living" (Mt 23:32), Jesus means that God "has these living persons with him, both as embodied and 'risen from the dead' and as enspirited."[77] If this is so, then certainly many of the dead, in addition to Mary, have been bodily assumed into heaven. More likely, all the dead have been bodily assumed (or raised), because as Balthasar insists, "No temporal hiatus is posited [by Jesus or by Scripture] between being with the living God and resurrection."[78] Balthasar proclaims that "the resurrection of the dead, or their glorification in God, has already begun with his Resurrection and the resurrection of those who rose together with him."[79] In other words, although we cannot with certitude coordinate "heavenly super-time" with earthly historical time, we can know enough to say that upon their death, many or (more probably) all people enter directly into judgment and eternal life in their soul-body totality. In her Assumption, Mary is one of those people, even as she is the exemplar of the whole people of God.[80] Balthasar does not discuss the question of where, in historical time and historical place, Mary's body (or John's, or the other saints') is now.

Further elements of Balthasar's position can be gleaned from the third volume of his *Theo-Drama*, originally published in 1978. Regarding Mary and all others who have a secondary share in Jesus' mission, Balthasar states, "It is impossible to discover which is prior in God's plan: the election of the individual for his universal mission or the election of the 'great nation' that is to result from the mission."[81] Reflecting on Jesus as the "last Adam" (1 Cor 15:45) or the "second Adam," Balthasar remarks: "[I]f he is the 'Second Adam', surely he is incomplete until God has formed the woman from his side?"[82] In this case, the woman must both be an individual—since Jesus is an individual—and represent humankind, which is "feminine" in relation to God.[83] The woman must in some sense come forth from the second Adam's side, and yet "as woman was made from man, so man is now born of woman" (1 Cor 11:12). Mary fits these requirements. She is mother of God and mother of the Church, and she is also a member of the Church in her self-surrendering love.

Many of the Fathers—Balthasar names Justin, Irenaeus, and Tertullian—depict Mary as the new Eve. They do so, however, only insofar as her obedience contrasts with Eve's disobedience; when Eve is considered as Adam's bride and helpmate, the new Eve is the Church. Mary is like the Church because the Church gives birth to Christ's members, but the Fathers do not equate Mary with the Church. Yet there is an important "parallelism between Mary as Mother of the Head and the Church as the Mother (Bride) of the Body," a parallelism that in Irenaeus can even be an "assimilation to the point of identity."[84] The medieval theologians press this parallel so that Mary also becomes the new Eve as Christ's bride and, in some sense, as his helpmate. Balthasar traces various distortions that arise from this identification, largely ones in which Mary takes on too strongly the redemptive and mediatorial role of her Son, as if Christ were the strict judge and Mary the merciful one. After correcting these distortions, he appreciatively sets forth the Second Vatican Council's teaching in *Lumen Gentium* on Mary, focusing on Mary's motherhood and the parallels between her and Eve (and thus her status as a "type" of the Church).[85]

What does this have to do with the doctrine of Mary's Assumption? Balthasar explains, "After what we have said about the typology between Mary and the Church (a typology that goes as far as identity), it is impossible to avoid seeing a Marian side in the picture of the Woman of the Apocalypse."[86] Revelation 12:1 depicts "a woman clothed with the sun, with the moon under her feet, and on her head a crown of twelve stars"; in verse 5 this woman brings "forth a male child, one who is to rule all the nations with a rod of iron, but her child was caught up to God and to his throne"; finally in verses 13–15 the "dragon" pursues the "woman," who flies to a protected place in the wilderness, with the result that "the dragon was angry with the woman, and went off to make war on the rest of her offspring, on those who keep the commandments of God and bear testimony to Jesus." Balthasar observes that an allegory of this kind could hardly have been written in the late first century without some awareness of Mary, the mother of Jesus. In Balthasar's view, it is at least clear that "the Woman is oriented to eternity"—as is shown by her child Jesus, by the rest of her children (the Church), and by her own attributes ("clothed with the sun" and so forth).[87] Given her orientation to heaven, it follows that "the question of her translation (*transitus*) to heaven arises automatically," not only in the sixth century but, Balthasar thinks, well before (in legendary form).[88] Her position in salvation history—which is presented in Revelation 12 in terms of her sanctity, her suffering with her Son, and her status as mother of the Church—means that Mary cannot be corrupt in either soul or body. For Balthasar, this is the meaning of Pope Pius XII's dogmatic definition.[89] Balthasar does not define "the nature of Mary's transition to heaven," other than to say that she died and entered body and soul into eternal life with Christ.[90]

To summarize Balthasar's position: Christ's Resurrection and Ascension have established "space" for our eternal life. Eternal life does not correspond to historical time; there is no intermediate state of separated souls awaiting the general resurrection. It is therefore possible and even likely that all the dead have been raised with Christ, although in historical time their corpses remain in the grave. Regarding Mary's special place in Catholic dogma, Balthasar explores her motherhood and her status as the second Eve. In this regard, he reflects on such themes as Mary being one flesh with Christ, Mary's self-surrender as "giving birth" to her entrance into heaven in her totality, the necessity that the second Adam not be alone, and the importance of the fact that we do not relate to Mary as to a pure spirit. He also argues that Revelation 12:1–15 is an allegory not only about the Church but also about Mary. The Church has the authority to speak truths about Mary that are not found explicitly in Scripture or in the early patristic tradition because some truths are unfolded by the Church over time, as the various biblical texts are gathered together and pondered by both theologians and the whole people of God.

In certain ways, Balthasar's theology of Mary's Assumption follows Rahner's. This is the case, for example, with his insistence that human "embodied sociality" requires that the ascended Christ not remain alone in his glorified flesh at the right hand of the Father. This is also the case with Balthasar's rejection of the intermediate state and his insistence upon resurrection-in-death. In my view, the strongest parts of Balthasar's theology of Mary's Assumption arise from his typological connection of Mary with the Church. Here his use of biblical texts, including Revelation 12, Ephesians 5, and 1 Corinthians 11 and 15, stands out.

Louis Bouyer

Louis Bouyer is best known for his contributions to the mid-century liturgical movement, but he also composed a number of major works of dogmatic theology. His *The Seat of Wisdom: An Essay on the Place of the Virgin Mary in Christian Theology* was written after the definition of the dogma of Mary's Assumption but before the Second Vatican Council. In this book, Bouyer focuses on three main biblical themes: Eve in relation to Adam, the people of God as the bride of the Lord, and the feminine personification of divine Wisdom. Each of these themes, he argues, is instructive both about the Church and about Mary. He begins with a careful sketch of these themes in the Old Testament, from which he draws three conclusions. First, woman is "the inseparable companion of man both for his blessing and for his downfall," and she is "the bearer of the promise of redemption."[91] Man is "radically incomplete without woman."[92] The main Old Testament texts that Bouyer notes in this regard are Genesis 2–4, Genesis 49:22–25, and Psalm 128:1–3. Second, although God does not need human companionship, and indeed although humans have turned away from God, nonetheless by making covenant with Israel God seeks to build up a people who will be his "bride." The main Old Testament texts here are Hosea 1–3, Ezekiel 16, Isaiah 54–55, the Song of Solomon, and Psalm 45. Third, before the creation of anything else, God created the pattern of his wisdom, a pattern that reflects himself and that is personified in feminine form. God configures his people to this pattern, so that "[s]he who is to ascend to him from the desert at the end of time is she who came down from him at the beginning."[93] Here Bouyer points especially to Job 18, Baruch 3–4, Daniel 2, Proverbs 8, Sirach 24, and Wisdom of Solomon 7–8. Bouyer concludes, "What the Old Testament does is to lay down the lines of thought that must be followed in order to understand the significance of the New," even though "the themes previously treated underwent a transposition which was made possible only by the new factors brought in by the Gospel."[94]

Along these lines, Bouyer argues that the account of the Annunciation (Lk 1:26–38) should be read in light of the Genesis account of Adam and Eve's temptation. The contrast between Mary's belief and obedience and Eve's disbelief and disobedience is evident, as is the contrast between the sons to whom they give birth. The angel tells Mary that she will conceive the Messiah by the Holy Spirit—"The Holy Spirit will come upon you, and the power of the Most High will overshadow you; therefore the child to be born will be called holy, the Son of God" (Lk 1:35)—and this overshadowing by the Holy Spirit corresponds to the "Spirit of God" that "was moving over the face of the waters" (Gen 1:2) at the first creation as well as to "the breath of life" by which God made Adam (Gen 2:7). Bouyer holds that "it is, in fact, a new creation that takes place in Mary, in the creation of this new man that Jesus is,"[95] and this new creation includes Mary. When Elizabeth tells her, "Blessed are you among women, and blessed is the fruit of your womb!" (Lk 1:42), Mary responds with her Magnificat, which, in its anticipation of Jesus' beatitudes, shows "that the Gospel of her Son finds its first and perfect fulfilment in herself."[96]

The same approach characterizes Bouyer's treatment of Revelation 12. The "woman clothed with the sun, with the moon under her feet, and on her head a crown of twelve stars" is the mother of "a male child, one who is to rule all the nations with a rod of iron" (Rev 12:1, 5). She is, then, the mother of Christ. She is also the Church, since the "dragon" makes "war on the rest of her offspring" (Rev 12:17). The parallel between the "great dragon," "that ancient serpent, who is called the Devil and Satan, the deceiver of the whole world" (Rev 12:9), and the serpent of Genesis 3 is clear. As Bouyer says, "This is yet another feature that emphasises the parallel continuously present in the minds of the early Christians between the Virgin Mary (or the Church) and Eve."[97] The water that comes forth from the serpent symbolizes chaos and death, in contrast to baptismal water; the child being taken up "to God and to his throne" (Rev 12:5) represents the Ascension of Christ. The cosmic participation in redemption appears in the earth's coming "to the help of the woman" (Rev 12:16).[98] In the new creation, Mary plays the role of the second Eve, thwarting the devil as part of the triumph of the second Adam.

In addition to this theme of the second Eve, there is also the theme of the "bride" of the Lord. Revelation 12 speaks not only of Israel/Church but also of Mary, since she (as the mother of Christ) is the one who "fled into the wilderness, where she has a place prepared by God" (Rev 12:6) and who received "the two wings of the great eagle that she might fly from the serpent into the wilderness" (Rev 12:14). Bouyer states, "As the new Eve intimately associated with the struggle and triumph of the new Adam, Mary is revealed to us as the perfect realization of the Church, in so far as she is the heavenly spouse, and as more than the Church, being mother of the heavenly king himself."[99] Mary embodies the "heavenly spouse" in her bridal motherhood. Bouyer also discusses the marriage feast at Cana, where Mary's interaction with Jesus is summed up by her command to the servants, "Do whatever he tells you" (Jn 2:5), exemplifying the obedience of faith. At the marriage feast, Mary teaches us the obedience of the bride of the Lord. Furthermore, when Mary and the beloved disciple are together at the foot of the Cross, Jesus tells them: "Woman, behold your son! . . . Behold your mother!" (Jn 19:26–27). This shows that Mary's motherhood is intimately linked both with the Church and with the Cross. The Church is the bride of Christ (Eph 5); thus Mary's motherhood is bridal. The Church is also, as configured to the Cross, the revelation of the wisdom of Christ (1 Cor 1–2, Col 2). Patristic liturgies and iconography connect Mary and the Church with the texts that personify (feminine) wisdom. This point will be especially important in Bouyer's treatment of Mary's Assumption.

After treating a variety of Marian doctrines, Bouyer focuses on Mary's Assumption in his final chapter, "Wisdom and the Assumption." As noted above, the Old Testament personifies wisdom as a feminine figure who was the first of God's works, the pattern and goal of creation, and the agent through whom God accomplishes the salvation of his people. As a creature, this wisdom could not be Christ. The image of the mother of Christ as "clothed with the sun, with the moon under her feet, and on her head a crown of twelve stars" (Rev 12:1) therefore led the Church to think of this feminine wisdom as, in certain ways, a depiction of Mary. The problem that arises for this connection, however, is whether it is "possible to transpose [Mary] absolutely to the plane, at once precosmic and eschatological, of the Wisdom who is the architect of the universe, of that other self who is the Spouse God finds for himself in history, who was not to be found in eternity, but who, nevertheless, in some aspects, overflows and anticipates the world of time."[100]

It would seem that the likely answer would be no. Yet Mary's motherhood, in God's eternal plan for the Incarnation of the Son and the eschatological redemption of the world, does indeed have both historical and trans-historical dimensions. With respect to wisdom as a divine attribute, Bouyer affirms the connection between wisdom and the Word: "In God himself, Wisdom has no transcendent and independent actuality, but is realised only in the person of the Son, the Word."[101] But insofar as the Word becomes incarnate and unites all creation to himself, bringing it back to the Father through the Holy Spirit, wisdom involves something on the side of creation as well.[102] On the side of creation, there is a feminine wisdom, characterized by the receiving of God and a unification of all things. The Church at the end of time is the embodiment of this responsive wisdom, "the holy city, new Jerusalem, coming down out of heaven from God, prepared as a bride adorned for her husband" (Rev 21:2). Like the Church, says Bouyer, "Mary is truly the Seat of Wisdom, of the uncreated Wisdom shown forth as a creature in her Son who is, at the same time, Son of the Father."[103] In Mary, the creation (in faithful self-surrender) is made rich by the Son's divine self-surrender. Mary's responsive and receptive wisdom mirrors the Wisdom of the Son; without Mary, there could be no Church.[104] Like the ark of the covenant and the Temple, Mary receives the glory of God into her dwelling, and this glory is not simply for her but for the glorification of the whole people of God.

How does this relate to her bodily Assumption? Bouyer links the reception of divine Wisdom, from the side of mere creatures, with Mary and with the Church (and thus with each of the blessed). Indeed, in her motherhood and charitable participation in Christ, Mary already possesses what the whole Church, when brought to fulfillment at the end of history, will possess.[105] The relationship between Mary and the Church sheds light on her being healed from sin and death: because God elects her to be the mother of his Son, Mary is most perfectly healed from sin before all others, and she is likewise restored from death before all others. She receives these graces on behalf of the Church, and so she is a symbol that the whole Church will also attain to perfect purity and to bodily glorification. In Mary, Christ has already united the Church to himself in the flesh, so that the Church's prayer is already perfectly united to his: Mary's intercession shares in Christ's rather than competing with it, as she prays that we, her children, "may come to be united to her in her Son."[106] Bouyer concludes that Mary, "united to [Christ] in glory, is still in the pangs of childbirth, till the marriage of the Lamb is consummated, and the last of the elect is born from the Cross to glory."[107]

In sum, Bouyer argues that Mary can be best understood in light of three biblical types: Eve in relation to Adam, the people of God as God's bride, and the feminine personification of Wisdom. He shows the typological relationship of Mary to Eve through various examples, such as the Annunciation story, in which Mary's belief and obedience contrasts with Eve's disbelief and disobedience, as well as the explicitly typological language of Revelation 12. Through this typology, he depicts Mary's motherhood as bridal, intimately united with the work of her Son. Mary's virginity, mentioned by Luke and Matthew, shows that her motherhood inaugurates a new creation, again a typological parallel with Eve. As the new ark and temple, the one who reflects the divine Wisdom that dwells within her, she receives beforehand the restoration from sin and death that God wills to give creation through Jesus Christ. She uniquely shares in the glorification that Christ accomplishes for his bride, the new Eve. Bouyer's central point is that it is the Bible itself that requires us to understand Mary typologically. It is this emphasis that makes Bouyer's work valuable for the theology of Mary's Assumption.

Joseph Ratzinger: Mary as Wholly Baptized into Christ

The most famous exponent of the *nouvelle théologie*, although a full generation younger than the others, is Joseph Ratzinger, whose stature as a theologian was secured by his election as pope in 2005. What does

Ratzinger offer to the theology of Mary's Assumption? Perhaps his most important contribution is his insistence that the blessed undergo a period of waiting prior to the general resurrection, as opposed to the position—adopted as we have seen by Rahner and Balthasar—"that death itself leads out of time into the timeless."[108] In his *Eschatology*, Ratzinger notes that the theory that death is a direct portal into the general resurrection, if it were true, would remove the difficulties of the doctrine of Mary's Assumption by offering a portrait of life after death (and of the "end of time") that requires neither an immortal soul, nor an intermediate period, nor an actual end of temporal history. According to those who hold this theory, "The person who dies steps into the presence of the Last Day and of judgment, the Lord's resurrection and parousia," with the result that "what the dogma of the assumption tells us about Mary is true of every human being."[109]

Ratzinger identifies at least three serious problems with this theory. First, the result of this view is that people whose bodies are now lying in their graves are said to be alive in the flesh. If their bodies are risen, then how are their bodies in the grave? How can their bodies be both completely dead and alive? Ratzinger observes that this position does not really take bodies seriously. To claim that the dead body is dead in historical time but that the dead person also now possesses his or her body in eternal life is to undermine the significance of our historical bodiliness, one component of which is that when a person's body is dead, that person's body is certainly not alive. Ratzinger rightly remarks, "What we have here is a covert assumption of the continuing authentic reality of the person in separation from his or her body."[110] In attempting to solve this problem without the spiritual soul, theologians make the problem worse by positing a glorified body that has no real relation to the decomposing body in the tomb.

Second, Ratzinger asks: "Are we really confronted with a choice between the stark, exclusive alternatives of physical time on the one hand, and, on the other, a timelessness to be identified with eternity itself?"[111] Eternal life has a beginning for us, rather than being eternal in the strict sense. Although it is not an extension of historical time, our eternal life therefore does not utterly do away with before and after. For this reason, a waiting period prior to the general resurrection is not ruled out by the concept of eternal life. To suppose otherwise would be to suppose that death is not the beginning of our eternal life, but instead that we have always (or eternally) experienced eternal life on the eternal level, even while on the historical level we experience a temporal life. In fact, such a view would simply take to its furthest consequences the split between the historical level and the eternal level that results from the theory that death ushers us immediately into resurrection life.

Third, while making it easier to account for Mary's bodily Assumption, this theory calls into question what it means to say that Jesus died, was buried, and rose from the dead on the third day. It would seem that Jesus' death would accomplish his resurrection immediately on the eternal level. If so, then his Resurrection on the third day would be a mere manifestation of the reality that had already occurred at the very moment that his followers were grieving over his death. His burial and "descent into hell" would have no real meaning. By contrast, for the New Testament, Jesus does indeed undergo an intermediate period between his death and his resurrection.[112] Furthermore, if we die into resurrection life, then Jesus' Resurrection would be nothing more than a manifestation of what actually happens to every single person, rather than the radical inbreaking of God's salvation that the first followers of Jesus proclaimed.

Two years after the publication of Ratzinger's *Eschatology*, his critique of the theory of resurrection-in-death was echoed by the Congregation for the Doctrine of the Faith in its "Letter on Certain Questions Regarding Eschatology" (May 17, 1979).[113] This Letter concludes that Rahner's way of making sense of the dogma of Mary's Assumption—namely, as the expression of what happens to all of us when we die—does not work as a matter of Catholic doctrine.

In 1977, Ratzinger also published a book-length study of Mary, *Daughter Zion: Meditations on the Church's Marian Belief*.[114] This study contains his central constructive insights regarding Mary's Assumption, which he develops within a profoundly biblical (and typological) theology of Mary. As we will see, the tenor of his approach is quite similar to Bouyer's. Ratzinger first remarks that Marian doctrine can appear to be a "scaled-down duplicate of Christology" or simply a Christian version of pagan goddess worship, arising from a need for a feminine dimension in worship.[115] If this were the truth about Marian doctrine, he says, then it would have to be rejected entirely, but in fact it has a rich biblical grounding. He remarks that "the image of Mary in the New Testament is woven entirely of Old Testament threads," and—much like Bouyer in his placement of three biblical types at the forefront of his exposition—he identifies three Old Testament figures in particular: Eve, Hannah, and Israel as daughter Zion.[116] In a characteristically typological manner, the New Testament draws on each of these figures in portraying Mary.

Ratzinger first takes up the figure of Eve. God makes Eve from Adam's rib, because it is "not good" for Adam to be alone (Gen 2:18). Humans are "fulfilled in the oneness of man and woman," just as it is as "male and female" that humans image God (Gen 1:27).[117] Eve is so named "because she was the mother of all living" (Gen 3:20), preserving her life-giving power even after the Fall. Eve's relation with Adam and her association with life, Ratzinger says, will be typologically "taken up again in the dogma of the Assumption."[118]

The second figure is Hannah. Hannah belongs in the Old Testament's line, beginning with Sarah, of infertile women who play a decisive role in transmitting the covenantal blessing of Israel. The blessing of the infertile woman shows that it is God's promise, not physical fertility, that ultimately gives life. To be blessed by God, we must rely on God's promise rather than on the resources of physical life. Hannah's song affirms that God not only makes the infertile woman a mother of many children but also "lifts the needy from the ash heap, to make them sit with princes and inherit a seat of honor" (1 Sam 2:8). All pride and arrogance are put to shame: the first will be last. This figure is taken up in Mary's Immaculate Conception (election and grace) and virgin motherhood.

The third figure or type is that of Israel as daughter Zion. Ratzinger finds this type in such women as Esther and Judith. Although Israel is enduring oppression, these women are spiritually strong and capable of overcoming Israel's enemies. Their strength comes solely from the Lord, and in this way they embody the true Israel, daughter Zion. In this light, Ratzinger notes that Israel is almost always personified as feminine in relation to God. He cites Hosea in particular, in which God depicts his indestructible love for his unfaithful wife Israel. The covenant between God and Israel (Zion) is presented in terms of a marital covenant. As Ratzinger comments, "In the women of Israel, the mothers and the saviors, in their fruitful infertility is expressed most purely and most profoundly what creation is and what election is, what 'Israel' is as God's people."[119] The acceptance of the Song of Solomon into the canon also exhibits this theology of Israel as God's bride. In the New Testament, the figure of daughter Zion finds its fulfillment in Mary, virgin and mother; Mary stands for Israel in assenting to the Incarnation. Ratzinger adds that the feminine personification of Wisdom, as the first creature or as the "answer" to God from the side of creatures, fits into the figure of daughter Zion as well. He states, "From the viewpoint of the New Testament, wisdom refers, on one side, to the Son as the Word, in whom God creates, but on the other side to the creature, to the true Israel, who is personified in the humble maid whose whole existence is marked by the attitude of *Fiat mihi secundum verbum tuum*."[120]

In sketching these three figures, Ratzinger's interpretation of the Old Testament is both literal and thoroughly typological. He argues that absent reflection on Mary, the full meaning of these Old Testament figures cannot be grasped. At the same time, study of New Testament texts alone cannot provide the foundation for the Marian doctrines; they require for their intelligibility the whole of Scripture. As Ratzinger observes, "They can become visible only to a mode of perception that accepts this unity, i.e., within a perspective which comprehends and makes its own the 'typological' interpretation, the corresponding echoes of God's single history in the diversity of various external histories."[121] Since historical-critical biblical scholarship easily divides Old and New Testament texts without seeing their (often typological) unity, the biblical foundations of the Church's Marian doctrines tend to be less evident to exegetes and theologians today.

Even if one grants that the New Testament's typology indicates that Mary is the new Eve, the New Testament does not draw the conclusion that Mary is sinless or that she was assumed into heaven. Such conclusions involve a further typological extension, now made not by the New Testament authors on the basis of Old Testament figures, but by the Church on the basis of reflection on the New Testament exposition of the Old Testament figures. Does this extension of the Marian typology count as biblical exegesis, inspired by the Holy Spirit, or is it simply the Church's imagination?

In response, Ratzinger takes up the three central Marian doctrines in the following order: Mary as virgin and mother, indeed mother of God; Mary's sinlessness; and Mary's unique participation in her Son's Resurrection. Regarding the first, the Apostle Paul emphasizes the priority of the promise and says that Jesus is "born of woman" (Gal 4:4). Mary's virgin motherhood is presented in the Gospels of Matthew and Luke. Ratzinger notes that in Luke the annunciation of John the Baptist's conception occurs in the Temple whereas, given Jesus' status as the new temple, the annunciation of Jesus' conception occurs in Nazareth.[122] The angel's greeting to Mary corresponds to Zephaniah 3, with Mary in the role of daughter Zion: "Sing aloud, O daughter of Zion; shout, O Israel! Rejoice and exult with all your heart, O daughter of Jerusalem! The Lord has taken away the judgments against you, he has cast out your enemies. The King of Israel, the Lord, is in your midst" (Zeph 3:14–15). The Holy Spirit that will overshadow Mary alludes to the creation (Gen 1:2) and to the cloud of glory overshadowing the Temple (1 Kgs 8:10–11). Mary is the infertile daughter Zion who bears the Savior of the world.

When Ratzinger turns to Mary's Immaculate Conception, he raises the central objection at once: "Facts . . . cannot be deduced through speculation, but can be known only through some communication (revelation). But such a communication regarding Mary does not exist."[123] A second objection asks how, if Mary is immaculately conceived, she can be said to need redemption. Along these lines, Karl Barth (for example) insists that God accepts the sinner Mary as the conceiver of her Son. Ratzinger responds that the priority of God does not require that there be no holy receptivity on the part of Israel. God promises Israel a righteous "remnant" (Isaiah 37 and elsewhere) and Paul argues that this holy remnant (Rom 11:7) has indeed received Christ. Mary embodies this holy remnant, and she unites the Old and New Covenants by offering a holy response to God's word. Her response derives entirely from God, and yet it is a true creaturely response (since God does not encounter opposition in her).[124] This brings Ratzinger back to the first and most difficult issue: how can we justify affirming that Mary is the sinless "remnant"?

The only way, he thinks, is through typological reasoning. As he points out, original sin itself is a typological doctrine. When Paul teaches that "one man's trespass led to condemnation for all men" (Rom 5:18), he does so through a typological argument based on Adam. If original sin can be accepted on the basis of Paul's typological exegesis, then the question is whether the New Testament offers any typology that would support the doctrine of Mary's Immaculate Conception. Ratzinger's answer is Ephesians 5. Here Paul states that Christ sanctifies the Church so that she may be "without spot or wrinkle or any such thing" and "holy and without blemish" (Eph 5:27). On the basis of Luke's and John's "typological identification of Mary and Israel," these statements in Ephesians about the Church are transferable to Mary, so that Mary is seen to embody personally "the rebirth of the old Israel into the new Israel, of which the Epistle to the Ephesians spoke."[125] The Mary-Church typology, argues Ratzinger, belongs as much to the New Testament as does the Adam-Christ typology that undergirds the doctrine of original sin. An example is the connection of Mary in Luke 1:28 with "daughter Zion" of Zephaniah 3:14. For Mary to be preserved from original sin means that "Mary reserves no area of being, life, and will for herself as a private possession: instead, precisely in the total dispossession of self, in giving herself to God, she comes to the true possession of self."[126] Her virginal dispossession, her barrenness, enables her to bear the Savior. Mary truly is the holy Church, in person, who responds fully and freely to the Lord thanks to his grace. The link between the Mary-Church typology and Paul's typological presentation of Christ and the Church in terms of marriage (Eph 5) is a link that Paul himself does not make. Instead, the Church perceives this link by tracing and connecting the biblical typologies.

Turning to Mary's Assumption, Ratzinger observes that the dogma does not attest to a "historical tradition of an historical fact," since there was no such tradition and since the event was not "historical" in the public sense that Jesus' Resurrection was.[127] In light of the crucial distinction between Jesus' publicly witnessed Resurrection and Mary's hidden Assumption, Mary's Assumption is not termed "Resurrection" by Pius XII. The dogmatic definition does not present itself as the defense of Mary's Assumption on historical grounds, but rather confirms the truth of centuries of liturgical veneration of Mary. Both the dogma of Mary's Immaculate Conception and the dogma of her Assumption are first and foremost acts of praise and veneration. Mary is recognized as most fully a "saint."

With this in mind, Ratzinger finds the biblical roots of Mary's Assumption first in the mandate that the Church venerate Mary, as in Luke 1:42, 45, and 48. In the Old Testament, extolling Abraham, Isaac, and Jacob means extolling the divine name; and the same is true in the New Testament for Mary. In Mark 12:26–27, Jesus makes clear that those who are venerated in this way will be resurrected. Death cannot keep them, because their God is the God of life. Given the connection between birth and death (Gen 3:16), Ratzinger considers it significant that Mary "bears him who is the death of death and is life in the full sense of the word."[128] As mother of God, she bears the one who breaks the cycle of death; and her motherhood belongs within this victory. This argument is essentially typological, rooted in and extending Jesus' insistence that God "is not God of the dead, but of the living" (Mk 12:27). Her motherhood breaks the cycle of birth and death, and her fullness of grace enables her assent to this motherhood. Mary's fullness of grace, her total self-dispossession, means that "death is absent, even if the somatic end is present. Instead, the whole human being enters salvation, because as a whole, undiminished, he stands eternally in God's life-giving memory that preserves him as himself in his *own* life."[129] In this way, Mary's Immaculate Conception implies her Assumption.

Ratzinger holds that it is to Mary alone, as the perfect Christian, that we can fully apply Colossians 3:3, "For you have died, and your life is hid with Christ in God," and Ephesians 2:6, "[God] raised us up with him, and made us sit with him in the heavenly places in Christ Jesus."[130] Because of her spiritual and physical motherhood, she possesses all the blessings of faith and baptism; she dies with Christ so as to be raised with him. She is most "blessed" (Lk 1:45) ultimately because, given her perfect self-dispossession, God has raised her up to sit with Christ in heaven (Eph 2:6). Along these typological lines of reasoning, it follows that "she who is wholly baptized, as the personal reality of the true Church, is at the same time not merely the Church's *promised* certitude of salvation but its *bodily* certitude also."[131] In her, we see that the new Israel will not fail or be cut off.

Ratzinger concludes with one final typological connection. King David, leading the ark of the covenant into Jerusalem, leaps and dances with joy before the ark (2 Sam 6:14–16). The Hebrew term for leaping, when translated into Greek, is the same word as that found in Luke 1:44, where Elizabeth tells Mary that "when the voice of your greeting came to my ears, the babe in my womb leaped for joy." To understand Marian doctrine, we require this sense of joyous veneration, of leaping and dancing before the ark of the covenant which Mary truly is.[132]

For Ratzinger, then, the Marian doctrines flow from the Church's typological exegesis and liturgical praise of Mary. These doctrines would fall to the ground without the acceptance of typology as a real way in which God has communicated truth about the mysteries of salvation. That God has used typology in this way is shown to us by Scripture, and indeed by Jesus himself. Guided by the same Holy Spirit, the Church over the centuries has liturgically and theologically interpreted Scripture's typological portraits of Mary by making typological connections that illumine the full reality of Mary's motherhood and her sharing in Christ's mission.

This chapter sheds particular light upon the content and style of the theology of Mary that we found in *Lumen Gentium* and even more in *Redemptoris Mater*. With the exception of Rahner, the theologians treated in this chapter rely upon biblical-typological arguments. Balthasar, Bouyer, and Ratzinger cite texts from the whole of Scripture in order to present Mary as a type of the Church (the new Eve, daughter Zion) and as participating uniquely in Christ's work. It might seem, however, that this focus on biblical typology neglects arguments based upon the Church's authority as interpreter of revelation, as found in the Church's liturgical and theological tradition. Likewise, the fittingness of Mary's Assumption in relation to other doctrines—for example, to her Immaculate Conception—also seems to receive somewhat less attention in these authors.

These appearances can be misleading. For example, Rahner's assertion of resurrection-in-death as the key unlocking the doctrine of Mary's Assumption leads to reflection on the Church's traditional teaching about the intermediate state and the final judgment, and Balthasar's emphasis on self-surrender (our "birth" into heaven) relates Mary's Assumption to Christ's *kenosis*. Bouyer's use of Genesis 2–4, Hosea 3, and Proverbs 8 connects a number of long-standing ways of thinking about

Mary—the new Eve, the type of the bridal Church, the feminine figure of personified Wisdom—in a manner that illumines how Mary's Assumption flows from her unique participation in the work of her Son. Ratzinger builds upon the Church's long-standing veneration of Mary (see Lk 1) in his typological reasoning about Mary's Assumption.

Even so, the heavy employment of biblical typology and typological reasoning by these theologians can appear to be quite a shaky reed upon which to ground a dogma of faith, even one that is also founded upon the authority of the Church and upon fittingness in the whole plan of salvation. With regard to Mary's Assumption, the Church has identified typological portraits of Mary in the New Testament and has reasoned typologically (in a liturgical context) from these and other biblical passages to the reality of Mary's Assumption. But to see these typologies in Scripture—even typologies such as Eve-Mary in the Gospels of Luke and John—generally requires reading with a prior appreciation for typology. The question inevitably arises regarding whether there are legitimate grounds for employing typological interpretation to make claims about events in history such as the Assumption of Mary. Correspondingly, what is the rationale for accepting the Church as the authoritative interpreter of divine revelation, able to identify the various elements of God's wise plan and perceive their harmony?

In the three chapters that follow, therefore, I undertake a constructive inquiry into the status of the three pillars of the doctrine of Mary's Assumption: biblical typology and typological reasoning, the Church's authority as interpreter of revelation under the guidance of the Holy Spirit, and doctrinal fittingness. If these pillars are scripturally sound, then, so my argument goes, faith in Mary's Assumption is scripturally sound as well. Having gained a sense for the twentieth-century Catholic conversation about Mary's Assumption, we are ready to turn to the first of our three pillars, biblical typology. I will ask whether Paul's use of typological reasoning about scriptural events should be seen as justification for the Church's use of typological reasoning to identify Mary's Assumption as a real event within the history of salvation.

PART II

CHAPTER 4

The Validity and Scope of Typological Exegesis

In his *Essay on the Development of Christian Doctrine*, John Henry Newman argues that for the Fathers, typology played a significant role in
doctrinal formulation.[1] Both in Scripture and in the Fathers, typological
reasoning seeks insight into a particular biblical person or event by
identifying biblical "figures" or "types" of that person or event.[2] With regard to the Nicene debates, Newman points to the Fathers' typological
interpretation of the following biblical texts: "'My heart is inditing of a
good matter,' or 'has burst forth with a good Word;' 'The Lord made' or
'possessed Me in the beginning of His ways;' 'I was with Him, in whom
He delighted;' 'In Thy Light shall we see Light;' 'Who shall declare His
generation?' 'She is the Breath of the Power of God;' and 'His Eternal
Power and Godhead.'"[3] The Fathers considered these texts to speak of
Christ. When Scripture is not read in this way, Newman thinks, the fulfillment that Christ brings will not be apparent.[4] He adds that even the
Council of Trent, whose arguments are often seen as strictly scholastic
and as having little place for typological reasoning, "appeals to the peace-
offering spoken of in Malachi in proof of the Eucharistic Sacrifice; to the
water and blood issuing from our Lord's side, and to the mention of
'waters' in the Apocalypse, in admonishing on the subject of the mixture
of water with wine in the Oblation."[5]

For Newman, therefore, the use of typological reasoning in Marian doctrine is what we should expect of orthodox Christian faith. In this regard, he draws attention to the typology found in Revelation 12. Identifying the "serpent" of Genesis 1 with Satan, Revelation 12 explicitly takes up the prophecy of Genesis 3:15, "I will put enmity between you and the woman, and between your seed and her seed; he shall bruise your head, and you shall bruise his heel." Recall that in Revelation 12 the "woman clothed with the sun, with the moon under her feet, and on her head a crown of twelve stars"—that is to say, the greatest mere creature— "was with child" and "brought forth a male child, one who is to rule all the nations with a rod of iron" (Rev 12:1–2, 5). Granting the references here to Israel and the Church, Newman also perceives a reference to Mary as the new Eve, who participates in the victory over the "serpent."[6] As he says in his *Essay on the Development of Christian Doctrine*, "If then there is reason for thinking that this mystery at the close of the Scripture records answers to the mystery in the beginning of it, and that 'the Woman' mentioned in both passages is one and the same, then she can be none other than St. Mary, thus introduced prophetically to our notice immediately on the transgression of Eve."[7]

Typological reasoning of this kind clearly played a significant role in fostering Christian proclamation that Mary was assumed bodily into heaven. Setting to the side for now the question of whether the Holy Spirit guided the Church in this doctrinal discernment, this chapter asks whether typological reasoning has a legitimate place within the Church's interpretation of divine revelation.[8] Can typological interpretation— both in Scripture *and* as a mode of the Church's exegesis—instruct us about the persons and events of salvation history? Or does typology, while useful enough for moral exhortation and imaginative stimulation, need to be kept at a distance with regard to events that occurred (or are said to have occurred) to real people in history?

In what follows, I address this question by surveying three contemporary Protestant approaches to typological exegesis by Richard B. Hays, Peter Enns, and Peter Leithart. Hays is a leading New Testament scholar; Enns is an Old Testament scholar whose work focuses on how Christian scholars should interpret the Old Testament; Leithart is a Reformed theologian. In different ways, all three recognize the importance of typology in Scripture and encourage its appropriation by contemporary exegetes. None of the three, I hasten to add, would have sympathy with the doctrine of Mary's bodily Assumption.

Hays and Enns demonstrate the value of typological exegesis both for the New Testament authors and for addressing certain problems facing the Church today, such as how to form believers as the people of God and how to read the Old Testament. They argue that Christians today cannot deny the validity of this mode of interpretation, even if, in Enns's view, we should distance ourselves from it as a culturally conditioned mode of interpretation. For both Hays and Enns, however, typological reasoning cannot teach us about the past. Instead, it should form us in the present by enabling us to perceive Christ as the fulfillment of Israel's story and ours. For his part, Leithart insists that typological reasoning can attain to real insight about the past because history itself is providentially patterned and typological reasoning uncovers these patterns. But Leithart leaves one wondering how true typological renderings of the past can be distinguished from fanciful ones. His performative understanding of how such discernment occurs in the Church indicates, in my view, the need for the Church's Magisterium, but otherwise I think he is right. Drawing upon these three Protestant scholars, I hope to show that on biblical grounds the typological reasoning that we find in the theology of Mary's Assumption is warranted in its doctrinal use.

Richard B. Hays: Typological Imagination and the Church's Practices

In his *First Corinthians*, Richard Hays observes that in 1 Corinthians 10, "By speaking of Israel as 'our fathers' and by reading the wilderness narrative as a typological prefiguration of the church's experience, Paul blurs the boundary between past and present and invites his readers to reimagine their lives as belonging to that story."[9] In this reimagining, Hays explains, the Corinthians' claim to belong to the story of Israel depends upon their union with Israel's Messiah, as well as upon the corresponding claim that Israel has always been ordered eschatologically by God toward fulfillment in the Messiah and his community. The latter claim raises the question of whether or in what way Paul's blurring of "the boundary between past and present" is legitimate. Does the wilderness narrative (Exodus and Numbers) intrinsically possess a typological character, or has Paul added typology in a manner extrinsic to the event and/or the narrative? In other words, is there a basis in Israel's past for the typological connection with the Gentile converts of Corinth?

In answer, Hays argues that when Paul describes the Israelites on the exodus journey as being baptized and eating supernatural food, biblical interpreters "should not make the mistake of supposing that the Old Testament itself interprets these events as sacramental symbols or that Jewish tradition before Paul had conceived of these events as figurative foreshadowings of future realities."[10] Rather, Paul is simply "thinking metaphorically, perceiving illuminating likenesses between dissimilar entities."[11] Paul's statements should not be used to claim that sacramental grace was at work in Israel. This would be anachronistic and would miss the point that in developing his typological metaphors, "Paul is reading Israel's story through the lens of the church's experience and discovering figurations of God's grace."[12] The "figurations" help to explain the Church's experience in Christ and the Holy Spirit, but do not describe the persons and events of Israel's Scriptures.

Hays points out that Paul's typological metaphors belong to a genre of scriptural interpretation common in his day. As Hays notes, Wisdom of Solomon 11:4 suggests that Wisdom arranged to give the journeying Israelites water "out of flinty rock, and slaking of thirst from hard stone" (cf. Exod 17:6). In 1 Corinthians 1:30, Paul states that God made Christ "our wisdom." This may be the link by which Paul arrives at the view that "the Rock was Christ." Philo, too, identifies the rock with the wisdom of God.[13] Hays concludes that Paul's statement should be taken as an evocative metaphor rather than as a claim about the past. Paul's goal is to issue a moral warning to the Corinthians: if they continue to share in sacrificial meals offered to pagan gods, they will be judged and condemned to death for their idolatry, just as were most of the Israelites on the exodus journey.

For Hays, therefore, the key is not the particular types, which are metaphors, but rather the insistence that the Corinthians should make decisions today by locating themselves typologically within the scriptural narrative. In his view, typological reasoning of this kind should be practiced by all Christians. Typology helps us to inhabit the biblical stories and to be formed by them in our individual and communal decision-making. Thus Hays encourages his fellow preachers "to let our metaphorical imagination work boldly as we seek to discover previously undiscerned correspondences between our world and the scriptural story."[14] The purpose of these metaphorical types is not to learn more about the biblical world itself, but to learn how to inhabit the biblical story ourselves and to be configured to its patterns. Hays affirms, "Thinking typologically is a necessary survival skill for adult Christians. . . . Rather than seeking to make the text relevant, Paul seeks to draw his readers *into* the text in such a way that its world reshapes the norms and decisions of the community in the present."[15] Typology encourages us to affirm that the people of God that we encounter in Scripture is the people of God that we are today, and to learn how to live as God's eschatological people by inhabiting the stories of God's people Israel.

If Paul means only to stimulate the metaphorical imagination of his congregation, however, why does he say that certain events *happened to Israel* as types? The answer, Hays thinks, is Paul's eschatological perspective. Paul holds that everything God accomplished within his people in the past was done in view of the eschatological fulfillment that has now occurred in Christ and the Holy Spirit. As Hays says, "From the privileged perspective of the new eschatological situation in Christ, Paul rereads the Old Testament stories and finds that they speak in direct and compelling ways about himself and his churches, and he concludes that God has ordered these past events 'for our instruction.'"[16] But could God have ordered the events of Israel's history so that these events actually were the types that Paul thinks they were?

In answering this question, it is instructive to compare Hays's reading of 1 Corinthians 9:9–10, where Paul claims that a Mosaic law about oxen "was written for our sake," with Hays's interpretation of 1 Corinthians 10:1–4. With respect to 1 Corinthians 9:9–10, Hays comments that "a careful look at the context of Deuteronomy 25:4 lends some credence to Paul's claim about this particular text. The surrounding laws in Deuteronomy 24 and 25 (especially Deut. 24:6–7, 10–22; 25:1–3) almost all serve to promote dignity and justice for human beings; the one verse about the threshing ox sits oddly in this context."[17] This differs, Hays thinks, from Paul's typological reading of Exodus 17:6 (and the exodus journey) in 1 Corinthians 10:4, where Paul teaches that "the Rock was Christ." But it seems to me that Hays does not pay sufficient attention to

Exodus 12–17, which contains the major "types" of Christian sacramental theology: the Passover lamb and Passover meal (Exod 12), the crossing of the Red Sea (Exod 14–15), the manna (Exod 16), and the water from the rock (Exod 17), as well as the pillars of cloud and fire (Exod 13) that symbolize the Holy Spirit.[18] So long as sacraments are understood analogously, Exodus 12–17 provides a context highly favorable to Paul's claim about Israel that "all ate the same supernatural food and all drank the same supernatural drink" (1 Cor 10:4), despite Hays's warning against "supposing that the Old Testament itself interprets these events as sacramental symbols."[19] Why does Hays attend to Deuteronomy 25:4's context but not to Exodus 17:6's?

The same chapter of 1 Corinthians includes the following sacramental text: "The cup of blessing which we bless, is it not a participation in the blood of Christ? The bread which we break, is it not a participation in the body of Christ? Because there is one bread, we who are many are one body, for we all partake of the one bread" (1 Cor 10:16–17). Hays argues that Paul means that the participants in the meal "are brought into partnership or covenant (cf. 11:25) with Christ."[20] For Hays, Paul's words "have nothing to do with mysteriously ingesting Christ in the meal."[21] Paul has in view neither Jesus' real presence in the Eucharist, nor a sacramental eating of Jesus' body and blood that would configure us to Jesus. To emphasize this point, Hays states that "Paul is not thinking of some sort of mystical union effected through the meal—an idea foreign to the Old Testament."[22] Hays's conclusion here is arguably shaped by his view that Paul's sacramental types have no basis in Israel's history or in Israel's narrative. I would suggest to the contrary that Paul's types do suggest "some sort of mystical union." If the Israelites in some sense "drank from the supernatural Rock" and ate "supernatural food," then one might suppose that the eschatological fulfillment of this supernatural nourishment (and supernatural presence) would indeed be a "mystical union" with Christ "effected through the meal."[23]

In sum, comparison of Hays's discussion of Paul's typological reading of Deuteronomy 25:4 (1 Cor 9:9–10) with his discussion of Paul's typological reading of the Exodus narrative (1 Cor 10:1–4) suggests that Hays is more comfortable with typology when it has to do with the community's moral practices than when it bears upon sacramental doctrine. Paul's typological use of Exodus, with its sacramental overtones, raises issues for Hays that do not arise when Paul uses Deuteronomy typologically for the purpose of shaping the community's treatment of those who preach the Gospel. Hays's assumption that Paul is not right about the supernatural or sacramental character of the manna and water can be challenged on the basis of Hays's more fully appreciative account of typological reasoning when applied to the moral practices of Israel and the Church. Why does Hays not allow that Paul's typological extension of Christian sacraments (baptism and the Eucharist) can uncover something true about Israel's past?

Discussing 1 Corinthians 10:1–13 in *Echoes of the Scripture in the Letters of Paul*, Hays makes many of the same moves that we have seen in his commentary. He notes that Paul has in view "Israel's experiences in the wilderness."[24] Paul's interpretation of these experiences as "types" (1 Cor 10:6) means, Hays thinks, that we should not read Paul's interpretation as descriptive of Israel's actual experiences in the wilderness. Rather, Paul's interpretation is a work of imagination whose aim is to interpret the present experiences of his Corinthian congregation. Hays states that "Paul fancifully explores the figurative possibilities inherent in the imaginative act of reading Exodus as metaphor for early Christian experience."[25] He grants that Paul's "fanciful analogies" have a "serious point"—namely, to exhort the Corinthians to take seriously their responsibility to avoid idolatry.[26]

Among the "fanciful analogies" are Paul's claims that the Israelites "were baptized into Moses in the cloud and in the sea" (1 Cor 10:2), that the Israelites consumed "supernatural food" and "supernatural drink" (1 Cor 10:3–4), and that a "supernatural Rock" (Christ) followed them (1 Cor 10:4). These types transpose the Corinthians' present experiences of baptism, the Eucharist, and Christ's presence to the past journeying of the Israelites under Moses. According to Hays, these types instruct the Corinthians that "participation in spectacular spiritual experiences does not relieve the people of God from ethical responsibility."[27] By placing the Corinthians in the shoes of the Israelites who experienced such wondrous miracles but whose later rebellion against God prevented them from entering the promised land, Paul exhorts the Corinthians to live according to the moral of the scriptural story rather than continuing to live from within pagan narratives about food offered to idols. Paul aims to move the Corinthians by means of "explicit and startling figurative claims; the effect of the passage is achieved through an outpouring of explicit figurations."[28] We would be missing the point if we concluded that Moses "passed out baptismal certificates."[29]

Hays desires to show that Paul's typology in 1 Corinthians 10 does not efface historical Israel. Recognizing the problem caused by denying that the types have a basis in Israel's history/narrative, Hays asks: "If Israel's story is a metaphor for Christian experience, has Paul so usurped the meaning and claims of the precursor story that he has in effect annihilated it, deprived it of a right to independent existence? . . . Does the Pauline Israel/church typology annihilate Israel and subordinate Scripture to Paul's own belated conceptions?"[30] In response, Hays emphasizes that "Paul thinks of the Corinthian Christians as Gentiles no longer; they have been incorporated into Israel."[31] The Scriptures of Israel directly address the Corinthian Christians as members of the one Israel. When Paul speaks in 1 Corinthians 10 of the consequences of Israel's unfaithfulness, he does so to show the Corinthians the moral path that they themselves are on, not to negate the "independent existence" of Israel's story of the exodus. Hays explains that this "is surely one reason for Paul's fanciful reading of Christ back into the exodus: if Christ was present to Israel in grace and judgment just as he is now present to the church, the Corinthians have no remaining ground for supposing themselves to possess an immunity from judgment that Israel did not possess."[32] This does not detract from the significance of the events of Israel's actual history. As Hays says, "The church discovers its true identity only in relation to the sacred story of Israel, and the sacred story of Israel discovers its full significance—so Paul passionately believed—only in relation to God's unfolding design for salvation of the Gentiles in the church."[33]

The final chapter of *Echoes of the Scripture in the Letters of Paul* provides a general assessment of Paul's mode of reading Scripture. Again stressing Paul's eschatological perspective, Hays observes that for Paul, "Scripture is construed metaphorically: it signifies far more than it says. Its latent sense is disclosed only to those who 'turn to the Lord.'"[34] Hays recognizes that Paul's typological exegesis "generates novel interpretations that nonetheless claim to be the true, eschatologically disclosed sense of the ancient texts."[35] Paul does not think of himself as exposing truths that should have been apparent to the original authors and agents.

Paul knows that without the guidance of the Holy Spirit, he could not find these typological connections to Christ, the Church, and the sacraments in Israel's Scripture. But Paul presents his interpretation of Israel as the true one, "the hermeneutical key that unlocks all the mysteries of God's revelation in the past."[36] By interpreting Israel's Scripture in this way, Paul taps into and imitates the intertextual allusions and echoes that characterize Israel's Scripture.[37] Paul also engages central themes in Israel's Scripture, above all the righteousness and covenant faithfulness of God.

Hays emphasizes once more that Paul does not negate or annul Israel's Scripture but instead interprets Scripture as bearing witness to the gospel. Scholars such as Adolf von Harnack and Rudolf Bultmann argue that Paul is a supersessionist both in the sense of repudiating Old Testament Israel and in the sense of caring next to nothing for the actual history of Israel. Hays points out that far from denigrating Israel's history, Paul finds a strong eschatological dynamism in the portrait of Israel's history given by Scripture. Believing that God's action in Jesus Christ and the Holy Spirit is fulfilling the eschatological dynamism of Israel's history, Paul undertakes "a dialectical struggle to maintain the integrity of his proclamation in relation to Scripture and the integrity of Scripture in relation to that proclamation, to justify his startling claims about what the God of Israel had elected to do in Jesus Christ."[38]

Hays recognizes that some contemporary scholars criticize Paul for offering "helter-skelter intuitive readings, unpredictable, ungeneralizable."[39] Hays denies that this is the case, but he gladly affirms that Paul does not have an abstract method that he applies to all scriptural texts. Rather, Paul has a guiding principle: the righteousness of God to which all Scripture attests has now been made manifest in the life, death, and Resurrection of the Messiah. As Hays remarks, "Paul reads Scripture under the conviction that its story prefigures the climactic realities of his own time."[40] Paul's interpretation of Scripture is fundamentally typological.

For Hays, a proper understanding of typology gets around the question of the historical accuracy of Paul's interpretations of Israel's (or the scriptural narrative's) past. Paul's metaphors assert figural connections rather than things that happened in the past. Hays states, "Typology forges imaginative correlations of events within a narrative sequence;

not all narrative sequences, however, are historical."[41] Through his "imaginative correlations," Paul aimed to show that the Church, even as communities of Gentile converts, is in continuity with Israel. His readings succeed as "historical" ones if they suggest accurately why Israel's story is the Church's story. For this reason Paul relies in particular on Deuteronomy and Isaiah, which already interpret "the history of Yahweh's dealing with Israel typologically, as a prefiguration of a larger eschatological design."[42] Since Israel's Scripture presents itself as having the power to speak anew to the present, Paul has ample grounds for his own imaginative readings of Scripture. These imaginative readings are not intended to describe what happened in the past, but instead are intended—as such readings were in Israel's Scripture itself—to form the practices of the present-day community. Given the eschatological character of the Messianic community, Paul's typological readings of Scripture are necessary so as to do justice to God's accomplishment of his plan in Christ and the Spirit. In this respect the scriptural pattern of reversal provides Paul with a way of making sense of the election of the Gentiles and the rejection of Jesus by many Jews.

Because of his eschatological perspective, Paul holds that "[a]ll that God has ever done in the past converges toward the eschatological community, and all past words of Scripture find their sense rooted in the present graced time."[43] Drawing upon the work of James Kugel, Hays suggests that this sense of time is quite different from that of Rabbinic midrash. Like the prophets, Paul believes that God is speaking through him: God has given him the mission to proclaim the gospel of Jesus Christ, and in so doing God has illumined for him the interior meaning of Israel's history, now fulfilled in Christ and the Church.

Responding to Paul's eschatological claim to be able to understand previously hidden dimensions of Israel's past, Hays affirms with Paul that the decisive eschatological event has occurred in the Crucifixion and Resurrection of Jesus Christ. This eschatology validates Paul's typological interpretations of Scripture, because such interpretations arise from the truth that the righteousness of God depicted in Scripture has been definitively accomplished in Jesus Christ. When Paul interprets Israel's Scripture in a manner that goes beyond what the scriptural text itself affirms, Hays rejects the historical validity of such interpretation

while accepting its imaginative validity for building up the eschatological community by illuminating "the witness of the Law and the
Prophets to the gospel of God's righteousness."[44]

The final pages of Hays's book ask the question: Are Christians
today justified in reading Scripture in the way that Paul did? Richard
Longenecker's negative answer to this question provides Hays with a
foil. For Longenecker, Paul's typological interpretations are true both as
regards Israel's past and the Church's present, but biblical scholars and
pastors today do not have warrant to interpret Scripture typologically.
On the one hand, Longenecker's acceptance of Paul's typological exegesis as historically accurate with respect to Israel's past seems to Hays to
put "Paul on a theological pedestal," insofar as (ahistorical) theology is
generally more inclined to find in Paul's "fanciful analogies" binding
truth about Israel's past.[45] On the other hand, Longenecker's rejection of
the use of typological exegesis today seems to Hays to cut off contemporary Christians from the very exegesis that is practiced within Scripture.
Hays urges us to create "new figurations out of the texts that Paul read"
and to weave "Paul's own writings into the intertextual web, perhaps dis-
cerning correspondences that did not occur to Paul himself."[46]

In arguing for typological exegesis today, Hays does not wish to encourage a postmodern free-for-all with regard to the meaning of Scripture. He identifies three Pauline criteria for exegetical fidelity: God's
faithfulness to his covenant promises, Jesus' Pasch as the fulfillment of
God's covenantal righteousness, and the power of Scripture to configure
its readers "into a community that embodies the love of God as shown
forth in Christ."[47] Grounded in this understanding of Scripture, good
typological exegesis will "bring Scripture's witness to God's action in the
past to bear as a critical principle on the present," thereby helping to
form the Church in love.[48] It will enable "God's present action among us
to illumine our understanding of his action in the past."[49] By this, Hays
means that we can find in Scripture certain "prefigurings" of God's
grace, metaphorically speaking, and also that we should learn to understand all of Israel's history as pointing to Christ and the Church. In this
way, we can discover ourselves as living in the eschatological age or
"God-dominated time," and we can learn how to be Christians not only
through doctrinal logic but also through rhetorical and metaphorical

imagination, granting "a broad space for the play of echo and allusion, for figurative intertextual conjunctions, and even—if our communities were sufficiently rooted in Scripture's symbolic soil—for metalepsis."[50]

Along these lines, Hays argues that all truth need not be, and indeed is not, logical or doctrinal. We need more room for metaphorical truth, which (if we can avoid turning it into logical or doctrinal truth) will help us to avoid narrow literalism. He concludes that historical criticism "should not be burdened with theological responsibility for screening the uses of Scripture in Christian proclamation. If it were entrusted with such a normative task, many of Paul's readings would fail the test."[51]

In a response to Hays's criticism of his position, Longenecker argues that Hays mistakenly downplays Paul's use of midrash, pesher, and allegory, none of which would today be suitable for understanding the apostolic witness to Jesus Christ. For Longenecker, Hays's encouragement of imaginative and ecclesial readings of Scripture would lead us back into the "disastrous results" that Christians have obtained when they have "claimed to be inspired by Christ living within me, by the Spirit illumining me, or by the Church conditioning me."[52] Among other things (including eccentric private judgment about the content of faith), Longenecker presumably has in mind the typological reading of Mary as the new Eve that fostered the Catholic and Orthodox teaching that Mary shares in Christ's victory and is now bodily present with Christ in heaven.

As we have seen, Hays recognizes that Paul interprets Scripture as filled with types of Christ and the Church. Since Hays is committed in faith to Jesus' inauguration of the eschatological age, Hays accepts Paul's authority to interpret the whole of Scripture in light of this eschatology and under the guidance of the Holy Spirit. Hays also appreciates the rhetorical play that makes Scripture more than a wooden textbook of doctrinal propositions. But Hays conceives of typology—both Paul's and the form that would be acceptable exegetically today—fundamentally in terms of helping the present-day community of believers shape their moral practices. As a way of shaping Christian practices, typology functions to insert Christian communities within the biblical stories and to bring about a more faithful Christian witness. By contrast, Paul himself claims a good deal more than this. Paul thinks that his eschatological mandate as an apostle, filled with the Holy Spirit, enables him to interpret the events recorded in Scripture in a manner that enhances our understanding of the events. Paul's typological exegesis about the exodus—which is already typologically significant in Old Testament Scripture—has to do with Israel's past as well as with the present-day Church. When Hays limits typology in the way that he does, he rules out Paul's own view of his exegesis, and it is unclear why this limitation is not arbitrary. In this regard, despite his insistence otherwise, Hays's position is quite similar to Longenecker's, although Longenecker accepts Paul's apostolic ability to teach typologically about the past but supposes that the Holy Spirit strictly limits this ability to the apostolic age. Thus insofar as Hays's critique of Longenecker's position is persuasive, as I think it is, his critique equally applies to his own position. Given the importance that Hays has shown typology to have, is there a way to employ it without arbitrarily limiting its reference to present-day moral exhortation?

Peter Enns: Historical Criticism and the Meaning of the Old Testament

Before addressing the question raised by my overview of Hays's work, I wish to reflect a bit further on why typological reasoning has been eclipsed in contemporary biblical exegesis. The key problem seems to be the nature of history and the historicity of the biblical text. This can be seen from Peter Enns's *Inspiration and Incarnation: Evangelicals and the Problem of the Old Testament*, which I will survey here. The central point of Enns's book is that conservative evangelical response to historical-critical scholarship on the Old Testament shares an assumption with modern disbelievers in the Bible's authority: namely, the assumption that "the Bible, being the word of God, ought to be historically accurate in all its details (since God would not lie or make errors) and unique in its own setting (since God's word is revealed, which implies a specific type of uniqueness)."[53] Enns, however, suggests that the Incarnation of the Son of God points in the opposite direction. Just as the incarnate Word is fully human, so also the biblical word of God is fully human.[54] In revealing himself, God accommodates himself to our historical mode of existence.[55] It follows that the truth of the Old Testament, as a whole, appears not in its historical facts or its doctrines, but in the apostles' re-reading of the whole story in light of what God has done in Jesus Christ. In this regard Enns emphasizes that it is to Christ "that the Bible as a whole bears witness."[56]

Enns defends his acceptance of historical and doctrinal errors in the Old Testament partly by means of a lengthy chapter that investigates the New Testament authors' interpretation of Scripture (the Old Testament). He aims to show that with respect to the interpretation of Old Testament texts, Jesus and the apostolic authors do not display the concern for factual accuracy that modern scholars value so highly. Enns sets the stage by pointing out that many readers find the New Testament's approach to be "somewhat troubling, for it seems to run counter to the instinct that context and authorial intention are the basis for sound interpretation."[57] As an example, he gives Jesus' debate with the Sadducees as reported in Luke 20. The Sadducees deny the resurrection of the dead, but Jesus corrects them by means of Exodus 3:6: "That the dead are raised, even Moses showed, in the passage about the bush, where he calls the Lord the God of Abraham and the God of Isaac and the God of Jacob. Now he is not God of the dead, but of the living; for all live to him" (Lk 20:37–38). In Exodus 3:6, however, God names himself "the God of Abraham, the God of Isaac, and the God of Jacob" without mentioning their resurrection, and historical-critical scholars of the Old Testament consider that the book of Exodus lacks a doctrine of the resurrection of the dead. Why then does Jesus' argument seem persuasive to his audience? To answer this question, Enns examines intra-biblical exegesis within the Old Testament as well as Second Temple modes of interpretation.

Before doing so, he briefly reviews the positions that he is opposing. Evangelical scholars defend in three ways the New Testament's use of the Old: by arguing that the New Testament authors are responding to a contextual clue about the original author's intention; by claiming that the New Testament authors aim solely to apply, not to interpret, the scriptural text; and/or by proposing that the New Testament authors, as inspired by the Holy Spirit, can go beyond the original authorial intention and context in ways that are not in fact unfaithful to the original intention and context. These three ways, says Enns, ultimately do not work, largely because they neglect "the historical context for apostolic hermeneutics."[58] Instead, Enns hopes to show that although the New Testament authors do not care about the original authorial intention and context, they nonetheless understand themselves to be exposing what the scriptural text meant and means "*in light of Christ's coming*," and their approach to the Old Testament's truth should be adopted by the Church today.[59]

Enns takes the example of Daniel's interpretation of Jeremiah's prophecy that the Babylonian captivity would last seventy years. In Daniel 9:22, the angel Gabriel comes to explain this prophecy to Daniel. Gabriel tells him, "Seventy weeks of years are decreed concerning your people and your holy city, to finish the transgression, to put an end to sin, and to atone for iniquity, to bring in everlasting righteousness, to seal both vision and prophet, and to anoint a most holy place" (Dan 9:24). A "week" of years is seven years; thus the total is 490 years. Enns suggests that Daniel's reinterpretation of Jeremiah's prophecy parallels what we find in New Testament interpretation of Scripture. Just as Gabriel explains to Daniel the inner meaning of Jeremiah's prophecy, so also does the risen Jesus explain the inner meaning of Scripture to his two disciples on the road to Emmaus (Lk 24:25–27) and to all of his apostles in the upper room (Lk 24:44–47). To do this, Jesus "opened their minds" (Lk 24:45) so that they could perceive what would otherwise be hidden or unclear. Jesus makes clear that the (Old Testament) Scriptures have their meaning in their fulfillment in himself and in the Church that proclaims him: "Thus it is written [in the Old Testament], that the Christ should suffer and on the third day rise from the dead, and that repentance and forgiveness of sins should be preached in his name to all nations, beginning from Jerusalem" (Lk 24:46–47). As Enns points out, Jesus is not here calling upon his apostles to recognize a few proof texts (for instance, Hosea 6:2). Instead, Jesus is claiming that the whole Old Testament is about him when read through the eyes of faith. Jesus "is saying that *all* Scriptures speak of him in the sense that he is *the climax of Israel's story.*"[60]

To interpret Scripture in this way, it would seem, requires divine authority—either as one commissioned by God (such as the angel Gabriel) or as Jesus Christ, the incarnate Son. But in fact this mode of interpretation can be found in numerous Second Temple texts. For example, in Wisdom of Solomon 10, pseudo-Solomon interprets Genesis and Exodus to show how God cares for his chosen people. Regarding Cain, pseudo-Solomon observes that "the earth was flooded because of him" (Wis 10:4), a causal link that Genesis itself does not explicitly state. Pseudo-Solomon also makes a connection between Abraham and Babel (Wis 10:5), and this connection is more explicitly made in the first-century AD *Book of Biblical Antiquities*. Pseudo-Solomon observes about Jacob that wisdom "kept him safe from those who lay in wait for him" (Wis 10:12). Genesis does not explicitly describe any of Jacob's enemies, whether Esau or Laban, as lying in wait for him. But in *Jubilees* (second century BC), we find the story of Esau preparing an ambush for Jacob. Enns gives numerous other examples from Wisdom of Solomon, and he concludes that its author drew upon interpretations that were common in the culture of his time. Enns also treats Qumran's pesher on Habakkuk 1:5, which makes the claim—somewhat similar to Jesus in Luke 24—that the true meaning of Habakkuk can only be known through the Teacher of Righteousness. The key point for Enns is that neither Wisdom of Solomon nor Qumran interprets Scripture with the purpose of discovering the original authorial intention.[61]

With this background, Enns returns to the scriptural interpretation employed by Jesus and the apostolic authors. Treating Matthew's use of Hosea 11:1, "Out of Egypt I called my son," he emphasizes that "Hosea himself is not talking about the boy Jesus, nor is he thinking of a future messiah."[62] In Hosea 11:1–4, God is bemoaning that Israel, his "son," turned away from him despite all that he did for Israel, including the exodus from Egyptian slavery.[63] Hosea 11:1 refers to Israel's past idolatry and disobedience, not to Jesus' future coming and flight into Egypt. Admittedly, there is a possible parallel between Jesus and Hosea 11 viewed as a whole. God in Hosea 11:8 proclaims his love and compassion for Israel: "How can I give you up, O Ephraim! How can I hand you over, O Israel! . . . My heart recoils within me, my compassion grows warm and tender." As Enns says, "Israel came out of Egypt, was disobedient, deserved punishment, yet was forgiven by God (Hos 11:8–11). Christ came out of Egypt, led a life of perfect obedience, deserved no punishment, but was crucified—the guiltless for the guilty."[64] Jesus embodies both the compassion of God for Israel, and Israel as God's "son." Enns does not deny that Matthew's use of Hosea has an internal logic that expresses Matthew's understanding of God, Jesus, and Israel. Rather, what Enns contests is that Hosea's text could be properly read in this way without faith in Christ. In its historical context, the text from Hosea means something quite different. Enns's point is not that we need to reject Matthew's use of Hosea; Enns aims only to show that Matthew, as a Christian interpreter of Scripture, is not worried about the authorial intention and original context of Hosea's words. The truth of Hosea's words is found not in their original context but in the light of Jesus Christ.

With similar conclusions, Enns examines Paul's use of Isaiah 49:8, "In a time of favor I have answered you, in a day of salvation I have helped you." Paul refers these words to God's grace and eschatological salvation in Jesus Christ. Enns points out, however, that Isaiah has in view the rebuilding and repopulation of Israel's war-ravaged land after the Babylonian captivity. From the same vantage point, Enns considers Paul's argument that "the promises were made to Abraham and to his offspring. It does not say, 'And to offsprings,' referring to many; but, referring to one, 'And to your offspring,' which is Christ" (Gal 3:16).[65] Paul appears to have in mind God's promise to Abraham in Genesis 12, 13, and 24; but the Hebrew word for "offspring" is, though singular in form, plural in meaning. Furthermore, God promises Abraham land, not reconciliation. Enns affirms the point that Paul is making, that "Christ alone is truly Abraham's seed, the one who embodies Israel's ideal."[66] But as an interpretation of Genesis, Paul's argument cannot stand, unless we argue that the truth of Genesis is found not in its original intention and context but in its Christological fulfillment. Skipping over Enns's discussion of Isaiah 59 in Romans 11, we can mention a last example, Hebrews 3:9's fruitful misquotation of Psalm 95:10. In Hebrews 3:17, the author alludes to the correct text of Psalm 95:10, showing that the misquotation was deliberate.[67] It serves the purpose of exhibiting the relationship between Jesus, Israel, and the Church, but it is not an interpretative move that we could make today.

Enns also describes instances in which the New Testament authors adopt traditions that were current in Second Temple literature, but that had no solid basis in Scripture. For example, 2 Timothy 3:8 names the magicians of Pharaoh's court, who were unnamed in Exodus; 2 Peter 2:5 calls Noah "a preacher of righteousness" whereas Genesis does not ascribe preaching to Noah; Jude 9 mentions a dispute between the devil and the archangel Michael over Moses' body; and Jude 14–15 quotes 1 Enoch as though it conveyed the words of the scriptural figure Enoch.

Among the further examples that Enns gives, 1 Corinthians 10:4 stands out for our purposes. Evidently referring to the rock that Moses struck to provide water for the Israelites on the exodus journey (Exod 17 and Num 20), Paul states that "they drank from the supernatural Rock which followed them, and the Rock was Christ." Paul's argument seems to be that Christ sustained the Israelites in the wilderness, just as Christ sustains the Corinthians. Enns inquires into the source of Paul's idea that the Rock "followed" the Israelites, since Exodus and Numbers do not say that the Rock actually moved. He finds that there is widespread Second Temple tradition about the Israelites on the exodus possessing a mobile source of water. Versions of this tradition can be found in the *Targum Onqelos* (on Num 20–21), in the Tosefta (*Sukkah* 3.11), and in the *Book of Biblical Antiquities*.[68] Enns once more draws the conclusion that the New Testament authors read Scripture much more loosely, as regards their attitude to the original texts, than we do today.

On the basis of faith in Jesus Christ, the New Testament authors read certain meanings into Scripture that were not the meanings that the original authors intended, and they were even willing to adjust Scripture and to read it through extra-biblical traditions. Enns explains that "the New Testament authors take the Old Testament out of *one* context, that of the original human author, and place it into *another* context, the one that represents the final goal to which Israel's story has been moving."[69] Enns thus thinks that had Hosea been in Matthew's position, Hosea would have been able to see how his words in fact speak of Jesus Christ. Nor is this merely an extrinsic connection: Enns observes that the divine author of Scripture, who is guiding the eschatological unfolding of history, can inspire words that in their own historical context mean one thing and in light of Christ mean quite another thing.

In Enns's view, it would be a mistake to find Christ in every Old Testament passage. Instead, we should recognize that the Old Testament as a whole has its fulfillment in Christ and the Church, and so we should employ a "christotelic" and "ecclesiotelic" hermeneutic. It follows that there are two acceptable ways of reading the Old Testament. First, we can read it "on its own terms," seeking the original authorial intention and context.[70] Reading in this way, we may not be able to make the connections that the New Testament authors do, but we will see that the Old Testament has a basic storyline that remains unfulfilled within the

Old Testament itself. Second, we can read the Old Testament in light of its eschatological fulfillment in Christ and in the Church. This way of reading allows for interpretations that go beyond what the Old Testament says in its own contexts. These interpretations go beyond the Old Testament meaning precisely by arguing that the fulfillment has come, a fulfillment that makes present what the Old Testament authors were unconsciously pointing to. Genesis 12.7, for example, which in its own context is about descendents and land, is (as fulfilled) truly about Christ and the Church, as Paul suggests in Galatians 3.[71]

This emphasis on fulfillment gets at the core of what typological interpretation involves. Typology expresses the fulfillment in Christ and the Church of the Old Testament stories, prophecies, prayers, and wisdom. Where Enns speaks of "Christotelic" and "ecclesiotelic" hermeneutics, he might equally have spoken of typological exegesis. Thus Enns sees Romans 15:4, where Paul asserts that "whatever was written in former days was written for our instruction," as an example of reading Psalm 69:9 "in its christotelic fullness."[72] Romans 15:4 elucidates the principle behind typological exegesis. Enns recognizes that not all New Testament interpretation of Scripture is typological (or, as he puts it, "christotelic and ecclesiotelic").[73] His main point is that we cannot pretend that the New Testament authors' shared our "grammatical-historical" approach to Scripture.

In dialogue with Richard Longenecker, Enns then takes up the issue of whether we are justified in reading Old Testament Scripture typologically today. He seeks a middle ground between simply copying the New Testament authors' exegesis, on the one hand, and rejecting it as entirely inappropriate today, on the other. His proposal is to "distinguish between *hermeneutical goal* and *exegetical method*."[74] Today we should share the New Testament authors' hermeneutical goal—namely, to read the Old Testament in light of the fulfillment that Christ brings about. Contemporary interpreters should "bring the death and resurrection of Christ to bear on the Old Testament" by insisting that these events should inform our understanding of the Old Testament.[75] Moreover, we cannot suppose that our grammatical-historical exegetical method must be the universal standard for exegesis. At the same time, however, we cannot imitate the New Testament authors in changing Old Testament words or in reading Old Testament realities (such as the rock of Exodus

17:6) in a manner that goes well beyond what the Old Testament says about them.

On the basis of these reflections, he suggests that focusing on exegetical method is not the best approach.[76] The New Testament authors did not adhere to one method or another; rather, they read Scripture through various lenses. Enns describes their scriptural interpretation as "an intuitive, Spirit-led engagement of Scripture, with the anchor being not what the Old Testament author intended but how Christ gives the Old Testament its final coherence."[77] They were excited about God's fulfillment of Israel in Christ, and they read Scripture in this new light, by which the goal of the divine author was revealed. We should do the same, rather than focusing on retrieving the Old Testament's original, historical meaning. But we do not need to follow their particular Second Temple interpretative modes; these modes are determined by their context, as ours are by our context. God revealed himself in Christ Jesus within a particular (Second Temple) historical context, and this context is reflected in the apostolic writings that bear witness to Christ. We have to bear witness to Christ in our own historical context, and our context will shape our witness.

Enns also comments briefly on patristic and medieval typological exegesis, which found (for example) in Rahab's "scarlet cord" (Josh 2:21) the blood of Christ. In Enns's view, such typological exegesis deserves the benefit of the doubt in general, even if not necessarily in specific cases, because God's word should be expected to have "multiple layers of meaning."[78] Given that the text is God's word, interpretation must go beyond analysis of the text in its ancient Near-Eastern context; interpretation must be illumined by Christ's coming. In order to be illumined in this way, interpretation must recognize its participation in an ecclesial context, "the witness of the church through time (with the hermeneutical trajectory set by the apostles as a central component), as well as the wisdom of the church in our time."[79] The goal of scriptural interpretation consists in encountering the God who reveals himself in Christ, and we encounter this God not merely individually but as a community of believers.

Enns, then, agrees with Hays that the New Testament authors often read Scripture typologically with the goal of asserting something true about the fulfillment in Christ, rather than about Israel's past. Typological exegesis belonged to the cultural context of the ancient world. It was their way of saying that "[t]he reality of the crucified and risen Christ is both the beginning and the end of Christian biblical interpretation."[80] Although we can appreciate the apostles' typological reading of Scripture, we cannot "ignore the cultural distance between us and Second Temple interpreters."[81] Despite this cultural distance, however, we must be able to see Christ in the Old Testament. We cannot do without typology. Yet, with Longenecker, we have to admit that certain New Testament exegetical modes are no longer open to us.

This approach is in many ways quite similar to that of Hays, even if Enns lacks Hays's emphasis on moral formation and does not exhort the Church to employ typological reasoning anew. With his focus on distinguishing the New Testament authors' approach from that of modern historical readers, Enns demonstrates the omnipresence of typological reasoning in Scripture. As an Old Testament scholar, it matters to him whether Paul's (and the other New Testament authors') reading of Israel's past is accurate. He argues that we can accept Paul's reading of Scripture as true, because in God's plan Scripture (the Old Testament) does indeed point to Christ, even though the authors of the original texts were unaware of the claims that the New Testament authors make. Enns does not think that typology can inform us about Israel's past, other than in the sense that whatever happened in Israel points to Christ and the Church. Yet, I would observe that if Israel's past has really been fulfilled by Jesus Christ, then we cannot rule out that typological reasoning can speak truly about the past (as well as about the present), nor can we suppose that typology is simply a culturally conditioned exegetical mode that happened to be present around the time of Jesus. At issue is not whether typological exegesis refers accurately to the historical past in every instance, but rather what the Church can hope for from typological exegesis under the guidance of the Holy Spirit. Once one takes seriously the biblical-typological worldview as a truthful witness to God's work in Israel (culminating in Jesus Christ and the Church), then the truth-bearing potential of typological reasoning cannot be easily restricted.

Peter Leithart: Typology and the Fabric of History

Hays helps us to see how necessary typological exegesis is for the Church's inhabiting of Scripture; Enns shows the extraordinary extent to which the New Testament authors used typological reasoning in order to understand the meaning of Scripture. I now bring these reflections to a close by briefly examining Peter Leithart's *Deep Exegesis: The Mystery of Reading Scripture*, which strongly affirms the ability of typology to refer not only to the present but also to the past. As Leithart shows, given the nature of texts and temporality under God's providence, typological reasoning is never out of date.[82]

Leithart begins by arguing that the words of the Bible, including the particularity of the modes of biblical language, are no mere husk from which interpreters extract kernels of meaning. He reviews various Enlightenment attempts to propose that biblical texts teach spiritual truths even though the form in which the truths are taught can now be rejected as misleading. Such attempts allow reason to sit in judgment over Scripture's husk, while locating in the scriptural husk a kernel of enduring truth. Leithart observes that those who sought to liberate Scripture's kernel generally "shared an antipathy to priestcraft, a suspicion of the dogmas, rites, and texts of positive religion, and a conviction that the central thrust of religion is morality."[83] As a particularly clear example of this view, he examines Immanuel Kant's *Religion within the Limits of Reason Alone*, in which Kant identifies the husks as the Jewish elements of ecclesiastical Christianity and identifies the kernel as an ethical community rooted in universal reason.[84] Leithart comments that Kant "does not consider the possibility that the Bible is pointing us to the historicity of reason itself. He does not consider the possibility that the Bible might be indicating that we reason temporally."[85]

Leithart then turns explicitly to our topic. He quotes two lengthy passages from Richard Longenecker, in which Longenecker warns (as we have seen) against using today the modes of biblical exegesis employed by Jesus and the apostles. In Leithart's view, Longenecker is falling into the husk/kernel error.[86] The husk here is the mode of biblical interpretation employed by Jesus and the apostles, which Longenecker links with Jewish midrash and allegory; the kernel is the doctrines that they taught. As Leithart says, for Longenecker, "We are supposed to follow Pauline doctrine, but not Pauline exegesis."[87] Leithart considers this to be a serious mistake, not least because the words of Scripture have transformative power in the particular form that God has given them. We need to study the form and to allow it to teach us how to read.

This might seem like an unpromising venture. Consider again Hosea 11:1–2: "When Israel was a child, I loved him, and out of Egypt I called my son. The more I called them, the more they went from me." On what grounds, historically speaking, can one hold that the "son" in the first verse is actually Jesus (Mt 2:15)? Likewise, although Paul claims that the Israelites "drank from the supernatural Rock which followed them, and the Rock was Christ" (1 Cor 10:4), Exodus and Numbers do not appear to support the view that a "Rock" followed Israel. In Galatians 4, Paul allegorizes the figures of Abraham, Hagar, and Sarah, and in this case Paul admits that he is allegorizing (see Gal 4:24). But the allegory veers quite far, it appears, from the actual biblical portrait of Abraham, Hagar, and Sarah in Genesis.[88]

For Leithart, this use of typology and allegory suggests that in some way, the meaning of biblical texts (say, Exod 12:6 or Gen 16) can change over time. Before spelling out his solution, he first surveys the various options for handling the problem of New Testament typology. One option is to say that Paul drew on the Jewish exegesis (midrash, pesher) of his day for his understanding in 1 Corinthians 10 of the mobile Rock. Leithart grants that this is so, but notes that it merely pushes the problem one step back: on what grounds did the Jewish exegetical tradition come up with this conclusion, and why does Paul adopt their conclusion? A second option is to appeal to the fact that God and humans are equally the authors of Scripture: the divine author may intend something that the human author does not intend. Again, however, the question is why the human author—in this case Paul—felt justified in arguing in this way. Third, we can say that the apostles were inspired by the Holy Spirit and so their exegesis is accurate, even though their exegetical mode escapes us. The problem here is whether we can read Scripture adequately when deprived of the lens with which the apostles saw things in Scripture that we cannot see.

Leithart then sets forth his own solution, one that Enns considers unpersuasive: the apostles "were following hints from the Old Testament itself."[89] Regarding the Rock of 1 Corinthians 10, for example, Leithart observes that Exodus 14:19 does say that Israel was followed by a "pillar of cloud." Given that something was following Israel, how did Jewish exegetes (including Paul) conclude that this something was the "Rock"? The Song of Moses in Deuteronomy 32 repeatedly proclaims YHWH to be "the Rock." When YHWH led the Israelites out of Egypt, further-more, Moses' Song says that YHWH made them "suck honey out of the rock, and oil out of the flinty rock" (Deut 32:13). Furthermore, when YHWH commands Moses to strike the rock, YHWH states that he him-self will stand upon the rock: "Behold, I will stand before you there on the rock at Horeb; and you shall strike the rock, and water shall come out of it, that the people may drink" (Exod 17:6). If we recall that the Song of Moses names YHWH "the Rock," and connect this with the fact that the Israelites were being followed on the exodus and with the fact that YHWH is standing on the rock that Moses strikes, then Paul's conten-tion (in accord with Jewish exegesis of the day) that the "Rock was Christ" seems more plausible as scriptural interpretation. What the Jew-ish exegetes and Paul have done is to weave together typologies and im-ages that are present in the various scriptural texts about the exodus journey.

What about Paul's allegorical interpretation of Abraham, Sarah, and Hagar? Paul presents Sarah's son Isaac as a type of those who are "born according to the Spirit" and Hagar's son Ishmael as a type of those who are "born according to the flesh" (Gal 4:29).[90] Does this interpretation have a basis in Scripture? Leithart answers in the affirmative. Ishmael is born before Abraham's circumcision—which serves for Abraham as a sign of dependence on God's "everlasting covenant" (Gen 17:13)—whereas Isaac is born after that event. Similarly, Abraham's casting out of Ishmael and Hagar into the wilderness (Gen 21) structurally parallels Abraham's near sacrifice of Isaac (Gen 22). Ishmael's history, too, paral-lels the history of Jacob/Israel; thus Ishmael also has twelve sons. As Leithart says with Paul's typology in view, "That Ishmael decreases so that Isaac might increase does not mean that Ishmael was nothing."[91] In other words, Paul's typology has a foundation in the way that Genesis relates Isaac to Ishmael.

Having defended apostolic typological reading as a legitimate weav-ing together of Scripture's typologies and images, Leithart then asks whether this mode of reading is legitimate only with regard to the Bible. Typological reading particularly fits the Bible due to the implications of its dual authorship, God and human. But Leithart considers that all major texts can and should be read typologically.[92] He points out that historical events can be said to change over time because their effects and significance change. Similarly, the same words, used in different contexts, can mean different things. Their meaning can be changed by events or by later texts. We can read the same words in different times of our lives and gain different meanings from these words. Typology relies upon sets of relationships that develop over time, and in fact all events and texts accrue meaning over time.

After examining various historical events and literary works in this light, he returns to the biblical example of Matthew's use of Hosea 11:1. In Matthew 2, Herod, the ruler of Israel, acts like Pharaoh, and Jesus is the new Moses who redeems Israel. When Matthew says that the flight of Joseph, Mary, and their child to Egypt fulfills the prophecy that "Out of Egypt have I called my son," therefore, this means that Jesus is called out of Herod's "Egypt," and Jesus is the "son" as Israel's Redeemer. Is this a distortion of Hosea? Only if we imagine that Hosea considered himself to be speaking only to his contemporaries. In fact, however, Hosea "surely did not think that the exodus from Egypt was the final word in Yahweh's salvation. . . . Like all faithful Israelites, he hoped for a redemption far beyond what Israel had already experienced."[93] Hosea would not have been surprised by a new "exodus" in which a future "Pharaoh" would be overcome and Israel be redeemed. Thus, says Leithart, "Matthew gives new meaning to Hosea, but the meaning he gives does not violate Hosea's original meaning. The meaning changes as Hosea's prediction comes to fulfillment, but the change is consistent with the original sense."[94] Indeed, many authors anticipate being read for centuries and recognize that the passage of time will enrich the meaning of their texts in ways that they cannot now know.

With Augustine, Leithart holds that "Scripture is about Christ, but the Christ of Scripture is not only himself but also his body. The Christ who is the subject matter of Scripture is the *totus Christus*."[95] This means that the story of Cain and Abel, for example, is not only about Cain and Abel, but also about Jesus and about the persecution of the Church (both typologically figured by Abel). It means, too, that as Paul says in

1 Corinthians 10, the story of the exodus speaks of the sacraments: "The sea is baptism, and the manna and water foreshadow the Eucharist."[96] The moral application of scriptural passages to the life of Christians is justified by the fact that Scripture, in speaking of Christ, speaks also of his members. Leithart shows how this works by means of an extended analysis of John 9 in the context of the Old Testament as well as of the whole Gospel of John.[97] Read typologically, John 9 is about the sacrament of baptism. In Leithart's view, because Jesus is the head of all things, the typological implications of John 9 can even be extended to the realm of literary interpretation, as can be seen by reading together Sophocles' *Oedipus the King* and John 9. Here the motif of blindness and sight leads onward into Nietzsche's critique of Socrates; sight is fraught with political weight. The blind man of John 9 provides typological insight into Jesus, into discipleship and power, and into the eschatological judgment and the new creation. Texts resonate with earlier texts in a manner that is inevitably and richly typological; there is no "timeless" text.

Leithart concludes that the fourfold sense of Scripture practiced by the Fathers and medievals was on the right track. He summarizes their approach: "For the medievals, the literal sense of the text opened out into a christological allegory, which, because Christ is the head of his body, opened out into tropological instruction and, because Christ is the King of a kingdom here yet also coming, into anagogical hope."[98] In defending typological exegesis, he argues not only that the biblical authors are justified in reflecting typologically upon scriptural types and images (as Paul does in 1 Corinthians 10), but also that post-biblical interpreters should learn to draw connections between the scriptural types and images. By reading typologically, post-biblical interpreters (such as the Fathers) enter into the mindset of the biblical authors themselves and see more deeply into the realities revealed in the whole Scripture. Typology, Leithart emphasizes, is not something enjoyed and practiced only by Second Temple Jews or by other ancient cultures. Rather, it is something that is intrinsic to the temporality of texts, and to the temporality of Israel, Christ, and the Church under God's providence.

How then does Leithart think that false typological interpretations can be avoided? He emphasizes that interpreters must become attuned to Scripture's truth. We attain such attunement "[w]hen the text is seen as an event, as a joke, as music; when words are seen as players; when the letter is not seen as a husk but as a necessary and nourishing part of God's verbal bread."[99] He compares biblical interpretation to a performance in which the performer seeks not only to get the notes right and to play them as beautifully as possible but also awaits the judgment of the audience (the community of believers). This comparison suggests to me the function of the Church's Magisterium, properly understood as being attuned (under the Holy Spirit's guidance) to the liturgical and theological tradition of the Church rather than being merely extrinsic decision making on the part of a pope or council.[100]

Leithart's main contributions to our study are twofold: his encouragement of typological reasoning by post-biblical interpreters without the restrictions that Hays and Enns impose; and his insistence that typological reasoning can speak truly about both the past and the present (even if, as I think, biblical typology can also be "fanciful" in Hays's sense).[101] As should be apparent from my brief discussion of his book, his readings are often ingenious, and his sensitivity to typology reminds us that its logic was not foreign to the biblical author even where we would not expect it. In this way, he helps us to see that typology and history are not necessarily opposed. Indeed, were we to presume such an opposition, we would rule out the historical reference of much of the New Testament. For, as Anthony Le Donne remarks, "one should expect among Jesus' contemporaries that the application of scriptural paradigms and typologies was an integral aspect of historical interpretation. . . . History is often seen through the lens of typology. The history of Jesus is no exception."[102]

In different ways, Hays, Enns, and Leithart show that contemporary Christians cannot exclude typological exegesis from the task of understanding divine revelation. Even so, Stanley Gundry warns that "whenever typology is used to show the Christocentric unity of the Bible, it is all too easy to impose an artificial unity (even assuming that there is a valid use of the basic method). Types come to be created rather than discovered, and the drift into allegorism comes all too easily."[103] It may seem that, having rejected Hays's limitation of typology to the formation of the community's practices and having argued that we cannot envision typology as merely a culturally conditioned or disposable mode of exegesis, I lack sympathy for such warnings against typological reasoning. On the contrary, although I value typology (and for that matter allegory as well), I think that the Church needs a way of measuring the truth of typological reasoning.[104] This is especially the case, it seems to me, with regard to a claim such as the Assumption of Mary. Although it is based upon connections between the various typological portraits of Mary in the New Testament, particularly those that depict Mary's participation in the mission of her Son in light of Genesis 3, the claim that Mary was assumed bodily into heaven could easily be an instance of the misuse of typology. If this were so, then the doctrine of Mary's Assumption would simply extend to the late patristic period what Enns finds to be the New Testament authors' lack of interest in historical accuracy.

What the Church requires, then, is a way of gauging the performance of its biblical interpreters. Because of the presence of typology in the literal sense of Scripture, we should expect typological connections still to be in play among Christians in the task of understanding and proclaiming divine revelation, but such typological exegesis cannot stand on its own. It must be shown to attest to God's saving power in Jesus Christ and must have its truth confirmed liturgically and theologically by the community of believers (the Church), guided by the Holy Spirit.[105]

This is the task of the Church's Magisterium, and it is what Pope Pius XII has in view when he appeals in *Munificentissimus Deus* to "the universal agreement of the Church's ordinary teaching authority" as "a certain and firm proof, demonstrating that the Blessed Virgin Mary's bodily Assumption . . . is a truth that has been revealed by God and consequently something that must be firmly and faithfully believed by all children of the Church" (§ 12).[106] At this stage, therefore, we need to look more closely into the Church's authority as interpreter of revelation under the guidance of the Holy Spirit.

CHAPTER 5

The Authority of the Church as Interpreter of Revelation

In a homily delivered a few years after his entrance into the Catholic Church, John Henry Newman preached on Mary's Immaculate Conception and bodily Assumption. Toward the end of this homily, he observes: "I am not proving these doctrines to you, my brethren; the evidence of them lies in the declaration of the Church. The Church is the oracle of religious truth, and dispenses what the apostles committed to her in every time and place. We must take her word, then, without proof, because she is sent to us from God to teach us how to please him."[1] Having devoted many pages to persuading his audience of the fittingness of Catholic doctrine about Mary, he is not here advocating a "blind" faith. Nor does he suppose that the Church possesses the authority to go beyond the faith revealed to the apostles. But he affirms that this faith is known in its fullness only when we receive it from the Church. God gave the apostolic Church the mission of proclaiming his revelation, and the Church in every age retains this mission.[2]

Prima facie, however, it seems unlikely that the revelation of God "in these last days" (Heb 1:2) could be carried forward unsullied through centuries of widely diverse cultural and religious contexts by the Catholic Church, which has shared in the vicissitudes of history. If even the Bible can be recognized as a diverse set of historically conditioned texts by those who affirm its fundamental unity as divine revelation, then the Church, too, must be seen as historically conditioned in a manner that, it seems, would put quite a bit of distance between the Church today and the Jesus of Nazareth who lived and taught in first-century Galilee and Judea. To put the matter succinctly, why should we suppose that the Church's doctrines about the papacy, bishops, Eucharistic sacrifice, transubstantiation, the seven sacraments, Mary's Immaculate Conception and bodily Assumption—or for that matter the co-equal divinity of the Father, Son, and Holy Spirit—belong to the same revelation that Jesus and his apostles taught?[3] What grounds do we have for holding that the Catholic Church is (by the guidance of the Holy Spirit) a true authority in matters of faith, so that we should "take her word," as Newman says? Why not instead agree with David Steinmetz that, in a strong sense, the Church "is not only a custodian of God's truth; it falsifies the Word of God as well"?[4]

To say the least, this topic is too big for one chapter.[5] Yet the topic of the Church's authority as interpreter of divine revelation must be treated here, because the doctrine of Mary's Assumption depends not only on typological reasoning but also on the authoritative judgment of the Church, guided by the Holy Spirit. The Church's interpretative authority manifests the work of the eschatological Spirit in the Church. As the Protestant biblical scholar David Seccombe says with regard to Luke/ Acts: "The primary spiritual distinctive of the new community is its possession of the Holy Spirit. . . . [T]he age of the Holy Spirit has dawned."[6] "For Luke," Seccombe adds, the Holy Spirit's "presence is inalienable."[7] Surely the presence of the Holy Spirit has profound implications for the Church's ability to retain visible unity and to proclaim the gospel truly. Indeed, Seccombe finds that Luke "is deliberately associating the assembly at Sinai and the Christian εκκλησία."[8]

Luke's insistence on the inalienability of the Holy Spirit in the Christian community is the basis for the Catholic view of the Church's authority. Yet given the apparent distance between Luke and the contemporary Church, the first task of this chapter is to present a representative critique of the Church's teaching regarding Mary's Assumption. For this purpose, I examine the young Jaroslav Pelikan's criticisms of Pope Pius XII's dogmatic definition of Mary's Assumption.[9] In light of the concerns that Pelikan raises, I then explore the place of the "assembly" (Israel/

Church) in the reception and transmission of revelation, by which God unites a people to his triune life. I investigate how the Old and New Testaments conceive of prophetic authority, Jesus Christ's authority, and apostolic authority. As a final step, I reflect on the relationship of Church, dogma, and liturgy with an eye to Mary's Assumption.

A Papal Usurpation of Authority?

Shortly before the Second Vatican Council, the Lutheran theologian Jaroslav Pelikan wrote a book titled *The Riddle of Roman Catholicism*. Although Pelikan writes with an ecumenical appreciation for his topic, when he takes up the Marian dogmas he registers profound concern and even alarm. Pope Pius XII's proclamation of the dogma of Mary's Assumption, in Pelikan's view, demonstrates how far the Catholic Church has moved from both Scripture and Tradition. Pelikan gives the following genealogy of Tradition and papal authority.[10] First, when the Fathers of the Church did not agree with each other, the notion of Tradition arose. The Bible lost much of its authority because the judgments formed over time by the Church ("Tradition") trumped the Bible's own words.[11] Second, when Tradition proved as ambiguous as the Bible, the medieval Church invoked papal authority. The popes claimed the authority to make infallible judgments regarding the content of both Scripture and Tradition, so as (in Pelikan's words) to "substitute clear and distinct doctrines for the ambiguous statements of Scripture and tradition."[12] The early Pelikan considers that in this way the Catholic Church marginalized both Scripture and Tradition.

Having arrived at this unfortunate position, says Pelikan, the Church at the First Vatican Council took the logical next step by formally recognizing papal infallibility. Pelikan comments: "So traumatic was the effect of the dogma of papal infallibility that the pope did not avail himself of this privilege for eighty years. But when he finally did, by proclaiming the assumption of the Blessed Virgin Mary on November 1, 1950, he confirmed the suspicions and misgivings of the dogma's critics."[13] Pelikan rejects both the content of the dogma and Pius XII's claim to teach it via his charism of infallibility. Regarding the Assumption of Mary, Pelikan argues that the doctrine has no grounds in either Scripture or apostolic Tradition: "Not only is Scriptural proof obviously lacking for this notion, but the tradition of the early Christian centuries is also silent about it."[14]

As a Lutheran, Pelikan could hardly be expected to support papal authority or the doctrine of Mary's Assumption.[15] In "The Pagan Servitude of the Church" (1520), Martin Luther remarks that in 1518, while denying "divine jurisdiction to the papacy," he still accepted a certain "human jurisdiction" of the papacy.[16] Upon reading the arguments of Catholic theologians who urged him to accept the pope's doctrinal authority, however, he came to reject any notion of papal authority. As he puts it, "I saw clearly that the papacy was to be understood as the kingdom of Babylon and the régime of Nimrod, the mighty hunter."[17] In 1520 Luther also published "The Freedom of a Christian," with its accompanying "Open Letter to Pope Leo X." In this letter he states that in matters of faith he must obey solely "the Word of God."[18] He emphasizes that "I acknowledge no fixed rules for the interpretation of the Word of God, since the Word of God, which teaches freedom in all other matters, must not be bound."[19] In his view, by binding the Word of God to the Church's authority, the popes became the "vicars" of an absent Christ rather than the humble "servants of the present Christ."[20] In 1522, Luther preached on the Feast of Mary's Assumption and argued that Scripture does not reveal how Mary (or any other saint) is in heaven, although we can know that Mary and the other saints are alive in Christ. He concluded that we should not go beyond these biblical bounds, since the Bible teaches clearly all that we need to know.[21]

For Pelikan, as for Luther, the underlying problem is the pope's doctrinal authority (a problem that Vatican I's definition of papal infallibility simply amplifies). Pelikan therefore expresses the hope that, like the Catholic monk Martin Luther, Catholics today will recognize "the conditioned and temporary character of the church's decisions."[22] The Church, like a human mother, should be honored; we receive our spiritual life through the instrumentality of the Church. But like our human mothers, the Church makes significant mistakes. The dogma of Mary's Assumption demonstrates nothing more than that the Church's teaching is fallible.[23] Unlike Luther, however, Pelikan does not claim that the Bible provides us with everything that we need, both because Pelikan considers the scriptural books to be historically conditioned and because he thinks that it was incumbent upon the Church to provide certain elements that Jesus did not spell out.[24]

In the young Pelikan's view, therefore, the "mature Roman Catholic"[25] will recognize the Church's fallibility and reject the First Vatican Council's dogma of papal infallibility. The mature Roman Catholic will also reject both the infallible character of Pope Pius XII's dogmatic statement of Mary's Assumption and the assured truthfulness of the dogmatic teaching of the councils of the Church (including Vatican I). And if neither the councils nor the Pope can be counted upon to communicate Christ's truth, then one cannot avoid the view that the Church often stands in the way of the reception of Jesus Christ. At the least, as Luther recognized, such a Church would need to cede real authority to mediate the truth of salvation. It follows that for Pelikan, Luther is a model of the "mature Roman Catholic," although Pelikan expresses much less confidence than Luther about the truth and sufficiency of Scripture.[26]

In short, Pelikan helps us to see that the theologically primary issue is not the pope's exercise of infallibility in the proclamation of Mary's Assumption but rather the whole basis of the Church's teaching authority.[27] Pelikan's view of the "mature Roman Catholic" requires that each believer evaluate which doctrines of the Church (and/or of the Bible) are true.[28] This view of revelation and reason, which Newman termed "private judgment," involves a range of problems, as Pelikan came to realize later in his career.[29] Most problematically, it centers upon individual reception and transmission of divine revelation. Are there biblical grounds for expecting that the individual, rather than the community, should play the central role? It seems to me that the opposite is the case: God wills that the Church be the authentic interpreter of revelation. In the Holy Spirit, the Church receives and interprets God's word so as to be constituted as the historical and eschatological body of Christ, "a sacrifice of praise to God" (Heb 13:15) and "a chosen race, a royal priesthood, a holy nation, God's own people" (1 Pet 2:9).[30] In this sense, as Paul Evdokimov says, "The Church is indeed the extension and the fullness of Christ incarnate. What Christ has *given* is supplemented by what is *done* on earth through the Spirit: it *fills* the witnesses, establishes the bishops; the Fathers of the Councils . . . are brought together with the Holy Spirit who presides over them and enlightens them; everything is charismatic in the Church."[31] In what follows, therefore, I explore the

Church's interpretative authority from three angles: the ministry of the prophet Elijah in relation to "the Israel of God" (Gal 6:16); the New Testament's portraits of Jesus' teaching and commissioning of his disciples/apostles; and the Church according to the New Testament.

Scripture, Community, Doctrine

Elijah and the Prophets of Baal: "I, even I only, am left"

Can Elijah's prophetic mission shed light on the transmission of divine revelation in and through the Church, the authoritative people of God? Elijah seems to be a solitary figure who alone proclaimed the truth amidst a people that had entirely fallen away from YHWH.[32] YHWH inspired the prophet Elijah during the long reign of King Ahab, who with his wife Jezebel strongly encouraged the worship of Baal. In this context, Elijah confronted his fellow Israelites: "How long will you go limping with two different opinions? If the Lord is God, follow him; but if Baal, then follow him" (1 Kgs 18:21). Since the people wish to worship both YHWH and Baal, Elijah seeks to resolve the issue by challenging the prophets of Baal to a contest. The prophets of Baal go first, and Baal's failure to do anything shows that Baal does not exist.[33] By contrast, when Elijah calls upon YHWH, "the fire of the Lord fell, and consumed the burnt offering" (1 Kgs 18:38).[34] In response, the people confess that YHWH is God, and even Ahab participates in a ritual meal on top of Mount Carmel.

Prior to this triumph, Elijah had been complaining about how alone he was: "I, even I only, am left a prophet of the Lord; but Baal's prophets are four hundred and fifty men" (1 Kgs 18:22). Later, after the victorious contest, Jezebel threatens Elijah's life and he has to flee into the wilderness, where he ends up resting under a broom tree. His victory now seems to him to have been worthless, because he has not been able to persuade Israel to worship YHWH alone. Indeed, he despairingly begs God to grant him death. Subsequently, when YHWH asks him why he has come to Horeb, he replies, "I have been very jealous for the Lord, the God of hosts; for the people of Israel have forsaken thy covenant, thrown down thy altars, and slain thy prophets with the sword; and I, even

I only, am left; and they seek my life, to take it away" (1 Kgs 19:10). How should we understand Elijah's sense of solitude?

Peter Leithart rightly observes that Elijah in a certain sense is "moving through the history of Israel."[35] Elijah's insistence that the Israelites cannot worship both YHWH and Baal can be read as a reiteration of YHWH's naming himself "I am" at the burning bush (Exod 3:14). In his contest with Ahab and his prophets (who play the role of Pharaoh's magicians), Elijah's first action is to call the people to him and to repair "the altar of the Lord that had been thrown down" (1 Kgs 18:30). The altar represents covenantal Israel: he "took twelve stones, according to the number of the tribes of the sons of Jacob, to whom the word of the Lord came, saying, 'Israel shall be your name'; and with the stones he built an altar in the name of the Lord" (1 Kgs 18:31). Again, just as Abraham set in place a sacrifice through which the Lord sent "a smoking fire pot and a flaming torch" (Gen 15:17) that sealed the covenant, Elijah calls down fire upon the sacrificial altar (representing Israel) in order to renew the covenant. And in his flight from Ahab and Jezebel (who represent Pharaoh), Elijah receives divine nourishment for his forty-day journey to Mount Sinai/Horeb, just as YHWH nourished the Israelites on their forty-year exodus journey.

Leithart emphasizes that when Elijah arrives at Sinai/Horeb and stands in his role as prophet before YHWH, "Elijah does not intercede for Israel, but instead formally accuses Israel (19:10, 14)."[36] YHWH accepts the accusation as true and commands Elijah to overthrow Ahab. This is quite different from Moses' encounter with YHWH on Mount Sinai after the rebellion of the people of Israel, when Moses intercedes repeatedly on behalf of the people (see Exod 32:30, 34:8–9).

In my view, however, YHWH does in fact correct Elijah in a way that helps us understand the authoritative role of Israel/Church rather than of the prophetic individual. Elijah's words to YHWH—"the people of Israel have forsaken thy covenant, thrown down thy altars, and slain thy prophets with the sword" (1 Kgs 19:10)—call into question YHWH's power to sustain his people and to accomplish his purposes in Israel. Moses mediated between God and the people, but Elijah simply accuses the people and bemoans his solitude. But like Moses, who failed to credit God with the miracle at the waters of Meribathkadesh, Elijah underestimates the power of YHWH to preserve and nourish his people Israel.[37]

YHWH makes this clear in three ways. First, when the Lord passes by Elijah, "a great and strong wind rent the mountains, and broke in pieces the rocks before the Lord" (1 Kgs 19:11); this is followed by an earthquake and a fire. YHWH, however, is not in the wind, the earthquake, or the fire. Instead YHWH is in "a still small voice" (1 Kgs 19:12). By making himself present in the "still small voice," YHWH shows Elijah that divine power is not absent even when its effects cannot be easily perceived.

The second way that YHWH subtly corrects Elijah has to do with the rulers and prophets of Israel. When Elijah hears the "still small voice," he comes out to face YHWH, who repeats his earlier question as to why Elijah has come to Mount Sinai/Horeb. Elijah again answers that he has been very busy defending the Lord, because the people of Israel have abandoned the Lord. Elijah concludes once more, "I, even I only, am left; and they seek my life, to take it away" (1 Kgs 19:14). In response, YHWH commands Elijah to go to Damascus and anoint Jehu to be the new king of Israel, as well as Hazael to be the new king of Syria. In other words, YHWH holds the power of kings in his hand. Elijah had been right to be "very jealous for the Lord, the God of hosts"; but he had not been right to despair about overcoming the power of Ahab and Jezebel. YHWH then adds another command, that Elijah anoint Elisha "to be prophet in your place" (1 Kgs 19:16).

Third, Elijah's failure to intercede for the people, as Moses had, would not be an issue if in fact there were no faithful Israelites other than Elijah. But YHWH tells Elijah that a perfect number of Israelites, a remnant of seven thousand, has in fact been preserved in Israel. YHWH will not punish these faithful Israelites when he punishes Israel: "Him who escapes from the sword of Hazael shall Jehu slay; and him who escapes from the sword of Jehu shall Elisha slay. Yet I will leave seven thousand in Israel, all the knees that have not bowed to Baal, and every mouth that has not kissed him" (1 Kgs 19:17–18). The number seven thousand is significant because of the perfection of the numbers seven and ten. The fullness of Israel remains present in the remnant, despite the infidelity of so many. Elijah never was as solitary as he imagined.

Leithart observes that "Yahweh does not rebuke Elijah for his loss of confidence, but concurs with Elijah's accusation and gives him three tasks to overthrow Ahab's house"—namely, the anointing of Hazael,

Jehu, and Elisha.[38] This is true as far as it goes, but it neglects the fact that Elijah stood before God not as a solitary prophet aloof from God's people, but as a member of God's covenantal people. No matter how many Israelites abandoned YHWH (and rejected Elijah), the community of holy Israel was always present, hearing and affirming the prophetic judgment under the guidance of YHWH. Elijah's teaching was true, but he also had much to learn about the exercise of YHWH's power and authority in and through, not simply a solitary prophet, but YHWH's holy people Israel.

Jesus Christ and the People of God

What about the case of Jesus? Is he the solitary prophet that Elijah sometimes thought himself to be? The biblical scholar Nicholas Perrin remarks that in light of Jesus' Second Temple Jewish context, "the historical Jesus comes to us as an exotic figure."[39] One might add that Jesus seemed very strange to his contemporaries as well. In his analysis of Jesus' Sermon on the Mount (Mt 5–7), Jacob Neusner helps us to see why this was so.[40] In the Sermon on the Mount, Jesus affirms that he has not "come to abolish the law and the prophets; I have come not to abolish them but to fulfil them" (Mt 5:17). What surprises Neusner, however, is the tone that Jesus takes. Jesus claims the authority to teach on his own ("but I say to you") rather than transmitting God's word as Moses did.[41] Furthermore, according to the Gospel of Matthew, Jesus shows power over diseases, over the weather, and over demons. Above all, he teaches that "the Son of man has authority on earth to forgive sins" (Mt 9:6) and, although God's name dwelt in the Temple, he proclaims that "something greater than the temple is here" (Mt 12:6).[42] He accepts the worship of his disciples, who say to him, "Truly you are the Son of God" (Mt 14:33). Matthew's Gospel concludes with the risen Jesus' proclamation that he possesses "all authority in heaven and on earth" (Mt 28:18).[43]

When Neusner criticizes Jesus for not recognizing the importance of the family and of the Sabbath, then, at stake is whether Jesus has the authority (as Joseph Ratzinger puts it) "to create a new and broader context for both."[44] Jesus can fulfill Israel's Scriptures without negating the authority of God's word only if, as the divine Son, he has the authority to reconfigure Israel. By choosing twelve disciples to constitute Israel anew around himself, Jesus claims this authority. His reconstitution of Israel is not a negation of Israel's authoritative mediation of God's revelation but rather is its eschatological fulfillment and extension to the whole world. Jesus promises Simon (Peter) and Andrew that "I will make you fishers of men" (Mt 4:19). After Simon confesses him as the Christ, Jesus gives him the new name Peter ("rock") and says that "on this rock I will build my church, and the powers of death shall not prevail against it" (Mt 16:18).[45] Further, Jesus gives Peter "the keys of the kingdom of heaven," so that "whatever you bind on earth shall be bound in heaven, and whatever you loose on earth shall be loosed in heaven" (Mt 16:19).[46] These teachings about apostolic and Petrine authority fit with Jesus' aim (in Perrin's words) "to establish a new temple and a correspondingly new priesthood."[47]

According to the Gospel of Matthew, the authority that Jesus gives to the apostles is inseparable from Jesus' authority.[48] Thus God proclaims from within the cloud at Jesus' Transfiguration, "This is my beloved Son, with whom I am well pleased; listen to him" (Mt 17:5). The risen Jesus instructs his apostles to teach all nations "to observe all that I have commanded you" (Mt 28:20).[49] In this task, they will never be bereft of Jesus' presence: "I am with you always, to the close of the age" (Mt 28:20). It is only in light of Jesus' eschatological rule, therefore, that the Church in and through which Jesus rules has authority.

In the Gospel of John, Jesus explains the apostles' teaching authority by promising that they will receive the Holy Spirit, "whom the Father will send in my name" (Jn 14:26).[50] Prior to their reception of the eschatological Spirit, there are many things that the disciples do not understand. At his last supper, Jesus tells them that "I have yet many things to say to you, but you cannot bear them now" (Jn 16:12). He reassures them, however, that the Holy Spirit "will teach you all things, and bring to your remembrance all that I have said to you" (Jn 14:26). The Holy Spirit "will guide you into all the truth; for he will not speak on his own authority, but whatever he hears he will speak, and he will declare to you the things that are to come. He will glorify me, for he will take what is mine and declare it to you" (Jn 16:13–14).[51] The Holy Spirit will teach the apostles many things that they could not "bear" during Jesus' earthly ministry, and in this sense the Holy Spirit will reveal new things to them. But all these things will be rooted in what Jesus taught during his earthly ministry. The Holy Spirit does not speak on his own: rather, his teaching is united to Jesus' teaching, just as Jesus' teaching comes from the Father. Jesus promises, "If you continue in my word, you are truly my disciples, and you will know the truth, and the truth will make you free" (Jn 8:31–32).[52]

The Gospel of John also describes Jesus' prayer for his Church's unity in truth. He prays to the Father: "Sanctify them in the truth; your word is truth. As you sent me into the world, so I have sent them into the world" (Jn 17:17–18).[53] In short, the apostles' mission in the world extends that of Jesus. Since believers are to be united in truth and love, Jesus prays "that they may be one even as we are one, I in them and thou in me, that they may become perfectly one, so that the world may know that you have sent me and have loved them even as you have loved me" (Jn 17:22–23). Among the apostles, Simon Peter receives a particular ministry in the service of unity. The risen Jesus three times urges him, "Feed my sheep" (Jn 21:17).[54]

According to the Book of Acts, the risen Jesus promises his apostles before his Ascension that "you shall receive power when the Holy Spirit has come upon you; and you shall be my witnesses in Jerusalem and in all Judea and Samaria and to the end of the earth" (Acts 1:8).[55] At Pentecost, the apostles receive this power to be Jesus' witnesses. The Book of Acts records the preaching of the apostle Peter and of the deacons Stephen and Philip. Paul receives his authority from a direct revelation of Jesus, but Paul also spends two weeks in Jerusalem with Peter and later seeks approval from James, Peter, and John (Gal 2:9; Acts 15:2).[56] In their travels, Paul and Barnabas take care to appoint "elders" for each church (Acts 14:23). Paul is not merely a charismatic preacher called by Jesus; rather, he is accountable to the apostolic community and he ensures that the churches that he founds have elders who are united to the apostles.

One danger, however, is that a particular church might come to associate itself with a particular apostle rather than with Jesus Christ. Paul therefore warns the Corinthians: "What then is Apollos? What is Paul? Servants through whom you believed, as the Lord assigned to each. I planted, Apollos watered, but God gave the growth" (1 Cor 3:5–6). Paul calls himself and the other apostles "God's fellow workers," and he describes their churches as "God's field, God's building," whose foundation can only be Jesus Christ (1 Cor 3:9, 11). Rather than denying the authority of the apostles, Paul says that the apostles are "servants of Christ and stewards of the mysteries of God" (1 Cor 4:1). He himself is the Corinthians' "father in Christ Jesus through the gospel" (1 Cor 4:15).

Indeed, Paul tells the Corinthian church that he has the authority to "come to you with a rod" if necessary (1 Cor 4:21).[57] His authority, in preparation for Christ's return, is such that he can pronounce "judgment in the name of the Lord Jesus" upon members of the community who are living in grave sin (1 Cor 5:3–4). With regard to one such person, he states, "When you are assembled, and my spirit is present, with the power of our Lord Jesus, you are to deliver this man to Satan for the destruction of the flesh, that his spirit may be saved in the day of the Lord Jesus" (1 Cor 5:4–5).[58]

What happens when Paul is unable to be present in his churches? Addressing the Corinthians, Paul recalls that "I sent to you Timothy, my beloved and faithful child in the Lord, to remind you of my ways in Christ, as I teach them everywhere in every church" (1 Cor 4:17).[59] He also speaks of another visit that Timothy is going to make to the Corinthians: "When Timothy comes, see that you put him at ease among you, for he is doing the work of the Lord, as I am" (1 Cor 16:10).[60] Writing to the Philippians, he greets them in the name of both himself and Timothy. His plan is "to send Timothy to you soon, so that I may be cheered by news of you. I have no one like him, who will be genuinely anxious for your welfare" (Phil 2:19–20). In a similar way, Paul reminds the Thessalonians how he sent Timothy to them, and he informs them that Timothy has returned "and has brought us the good news of your faith and love and reported that you always remember us kindly and long to see us, as we long to see you" (1 Thess 3:6).

The First Epistle to Timothy, then, shows Paul instructing Timothy on how to fulfill his office in "the household of God, which is the church of the living God, the pillar and bulwark of the truth" (1 Tim 3:15).[61] Paul urges Timothy to "be a good minister of Christ Jesus, nourished on the words of the faith and of the good doctrine which you have followed" (1 Tim 4:6). Timothy should "attend to the public reading of scripture, to preaching, to teaching" (1 Tim 4:13). He has the responsibility to do these things in the Church because the elders, guided by "prophetic utterance" (1 Tim 4:14), laid hands on him. The same letter also reviews the requirements for the offices of bishop and deacon in the Church (1 Tim 3:2–3).[62]

In addition, Paul's struggles with popular factions in his churches display the exercise of apostolic authority among Jesus' people.[63] On the eve of Paul's third visit to Corinth, for example, he writes of his fear "that perhaps I may come and find you not what I wish, and that you may find me not what you wish; that perhaps there may be quarreling, jealousy, anger, selfishness, slander, gossip, conceit, and disorder" (2 Cor 12:20). Paul warns the Corinthians that although he hopes not to have to be severe, he will use "the authority which the Lord has given me for building up and not for tearing down" (2 Cor 13:10).[64] Paul has a similar experience with the Galatians, some of whom have been persuaded to turn away from the Gospel that Paul preached. After sternly correcting the Galatians, Paul asks rhetorically: "Am I now seeking the favor of men, or of God? Or am I trying to please men?" (Gal 1:10). He answers his own question: "If I were still pleasing men, I should not be a servant of Christ" (Gal 1:10).[65] The point is that the Church's authority is real even when those who exercise it are not popular.

Even so, since the Church's leaders are merely human, some of the elders of the Church will "persist in sin" and will need to be rebuked "in the presence of all, so that the rest may stand in fear" (1 Tim 5:20).[66] It is the Holy Spirit, not mere humans, who ensures that the Church remains Christ's body, "the pillar and bulwark of the truth" (1 Tim 3:15). Thus, Paul in the Book of Acts takes final leave of the elders of Ephesus with these sobering words: "Take heed to yourselves and to all the flock, in which the Holy Spirit has made you guardians, to feed the church of the Lord which he obtained with his own blood. I know that after my departure fierce wolves will come in among you, not sparing the flock; and from among your own selves will arise men speaking perverse things, to draw away the disciples after them" (Acts 20:28–30).[67]

How could Jesus ascend to the right hand of the Father and allow "fierce wolves" to attain positions of authority even within his Church? Given this situation, wouldn't believers be better off to rely solely on "the sacred writings which are able to instruct you for salvation through faith in Christ Jesus" (2 Tim 3:15)?[68] To rely on the Bible, however, is to recognize the teaching authority of the Church. Jesus Christ's living authority is present and active in both. The question then is why Jesus willed this ecclesial mediation of his authority.[69]

In answer, we should recall first the extraordinary humility that the Son of God manifests in his historical mission.[70] He dares to associate with sinners. Paul urges us to "have this mind among yourselves, which was in Christ Jesus, who, though he was in the form of God, did not count equality with God a thing to be grasped, but emptied himself, taking the form of a servant, being born in the likeness of men" (Phil 2:5–7). In his humility, Jesus prepares mere humans to receive the dignity of a participation in his authority, something that is only possible due to the work of the Holy Spirit. Second, Jesus' choosing of his twelve disciples, and his frequent highlighting of the unique role of Peter among the twelve, needs to be given weight. This apostolic structure characterizes the visible unity of the Church. It is not a secondary element that can be discarded.[71] Third, although we know that "fierce wolves" will take their place among the Church's leaders, we also know in faith that the Church, as the body of Christ, will not cease to be "the pillar and bulwark of the truth" (1 Tim 3:15) that is guided "into all the truth" (Jn 16:13) by the Holy Spirit. This is so because Christ continually "nourishes and cherishes" the Church (Eph 5:29) and ensures that "there shall be one flock, one shepherd" (Jn 10:16). In fulfillment of God's promise that "I myself will be the shepherd of my sheep" (Ezek 34:15), Christ the good shepherd builds up his Church in the Eucharistic liturgy: "The bread which we break, is it not a participation in the body of Christ? Because there is one bread, we who are many are one body, for we all partake of the one bread" (1 Cor 10:16–17).[72]

Church, Liturgy, Dogma

Yet, is the Church of the fourth century, or of the eleventh century, the same authoritative Church that is described in the New Testament as "the pillar and bulwark of the truth"?[73] If we accept in faith the New Testament's testimony to the Church, then we can anticipate that the answer will be yes and, with Joseph Ratzinger, affirm "the enduring subjecthood of the Church in the midst of temporal change."[74] The Church is a living, ongoing "subject," visible in the world and able to internalize and unite the diversity of texts and historical situations. Otherwise, as Ratzinger says, "one stands before a sequence of but partly reconcilable texts."[75] Without the Church's subjecthood, we find ourselves continually slipping away from a Jesus who recedes further and further into the past. The New Testament's testimony to the Church requires theology to (in Ratzinger's words) "find its way back to that ecclesial identity which holds all together. In this way, theology will be able to grasp faith in the living dynamic of its development."[76]

The Orthodox theologian Georges Florovsky makes a similar point. After approvingly quoting Newman on the nature of theology, Florovsky comments:

> A Catholic [Orthodox] theologian is not left alone with logic and erudition. He is led by the faith; *credo ut intelligam*. Faith illuminates the reason. And erudition, the memory of the past, is quickened in the continuous experience of the Church. A Catholic theologian is guided by the teaching authority of the Church, by its living tradition. But above all, he himself *lives in the Church*, which is the Body of Christ. The mystery of the Incarnation is still, as it were, continuously enacted in the Church, and its "implications" are revealed and disclosed in devotional experience and in sacramental participation.[77]

Theology, then, is rooted in the Church's life of faith, and its true developments "are revealed and disclosed in devotional experience and sacramental participation." This can be seen not least with respect to the doctrine of the Trinity. Many scholars today do not think that the first Christians worshipped the Son; almost all scholars deny that the first Christians worshipped the Holy Spirit. In any case, the reality of God's triunity cannot be demonstrated by historical research. What is needed instead is an appreciation for the Church's ongoing life as the authoritative matrix in which Trinitarian doctrine developed. Illumined by liturgical worship, the Church in the fourth century made connections between various passages of Scripture and exhibited their Trinitarian reference.[78] Building upon scriptural and liturgical texts, for example, Basil the Great defends the divinity of the Holy Spirit on the grounds that "[t]he Holy Spirit cannot be divided from the Father and the Son in worship."[79] The bishops meeting at the Council of Constantinople confirmed this doctrine in 381.

In a comparable way, beginning especially with the recognition that Mary is the *Theotokos*, early Christians pondered liturgically upon the biblical portraits of Mary that suggest Mary's typological status as the new Eve and the new ark of the covenant.[80] The extraordinary grace that Mary received as the mother of her Son was evident to those who brought Christological and Trinitarian doctrine to full expression in the fourth and fifth centuries. By the sixth century, Mary's Assumption had already obtained a firm place in the Church's liturgy, and in the centuries that followed theologians such as John of Damascus began to undertake the long process of sifting the doctrinal truth of Mary's Assumption from the legendary stories about the event. Liturgically, the celebration of Mary's Assumption took hold in such a manner that this way of connecting the New Testament's typological texts about Mary came to be understood by the Church as flowing from the guidance of the Holy Spirit.[81]

A number of typologically rich biblical texts play a role in the Church's liturgical celebration of Mary's Assumption. In the Roman Missal in use today, the biblical texts for the Feast of the Assumption include Revelation 11:19 and 12:1–6, 10; Psalm 45:10–12, 16; 1 Corinthians 15:20–27; and Luke 1:39–56. Revelation 11:19–12:10 contains an abundance of imagery derived from Genesis 3:15, as well as from the symbolism of the temple, the ark of the covenant, and the theophany at Mount Sinai. Psalm 45 describes the victory of Daughter Zion. The "queen" stands at the right hand of the Messianic king, "and the king will desire your beauty" (Ps 45:11). Her children will all be princes.[82] The imagery in 1 Corinthians 15:20–27, like that of Revelation 12, relates to Genesis 3: "For as in Adam all die, so also in Christ shall all be made alive. But each in his own order: Christ the first fruits, then at his coming those who belong to Christ" (1 Cor 15:22–23). Finally, the Gospel passage from Luke 1:39–56, which includes Mary's Magnificat, presents Mary as Daughter Zion and as the new ark of the covenant.

In the Greek Orthodox liturgy, at Great Vespers on the Feast of Mary's Dormition, the biblical texts include Genesis 28:10–17, where Jacob's dream uncovers for him the "gate of heaven"; Ezekiel 43:72–44:1, which describes the gate of the eschatological temple through which only the Lord God enters; and Proverbs 9:1–11, which describes the "house" of Wisdom and her life-giving instruction.[83] Among mere creatures, Mary as *Theotokos* has become the eschatological temple and gate, and she is now fully united with her life-giving Son. The liturgy proclaims: "The divine tabernacles of heaven fittingly received you as a living heaven, all-pure Virgin; and as a blameless bride you stand radiantly adorned before your King and God."[84] Here we can recognize the tabernacle/ark and enthronement imagery of Psalm 45, Luke 1, and Revelation 11–12. As Alexander Schmemann observes, Mary's Assumption reveals the personal face of the fully redeemed human being, the "temple of God in a most particular and literal sense."[85] For Schmemann, "The accepted doctrine of the Church sees in 'the tradition of sacraments and sacred rites' an inviolable element of Tradition, and thus also one of the sources which theology must utilize if it seeks to expound fully the faith and life of the Church."[86]

Why, however, should Mary's Assumption be dogmatically defined and thus be included among the most significant mysteries of faith? Ratzinger's reflections are helpful here. The Incarnation, he notes, means that "God becomes small. He becomes man; he accepts thereby the limitations of human conception and childbirth. He has a mother and is thus truly woven into the tapestry of our human history, so that in fact a woman is able to say to him who is her child, a human child: The Lord of the world is within you."[87] In Christ, we see ever more keenly that God does not come among us without becoming "truly woven into the tapestry of our human history." Only Christ saves us, but we cannot rightly perceive that salvation when we exclude Mary (and Israel/Church) from the picture. Mary does not obstruct our discovery of her Son. On the contrary, she makes manifest the kind of Savior he is—namely, one who comes to make us into the family of God that we were intended to be. In his divine humility, he embraces real human bonds. Christ's preeminence appears precisely in his gifting: Mary truly is most blessed among women.[88]

Newman famously observes that "[a] revelation is not given, if there be no authority to decide what it is that is given."[89] His argument might appear to arise from nineteenth-century epistemological doubts, but in fact it rests on firm biblical grounds. As he points out, "Scripture expressly calls the Church 'the pillar and ground of the Truth,' and promises her as by covenant that 'the Spirit of the Lord that is upon her, and His words which He has put in her mouth shall not depart out of her mouth, nor out of the mouth of her seed, nor out of the mouth of her seed's seed, from henceforth and forever.'"[90] By contrast, the young Jaroslav Pelikan envisions a devolutionary process, in which biblical ambiguities led the Church to postulate the authority of "Tradition" and then ambiguities within Tradition led the Church to inflate the authority of the pope, thereby eviscerating Scripture's authority to challenge and correct the Church today. As noted earlier, Pelikan at this early stage of his career calls for recognizing the fallibility of the Church and returning in a chastened way to the central teachings of Scripture. He sees the use of papal infallibility in defining Mary's Assumption—a dogma that in his view lacks support from either Scripture or Tradition—as demonstrating the absurd position into which the modern Church has fallen.

In response, this chapter argued that the young Pelikan's vision of the "mature" Christian and the fallible Church is inadequate to Scripture's portraits of the believer and the Church. The prophetic ministry of Elijah is a case in point: YHWH reminds Elijah of the seven thousand faithful Israelites whom YHWH has preserved. It is Israel that carries forward the faithful reception of God's word, and the role of the prophet fits within Israel as God's people. This point holds for the Christian community as well, in a manner refracted by the newness brought by Jesus Christ. According to the New Testament, Jesus enabled the apostles to share in his authority through the outpouring of the Holy Spirit, and among the apostles he gave a particular role to Peter. This apostolic structure can be seen in the Church over the centuries. The Book of Acts and the Epistles help further to unfold Jesus' promise that the Holy Spirit will guide the Church into all truth.

As Ratzinger emphasizes, the dogmas of faith are what the Church as a living subject has identified as central to God's revelation. Although it might seem that dogmas would be highly fallible as products of particular epochs, the Holy Spirit ensures the truth of the Church's dogmatic teachings as part of sustaining the covenantal relationship between the living God and his people, which involves a unity of truth and love. Beginning in the late fifth century, Mary's participation in Christ's victory as the new Eve, the "woman clothed with the sun" (Rev 12:1), increasingly became a liturgical and theological theme. The claim that Mary was assumed bodily into heaven need not have been accepted liturgically and theologically by the Church, but it was accepted. By themselves, the typological connections in Scripture could not have sufficed for the dogma of Mary's Assumption. The reality of her Assumption had to be confirmed by the Church under the guidance of the Holy Spirit.

Over the centuries, the Church's Magisterium in various ways confirmed the reality of Mary's Assumption, culminating in the recognition of this doctrine's dogmatic status within the mysteries of the New Covenant. In the fullness of her configuration to her Son, Mary is the "type," the fullness, of what each Christian—each mere creature, each follower of Christ—will be. Her Assumption into heaven fits with her role in salvation history, as the unique covenantal partner that God made ready for his Son. In this way, Mary truly is, as Elizabeth proclaimed, supremely "blessed . . . among women" (Lk 1:42).

CHAPTER 6

The Fittingness of Mary's Assumption in God's Economy of Salvation

In his sermon "The Glories of Mary for the Sake of Her Son," John Henry Newman argues that the Church's doctrines about Mary reflect the unity of the economy of salvation. For Newman, just as the natural world forms an ordered whole, so too does the supernatural world of divine revelation. In this supernatural world, Mary's Assumption to heaven befits the life-giving power of the Incarnation. The Son's humility brings about the exaltation of creatures, first and foremost the one whose mission was so closely associated with his own. Newman remarks in this vein: "If the Creator comes on earth in the form of a servant and a creature, why may not His Mother, on the other hand, rise to be the Queen of heaven, and be clothed with the sun, and have the moon under her feet?"[1]

Newman defends and expands upon this approach in another sermon, "On the Fitness of the Glories of Mary." Here he observes that the New Testament itself appeals to fittingness in matters of doctrine.[2] For example, Jesus asks the disciples on the road to Emmaus, "Was it not necessary that the Christ should suffer these things and enter into his glory?" (Lk 24:26); and the Letter to the Hebrews states that "it was fitting that he, for whom and by whom all things exist, in bringing many sons to glory, should make the pioneer of their salvation perfect through suffering" (Heb 2:10). Thus both Jesus and the Letter to the Hebrews explain his suffering on the Cross, which was not expected of the Messiah, by means of its fittingness in light of the whole economy of salvation. This same fittingness, Newman suggests, applies to the Assumption of Mary into heaven. As Newman says, "we feel it 'ought' to be; that it 'becomes' her Lord and Son thus to provide for one who was so singular and special, both in herself and her relations to Him."[3]

In exploring this fittingness, Newman begins with Mary's motherhood: as the mother of Christ, she is the mother of the Word. She gave to Christ his human nature; she cared for him as an infant; and she knew him intimately for the thirty years prior to his public ministry. Her motherhood of the Word incarnate was an extraordinary grace and dignity bestowed upon her by God. She must indeed be the greatest mere creature that has ever been or ever will be. Newman concludes that it is fitting to suppose that "[n]othing is too high for her to whom God owes His human life; no exuberance of grace, no excess of glory, but is becoming, but is to be expected there, where God has lodged Himself, whence God has issued."[4] It is most fitting that she be configured most perfectly to her Son. Her Son fittingly treats her as does King Solomon his own mother (but without the sinful court intrigue!): "And the king rose to meet her, and bowed down to her; then he sat on his throne, and had a seat brought for the king's mother; and she sat on his right" (1 Kgs 2:19).[5]

Unlike other bodies, it would hardly be fitting for Mary's body to moulder in the grave. Among the reasons that Newman gives for this are her sinlessness and her Son's love for his mother. Indeed, the fittingness of Mary's Assumption has been confirmed over the centuries by "the consent of the whole Catholic world."[6] In Mary, God reveals to us "the personal type and representative image of that spiritual life and renovation in grace, 'without which no one shall see God' [Heb 12:14]."[7] As the type of the perfect Christian, she is now present body and soul with Christ in glory.

Building upon Newman's approach and upon the twentieth-century approaches that were surveyed above, this chapter explores the relationship of Mary's Assumption to other mysteries of faith. The Church calls this procedure the "analogy of faith," whose purpose is to reflect upon "the coherence of the truths of faith among themselves and within the whole plan of Revelation."[8] Among the many mysteries of faith that could be examined, I will highlight three: creation and fall, God's election of Israel, and the Incarnation of the Son of God. In each case, I will examine the biblical testimony to the mystery before drawing a connection to Mary's Assumption.

This procedure differs from arguments for Mary's Assumption based on biblical typology, although I use Scripture's typological portraits of Mary. Beginning with the doctrine of Mary's Assumption, I argue that this doctrine coheres, in an eminently fitting manner, with what Scripture teaches about creation and fall, the election of Israel, and the Incarnation of the Son. Certainly biblical typology and the Church's authority lay the foundations for the doctrine of Mary's Assumption. But fittingness within the unity of the mysteries of faith is also necessary, because were Mary's Assumption opposed to God's pattern of salvation, then Mary's Assumption could hardly be true. In fact, Mary's Assumption marvelously accords with the way in which God has "raised us up with him [Christ], and made us sit with him in the heavenly places in Christ Jesus, that in the coming ages he might show the immeasurable riches of his grace in kindness toward us in Christ Jesus" (Eph 2:6–7).

Creation and Fall

Echoing the work of Jon Levenson and others, the Old Testament scholar John Walton observes that "we should think of Genesis 1 in relation to a cosmic temple."[9] The creation exists in order to give holy praise to its Creator, who dwells in it. The Sabbath is the reason for the creation: all that exists is ordered to the holiness of God. God creates male and female human beings "in our image, after our likeness" (Gen 1:26). He gives them "dominion" (Gen 1:26) or governance of the whole earth, and he gives them the fruits of the earth for food. When they disobey God's command regarding the tree of the knowledge of good and evil, however, the temple is profaned. The curse that follows upon their transgression consists in suffering and death; as God tells Adam, "In the sweat of your face you shall eat bread till you return to the ground, for out of it you were taken; you are dust, and to dust you shall return" (Gen 3:19).[10]

This curse makes clear that for human beings, holiness and life are intrinsically related. This is what one would expect from the fact that creation is presented as a cosmic temple. Lacking holiness, Adam and Eve are exiled from the paradisal Garden of Eden and no longer live in the presence of God. Their firstborn son, Cain, murders their second son Abel. Far from being ordered to the worship of God, the earth becomes a land of injustice and bloodshed. Yet Adam and Eve have a third son, Seth, and his descendents include some who are holy. The case of Enoch bears witness to the bond between holiness and life, since he lived for a symbolically perfect number of years (365), as befits the fact that he "walked with God" (Gen 5:24). As one who walked with God in life, Enoch also experiences death in a different way from other fallen humans: "Enoch walked with God; and he was not, for God took him" (Gen 5:24).[11]

When God later finds "that the wickedness of man was great in the earth, and that every imagination of the thoughts of his heart was only evil continually" (Gen 6:5), God repents that he ever made human beings. Even then, however, the link between sin and death does not result in the destruction of all humans, because Noah is "a righteous man, blameless in his generation" (Gen 6:9) and so God spares Noah and his family. Nonetheless, "the earth was filled with violence" and "all flesh had corrupted their way upon the earth" (Gen 6:11–12). When Noah leaves the ark, he gets drunk and his son Ham sees Noah's nakedness, leading to a further spiral of violence. But God promises never to obliterate the human race. God tells Noah and his sons, "This is the sign of the covenant which I make between me and you and every living creature that is with you, for all future generations: I set my bow in the cloud, and it shall be a sign of the covenant between me and the earth" (Gen 9:12–13).[12]

The connection between life and holiness continues with Abram, whom God names Abraham. For Abraham, to have life is to have descendents, and God promises many descendents to Abraham if he exhibits holiness. We read that "the Lord appeared to Abram, and said to him, 'I am God Almighty; walk before me, and be blameless. And I will make my covenant between me and you, and will multiply you exceedingly'" (Gen 17:1–2). The catastrophe that befalls Sodom and Gomorrah also bears upon this theme: their lack of holiness leads to destruction. The hard-heartedness of Pharaoh leads to the slaughter of the firstborn of Egypt, and Israel's worship of the golden calf leads to a civil war and a plague. Moses urges the people of Israel to be holy and thereby to gain life: "I have set before you life and death, blessing and curse; therefore choose life, that you and your descendants may live, loving the Lord your God, obeying his voice, and cleaving to him; for that means life to you and length of days, that you may dwell in the land which the Lord swore to your fathers, to Abraham, to Isaac, and to Jacob, to give them" (Deut 30:19–20).[13] Joshua warns that the people cannot merely pretend to serve God. If they lack holiness, they will perish. As Joshua puts it in challenging them to serve God truly, "You cannot serve the Lord; for he is a holy God; he is a jealous God; he will not forgive your transgressions or your sins. If you forsake the Lord and serve foreign gods, then he will turn and do you harm, and consume you, after having done you good" (Josh 24:19–20). Holiness and life are inextricably bound.[14]

Israel is called to be renewed in God's image, to once more "be holy; for I the Lord your God am holy" (Lev 19:2).[15] Indeed, God is present in Israel as he was originally present to the cosmic temple. The "pillar of cloud" that guides Israel on its exodus journey stands at the door of the tent of meeting so as to indicate God's presence with Moses. God is present—both for life and (in cases of disobedience) for death—in the ark of the covenant that David brings into Jerusalem, when David dances before the ark. When Solomon builds the Temple in Jerusalem, God makes his presence known by means of a cloud that fills the Temple and overwhelms the priests with God's glory.[16] In light of God's abandonment of the first Temple due to the people's idolatry, Ezekiel prophesies the building of an eschatological temple from whose door healing and life-giving water will pour forth. God promises to "put my law within them, and I will write it upon their hearts" (Jer 31:33); and again he says, "A new heart I will give you, and a new spirit I will put within you" (Ezek 36:26).[17]

In Christian iconography, the cloud signifies the grace of the Holy Spirit, the "Spirit of God" that at creation was "moving over the face of the waters" (Gen 1:2). When Mary receives word that she is to bear the Messiah, she learns that the Holy Spirit will overshadow her, just as the Spirit moved over the face of the waters at the creation. Her Son will be conceived when, as the angel tells her, "The Holy Spirit will come upon you, and the power of the Most High will overshadow you; therefore the child to be born will be called holy, the Son of God" (Lk 1:35).

When Mary, pregnant with Jesus, goes to visit her cousin Elizabeth (pregnant with John the Baptist) in the hill country of Judea, John the Baptist "leaped for joy" in Elizabeth's womb, just as David danced before the ark. For Mary to be *Theotokos*, God-bearer, means that such connections with the Temple and the ark are appropriate.[18]

If Mary is the new temple and new ark, is she holy? This question will sound odd once we recognize that the Temple and the ark were places of preeminent holiness. The greeting "Hail, full of grace, the Lord is with you" (Lk 1:28) means that she has received not some worldly dignity but the favor of God.[19] To be favored by God is, as we have seen, to be holy (cf. Lev 19:2). Of the holy women of Israel, Mary is preeminent: as Elizabeth proclaims, "Blessed are you among women, and blessed is the fruit of your womb!" (Lk 1:42). Mary responds to Elizabeth by giving praise to God because "he has regarded the low estate of his handmaiden. For behold, henceforth all generations will call me blessed; for he who is mighty has done great things for me, and holy is his name" (Lk 1:48–49). She is blessed as the mother of the Messiah, and it is *she* who is blessed along with her Son: she is holy, set apart, so that the Son of the Most High might dwell in her.

By recognizing Mary as the new ark and the new temple, we do not overlook the fact that Jesus is the new temple from whom will flow "rivers of living water," that is, the Holy Spirit (Jn 7:38).[20] After cleansing the Temple in Jerusalem, Jesus prophesies, "Destroy this temple, and in three days I will raise it up," and "he spoke of the temple of his body" (Jn 2:19, 21). The Word of God tabernacles among us in Jesus Christ (Jn 1:14). The symbolism can apply to both Jesus and Mary, in different ways. Mary is presented as uniquely favored by God, most blessed among women, because she is the ark and temple that God's Spirit overshadows and that houses the Son of God. Mary's holiness is revealed in her obedience to God, which reverses Eve's disobedience: "Behold, I am the handmaid of the Lord; let it be to me according to your word" (Lk 1:38).[21] This obedience, again, is more than her agreement to go ahead with it. It is her complete self-giving to God, in which she fully embraces God's will—something possible only through the grace of the Holy Spirit working in her.[22] She need not know all that her mission (and Jesus') entails; thus she and his "brothers" do not seem to understand his preaching in Nazareth (Mk 3:31).[23] Repeatedly he emphasizes that her role as mother of the Messiah is not based simply on bodily ties.[24] He tells the crowd, "Whoever does the will of God is my brother, and sister, and mother" (Mk 3:35), and when a woman in another crowd "raised her voice and said to him, 'Blessed is the womb that bore you, and the breasts that you sucked!'" he corrects her immediately: "Blessed rather are those who hear the word of God and keep it!" (Lk 11:27–28). But Luke has already shown us that Mary is preeminently the one who hears and obeys the word of God: "Mary kept all these things, pondering them in her heart" (Lk 2:19).

If we avoid false antinomies, then, we can affirm Mary's unique holiness (flowing entirely from her Son's), which the Church affirms by proclaiming her to be immaculate from her conception. Does Mary's unique holiness continue the biblical connection between holiness and life that we have traced above? Jesus is utterly sinless (see 2 Cor 5:21, Heb 4:15), and he suffers and dies on the Cross in order to redeem us from sin and to enable us to share forever in the Trinitarian life. Mary does not possess a holiness that exempts her from following her Son's path of suffering and death. Holiness, in Christ, requires this path. Simeon prophesies to Mary that "a sword will pierce through your own soul also" (Lk 2:35).[25] Mary is found at the foot of the Cross, sharing in Christ's suffering. She is the "woman" who shares uniquely in the new Adam's victorious "hour" (Jn 2:4).

Although Mary's holiness does not preclude her suffering and death, her holiness is indeed connected with life. Not only is she the bearer of the life-giver, Jesus Christ, but she also receives glorified life in heaven as the culmination of her sharing with her Son in the mysteries of salvation. The doctrine of Mary's Assumption teaches that Mary, continuing her holy and unique participation in the mysteries of her Son, shares uniquely in Christ's victorious suffering and thus also uniquely in Christ's Resurrection. Mary's Assumption means that the new ark of the covenant did not corrupt—her Son did not simply discard the flesh that gave him flesh—but instead is now present bodily with her Son in heaven. Typologically, this means that "God's temple in heaven was opened, and the ark of his covenant was seen within his temple" (Rev 11:19). Mary's unique holiness, embodied in her participation in Christ's mysteries, means that she is perfected first among mere creatures. Her perfecting is representative of that of Israel and the Church. Holy Israel/Church is not simply an impersonal, abstract structure.[26] Rather, the Word becomes incarnate in a woman who is "full of grace" and uniquely blessed among women because she "believed that there would be a fulfillment of what was spoken to her from the Lord" (Lk 1:28, 45). She is the model of the Church in her participation in Christ's mysteries and in her radical openness to God's will: "[L]et it be to me according to your word" (Lk 1:38).

On the basis of her holiness, we can agree with Joseph Ratzinger when he suggests that Mary uniquely received the gift of life that Paul describes in Ephesians 2:4–6: "God, who is rich in mercy, out of the great love with which he loved us, even when we were dead through our trespasses, made us alive together with Christ (by grace you have been saved), and raised us up with him in the heavenly places in Christ Jesus." Similarly, since Mary gave her life entirely to God, Colossians 3:3 applies to her in a full manner: "For you have died, and your life is hid with Christ in God." Christ gave up his life in order to sanctify the Church, "that he might present the church to himself in splendor, without spot or wrinkle or any such thing, that she might be holy and without blemish" (Eph 5:27). The holiness of the Church will be completed when the entire Church enjoys full life with Christ in glory. Mary's holiness makes it fitting that Christ has brought about such full life in Mary.

The point of the "analogy of faith" is that one Christian belief sheds light on another. This is the case with the doctrine of creation and fall, in which we find the connection of holiness and life. Mary is holy; it is fitting that she, the new ark of the covenant, is fully redeemed, fully alive with her Son. She is the living model of holy Israel/Church.

The Election of Israel

The Jewish biblical scholar Joel Kaminsky, after examining the Cain/Abel and Ishmael/Isaac stories, concludes that "God's choice of the elect remains shrouded in mystery and is not dependent on human action."[27] He does think, however, that the Ishmael/Isaac story adds an element not found in the Cain/Abel story—namely, the significance of human choice. As he puts it, "being chosen demands a human response," so that "chosenness is brought to fruition by human action, creating a synergy between divine initiative and human response."[28] This human response, after the Fall, can be imperfect and mistaken, but even then it does not ultimately frustrate God's plan.

In this light, Kaminsky explores Israel's understanding of its divine election. Election does not mean that Israel (as God's elect people) will be saved and those outside Israel (i.e., non-elect people) will be damned. Furthermore, the election of the particular people of Israel is never superseded, even in the eschaton when the nations will come to recognize God's chosen people Israel as "a blessing in the midst of the earth" (Is 19:24). The other nations do not, Kaminsky thinks, come to share in Israel's elect status.[29] He recognizes that "major streams of New Testament thinking broadened the elect group to include those Gentiles who came to believe in Jesus as the Christ," although he rightly adds that Christians remained "particularists" because of the central focus on Jesus Christ.[30] (Whether it was "major streams of New Testament thinking" or the risen Jesus himself who "broadened the elect group" is of course the question.)

Mary's song of praise to God, in response to Elizabeth's greeting, centers upon Israel's election—and her own.[31] God's blessing of her is God's blessing of all Israel; and she responds on behalf of all Israel. She recognizes that she has been uniquely chosen. As she says, God "has regarded the low estate of his handmaiden. For behold, henceforth all generations will call me blessed; for he who is mighty has done great things for me" (Lk 1:48–49). As the mother of the Messiah, she is the elect bearer of the covenantal blessing. Through her, God's covenantal work in Israel will be accomplished, as it was through Abraham, Isaac, and Jacob. She accepts God's choice of her on behalf of the people Israel. In this vein, she affirms that God's "mercy is on those who fear him from generation to generation," so that her election exemplifies the pattern in Israel by which God "has put down the mighty from their thrones, and exalted those of low degree; he has filled the hungry with good things, and the rich he has sent empty away" (Lk 1:52–53). Indeed, God's choice of her confirms God's election of Israel, because the purpose of the election of Israel is now coming to fulfillment—namely, to make his people holy. God will accomplish this through the Redeemer, Jesus Christ. People could of course be united to the Redeemer prior to his coming, through implicit faith (see Heb 11). In this way people could be purified in advance through union with Jesus' future Pasch, as Mary was in a unique manner.[32] When the fullness of time had arrived, God demonstrated his covenant faithfulness by choosing Mary as the woman in and through whom the Redeemer would enter the world: "He has helped his servant Israel, in remembrance of his mercy, as he spoke to our fathers, to Abraham and to his posterity for ever" (Lk 1:54–55).

Mary's song of praise has evident similarities with the song of Hannah, the mother of the prophet Samuel. Hannah prays before the ark that she might have a child, for she is barren.[33] When she and her husband Elkanah conceive a son, she names her son Samuel and dedicates him to the service of God. After she has weaned her son, she presents him to Eli, the priest at the temple in Shiloh where the ark is. In her song, she proclaims that she "exults in the Lord" and that "my strength is exalted in the Lord" (1 Sam 2:1); she focuses not on herself but on the God of life.[34] She emphasizes that everything is in God's hands: those who oppose God will be utterly cut off, and the poor and needy will be blessed. As she says, "The Lord kills and brings to life; he brings down to Sheol and raises up. The Lord makes poor and makes rich; he brings low, he also exalts" (1 Sam 2:6).

What about earlier women whom God chooses to continue the covenant? Abraham's wife Sarah, mother of Isaac, laughs at the idea that she is to have a child because she has already entered menopause. She earlier seeks to give Abraham children by giving him Hagar, her slave, to beget a child who would then be (in an extended sense) Sarah's. This action backfires, however, because as Sarah says to Abraham, "I gave my maid to your embrace, and when she saw that she had conceived, she looked on me with contempt" (Gen 16:5). This obviously is not what God had in mind when he promised a son to Abraham. When Sarah does conceive and bear her son Isaac, she rejoices: "God has made laughter for me; every one who hears will laugh over me. . . . Who would have said to Abraham that Sarah would suckle children? Yet I have borne him a son in his old age" (Gen 21:6–7).[35] God, rather than either Sarah or Abraham, has chosen how to extend his covenant with Abraham.

Mary is in the line of women such as Sarah and Hannah. For Sarah, God has accomplished an act that will make all who hear rejoice with her; for Hannah, God has accomplished an act that shows that he alone is the God of life, who disposes everything according to his choice. For Mary, God has chosen and exalted her to such a degree that all generations will call her blessed, and this choosing confirms God's election of Israel. The generations of Israelites who were yearning for the holy God to make his people holy should also be mentioned here. Josiah institutes reforms, including putting "away the mediums and the wizards and the teraphim and the idols and all the abominations that were seen in the land of Judah and in Jerusalem" (2 Kgs 23:24), but God nonetheless allows the Babylonian exile to take place. Ezra sadly confesses on behalf of the people that "our iniquities have risen higher than our heads, and our guilt has mounted up to the heavens" (Ezra 9:6). In the time of the Maccabees, God permits an "onslaught of evil" such that "the temple was filled with debauchery and reveling by the Gentiles, who dallied with harlots and had intercourse with women within the sacred precincts, and besides that brought in things for sacrifice that were unfit" (2 Macc 6:3–4). Judas Maccabeus and his supporters find that even within their own ranks there are those who trusted in the "sacred tokens of the idols of Jamnia" (2 Macc 12:40). Like Ezra, Judas Maccabeus and his followers "turned to prayer, beseeching that the sin which had been committed might be wholly blotted out" (2 Macc 12:42). The people are not yet what God has promised they will be.[36]

Particularity is the hallmark of divine election. Elect Israel is to be God's dwelling place, God's pure bride, God's faithful daughter. As Ratzinger emphasizes, therefore, it should not surprise us that Mary, a particular woman, is depicted as Daughter Zion.[37] Mary embodies concretely the faithful bride about whom Hosea speaks prophetically and who is figured in the Song of Solomon. As Israel/Church, Mary shares with her Son in the mysteries of his life, and she prays with the apostles in the upper room in preparation for the outpouring of the Holy Spirit at Pentecost. As Israel/Church, she is the mother not only of Jesus but, at Jesus' command, also of the beloved disciple and thus of all disciples.[38] Certainly she (Israel/Church) is still on earth fighting Satan, who cannot destroy her but who persecutes her children, "those who keep the commandments of God and bear testimony to Jesus" (Rev 12:17). But she is also the one who in heaven is "clothed with the sun, with the moon under her feet, and on her head a crown of twelve stars" (Rev 12:1). She is the greatest of all mere creatures, and she is fully victorious with her Son in heaven.

The particularity of election, in this view, means that God's exaltation of Mary (through her motherhood of the Son) does not decrease as her Son increases. Jesus Christ is not in competition with his elect, who are called to imitate his kenotic love. When he "increases" by kenotic love, his elect people also increase—and this by means of Mary's injunction, "Do whatever he tells you" (Jn 2:5).[39] Mary is more than a precursor of Christ like John the Baptist; her role does not disappear when Christ appears. Christ's intimacy with his elect is reflected in his drawing of Mary, blessed among women, into the fullness of salvation, body and soul. Mary's Assumption guarantees the truth that "to all who received him, who believed in his name, he gave power to become children of God; who were born, not of blood nor of the will of the flesh nor of the will of man, but of God" (Jn 1:12–13). She has entered fully, as God's temple (and thus as Israel/Church), into eternal life.

Again, this is a conclusion of fittingness. In affirming Mary's Assumption, one sees that the doctrine of God's election of Israel sheds special light on Mary. God's choosing of Mary to be the mother of Israel's Messiah makes Mary the embodiment of holy Israel, God's temple and bride. By God's election, Mary (Israel/Church) receives the mission of accompanying her Son on his path of love. Mary's glorious Assumption to the right hand of Christ Jesus shows what God, through the missions of the Son and the Holy Spirit, accomplishes for his elect people, those who accompany him by kenotic love. God exalts his elect.

The Incarnation of the Word

As Ratzinger notes, Eve's life-giving power gives birth to humans who are doomed to die, whereas Mary's life-giving power gives birth to a Son who takes the sting out of death. As the one who gives life to the lifegiver, it is fitting that Mary receive the fullness of life at her death.

The doctrine of the Incarnation teaches that Mary's Son was in the beginning; he "was with God" and he "was God" (Jn 1:1). No less than the Father, the Son is the Creator: "[A]ll things were made through him, and without him was not anything made that was made" (Jn 1:3).[40] The Incarnation of the Son repairs fallen humanity by giving us the ability, through faith, to become adoptive children of God. Paul states: "We know that in everything God works for good with those who love him, who are called according to his purpose. For those whom he foreknew he also predestined to be conformed to the image of his Son, in order that he might be the first-born among many brethren" (Rom 8:28–29).[41]

Furthermore, Mary is mother not merely of Jesus in his humanity, but of the Person Jesus Christ. Jesus' human actions are the actions of the divine Son, incarnate in Israel. This means that Mary is mother of the divine Son; she has a unique relation—the relation of motherhood—to the Son.[42] The eternal Son does not of course have an eternal mother, which would be absurd. Instead, the eternal Son, by becoming incarnate, relates himself to his human mother. Her privilege can hardly be over-emphasized.[43] Only Mary gives him his human constitution, experiences his growth in the womb and his infancy, and knows him intimately throughout his hidden life in Nazareth and over the course of his public ministry. What could be a greater privilege for a mere human being than to be the mother of the incarnate Son (and through him, the mother of all sons and daughters in the incarnate Son)?[44]

Yet, Jesus worked few miracles in Nazareth because the townspeople imagined that they already knew everything about him. They told each other: "Where did this man get this wisdom and these mighty works? Is this not the carpenter's son? Is not his mother called Mary? And are not his brethren James and Joseph and Simon and Judas? And are not all his sisters with us? Where then did this man get all this?" (Mt 13:54–56). In fact, as we read, "they took offense at him" (Mt 13:57). Could it be, then, that Mary's closeness to Jesus as his mother would have led her to overlook what sets him apart?

This seems unlikely if we accept what the Gospels of Matthew and Luke tell us. Miraculously, Mary's conception of Jesus is virginal, and indeed an angel tells Joseph in a dream, "Joseph, son of David, do not fear to take Mary your wife, for that which is conceived in her is of the Holy Spirit; she will bear a son, and you shall call his name Jesus, for he will save his people from their sins" (Mt 1:20–21).[45] In this light, Mary (and Joseph) would hardly have been likely to underestimate their Son, even if at times they may not have understood him.[46] The Gospel of Luke observes in a similar fashion that on the night of Jesus' birth, the shepherds tell Mary and Joseph what the angels had proclaimed to the shepherds—

namely, that her newborn Son is "a Savior, who is Christ the Lord" (Lk 2:11). Mary takes this proclamation seriously: she "kept all these things, pondering them in her heart" (Lk 2:19). This "pondering" marks Mary's relationship to her Son as an interior one from the outset.

Indeed, Luke makes especially clear that Mary's motherhood is never merely a bodily event. Rather than simply having an external relationship with her Son, her relationship to him is rooted in faith. She accepts the vocation to be the mother of the Messiah in a manner that expresses interior faith: "Behold, I am the handmaid of the Lord; let it be to me according to your word" (Lk 1:38).[47] This faith develops as she accompanies her Son through his public ministry and death on the Cross, so that after his Resurrection she is present in the upper room among the disciples and other believers gathered in prayer. Her faith is well expressed in her remark to the servants at the wedding feast, "Do whatever he tells you" (Jn 2:4). In a real sense, we are all servants at the wedding feast of the Lord, and faith consists in recognizing and obeying the Lord by doing whatever he tells us.

The Incarnation, then, gives Mary a unique closeness to her Son. Even so, it might seem that Peter, James, and John have a greater intimacy with Jesus than she does. God reveals to Peter that Jesus is "the Christ, the Son of the living God" (Mt 16:16). Jesus takes Peter, James, and John up the mountain where they see Jesus transfigured so that "his face shone like the sun, and his garments became white as light" (Mt 17:2). Peter, James, and John hear God's testimony to his Son: "[A] bright cloud overshadowed them, and a voice from the cloud said, 'This is my beloved Son, with whom I am well pleased; listen to him'" (Mt 17:5).[48] Along with the other disciples, Peter, James, and John hear Jesus' preaching, see his miracles, and are present at his Last Supper. It could appear that the adult Jesus (like most adults) leaves behind his intimacy with his mother, so that his mother's role becomes peripheral, at least in comparison with that of his closest disciples.

On further consideration, however, Mary's role stands out all the more in light of the privileges of Jesus' chosen disciples. What Peter, James, and John hear and see does not outpace what Mary hears and sees at the Annunciation and the birth of Jesus. Indeed, the intimacy of receiving the incarnate Son into her womb, of giving him flesh, marks Mary's experience as by far the more profound. Further, Mary's intimacy with her Son does not end after his birth and childhood. According to the Gospel of John, she is present at his first miracle, at the wedding at Cana. The disciples are also there, but it is Mary who understands that the wedding feast—which in John's Gospel symbolizes the marriage of God and his people—requires us to "[d]o whatever he tells you" (Jn 2:5).[49] The disciples abandon Jesus after his arrest, whereas Mary (with the beloved disciple) follows Jesus to the foot of the Cross. From the Cross, Jesus commands her to take the beloved disciple as her son and commands the beloved disciple to take Mary as his mother. Her intimacy with her Son, then, includes his Incarnation, public ministry, and Cross. This intimacy goes well beyond that enjoyed by his disciples.

It is also noteworthy that in Mary the Incarnation is connected with the Cross. John's symbolism makes this clear. The "good wine" (Jn 2:10) that Jesus gives is an image of the eschatological age, which will be fully inaugurated by his Pasch.[50] In his Pasch, the incarnate Son consummates God's eschatological marriage with his people (Israel/Church). Among those who followed Jesus, Mary alone is present at both the Incarnation and the Cross, by which Jesus glorifies the Father (see Jn 17). She shares profoundly in both events, and after Jesus' Resurrection she is with the disciples as they pray in the upper room. Her role does not diminish as it would if she were merely a mother whose mission is unconnected with her adult son's mission. Indeed, knowing her unique participation in the mysteries of his life, Jesus calls her not "mother" but "woman" at Cana and at the Cross. She is the "woman" prophetically signaled by God in his curse of the serpent, Satan: "I will put enmity between you and the woman, and between your seed and her seed; he shall bruise your head, and you shall bruise his heel" (Gen 3:15)—imagery that recurs in Revelation 12.

As Thomas Merton observes, Mary's Assumption manifests God's "desire to do honor to the beings He has made in His own image, and most particularly His respect for the *body* which was destined to be the temple of His glory. . . . If human nature is glorified in her, it is because God desires it to be glorified in us too, and it is for this reason that His Son, taking flesh, came into the world."[51] The Assumption of Mary does not compete with her Son's Incarnation, Passion, and Resurrection, but instead displays for us the goal of these mysteries in which Mary uniquely shares.[52] Mary does not give birth to Jesus and then get out of the way.

Her mission is much greater than that. As the mother of the incarnate Son, she lives her entire life according to her promise, "Behold, I am the handmaid of the Lord; let it be to me according to your word" (Lk 1:38). She is the "handmaid" of God, the embodiment of elect Israel/Church that God unites to himself. Her unique relationship to her Son continues in heaven, where she now dwells with her Son as a glorified human being (body and soul) and as the greatest mere creature, symbolically "clothed with the sun, with the moon under her feet, and on her head a crown of twelve stars" (Rev 12:1).

The doctrinal fittingness of Mary's Assumption is well expressed by Pope Benedict XVI in his homily on August 15, 2011, the Feast of the Assumption. He discusses Mary as the "true ark of the covenant" in light of Revelation 11:19–12:5, Luke 1:39–56, and 2 Samuel 6:16.[53] He affirms typological connections that were set forth centuries ago by John of Damascus in arguing for Mary's Assumption. Just as the original ark of the covenant held the word of God, the two tablets of the law, so also Mary received the Word of God into her womb and obeyed this Word with perfect holiness. According to Pope Benedict, Revelation 12:1 suggests that Christ does not allow his perfect ark—mentioned in the preceding verse (11:19)—to corrupt. Rather, as the "living ark of the covenant," Mary "has a destiny of extraordinary glory, because she is so closely united to the Son." This destiny is "to share fully in the glory of heaven." Like Elizabeth, we should exclaim at this living ark and proclaim her blessed among women; like John the Baptist (and before him David), we should leap for joy in the presence of this ark, the living ark who now dwells fully with her Son in heaven. In the one whom God has chosen to be the mother of his incarnate Son, holiness and life are joined.

In Mary, therefore, we see the fruit of God's love and the reward of faith. If, like Mary, we "allow ourselves to be illumined and guided by his word" and follow him to the Cross, we too will attain to union with him in heavenly glory. The living ark, Mary, is with Christ in heaven. Because this ark contains the Word of God, we can follow this ark—as the Israelites followed it across the Red Sea and the Jordan—"to our true Home, to communion of joy and peace with God."[54]

This fittingness of Mary's Assumption in relation to the other realities of faith, to be sure, is not enough by itself to assure us of the doctrine's truth. Was Mary really assumed bodily into heaven, and is she
really now there in her glorified body by her Son? The answer depends
upon all three pillars, beginning with Scripture, moving to the Church
that has proclaimed this truth for so many centuries, and finally arriving
at the ability of this mystery to shed light upon and confirm so many
other central realities of faith. Have we thereby proven Mary's Assumption? Certainly not, since faith is God's gift. But ours is not *blind* faith.
On the contrary, Mary's Assumption has a place among the central
teachings of faith for good reason.

Conclusion

What has this book achieved? On the one hand, the goal of the book was quite modest: to retrieve the twentieth-century arguments in favor of Mary's bodily Assumption and on this basis to introduce the three pillars on which the doctrine of Mary's Assumption rests for its plausibility. The idea was that Protestant, Catholic, and Orthodox readers would all benefit from an introductory study of how Christians today can give an account of their faith in Mary's Assumption. On the other hand, the book's goal was ambitious in the sense that defending Mary's Assumption—and in the process, inevitably, other Marian doctrines as well—is made difficult by the hiddenness that God willed for it. The New Testament places Jesus Christ and his Church at the center, as they should be. Mary's significance becomes apparent through connections with Christ and the Church that Scripture affirms but does not fully clarify. It took the Church's full recognition of Jesus' divine Sonship and of Mary as the Mother of God before the doctrine of Mary's Assumption emerged liturgically. Even then, legendary stories from well-meaning Christians, who sought to give the doctrine a historical flavor like that of Jesus' Resurrection, damaged the plausibility of this truth about Mary.

Given these difficulties, which are only made more severe in an ecumenical context in which judgments about biblical clarity often have no place for typology, it should come as no surprise that discussion of

Mary's Assumption largely disappeared in Catholic theology after the Second Vatican Council, especially among theologians who came of age in the years following the Council. The last significant theological discussion bearing upon Mary's Assumption was prompted by Karl Rahner's claim that this dogma means that all humans (including Mary) die into resurrection life. Rahner's view, as was noted in chapter three, prompted a negative response from the Congregation for the Doctrine of the Faith in 1979. If Mary's Assumption were merely an anthropological truth, as Rahner holds, then Jesus' Resurrection would also be essentially a truth about human existence after death rather than about the radical inbreaking of God's power in the raising of Jesus. Mary's Assumption would not merit elevation to a dogma of the Church if, in fact, her body merely turned to dust in the grave. Although the Church has continued to teach the doctrine catechetically and to celebrate it liturgically, Mary's Assumption has not been a significant topic in Catholic theology for a number of decades.[1]

Why, then, resurrect this topic today? One reason consists in Peter's injunction, "Always be prepared to make a defense to any one who calls you to account for the hope that is in you, yet do it with gentleness and reverence" (1 Pet 3:15). Mary's Assumption concretely reveals the saving power of Christ and his will to unite his elect intimately to himself.[2] In his supreme goodness, the incarnate Son does not will to be alone, either on earth or in heaven. The eschatological Church is already present, in an embodied way, with Christ at the right hand of the Father; the new Adam has crowned the new Eve. Mary's fiat, "Behold, I am the handmaid of the Lord; let it be to me according to your word" (Lk 1:38), might seem to be self-abnegating and self-diminishing. In fact, Mary shows us not to fear (in the words of Pope Benedict XVI) "that God might be a 'rival' in our life, that with his greatness he might encroach on our freedom, our vital space. She knew that if God is great, we too are great."[3]

Given the Reformation controversies, however, why must Catholics and Orthodox insist upon the truth of Mary's Assumption? The present book has attempted to answer this question. One part of the answer is ecclesiological, rooted in the work of the exalted Christ and his Holy Spirit in ensuring the Church's faithful mediation of divine revelation. The truth of Mary's Assumption has been received and handed down in the Church for well over a millennium, so the Holy Spirit's efficacious governance of the Church in the central task of teaching the Christian mysteries is at issue. Another part of the answer has to do with the interpretation of Scripture. Drawing upon the work of Protestant scholars, I have tried to show that typological reasoning (of the kind employed by Jesus and Paul) can and should be used doctrinally by the Church in response to the promptings of Scripture's own typological portraits of Mary. As Ralph Russell points out, echoing numerous other theologians, typological exegesis reveals the meaning of Mary's motherhood by enabling Scripture "to be seen in entirety. Then the 'Woman' in Genesis will be answered by the Woman in the Book of Revelation (ch. 12), the Fall will go with the Annunciation, Adam with Christ (cf. St. Paul), Eve with Mary."[4] Admittedly, typological exegesis of this kind—whose perspicacity will be most evident in the liturgy—often makes little sense to Christians today, who have been taught to seek a different kind of clarity in Scripture.

Third, I argued that the Church's affirmation of Mary's bodily Assumption is also eminently fitting. What we know of Christ Jesus accords with the belief that he did not discard the new ark of the covenant in which he dwelt, and also that he did not fail to reward the new Eve who, by his grace, shared uniquely in his Incarnation and Passion. Mary's motherhood was certainly not a merely physical reality from which the adult Jesus distanced himself. As Benedict XVI says, because Mary "had made room for the Lord in her soul," she "really became the true Temple where God made himself incarnate."[5] Her body can never lose this dignity: "Mary is 'blessed' because—totally, in body and soul and for ever—she became the Lord's dwelling place."[6] Her bodily Assumption, then, precedes the general resurrection because of her unique participation in her Son's Incarnation and thus also (as his mother) in his public ministry and Crucifixion. Having uniquely dwelt with her, her Son uniquely exalts her.

I do not expect my arguments in this book to necessarily persuade those who do not presently believe in Mary's Assumption, although I do hope that the biblical character of my arguments is appreciated. Speaking for Evangelical Christians who do not believe that Mary was bodily assumed into heaven, Tim Perry argues that the historical person of Mary can be found in Paul, Mark, and Matthew, whereas Luke and John, with their penchant for typology, overlay the historical Mary with "Mary the symbol."[7] According to Perry, "Mary the symbol" quickly overshadowed and ultimately nearly suffocated "Mary the person" in the history of the Church. To my mind, Perry thereby mistakenly denigrates the Gospels of Luke and John. He also undermines the biblical testimony to the Church as the "pillar and bulwark of the truth" (1 Tim 2:15). The exalted Christ is with his eschatological Church, upon which he has poured out his Spirit, "to the close of the age" (Mt 28:20). Nonetheless, by recognizing a strong "typological link between Mary and Israel in the pages of the New Testament" and by affirming that Mary's fiat involved a real cooperation with God's saving work, Perry opens up the possibility of fruitful discussion between Catholics, Orthodox, and Protestants about Scripture's typological portraits of Mary.[8]

Not surprisingly, contemporary Catholic criticism of the doctrine of Mary's Assumption tends to follow the same path as Protestant criticism, although with less appreciation for the authority and truth of Scripture. For instance, Elizabeth Johnson's *Truly Our Sister: A Theology of Mary in the Communion of Saints* presents Mary, in her death, as being simply like all the redeemed: "Her historical life having ended, she died and passed into the unimaginable, life-giving embrace of the living God. Now she joins the company of loving, faithful people who encourage those still running the race."[9] Indeed, Johnson warns against "the harmful Eve-Mary dichotomy" and criticizes *Lumen Gentium* for "the inadequacy of its biblical exegesis, which merges all marian texts together without regard for genre or author and which conflates biblical narrative with later dogmatic statements."[10] Since she rules out the typological comparison of Eve and Mary, she does not see the depth of Mary's participation in the mission of her Son. Her account of Mary's death lacks appreciation for Scripture's use of typology, as well as for the Church's ability to communicate the truth of divine revelation.[11]

But there is another problem that seems to arise from the claim that Scripture, as interpreted by the Church, typologically reveals Mary's Assumption. Namely, does this claim require that the authors of Luke, John, and Revelation—all of whom wrote after Mary's death—must have known that Mary had been bodily assumed into heaven and encoded this fact into their writings? The answer is no. One need simply hold that Mary's Assumption belongs to the apostolic deposit of faith, which includes the typological witness of Scripture. Insofar as the truth of Mary's Assumption is rooted in the New Testament's typological portrait of Mary, then the truth of Mary's Assumption belongs to the apostolic deposit of faith. The same Holy Spirit who taught this truth through the typological portraits of Mary, especially as found in Luke 1–2, John 2 and 19, and Revelation 11–12 (in light of Genesis 3:15), also taught this truth in the Church beginning in the late fifth century as part of unfolding and developing the deposit of faith (see Jn 16:12–14).

How does the development of the doctrine of Mary's Assumption compare with the development of other Christian doctrines? It is not as though most other Christian doctrines followed an easy path of development or have been widely accepted by contemporary biblical scholars. The leading Christian biblical scholars today, for example, argue that the faith of the New Testament is not Trinitarian but binitarian (Larry Hurtado) or unitarian (James D. G. Dunn).[12] Study of the fourth-century controversies about the divinity of the Son and Spirit demonstrates that the biblical portraits of the Father, Son, and Holy Spirit, like the biblical portraits of Mary as the new Eve and new ark of the covenant, needed to be reflected upon liturgically and theologically in order for their full meaning to become manifest. Thus the messy human history of belief in Mary's Assumption, not least the legendary elements that color the early presentations of the doctrine, does not negate the truth of the doctrine. Although Mary's Assumption is not explicitly mentioned in Scripture, Mary is mentioned, and the mysteries of her life demand the typological reflection that we find wherever she is present, including Revelation 12. Demand for biblical clarity before a doctrine is accepted cannot rule out the typological reasoning omnipresent among the biblical authors and Jesus himself. It should also recognize the clarity of Scripture's testimony to the Church's ongoing interpretative authority.

Even so, now that the doctrine of Mary's Assumption is a marker of division, would the Church be better off without this doctrine? By no means, no more than Christ on earth (or in heaven) would be better off without Mary. A helpful approach in this regard is adopted by the Anglican theologian John Macquarrie, who holds that Mary's Assumption sheds light on "the beginning of a vaster (dare we even say, cosmic or universal?) assumption. That vaster assumption is in progress now. Wherever in the Church militant here on earth there is a gleam of true glory, a faithful act of discipleship, a prayer offered in faith, a hand stretched out in love, there is assumption, human life is being lifted up to God by God."[13] Although Mary's Assumption is unique, it is also representative. We too are in the process of being glorified; indeed the whole creation is in the process of coming to share in Christ's glory. As Paul says, "the creation itself will be set free from its bondage to decay and obtain the glorious liberty of the children of God. We know that the whole creation has been groaning in travail together until now; and not only the creation, but we ourselves who have the first fruits of the Spirit groan inwardly as we wait for adoption as sons, the redemption of our bodies" (Rom 8:21–23).[14] The Church needs to insist more, not less, upon Christ's eschatological conquest of corruption and death, a conquest whose fruits already characterize in his eschatological Church.

Although the Reformed theologian Kevin Vanhoozer does not share Macquarrie's positive view of the Church's Marian teaching, he provides an illuminating description of doctrine that at least helps us to understand the place of the Marian doctrines. Vanhoozer states that Christian "doctrine is both *instruction for understanding* the drama and *direction for participating fittingly* in it."[15] As a reality of faith, the Assumption of Mary instructs us about the saving drama and calls us to intimate participation in it. Indeed, the Assumption of Mary shows us that Christ invites the most intimate possible sharing in his victorious Pasch. Reversing Eve's disobedience, Mary shares in the Paschal victory of the new Adam: Christ has made for himself a real partner in the work of salvation, a partner who already shares in his exaltation by the power of his Pasch and by his superabundant grace. This partner is not merely Mary the individual, but rather is Mary the type of the Church: Daughter Zion. Each August 15, then, the Church liturgically celebrates the wondrous truth that, through Jesus and his Holy Spirit, Mary has become the first to receive the fullness of the promise that we are to be "heirs of God and fellow heirs with Christ, provided we suffer with him in order that we may also be glorified with him" (Rom 8:17). "When the perishable puts on the imperishable, and the mortal puts on immortality, then shall come to pass the saying that is written: 'Death is swallowed up in victory'" (1 Cor 15:54). This victory—Christ's victory—is already having its effect.

Notes

Introduction

1. For background see Stephen J. Shoemaker, *Ancient Traditions of the Virgin Mary's Dormition and Assumption* (Oxford: Oxford University Press, 2002). Regarding the earliest traditions, Shoemaker argues that the *Liber Requiei*, in which Mary is transferred or assumed into heaven at her death, belongs to a Gnostic theological milieu and should be dated no later than the fourth century, and perhaps even to the second century. Shoemaker here benefits particularly from Richard Bauckham, *The Fate of the Dead: Studies on Jewish and Christian Apocalypses* (Leiden: Brill, 1998), and Joan E. Taylor, *Christians and the Holy Places: The Myth of Christian Origins* (Oxford: Clarendon Press, 1993). See also the earlier research of Bernard Capelle, "Les Homélies liturgique de prétendu Timothée de Jérusalem," *Ephemerides liturgicae* 63 (1949): 5–26; Carolus Balić, O.F.M., *Testimonia de Assumptione Beatae Virginis Mariae ex omnibus saeculis. Pars prior: ex aetate ante concilium tridentine* (Rome: Academia Mariana, 1948); Antoine Wenger, A.A., *L'Assomption de la T. S. Vierge dans la tradition Byzantine du VIe au Xe siècle* (Paris: Institut Français d'Études Byzantines, 1955); Roberto Caro, S.J., *La Homiletica Mariana Griega en el Siglo V*, 3 vols. (Dayton, OH: University of Dayton Press, 1971–73); Bellarmino Bagatti, O.F.M., M. Piccirillo, and A. Prodomo, O.F.M., *New Discoveries at the Tomb of Virgin Mary in Gethsemane* (Jerusalem: Franciscan Printing Press, 1975); Emmanuele Testa, O.F.M., "Lo sviluppo della 'Dormitio Mariae' nella letteratura, nella teologìa e nella archeologìa," *Marianum* 44 (1982): 316–89; Frédéric Manns, O.F.M., *Le Récit de la dormition de Marie (Vatican grec 1982): Contribution à l'étude de origins de l'exégèse chrétienne* (Jerusalem: Franciscan Printing Press, 1989); Michel van

Esbroeck, *Aux origines de la Dormition de la Vierge: Études historique sur les traditions orientales* (London: Variorum, 1995); Simon Claude Mimouni, *Dormition et assumption de Marie: Histoire des traditions anciennes* (Paris: Beauchesne, 1995); and Simon Claude Mimouni, *Les traditions anciennes sur la Dormition et l'Assomption de Marie: Études littéraires, historiques et doctrinales* (Leiden: Brill, 2011). On these authors, see especially Shoemaker's critique of the positions of Mimouni, Bagatti, Testa, and Manns (whose viewpoint is advocated by Jean Daniélou, S.J., in his *The Theology of Jewish Christianity*, trans. John A. Baker [London: Darton, Longman & Todd, 1964]).

2. For the legends about Mary's Assumption, and for the criticisms of them from the patristic period onward, see Joseph Duhr, S.J., *The Glorious Assumption of the Mother of God*, trans. John Manning Fraunces, S.J. (New York: P. J. Kenedy & Sons, 1950), chapter 3. Duhr observes, "In the name of history the legend-makers of earlier ages pretended to establish it [Mary's Assumption]; it was likewise in the name of history that these more recent critics denied it or at least cast doubt on it" (ibid., 51). See also Duhr's succinct discussion of the history of the doctrine of Mary's Assumption in *The Glorious Assumption of the Mother of God*, chapter 4.

3. René Laurentin, *A Short Treatise on the Virgin Mary*, trans. Charles Neumann, S.M. (Washington, NJ: AMI Press, 1991), 248. On this point see also Alexander Schmemann, *The Virgin Mary*, with selections translated from the Russian by John A. Jillions (Crestwood, NY: St Vladimir's Seminary Press, 1995), 39, and Donal Flanagan, *The Theology of Mary* (Hales Corners, WI: Clergy Book Service, 1976), 67–68. Further helpful clarification is found in Thomas A. O'Meara, O.P., *Mary in Protestant and Catholic Theology* (New York: Sheed and Ward, 1966), 79.

4. Dwight Longenecker holds that "there was a core tradition that was later elaborated" (Dwight Longenecker and David Gustafson, *Mary: A Catholic-Evangelical Debate* [Grand Rapids, MI: Brazos Press, 2003], 123), but Stephen Shoemaker has conclusively shown that this claim—even if it were so—cannot be substantiated historically. There certainly were early traditions such as the *Liber Requiei*, but their historical and theological unreliability make them unworthy of constituting a basis for a historical reconstruction of the event of Mary's Assumption, and in fact such a historical reconstruction based on the legends would be a mistake. Thus Kilian J. Healy, O.Carm., is right to distance the argument of Theoteknos of Livias's sixth-century homily on Mary's Assumption from the earlier legends. See Healy, *The Assumption of Mary*, ed. William J. Harry, O.Carm., and Michael M. Gorman (Darien, IL: Carmelite Media, 2011), 47–48. On Theoteknos see also Manfred Hauke, "The Immaculate Conception of Mary in the Greek Fathers and in an Ecumenical Context," *Chicago Studies* 45 (2006): 327–46, at 338–40. John Henry Newman, too, reports the legends (and commends their piety) but carefully does not draw theological or his-

torical conclusions from them. See Newman, "On the Fitness of the Glories of Mary," in *Mary: The Virgin Mary in the Life and Writings of John Henry Newman*, ed. Philip Boyce (Grand Rapids, MI: Eerdmans, 2001), 163.

5. Kallistos Ware, "The Mother of God in Orthodox Theology and Devotion," in *Mary's Place in Christian Dialogue: Occasional Papers of the Ecumenical Society of the Blessed Virgin Mary, 1970–1980*, ed. Alberic Stacpoole, O.S.B. (Middlegreen, England: St. Paul Publications, 1982), 169–81, at 179.

6. For further reflection, see the discussion of development of doctrine in Jaroslav Pelikan, *Mary Through the Centuries: Her Place in the History of Culture* (New Haven, CT: Yale University Press, 1996), 9–11, 210. Pelikan observes:

> From the apparently simple statements "This is my body" and "This is my blood" in the words of institution of the Lord's Supper, for example, had come not only the resplendent eucharistic liturgies of Eastern Orthodoxy and the Latin Mass with all its concomitants, including the reservation of the consecrated Host and devotion to it, but the long and complicated history of the development of the doctrine of the real presence of the body and blood of Christ in the Sacrament, leading in the Western church to the promulgation of the doctrine of transubstantiation at the Fourth Lateran Council in 1215 and its reaffirmation by the Council of Trent in 1551. If the First Council of Nicaea was a legitimate development and the Fourth Council of the Lateran an illegitimate development, what were the criteria, biblical and doctrinal, for discerning the difference? (ibid., 10)

7. From a more historical perspective, Trent Pomplun insightfully shows that "the logic that underlies Roman Catholic doctrines of Mary . . . comprises three elements: the spiritual exegesis of the fathers, the aesthetic arguments of the schoolmen, and the spiritual theology of the early modern Church." Pomplun, "Mary," in *The Blackwell Companion to Catholicism*, ed. James J. Buckley, Frederick Christian Bauerschmidt, and Trent Pomplun (Oxford: Blackwell, 2007), 312–25, at 312.

8. For this development see Stephen Shoemaker's *Ancient Traditions of the Virgin Mary's Dormition and Assumption*, along with other historical studies mentioned in note 1 above. See also Luigi Gambero, S.M.'s two volumes on the patristic and medieval development of Marian doctrine, *Mary and the Fathers of the Church: The Blessed Virgin Mary in Patristic Thought*, trans. Thomas Buffer (San Francisco: Ignatius Press, 1999), and *Mary in the Middle Ages: The Blessed Virgin Mary in the Thought of Medieval Latin Theologians*, trans. Thomas Buffer (San Francisco: Ignatius Press, 2005), as well as such recent works as Klaus Schreiner, *Maria: Jungfrau, Mutter, Herrscherin* (Munich: Carl Hanser Verlag, 1994), and Miri Rubin, *Mother of God: A History of the Virgin Mary* (New Haven, CT: Yale University Press, 2009).

9. Kilian Healy's *The Assumption of Mary*, reprinted by Carmelite Media in 2011, was originally published in 1982 by Michael Glazier.

10. For the general tendency of the pre-1950 period, see, e.g., Caspar Freithoff, O.P., "The Dogmatic Definition of the Assumption," Gabriel M. Roschini, O.S.M., "The Assumption and the Immaculate Conception," and Kilian J. Healy, O.Carm., "The Assumption among Mary's Privileges," *The Thomist* 14 (1951): 41–58, 59–71, and 72–92, respectively. All three essays underscore the link between Mary's Immaculate Conception and Assumption.

11. See John Henry Newman, *An Essay in Aid of a Grammar of Assent* (Westminster, MD: Christian Classics, 1973), 409–15 and elsewhere. In explaining his view that "from probabilities we may construct a legitimate proof, sufficient for certitude" (411), Newman states: "It is not wonderful then, that, while I can prove Christianity divine to my own satisfaction, I shall not be able to force it upon any one else. Multitudes indeed I ought to succeed in persuading of its truth without any force at all, because they and I start from the same principles, and what is proof to me is a proof to them; but if any one starts from any other principles but ours, I have not the power to change his principles, or the conclusion which he draws from them, any more than I can make a crooked man straight" (413). Arguments from converging probabilities depend upon what Newman calls Informal Inference, and the task of drawing conclusions from converging probabilities requires what Newman calls the Illative Sense. See also the arguments that Newman makes for the faithful development (rather than corruption) of particular doctrines in his *An Essay on the Development of Christian Doctrine*, 6th ed. (Notre Dame, IN: University of Notre Dame Press, 1989).

12. Brian E. Daley, S.J., "Woman of Many Names: Mary in Orthodox and Catholic Theology," *Theological Studies* 71 (2010), 846–69, at 848. See also for the same point, but with different implications, Hans Küng, "Mary in the Churches," in *Mary in the Churches*, ed. Hans Küng and Jürgen Moltmann (New York: Seabury Press, 1983), vii–xi, at vii–viii.

13. Ware, "The Mother of God in Orthodox Theology and Devotion," in Stacpoole, *Mary's Place in Christian Dialogue*, 179. See also John Meyendorff, *Byzantine Theology: Historical Trends and Doctrinal Themes*, 2nd ed. (New York: Fordham University Press, 1979), 148–49; Vladimir Lossky, "Panagia," in *The Mother of God: A Symposium*, ed. E. L. Mascall (London: Dacre Press, 1949), 24–36, at 35–36; and Schmemann, *The Virgin Mary*, 14–16, 61, 85–90.

14. Kallistos Ware, *The Orthodox Way*, rev. ed. (Crestwood, NY: St Vladimir's Seminary Press, 2002), 77–78. Schmemann observes: "If I am permitted a word here by way of a friendly ecumenical critique, the Catholics should never have permitted their theologians to 'elaborate' the mystery of the Assumption (as also that of the Immaculate Conception). They missed the whole point, for they tried to explain rationally—and in inappropriate terms—an eschatological mystery. The Orthodox Church does not 'explain' what happened when Mary died. It simply states that her death signifies the 'morning of a mysterious day,'

that Mary, in virtue of her total love for God and surrender to him, of her absolute obedience and humility, is the beginning of that common resurrection which Christ announced to the world" (Schmemann, *The Virgin Mary*, 63). But unless I am misunderstanding him, this is the Catholic view as well.

15. Thus Brian Daley remarks: "As a person of typological significance, a figure of icons, Mary is better encountered by vision than by the analytical mind. She offers us, in her own person, a glimpse of where God is and what God does. But we cannot understand her, or even speak appropriately of her except in typological terms—in icons and art, in the 'many names' of poetry and liturgy and biblical metaphor, and in the theological language that feeds on them" (Daley, "Woman of Many Names," 868). See also Lossky, "Panagia," in Mascall, *The Mother of God*, 24–27. For Mary's Assumption in the Catholic liturgy, see J. D. Crichton, *Our Lady in the Liturgy* (Collegeville, MN: Liturgical Press, 1997), 24–25, 52–59; Emmanuel Bourque, "Le sens de l'Assomption dans la liturgie" and Clément Morin, P.S.S., "The Assumption and the Liturgy," in *Vers le dogme de l'Assomption.* Journées d'études mariales, Montréal 12–15 Août 1948, ed. Adrien-M. Malo, O.F.M. (South Bend, IN: Fides, 1948), 151–202 and 391–97, respectively; and Bertrand de Margerie, S.J., "Ecumenical Problems in Mariology," trans. Aloysius J. Owen, S.J., *Marian Studies* 26 (1975): 180–203, at 194–99.

16. Nikos Nissiotis, "Mary in Orthodox Theology," in *Mary in the Churches*, ed. Hans Küng and Jürgen Moltmann (New York: Seabury Press, 1983), 25–39, at 26. This does not mean that all expressions in the West about Mary's participation will necessarily cohere with all such expressions in the East. See M. C. Steenberg, "The Mother of God as Mediatrix in Orthodox and Roman Catholic Thought," *Sobornost* 26 (2004): 6–26.

17. Avery Dulles, S.J., "The Dogma of the Assumption," in *The One Mediator, the Saints, and Mary: Lutherans and Catholics in Dialogue VIII*, ed. H. George Anderson, J. Francis Stafford, and Joseph A. Burgess (Minneapolis, MN: Augsburg Fortress, 1992), 279–94, at 291. For criticism of the preconciliar period see Flanagan, *The Theology of Mary*, 61–62; Thomas M. Thompson, S.M., "A Changed Context for Marian Doctrine," in *Mother, Behold Your Son: Essays in Honor of Eamon R. Carroll, O.Carm.*, ed. Donald W. Buggert, O.Carm., Louis P. Rogge, O.Carm., and Michael J. Wastag, O.Carm. (Washington, D.C.: Carmelite Institute, 2001), 195–213; and Anthony J. Tambasco, *What Are They Saying about Mary?* (New York: Paulist Press, 1984), 4–8. See also the nuanced reflections of Laurentin, *A Short Treatise on the Virgin Mary*, 142–52; and Joseph Ratzinger, "Thoughts on the Place of Marian Doctrine and Piety in Faith and Theology as a Whole," in *Mary: The Church at the Source*, by Joseph Ratzinger and Hans Urs von Balthasar, trans. Adrian Walker (San Francisco: Ignatius Press, 2005), 19–36.

18. Bernard Lonergan, S.J., "The Assumption and Theology," in Malo, *Vers le dogme de l'Assomption*, 411–24, at 412.

19. Joseph Ratzinger, "The Assumption of Mary," in *Dogma and Preaching: Applying Christian Doctrine to Daily Life*, trans. Michael J. Miller and Matthew J. O'Connell (San Francisco: Ignatius Press, 2011), 357–61, at 358.

20. Avery Dulles, S.J., "Mary at the Dawn of the New Millennium," in *Church and Society: The Laurence J. McGinley Lectures, 1988–2007* (New York: Fordham University Press, 2008), 248–61, at 248–49. In this essay Dulles is reflecting on Pope John Paul II's Mariology.

21. George H. Tavard, A.A., *The Thousand Faces of the Virgin Mary* (Collegeville, MN: Liturgical Press, 1996), 29. The biblical scholar John McKenzie, S.J., similarly remarks that "the meagre historical knowledge about the real Mary was no obstacle to the development of Mariology and Marian devotion; what Christians did not find they created. No doubt historical and biblical criticism has an iconoclastic effect upon Mariology." McKenzie, "The Mother of Jesus in the New Testament," in *Mary in the Churches*, ed. Hans Küng and Jürgen Moltmann (New York: Seabury Press, 1983), 3–11, at 10. See also Hans Küng, *Christ Sein* (Munich: Piper, 1974), 450–52. For an Anglican critique of the doctrine of Mary's Assumption, see Austin Farrer, "Mary, Scripture, and Tradition," in *The Blessed Virgin Mary: Essays by Anglican Writers*, ed. E. L. Mascall and H. S. Box (London: Darton, Longman & Todd, 1963), 27–52.

22. Tavard, *The Thousand Faces of the Virgin Mary*, 190, 261.

23. For recent contributions to the theology of Mary's Assumption, many of them ecumenically oriented, see the essays in *L'Assunzione di Maria Madre di Dio: Significato storico-salvifico a 50 anni dalla definizione dogmatica*, ed. Gaspar Calvo Moralejo and Stefano Cecchin (Vaticano City: Pontificia Academia Mariana Internationalis, 2001).

24. See John McHugh, *The Mother of Jesus in the New Testament* (Garden City, NY: Doubleday, 1975); Ben Witherington III, *John's Wisdom: A Commentary on the Fourth Gospel* (Louisville, KY: Westminster John Knox Press, 1995), 79, 99, 310; and Beverly Roberts Gaventa, *Mary: Glimpses of the Mother of Jesus* (Minneapolis, MN: Fortress Press, 1999), 86. See also Beverly Roberts Gaventa, "'Nothing Will Be Impossible with God': Mary as the Mother of Believers," in *Mary, Mother of God*, ed. Carl E. Braaten and Robert W. Jenson (Grand Rapids, MI: Eerdmans, 2004), 19–35; and Gaventa, "'Standing Near the Cross': Mary and the Crucifixion of Jesus," in *Blessed One: Protestant Perspectives on Mary*, ed. Beverly Roberts Gaventa and Cynthia L. Rigby (Louisville, KY: Westminster John Knox Press, 2002), 47–56. For Catholic and Orthodox typological readings see especially Laurentin, *A Short Treatise on the Virgin Mary*, 15–49, 269–83; Nissiotis, "Mary in Orthodox Theology," 25–39; and M. C. Steenberg, "The Role of Mary as Co-recapitulator in St. Irenaeus of Lyons," *Vigiliae Christianae* 58 (2004): 117–37. See also, from Protestant perspectives sympathetic to typology, Max Thurian, *Mary, Mother of the Lord, Figure of the Church*, trans. Neville B. Cryer (London: Mowbray, 1985), 49–55, 176–83; and J. A. Ross MacKenzie, "The Patristic Witness to the Virgin Mary as the New Eve," *Marian*

Studies 29 (1978): 67–78. The recent acceptance of typological exegesis by the Anglican-Roman Catholic International Commission in its statement *Mary: Grace and Hope in Christ* is also significant. See "A Response to 'Mary: Grace and Hope in Christ'" by the members of Anglican-Roman Catholic Commission in Canada, published in *One in Christ* 43 (2009): 167–82, at 167–68. For discussion see Timothy Bradshaw, "The Anglican Commentary," in *Mary: Grace and Hope in Christ. The Seattle Statement of the Anglican-Roman Catholic International Commission: The Text with Commentaries and Study Guide*, ed. Donald Bolen and Gregory Cameron (New York: Continuum, 2006), 133–65; Martin Warner, "*Mary, Grace and Hope in Christ*: A New Understanding of Scripture and Tradition?," *International Journal for the Study of the Christian Church* 5 (2005): 265–71; Frederick H. Borsch, "Mary and Scripture: A Response to *Mary: Grace and Hope in Christ*," *Anglican Theological Review* 89 (2007): 375–99; Paul Williams, "The Virgin Mary in Anglican Tradition," in *Mary: The Complete Resource*, ed. Sarah Jane Boss (Oxford: Oxford University Press, 2007), 314–39; and David Carter, "Mary in Ecumenical Dialogue and Exchange," in Boss, *Mary: The Complete Resource*, 340–60, at 355–58. For a high-church Anglican perspective on Mary's Assumption, see H. S. Box, "The Assumption," in Mascall and Box, *The Blessed Virgin Mary*, 89–102.

    25. Karl Barth, *Church Dogmatics*, vol. I, part 2, *The Doctrine of the Word of God*, trans. G. T. Thomason and Harold Knight (Edinburgh: T & T Clark, 1956), 143. See also Barth, "A Letter about Mariology," in *Ad Limina Apostolorum: An Appraisal of Vatican II*, trans. Keith R. Crim (Richmond, VA: John Knox Press, 1968), 57–62. For similar views see Gerhard Ebeling, "Zur Frage nach dem Sinn des mariologischen Dogmas," *Zeitschrift für Theologie und Kirche* 47 (1950): 383–91; and Stephen Benko, *Protestants, Catholics, and Mary* (Valley Forge, PA: Judson Press, 1968), especially 72–78. Benko concludes that "Roman Catholic Mariology denies that the grace of God is really all-sufficient. It holds that grace makes salvation possible only because Mary, as the archetype of the church, made salvation a reality by her active cooperation with God" (Benko, *Protestants, Catholics, and Mary*, 78). Citing Edward Schillebeeckx, O.P.'s *Mary, Mother of the Redemption*, trans. N. D. Smith (New York: Sheed and Ward, 1964), Benko argues that the Catholic position "leads to the conclusion that each time a person assents to the grace of God he is simply echoing Mary's *fiat*. Thus every human being becomes a coredeemer or coredemptrix in his or her own salvation. . . . Any such cooperation of man is impossible in the Protestant understanding of justification and grace" (Benko, *Protestants, Catholics, and Mary*, 78). See also David F. Wells, *Revolution in Rome* (London: Tyndale, 1973), 111–19, and (in response to Wells) John de Satgé, *Down to Earth: A Protestant Vision of the Virgin Mary* (Wilmington, NC: Consortium Books, 1976), 10–11, 68–69, 121–22. For detailed discussion of Barth's approach to Mary, see Andrew Louth, *Mary and the Mystery of the Incarnation: An Essay on the Mother of God in the Theology of Karl Barth* (Oxford: SLG Press, 1977); and Tim Perry,

"'What Is Little Mary Here For?' Barth, Mary, and Election," *Pro Ecclesia* 19 (2010): 46–68. For Catholic responses to Barth, see O'Meara, *Mary in Protestant and Catholic Theology*, 206–24; Yves Congar, O.P., *Christ, Our Lady and the Church: A Study in Eirenic Theology*, trans. Henry St. John, O.P. (London: Longmans, Green, 1957), 14–17, 35–37; and Donal Flanagan, "An Ecumenical Future for Roman Catholic Theology of Mary," in Stacpoole, *Mary's Place in Christian Dialogue*, 3–24, at 14–19. Joseph Ratzinger's remark is apropos: "Mariology demonstrates that the doctrine of grace does not revoke creation; rather, it is the definitive Yes to creation" (Ratzinger, "Thoughts on the Place of Marian Doctrine and Piety in Faith and Theology as a Whole," in Ratzinger and Balthasar, *Mary*, 31).

26. Barth, "A Letter about Mariology," 61.

27. Scot McKnight, *The Real Mary: Why Evangelical Christians Can Embrace the Mother of Jesus* (Brewster, MA: Paraclete Press, 2007), 116. Along these lines see also Heiko A. Oberman, "The Virgin Mary in Evangelical Perspective," *Journal of Ecumenical Studies* 1 (1964): 271–98, at 274–76, 292–93; Stephen Benko, *Protestants, Catholics, and Mary* (Valley Forge, PA: Judson Press, 1968), 64–69; David Parker, "Evangelicals and Mary: Recent Theological Evaluations," *Evangelical Review of Theology* 30 (2006): 121–40; and Kari Børresen, "Mary in Catholic Theology," in Küng and Moltmann, *Mary in the Churches*, 48–56, at 55. See also A. T. Robertson, *The Mother of Jesus: Her Problems and Her Glory* (New York: George H. Doran, 1925).

28. McKnight, *The Real Mary*, 116.

29. See Yves Congar, O.P., *Tradition and Traditions: An Historical and Theological Essay*, trans. Michael Naseby and Thomas Rainborough (New York: Macmillan, 1967).

30. Joseph Ratzinger, "Anglican-Catholic Dialogue: Its Problems and Hopes," in *Church, Ecumenism and Politics: New Essays in Ecclesiology*, trans. Robert Nowell (New York: Crossroad, 1988), 65–98, at 71. For a contrasting view, see John Webster, *Holy Scripture* (Cambridge: Cambridge University Press, 2003), 52.

31. Ratzinger, "Anglican-Catholic Dialogue," 71. In Ratzinger's view, "It is a universal tenet amongst Christians that scripture is the basic standard of Christian faith, the central authority through which Christ himself exercises his authority over the Church and within it. For this reason all teaching in the Church is ultimately exposition of scripture, just as scripture in its turn is exposition of the living word of Jesus Christ: but the ultimate value of all is not what is written but the life which our Lord transmitted to his Church, within which scripture itself lives and is life" (ibid.).

32. McKnight, *The Real Mary*, 123. David Parker notes that "the patristic idea of a symbolic connection between Mary and Eve" has not influenced evangelicals (Parker, "Evangelicals and Mary," 132). Parker observes that "evangelicals reject this Eve/Mary symbolism as an invalid transference of the typology

away from Jesus and Adam, contradicting and going beyond Scripture. Thus, whatever virtues Mary may have possessed as a woman of faith and whatever position she may have held by God's grace in salvation history, there is no justification for elevating her in the way the Eve/Mary symbolism does" (ibid., 133). By contrast, the Baptist theologian Timothy George, in an essay that Parker criticizes, recognizes Mary as "the Daughter of Zion" and "the kairotic representative of the eschatological and redeemed people of God," and he supports "reading Mary against the background of Old Testament foreshadowings." George, "The Blessed Virgin Mary in Evangelical Perspective," in Braaten and Jenson, *Mary, Mother of God*, 100–122, at 105. As George says, "It is this kind of typological reading that allowed the early church, from Justin Martyr and Irenaeus onward, to depict Mary as the new Eve, the one through whose obedience the disobedience of the first Eve was reversed" (ibid.). See also Gary A. Anderson, "Mary as Second Eve," chap. 4 in *The Genesis of Perfection: Adam and Eve in Jewish and Christian Imagination* (Louisville, KY: Westminster John Knox Press, 2001).

33. McKnight, *The Real Mary*, 123. See also Parker, "Evangelicals and Mary," 135; and Keith Weston, "Mary: An Evangelical Viewpoint," in Stacpoole, *Mary's Place in Christian Dialogue*, 158–66.

34. For this fuller portrait see, for example, Thomas Weinandy, O.F.M.Cap., "The Annunciation and Nativity: Undoing the Sinful Act of Eve," *International Journal of Systematic Theology* 14 (2012): 217–32; Ralph Russell, O.S.B., "The Blessed Virgin Mary in the Bible: The Scriptural Basis of Ecumenical Dialogue," in Stacpoole, *Mary's Place in Christian Dialogue*, 45–50; and Lucien Deiss, C.S.Sp., *Mary, Daughter of Sion*, trans. Barbara T. Blair (Collegeville, MN: Liturgical Press, 1972). On the diversity of New Testament portraits of Mary, see René Laurentin, "Pluralism about Mary: Biblical and Contemporary," *The Way*, Supplement 45 (1982): 78–92. See also Donald G. Dawe, "The Assumption of the Blessed Virgin in Ecumenical Perspective," *The Way*, Supplement 45 (1982): 41–54, especially 44–48, 52.

35. For his part, Barth connects Mary with the Church in his commentary on Luke 1, published in English as *The Great Promise: Luke I*, trans. Hans Freund (Eugene, OR: Wipf and Stock, 2004). As Tim Perry remarks, for Barth "the linking of Mary with the church does not become the occasion for Barth to decouple her from Christology and establish her relative theological independence. Rather, she is one of the means by which Barth brings ecclesiology more securely within the orbit of Christology" (Perry, "'What Is Little Mary Here For?,'" 62). The same rooting of ecclesiology "within the orbit of Christology" is the purpose of Catholic Mariology. But as David C. Steinmetz (who holds that medieval Mariology developed from the Church's negative view of sex and from believers' increasing inability to connect with a divine Jesus) observes, for Protestants "[t]he church does not offer anything to God, except perhaps gratitude and praise. God offers everything to believers, which they then gladly share with

their neighbors. Mary as co-worker and Mary as co-offerer are images traditional Protestants think unbiblical. . . . Protestants agree with Thomas Aquinas in opposing any Marian theology that seems to them to undercut the centrality of Jesus Christ. God found a faithful covenant partner only in his son." See Steinmetz's "Mary Reconsidered," in *Taking the Long View: Christian Theology in Historical Perspective* (Oxford: Oxford University Press, 2011), 45–51, at 50.

36. McKnight, *The Real Mary*, 131.

37. See also Marina Warner's account of the various legends regarding Mary's Assumption in Warner, *Alone of All Her Sex: The Myth and Cult of the Virgin Mary* (New York: Vintage Books, 1983), 82–87. Aware that Pope Pius XII's dogmatic teaching does not employ the legends, Warner concludes that the dogma instead "depended on the Christian equivalence between sex and death, and consequently between the Virgin's purity and her freedom from the dissolution of the grave. . . . Death, like birth, belongs to time; freedom from death, like freedom from sex, overcomes it" (ibid., 92, 94).

38. McKnight, *The Real Mary*, 133.

39. Ibid.

40. Paul J. Griffiths, *Song of Songs* (Grand Rapids, MI: Brazos Press, 2011), lvii.

41. Pomplun, "Mary," in Buckley, Bauerschmidt, and Pomplun, *The Blackwell Companion to Catholicism*, 314.

42. Ware, "The Mother of God in Orthodox Theology and Devotion," in Stacpoole, *Mary's Place in Christian Dialogue*, 180.

43. Hans Boersma, *Heavenly Participation: The Weaving of a Sacramental Tapestry* (Grand Rapids, MI: Eerdmans, 2011), 135–36. Boersma has in view Kevin J. Vanhoozer's *The Drama of Doctrine: A Canonical-Linguistic Approach to Christian Theology* (Louisville, KY: Westminster John Knox Press, 2005). As Gary Culpepper observes, "There is abundant evidence today that many evangelicals and Catholics are prepared to reconsider together the basic features of a scripturally governed understanding of Mary in God's plan of salvation." See Gary Culpepper, "'A Sword Will Pierce through Your Own Soul Also': The Sanctification, Conversion, and Exemplary Witness of the Blessed Mary," *Pro Ecclesia* 19 (2010): 28–45.

44. Boersma, *Heavenly Participation*, 136. Boersma relies here, in large part, on Congar, *Tradition and Traditions*.

45. Boersma, *Heavenly Participation*, 135. For a Protestant evaluation of the liturgical tradition with respect to Mary's Assumption, see Geoffrey Wainwright, *Doxology: The Praise of God in Worship, Doctrine, and Life* (New York: Oxford University Press, 1980), 237–40.

46. Yves Congar, O.P., notes in this regard that "metaphysics shows us how God alone is infallible [in the sense of literally being unable to sin]. All created reality, on the other hand, can fail to achieve what it ought to be or to do. If the church is holy and infallible in itself, that is only insofar as it is *from God*; it is so

according to the aspect that it comes *from God*, and to the degree that it is *of God*." Congar, *True and False Reform in the Church*, trans. Paul Philibert, O.P. (Collegeville, MN: Liturgical Press, 2011), 83. Congar affirms a "real communication of God's holiness to the church and to the faithful," one that is "due to the gift and communication of the Holy Spirit" (ibid.).

47. Adrienne von Speyr, *Mary in the Redemption*, translated from the third edition by Helena M. Tomko (San Francisco: Ignatius Press, 2003), 93. On Speyr's Mariology see Jacques Servais, S.J., "Mary's Role in the Incarnation," *Communio* 30 (2003): 5–25, at 18 20. Servais points out that for Speyr, Mary's participation in some way includes participating "in the constitution of the hypostatic union" (23), which strikes me as a gravely exaggerated formulation. For cautions regarding the articulation of Mary's role as second or new Eve, see John McHugh, "The Second Eve: Newman and Irenaeus," *The Way*, Supplement 45 (1982): 13–21.

48. For further reflection on the significance of Mary's Assumption for Christian faith in Christ's Incarnation and saving work, see Roch Kereszty, O Cist., "Toward the Renewal of Mariology," *Nova et Vetera* 11 (2013): 779–99; Bernard Leeming, S.J., "The Assumption and the Christian Pattern," *The Month* 19 (1951): 142–50; and Yves Congar, O.P., "Theological Notes on the Assumption," in *Faith and Spiritual Life*, trans. A. Manson and L. C. Sheppard (New York: Herder and Herder, 1968), 3–10, at 9.

Chapter 1
Twentieth-Century Magisterial Teaching on Mary and Her Assumption

1. It should be noted that I do not treat Pope Paul VI's apostolic exhortations *Signum Magnum* (1967) and *Marialis Cultus* (1974) in this chapter. *Signum Magnum* is relatively brief, and its purpose is to reinvigorate Marian devotion. *Marialis Cultus* is longer, and it has the same purpose: it emphasizes that "every authentic development of Christian worship is necessarily followed by a fitting increase of veneration for the Mother of the Lord" (*Marialis Cultus*, Introduction). The focus of *Marialis Cultus* is specifically on the liturgy, the Angelus, and the Rosary. With respect to the Solemnity of the Assumption of Mary (August 15), *Marialis Cultus* observes, "It is a feast of her destiny of fullness and blessedness, of the glorification of her immaculate soul and of her virginal body, of her perfect configuration to the Risen Christ; a feast that sets before the eyes of the Church and of all mankind the image and the consoling proof of the fulfillment of their final hope, namely, that this full glorification is the destiny of all those whom Christ has made His brothers, having 'flesh and blood in common with them' (Heb. 2:14; cf. Gal. 4:4)" (§ 6). Likewise, in § 11 *Marialis Cultus* states, "In the Assumption they [the liturgical texts] recognize the beginning that has already been made and the image of what, for the whole

Church, must still come to pass." *Marialis Cultus* contains an extraordinary paragraph (§ 26) on the relation of Mary to the Holy Spirit, as well as valuable insight into the relationship of devotion to Christ and devotion to Mary (cf. § 57).

2. I have taken the text of *Munificentissimus Deus* from www.vatican.va. For discussion of *Munificentissimus Deus* and the development of doctrine, see Dulles, "The Dogma of the Assumption," in Anderson, Stafford, and Burgess, *The One Mediator, the Saints, and Mary: Lutherans and Catholics in Dialogue VIII*, 279–94, at 285–91. On Pius XII's Mariology see H. E. Cardinale, "Pope Pius XII and the Blessed Virgin Mary," in Stacpoole, *Mary's Place in Christian Dialogue*, 248–60.

3. As Trent Pomplun puts it, "Perfect redemption . . . must entail most perfect triumph" (Pomplun, "Mary," in Buckley, Bauerschmidt, and Pomplun, *The Blackwell Companion to Catholicism*, 312–25, at 323). See also Donald J. Keefe, S.J., "Mary as Created Wisdom, the Splendor of the New Creation," *The Thomist* 47 (1983): 395–420, at 412: "The Assumption into the heavenly Kingdom of the Queen of Heaven is no mere sign of divine favor, no inference from a more or less sentimental love of the Son for his mother; it is the strict counterpart of her Immaculate Conception, of her substantial integrity."

4. For discussion see O'Meara, *Mary in Protestant and Catholic Theology*, 77, 286–87. See also J. M. R. Tillard, O.P., "Sensus Fidelium," *One in Christ* 11 (1975): 2–29.

5. On the relationship of the liturgy to theology, see Pope Pius XII, *Mediator Dei* (1948), §§ 45–46.

6. For discussion see George Bissonnette, A.A., "The Twelfth Chapter of the Apocalypse and Our Lady's Assumption," *Marian Studies* 2 (1951): 170–77, as well as his bibliographical references.

7. For discussion see O'Meara, *Mary in Protestant and Catholic Theology*, 75–76. O'Meara comments:

> It is significant that the Holy Father found that doctrine contained in a scriptural idea, Mary's association with Christ. Mary as the New Eve really means simply Mary's association under and with the New Adam in the world's redemption. It is not such a bold idea if we consider that Mary certainly co-operated through her *fiat*; she associated her life with Christ's, for we see her at Cana asking him for a favor, and standing at Calvary almost alone among all his associates to join with him in his sacrifice. Catholic tradition extends these brief evangelical pictures and interprets them as showing Mary not as an empty bystander, but as mother and associate with her son. This association with Jesus is the ultimate foundation upon which the doctrine of the Assumption rests as contained in the fact of revelation. (ibid., 76)

8. See Duhr, *The Glorious Assumption of the Mother of God*, 28–35.

9. On typology in the Old Testament and intertestamental literature, see especially James L. Kugel, *How to Read the Bible: A Guide to Scripture, Then and Now* (New York: Free Press, 2007); and Michael Fishbane, *Biblical Interpretation in Ancient Israel* (Oxford: Oxford University Press, 1985), 350–52.

10. See for example John W. O'Malley, S.J., *What Happened at Vatican II* (Cambridge, MA: Harvard University Press, 2008); and John W. O'Malley, S.J., "Vatican II: Historical Perspectives on Its Uniqueness and Interpretation," in *Vatican II: The Unfinished Agenda: A Look to the Future*, ed. Lucien Richard, Daniel T. Harrington, and John W. O'Malley (New York: Paulist Press, 1987), 22–32.

11. Joseph Ratzinger, "On the Position of Mariology and Marian Spirituality within the Totality of Faith and Theology," in *The Church and Women: A Compendium*, trans. Maria Shrady and Lothar Krauth (San Francisco: Ignatius Press, 1988), 67–81, at 72. See Emery de Gaál, *The Theology of Pope Benedict XVI: The Christocentric Shift* (New York: Palgrave Macmillan, 2010), 294–96.

12. Ratzinger, *Church, Ecumenism and Politics*, 20. De Gaál comments on Ratzinger's involvement in the debate at the Second Vatican Council over whether to produce a separate document on Mary or to include Mary in the document on the Church: Ratzinger "welcomed Cardinal König's intervention to incorporate Mariology into *Lumen Gentium.* . . . Later, Ratzinger would lament that this led to yet another misunderstanding. Rather than appreciating Mary as *Theotokos*, Mother of God, as the paradigm for the Church, Mariology was subsequently neglected. Yet, only via Mary does one understand the truth about both Jesus Christ and the Church. A balanced appreciation of Mary's role in salvation history prevents one from reducing the Savior to a mere human and from perceiving the Church as a mere congregation. For this reason, Ratzinger is now more favorably disposed to Marian titles than he perhaps was during the council" (de Gaál, *The Theology of Pope Benedict XVI*, 101).

13. Quotations from *Lumen Gentium* are taken from *Decrees of the Ecumenical Councils*, vol. 2, *Trent to Vatican II*, ed. Norman P. Tanner, S.J. (Washington, D.C.: Georgetown University Press, 1990), 849–900.

14. For discussion see Juan Luis Bastero, "El Espíritu Sancto y María en *Lumen Gentium* y en el Magisterio de Pablo VI," *Scripta Theologica* 38 (2006): 701–35; Laurentin, *A Short Treatise on the Virgin Mary*, 158–62; Cardinal Léon Josef Suenens, "The Relation that Exists Between the Holy Spirit and Mary," in Stacpoole, *Mary's Place in Christian Dialogue*, 69–78; Alan Clark, "The Holy Spirit and Mary," in Stacpoole, *Mary's Place in Christian Dialogue*, 79–88; Donal Flanagan, "An Ecumenical Future for Roman Catholic Theology of Mary," in Stacpoole, *Mary's Place in Christian Dialogue*, 3–24, at 21–23; and Jarislaw Jasianek, "La Presencia del Espíritu Santo en la Maternidad de María," *Scripta Theologica* 38 (2006): 671–700.

15. On Daughter Zion see, e.g., Thurian, *Mary, Mother of the Lord, Figure of the Church*, 13–19, 159–66. See also Joseph Ratzinger's *Daughter Zion:*

Meditations on the Church's Marian Belief, trans. John M. McDermott, S.J. (San Francisco: Ignatius Press, 1983), which I discuss in chapter 3.

16. For ecumenical discussion of this passage in *Lumen Gentium,* with regard to the nature of Mary's sharing in Christ's Cross, see John de Satgé and John McHugh, "Bible and Tradition in regard to the Blessed Virgin Mary," in Stacpoole, *Mary's Place in Christian Dialogue,* 51–58, at 55–57. See also Raniero Cantalamessa, *Mary: Mirror of the Church,* trans. Frances Lonergan Villa (Collegeville, MN: Liturgical Press, 1992), 97–105.

17. The contrasting view is well expressed by the Anglican exegete N. T. Wright:

> I do not, however, find in the New Testament or in the earliest Christian fathers any suggestion that those at present in heaven or (if you prefer) paradise are actively engaged in praying *for* those of us in the present life. Nor do I find any suggestion that Christians who are still alive should pray to the saints to intercede to the Father on their behalf. . . . It is true that if the Christian dead are conscious, and if they are "with Christ" in a sense that, as Paul implies, is closer than we are at the moment, there is every reason to suppose that they are at least, like the souls under the altar in Revelation, urging the Father to complete the work of justice and salvation in the world. If that is so, there is no reason in principle why they should not urge the Father similarly on our behalf. Or if, from another point of view, they are indeed "with Christ," and if part of the work of the ascended Christ is indeed to be ruling the world as the agent of his Father, we might indeed suppose that the dead are somehow involved in that, not merely as spectators of that ongoing work. But—and this is very important for those who, like me, believe that it's vital to ground one's beliefs in scripture itself—I see no evidence in the early Christian writings to suggest that the Christian dead are in fact engaged in work of that sort, still less any suggestion that presently alive Christians should, so to speak, encourage them to do it by invoking them specifically.
>
> In particular, we should be very suspicious of the medieval idea that the saints can function as friends at court so that while we might be shy of approaching the King ourselves, we know someone who is, as it were, one of us, to whom we can talk freely and who will maybe put in a good word for us. The practice seems to me to call into question, and even actually to deny by implication, the immediacy of access to God through Jesus Christ and in the Spirit, which is promised again and again in the New Testament. In the New Testament it is clear: because of Christ and the Spirit, every single Christian is welcome at any time to come before the Father himself. If you have a royal welcome awaiting you in the throne room itself, for whatever may be on your heart and mind, whether great or small, why would you bother hanging around the outer lobby trying to persuade someone there, however distinguished, to go in and ask for you? (Wright,

Surprised by Hope: Rethinking Heaven, the Resurrection, and the Mission of the Church [New York: HarperCollins, 2008], 173)

Wright goes on to suggest that prayers beseeching the intercession of saints might in fact, quite likely, be a return to semi-paganism. In his view, furthermore, no saint is closer to God than any other saint: "[I]n light of the basic and central Christian gospel, the message and achievement of Jesus, and the preaching of Paul and the others, there is no reason whatever to say, for instance, that Peter or Paul, Aidan and Cuthbert, or even, dare I say, the mother of Jesus herself is more advanced, closer to God, has achieved more spiritual growth, or whatever, than those Christians who have been martyred in our own day and indeed those who have died quietly in their beds" (ibid., 169–70). For historical background on these issues, sympathetic to the Catholic and Orthodox viewpoint but highly conversant with the theology of the Reformation, see Carlos Eire, *A Very Brief History of Eternity* (Princeton, NJ: Princeton University Press, 2010), 67–156. In response to Wright's view that Mary and the Christian who dies today are equal in closeness to God, see my *Jesus and the Demise of Death: Resurrection, Afterlife, and the Fate of the Christian* (Waco, TX: Baylor University Press, 2012), 17–19. The intercession of saints flows from the nature of the Church as the body of Christ and as the communion of saints: Jesus chooses that we approach him with and often through his friends, because of the communion that his Church is.

18. See John Paul II, *Redemptoris Mater*, in *The Encyclicals of John Paul II*, ed. J. Michael Miller, C.S.B. (Huntington, IN: Our Sunday Visitor, 2001), 318–63. For an overview, see Joseph Ratzinger, "The Sign of the Woman: An Introductory Essay on the Encyclical *Redemptoris Mater*," in Ratzinger and Balthasar, *Mary: The Church at the Source*, 37–60. Observing that the encyclical quite often "takes the form of a meditation on the Bible," Ratzinger emphasizes that "to interpret Scripture theologically means not only to listen to the historical authors whom it juxtaposes, even opposes, but to seek the one voice of the whole, to seek the inner identity that sustains the whole and binds it together. . . . In this sense, the methodological form that comes into play here is ultimately quite simple: Scripture is interpreted by Scripture" (ibid., 39–40).

19. Joseph Ratzinger, "The Sign of the Woman: An Introduction to the Encyclical 'Redemptoris Mater,'" in *Mary: God's Yes to Man; John Paul's Encyclical Redemptoris Mater* (San Francisco: Ignatius Press, 1988), 9–40, at 10.

20. For further discussion see Lawrence S. Cunningham, "Born of a Woman (Gal. 4:4): A Theological Meditation," in Braaten and Jenson, *Mary, Mother of God*, 36–48.

21. For reflection see Antonio López, "Mary, Certainty of Our Hope," *Communio* 35 (2008): 174–99.

22. Mary is mother of her Son physically and spiritually, whereas she is Christ's "bride" only spiritually, as the type of the Church. Eve is Adam's bride but obviously not Adam's mother, although she is mother of all the living. It

should go without saying that the biblical typology, rooted in Mary's reversal of Eve's disobedience, does not depend upon a physical equivalence.

23. On the election or predestination of Mary, see Daniel L. Migliore, "Woman of Faith: Toward a Reformed Understanding of Mary," in Gaventa and Rigby, *Blessed One*, 117–30, at 122–25; see also the Anglican-Roman Catholic International Commission's statement *Mary: Grace and Hope in Christ. The Seattle Statement of the Anglican-Roman Catholic International Commission: The Text with Commentaries and Study Guide*, ed. Donald Bolen and Gregory Cameron (New York: Continuum, 2006).

24. For further discussion of the meaning of "divine motherhood," see Laurentin, *A Short Treatise on the Virgin Mary*, 201–34; and O'Meara, *Mary in Protestant and Catholic Theology*, 49, 53–57.

25. For this comparison of Mary's faith with Abraham's, see also Thurian, *Mary, Mother of the Lord, Figure of the Church*, 60–64.

26. See the spirituality of Charles de Foucauld in *Charles de Foucauld: Writings* (Maryknoll, NY: Orbis Books, 1999).

27. See André Feuillet, "Les adieux du Christ à sa mère (Jn 19, 25–27) et la maternité spirituelle de Marie," *Nouvelle revue théologique* 86 (1964): 469–89.

28. For further discussion of John Paul II's teaching on Mary's mediation, see Ratzinger, "The Sign of the Woman," in Ratzinger and Balthasar, *Mary: The Church at the Source*, 53–59.

29. See William S. Kurz, S.J., "Mary, Woman and Mother in God's Saving New Testament Plan," *Nova et Vetera* 11 (2013): 801–18, at 809–15.

30. See Cantalamessa, *Mary: Mirror of the Church*, 123–29. See also the cautious approach taken by Jean-Pierre Torrell, O.P., with respect to Mary's spiritual motherhood and the title "Mother of the Church" in Torrell, *La Vierge Marie dans la foi catholique* (Paris: Cerf, 2010), 123–78.

31. For reflection see José Granados, D.C.J.M., "Through Mary's Memory to Jesus' Mystery," *Communio* 33 (2006): 11–42.

32. On *Redemptoris Mater*'s ecumenical intention vis-à-vis the Orthodox, in light of Pope John Paul II's references to the Greek Fathers in his Marian Catecheses (1995–97) and in light of early conciliar teaching on original sin, see Hauke, "The Immaculate Conception of Mary in the Greek Fathers and in an Ecumenical Context," 327–46.

33. See Anthony Le Donne, *The Historiographical Jesus: Memory, Typology, and the Son of David* (Waco, TX: Baylor University Press, 2009); Paul M. Hoskins, *That Scripture Might Be Fulfilled: Typology and the Death of Christ* (Maitland, FL: Xulon Press, 2009); and R. T. France, *Jesus and the Old Testament: His Application of Old Testament Passages to Himself and His Mission* (Vancouver, B.C.: Regent College Publishing, 1998). For classic reflection on the significance of biblical typology see Jean Daniélou, S.J., "Symbolism and History," in *The Lord of History: Reflections on the Inner Meaning of History*, trans. Nigel Abercrombie (Chicago: Henry Regnery, 1958), 130–46; and Jean Danié-

lou, S.J., *From Shadows to Reality: Studies in the Biblical Typology of the Fathers*, trans. Dom Wulstan Hibberd, O.S.B. (London: Burns & Oates, 1960), especially the first chapter, "Adam and Christ in Holy Scripture." Whereas Daniélou differentiates typology sharply from allegory, Henri de Lubac, S.J., rejects this sharp distinction: see de Lubac, "'Typologie' et 'allégorisme,'" *Recherches de science religieuse* 34 (1947): 180–226; de Lubac, *Scripture in the Tradition*, trans. Luke O'Neill (New York: Crossroad, 2000), 15–16. For discussion related to this debate, generally siding with de Lubac, see Walter J. Burghardt, S.J., "On Early Christian Exegesis," *Theological Studies* 11 (1950): 78–116; Herbert Musurillo, S.J., "Shadow and Reality: Thoughts on the Problem of Typology," *Theological Studies* 22 (1961): 455–60; Hans Boersma, *Nouvelle Théologie and Sacramental Ontology: A Return to Mystery* (Oxford: Oxford University Press, 2009), chap. 5; John J. O'Keefe and R. R. Reno, *Sanctified Vision: An Introduction to Early Christian Interpretation of the Bible* (Baltimore, MD: Johns Hopkins University Press, 2005), chaps. 4–5; Frances M. Young, *Biblical Exegesis and the Formation of Christian Culture* (Cambridge: Cambridge University Press, 1997), 152–57; Denys Turner, "Allegory in Christian Late Antiquity," in *The Cambridge Companion to Allegory*, ed. Rita Copeland and Peter Struck (Cambridge: Cambridge University Press, 2010), 71–82; and Lewis Ayres, "'There's Fire in That Rain': On Reading the Letter and Reading Allegorically," *Modern Theology* 28 (2012): 616–34. I agree with Paul J. Griffiths that we can and should make a distinction— if not always a sharp one—between typological or "figural" interpretation and allegory: see Griffiths, *Song of Songs*, lvi–lvii.

34. The Catholic theologian George Tavard, A.A., entirely misses the significance of typology in the New Testament when he writes: "Allegorical interpretations . . . have been the destiny of the New Testament texts about Mary. For it has seemed to later generations of Christians that the evangelists should have said more about the mother of the Lord" (Tavard, *The Thousand Faces of the Virgin Mary*, 15). Unfortunately, not only theologians but also contemporary Catholic biblical scholars generally neglect typology when it comes to the New Testament portraits of Mary. See, for example, Donald Senior, C.P., "Gospel Portraits of Mary: Images and Symbols from the Synoptic Tradition," in *Mary, Woman of Nazareth: Biblical and Theological Perspectives*, ed. Doris Donnelly (New York: Paulist Press, 1990), 92–108; Pheme Perkins, "Mary in Johannine Traditions," in Donnelly, *Mary, Woman of Nazareth*, 109–22; Joseph A. Fitzmyer, S.J., *The Gospel According to Luke (I–IX)* (Garden City, NY: Doubleday, 1981), 364; and Francis Moloney, S.D.B., *The Gospel of John* (Collegeville, MN: Liturgical Press, 1998), 71. The Protestant exegete Joel Green remarks that "Luke seems little concerned with typological hermeneutics in his birth narrative." Green, *The Gospel of Luke* (Grand Rapids, MI: Eerdmans, 1997), 87n23. Even so, Green presents what seem to me to be typological connections between Sarah and Abraham, on the one hand, and Zechariah, Elizabeth, and Mary on the other. But Green insists that because *both* Zechariah and Mary are depicted by Luke

as being like Abraham, it therefore follows that "Luke is making no straightforward typological argument here" (ibid., 56). Readers attuned to biblical typology would not expect typological arguments to be "straightforward" in this sense. See the helpful essay of Denis Farkasfalvy, O.Cist., "Reconstructing Mariology: Mary's Virginity and the Future of Mariology," *Communio* 37 (2010): 47–68.

35. Regarding Revelation 12, Stephen Shoemaker cautions against "certain Roman Catholic thinkers who, faced with the scandalous lack of any formal testimony regarding the end of the Virgin's life in the earliest Christian writings, have sought to identify here an implicit testimony to the Virgin's Assumption" (Shoemaker, *Ancient Traditions of the Virgin Mary's Dormition and Assumption*, 12–13). Although Shoemaker gives little place to typology and therefore misunderstands the way in which Revelation 12 functions as "testimony," he has on his side the fact that "the early church unanimously identified this apocalyptic woman with the church. For the most part this hermeneutic trend continues in later patristic literature, where the Virgin is only infrequently identified with this apocalyptic woman" (ibid., 13). The identification of the "woman" with the Church does not, however, negate the typological link to Mary. On this point see Raymond E. Brown, S.S., *The Gospel according to John (I–XII)* (Garden City, NY: Doubleday, 1966), 107–9, even though Brown distinguishes his exegetical remarks from later Mariological developments (and even though, unfortunately, he altered his position in his later *The Death of the Messiah: From Gethsemane to the Grave*, 2 vols. [New York: Doubleday, 1994], 2:1024). See also Albert Vanhoye, S.J., "Interrogation johannique et éxègese de Cana (Jn 2:4)," *Biblica* 55 (1974): 157–67; George T. Montague, S.M., "Eschatology and Our Lady," *Marian Studies* 17 (1966): 65–83, at 74–78; and Thurian, *Mary, Mother of the Lord, Figure of the Church*, 117–75.

Chapter 2
Early to Mid-Twentieth-Century Theologies of Mary's Assumption

1. For studies of Mary's Assumption published in the century before the 1950 definition (most of them in the 1940s), see Juniper B. Carol, O.F.M., "A Bibliography of the Assumption," *The Thomist* 14 (1951): 133–60.

2. See Duhr, *The Glorious Assumption of the Mother of God*; originally published as Duhr, *La Glorieuse Assomption de la Mère de Dieu* (Paris: La Maison de la Bonne Presse, 1948). See also Johann Ernst, *Die leibliche Himmelfahrt Mariä: Historisch-dogmatisch nach ihrer Definierbarkeit beleuchtet* (Regensburg: Manz, 1921); and Johann Ernst, "Neues zur Kontroverse über die Definierbarkeit der Himmelfahrt Mariä," *Bonner Zeitschrift* 6 (1929): 289–304; 7 (1930): 16–31. In the 1940s, Catholic critics of the definability of the dogma of Mary's

Assumption included Berthold Altaner, "Zur Frage der Definibilität der Assumptio B. V. M.," *Theologische Revue* 44 (1948): 129–40; 45 (1949): 129–42; 46 (1950): 5–20; and Joseph Coppens, "La définibilité de l'Assomption," *Ephemerides theologicae Lovanienses* 23 (1947): 5–35. For a survey of criticisms see Friedrich Heiler, "Assumptio," *Theologische Literaturzeitung* 79 (1954): 1–51. See also Juniper B. Carol, O.F.M., "The Definability of Mary's Assumption," *American Ecclesiastical Review* 118 (1948): 161–77; and J. Filograssi, S.J., "Theologia catholica et Assumptio B. V. M.," *Gregorianum* 31 (1950): 323–60.

3. Duhr, *The Glorious Assumption of the Mother of God*, 2.

4. Ibid., 3. For background to this approach to dogmatic reasoning, see Jan Hendrik Walgrave, O.P., *Unfolding Revelation: The Nature of Doctrinal Development* (Philadelphia: Westminster, 1972), 135–78.

5. Duhr, *The Glorious Assumption of the Mother of God*, 3. Duhr later observes:

> Guided and enlightened by the divine Spirit, Who never fails to assist her, and growing in age and wisdom as did her Founder, the Church has become ever more clearly conscious of this truth [Mary's Assumption], as of many others. Understand us well. We do not say—and this is of capital importance—that the theologian can conclude to the Assumption of Mary from the *abstract* notion of the divine Motherhood [Mary's motherhood of the divine Son incarnate]; but we say that the *Church of Christ*, thanks to a light that is hers alone, can discern clearly in the *concrete* notion of Mary's Motherhood—such as Christ conceived it and wished it to be, with its privileges and consequences—the privilege of the corporal Assumption. (ibid., 75)

6. Ibid., 7.

7. On Epiphanius of Salamis, see Shoemaker, *Ancient Traditions of the Virgin Mary's Dormition and Assumption*, 11–14.

8. Duhr, *The Glorious Assumption of the Mother of God*, 74. Léandre Poirier, O.F.M., denies that Revelation 12 has to do with Mary: see Poirier, "Le chapitre XII de l'Apocalypse fait-il allusion à l'Assomption?" in Malo, *Vers le dogme de l'Assomption*, 93–102. See also Adrien-M. Malo, O.F.M., "La Bible et l'Assomption," in Malo, *Vers le dogme de l'Assomption*, 103–22. For a study of Catholic exegetical interpretations of Revelation 12 from the patristic period through the mid-twentieth century, see Dominic J. Unger, O.F.M.Cap., "Did Saint John See the Virgin Mary in Glory?," *Catholic Biblical Quarterly* 11 (1949): 249–62, 392–405; 12 (1950): 75–83, 155–61, 292–300, 405–15. Unger concludes that "even though John does not say in so many words that Mary was assumed into glory and that this picture is proof of it, he clearly implies this by what he says of that glorious woman in literal and explicit language. We hold that Pope Pius X was quite right when he said, 'No one is ignorant that this woman signified the Virgin Mary. . . . So John saw the most holy Mother of God already

enjoying happiness.'" Unger, "Did Saint John See the Virgin Mary in Glory," *Catholic Biblical Quarterly* 12 (1950): 405–15, at 415.

9. Duhr, *The Glorious Assumption of the Mother of God*, 74. See also John D. Dadosky, "Woman without Envy: Toward Reconceiving the Immaculate Conception," *Theological Studies* 72 (2011): 15–40, at 39–40.

10. Duhr, *The Glorious Assumption of the Mother of God*, 82. See also Pelikan, *Mary Through the Centuries*, 41–44; and Hilda Graef, *Mary: A History of Doctrine and Devotion*, with a new chapter "Vatican II and Beyond" by Thomas M. Thompson, S.M. (Notre Dame, IN: Ave Maria Press, 2009), 29–32. For insight into Irenaeus's exegetical approach, see Thomas Holsinger-Friesen, *Irenaeus and Genesis: A Study of Competition in Early Christian Hermeneutics* (Winona Lake, IN: Eisenbrauns, 2009).

11. Duhr, *The Glorious Assumption of the Mother of God*, 83.

12. Ibid., 85.

13. Ibid., 11; cf. 13–14, 80–81. On the "ordinary universal Magisterium," see Avery Dulles, S.J., *Magisterium: Teacher and Guardian of the Faith* (Naples, FL: Sapientia Press, 2007), 67.

14. Aloïs Janssens, *The Assumption of Our Lady* (Fresno, CA: Academy Library Guild, 1954), 39. This book is a translation of *Maria's Hemelvaart* (1931), vol. 4 of Janssens, *De Heilige Maagd en Moeder Gods Maria* (4 vols.).

15. Janssens, *The Assumption of Our Lady*, 44.

16. Ibid.

17. Ibid.

18. Ibid., 45. For a Reformed Protestant critique of the view that Mary is the new Eve, see Nancy J. Duff, "Mary, the Servant of the Lord: Christian Vocation at the Manger and the Cross," in Gaventa and Rigby, *Blessed One*, 59–70, at 64.

19. On the latter point see Janssens, *The Assumption of Our Lady*, 147.

20. Ibid., 99. See also, along these lines, Otto Semmelroth, S.J., *Mary, Archetype of the Church*, trans. Maria von Eroes and John Devlin (New York: Sheed and Ward, 1963), 7–25.

21. Janssens, *The Assumption of Our Lady*, 103.

22. Ibid.

23. Ibid., 169.

24. In a lengthy essay on "The Fundamental Principle of Marian Theology," which describes the positions of numerous authors on this topic, Cyril Vollert likewise argues that the key principle of Mariology is Mary's motherhood, from which other elements such as her status as the new Eve follow. See Cyril Vollert, S.J., *A Theology of Mary* (New York: Herder and Herder, 1965), especially 111–12; see also Semmelroth, *Mary, Archetype of the Church*, 7–25; Laurentin, *A Short Treatise on the Virgin Mary*, 166–76; and Karl Rahner, S.J., *Mary, Mother of the Lord: Theological Meditations*, trans. W. J. O'Hara (New York: Herder and Herder, 1963), 32–41. John Courtney Murray, S.J., provides a

short preface to Vollert's book, in which he begins by praising Vollert and ends by condemning Vollert's method of theologizing as too propositional, too optimistic regarding the Church's Magisterium, and too ignorant regarding "the new world of interiority" enjoyed by individual Christians and by the whole believing community (see Murray, "Preface," in Vollert, A Theology of Mary, 11).

25. Réginald Garrigou-Lagrange, O.P., The Mother of the Saviour and Our Interior Life, trans. Bernard J. Kelly, C.S.Sp. (Charlotte, NC: TAN Books, 1993), 4. This book was first published in French as La Mère du Sauveur et notre vie intérieure (Lyon: Éditions de l'Abeille, 1941). For Garrigou-Lagrange on Mary's Assumption, see the brief discussion by Aidan Nichols, O.P., Reason with Piety: Garrigou-Lagrange in the Service of Catholic Thought (Ave Maria, FL: Sapientia Press, 2008), 39–40, 86.

26. For discussion see Jean-François Bonnefoy, O.F.M., "L'Assomption de la T. S. Vierge et sa predestination," in Malo, Vers le dogme de l'Assomption, 293–335. On predestination more broadly, see Réginald Garrigou-Lagrange, O.P., Predestination, trans. Dom Bede Rose, O.S.B. (Rockford, IL: TAN Books, 1998). See also my Predestination: Biblical and Theological Paths (Oxford: Oxford University Press, 2011).

27. Garrigou-Lagrange, The Mother of the Saviour and Our Interior Life, 9; cf. 11.

28. See also Charles De Koninck, Ego Sapientia: The Wisdom That Is Mary (1943), included in The Writings of Charles De Koninck, vol. 2, ed. and trans. Ralph McInerny (Notre Dame, IN: University of Notre Dame Press, 2009), 1–62.

29. Garrigou-Lagrange, The Mother of the Saviour and Our Interior Life, 13.

30. Ibid., 15. For contemporary discussion see Jean-Miguel Garrigues, "The 'Natural Grace' of Christ in St. Thomas," in Surnaturel: A Controversy at the Heart of Twentieth-Century Thomistic Thought, ed. Serge-Thomas Bonino, O.P., trans. Robert Williams (Ave Maria, FL: Sapientia Press, 2009), 103–15.

31. Garrigou-Lagrange, The Mother of the Saviour and Our Interior Life, 18; cf. 27–72 on Mary's Immaculate Conception.

32. Ibid., 24.

33. Ibid. See also John Duns Scotus, Ordinatio III, dist. 3, q. 1, "The Immaculate Conception of the Blessed Virgin," in John Duns Scotus, Four Questions on Mary, trans. Allan B. Wolter, O.F.M. (Saint Bonaventure, NY: Franciscan Institute, 2000), 30–62. For further discussion see, e.g., Rahner, Mary, Mother of the Lord, 74–76.

34. For further discussion see Réginald Garrigou-Lagrange, O.P., Grace: Commentary on the Summa theologica of St. Thomas, Ia IIae, q. 109–14, trans. Dominican Nuns of Corpus Christi Monastery (St. Louis, MO: B. Herder, 1952).

35. Garrigou-Lagrange, The Mother of the Saviour and Our Interior Life, 27 n. 1.

36. Ibid., 28.

37. Ibid.

38. Ibid., 29.

39. Ibid., 32. For the nineteenth-century theological discussion, see Matthias Joseph Scheeben, *Mariology*, 2 vols., trans. T. L. M. J. Geukers (St. Louis, MO: B. Herder, 1946–48).

40. Garrigou-Lagrange, *The Mother of the Saviour and Our Interior Life*, 33.

41. Ibid., 34. See John Duns Scotus, *Ordinatio* III, dist. 3, q. 1, "The Immaculate Conception of the Blessed Virgin," in John Duns Scotus, *Four Questions on Mary*, trans. Allan B. Wolter, O.F.M. (Saint Bonaventure, NY: Franciscan Institute, 2000), 30–62. For discussion see Léonard-M. Puech, O.F.M., "Une preuve scotiste: la mediation parfaite due Christ," in Malo, *Vers le dogme de l'Assomption*, 337–58; and George H. Tavard, A.A., "John Duns Scotus and the Immaculate Conception," in Anderson, Stafford, and Burgess, *The One Mediator, the Saints, and Mary: Lutherans and Catholics in Dialogue VIII*, 209–17.

42. Was Jesus too, then, the recipient of a preservative redemption thanks to God's foreknowledge of the merits of Jesus' Passion? In other words, was Jesus (as sinless) both Redeemer and redeemed? For two reasons, the answer is no. First of all, at the instant of his conception, the human nature of Jesus was united to the divine nature in the Person of the Word and nothing sinful can be attributed to the Word. Second, Jesus received his human nature not through natural conception, but from Mary's virginal conception.

43. Garrigou-Lagrange, *The Mother of the Saviour and Our Interior Life*, 36.

44. For further discussion see Leo Scheffczyk, *Maria: Mutter und Gefährtin Christi* (Augsburg: Sankt Ulrich Verlag, 2003), 150–56.

45. Garrigou-Lagrange, *The Mother of the Saviour and Our Interior Life*, 36–37.

46. Ibid., 37.

47. For background see Sebastian Brock, "Mary in Syriac Tradition," in Stacpoole, *Mary's Place in Christian Dialogue*, 182–91.

48. See Garrigou-Lagrange, *The Mother of the Saviour and Our Interior Life*, 161ff. For further discussion of the term co-redemptrix, with particular attention to what it does *not* mean and to Mary as type of the Church, see Semmelroth, *Mary, Archetype of the Church*, 63–89. On Mary's (and the Church's) mediation see ibid., 92–110. See also Laurentin, *A Short Treatise on the Virgin Mary*, 236–43, 256–58; Thurian, *Mary, Mother of the Lord, Figure of the Church*, 96–116; and O'Meara, *Mary in Protestant and Catholic Theology*, 85–88.

49. Garrigou-Lagrange, *The Mother of the Saviour and Our Interior Life*, 111.

50. See Walter J. Burghardt, S.J., "The Testimony of the Patristic Age Concerning Mary's Death," *Marian Studies* 8 (1957): 58–99; and John P. O'Connell,

"The Testimony of the Sacred Liturgy Relative to Mary's Death," *Marian Studies* 8 (1957): 125–42.

51. Garrigou-Lagrange, *The Mother of the Saviour and Our Interior Life*, 129.

52. Ibid., 131.

53. Ibid., 133.

54. Ibid. I agree with Bernard Lonergan on this point: "Though not explicitly revealed in Holy Scripture, nor, as far as we know with certitude, in any explicit, oral, apostolic tradition, still it [Mary's Assumption] is revealed implicitly" (Lonergan, "The Assumption and Theology," in Malo, *Vers le dogme de l'Assomption*, 411–24, at 424; cf. 413–14).

55. Garrigou-Lagrange, *The Mother of the Saviour and Our Interior Life*, 133–34. For the contention that much Catholic and Orthodox Mariology derives from goddess worship, see Stephen Benko, *The Virgin Goddess: Studies in the Pagan and Christian Roots of Mariology* (Leiden: E. J. Brill, 1993). While Benko (and Garrigou-Lagrange) presuppose that goddess worship is in error, Francis X. Clooney, S.J., suggests the opposite in *Divine Mother, Blessed Mother: Hindu Goddesses and the Virgin Mary* (Oxford: Oxford University Press, 2005). Clooney recognizes that "[t]here is no plausible way for a Christian simply to affirm the existence of goddesses or to participate easily in worship of them" (223), but his reliance on metaphor (rather than analogy) in God-talk arguably requires goddesses so as to include feminine qualities. Similarly restricting God-talk to metaphor, Elizabeth A. Johnson, C.S.J., sees Mariology as a means by which Christian believers have made contact with the feminine dimensions of God, although Christians do not envision Mary as God (and indeed Johnson worries that Mary's mediation has replaced the work of the Holy Spirit in Christian tradition). See Johnson, "Mary and the Female Face of God," *Theological Studies* 50 (1989): 500–526; and cf. Johnson, "The Incomprehensibility of God and the Image of God Male and Female," *Theological Studies* 45 (1984): 441–65. For a nuanced perspective, cited by Johnson, see Jean Daniélou, S.J., "Le culte marial et le paganisme," in *Maria: Etudes sur la Sainte Vierge*, ed. D'Hubert du Manoir (Paris: Beauchesne, 1949), 159–81. See also Andrew Greeley, *The Mary Myth: On the Femininity of God* (New York: Seabury Press, 1977).

56. Garrigou-Lagrange, *The Mother of the Saviour and Our Interior Life*, 134.

57. For a contemporary philosophical approach (from the perspective of analytic Thomism) that defends deductive theological reasoning on the basis of fittingness with regard to Mary's Assumption, see John Haldane, "Examining the Assumption," *Heythrop Journal* 43 (2002): 411–29.

58. Garrigou-Lagrange, *The Mother of the Saviour and Our Interior Life*, 138.

59. Ibid., 139.

60. Ibid.

61. Ibid.

62. Duhr, *The Glorious Assumption of the Mother of God*, 74.

63. Janssens, *The Assumption of Our Lady*, 44.

64. Ibid.

Chapter 3
The *Nouvelle Théologie* and Mary's Assumption

1. For discussion attuned to diverse perspectives see Bonino, *Surnaturel*. The publication of Lawrence Feingold's *The Natural Desire to See God according to St. Thomas Aquinas and His Interpreters*, 2nd ed. (Ave Maria, FL: Sapientia Press, 2010)—originally published in 2001—generated a wave of new reflection on this topic, including book-length studies by Steven A. Long, *Natura Pura: On the Recovery of Nature in the Doctrine of Grace* (New York: Fordham University Press, 2010) and John Milbank, *The Suspended Middle: Henri de Lubac and the Debate concerning the Supernatural* (Grand Rapids, MI: Eerdmans, 2005).

2. See Jean Daniélou, S.J., "Les Orientations présentes de la pensée religieuse," *Études* 249 (1946): 5–21.

3. See Marie-Michel Labourdette, O.P., "La Théologie et ses sources," *Revue thomiste* 46 (1946): 353–71. For the political context of the modernist controversy and the two world wars, the context in which the leading figures of the 1940s in Catholic theology were shaped, see William L. Portier's historical tribute to Blondelian theology: "Twentieth-Century Catholic Theology and the Triumph of Maurice Blondel," *Communio* 38 (2011): 103–37. For the contemporary theological situation and an effort to readdress the fundamental questions, see Reinhard Hütter, "Catholic Theology in America: Quo Vadis?," *Nova et Vetera* 9 (2011): 539–47; and Reinhard Hütter, "Theological Faith Enlightening Sacred Theology: Renewing Theology by Recovering Its Unity as *sacra doctrina*," *The Thomist* 74 (2010): 369–405. To my mind, the solution will require combining the strong points of neoscholastic theology with those of the *nouvelle théologie*. In this regard, Thomas Aquinas himself shows the way forward through his use of Scripture, the Fathers, and the liturgy. On this point see especially Aidan Nichols, O.P., "Thomism and the *Nouvelle Théologie*," *The Thomist* 64 (2000): 1–19. See also, for de Lubac's concerns about post-conciliar theology, Rudolf Voderholzer, *Meet Henri de Lubac: His Life and Work*, trans. Michael J. Miller (San Francisco: Ignatius Press, 2008), 93–97.

4. See Réginald Garrigou-Lagrange, O.P., "La Théologie nouvelle, où va-t-elle?," *Angelicum* 23 (1946): 126–45. See also Nichols, *Reason with Piety*, 128–30.

5. See, for example, Boersma, *Nouvelle Théologie and Sacramental Ontology*; Gabriel Flynn and Paul D. Murray, eds., *Ressourcement: A Movement for*

Renewal in Twentieth-Century Catholic Theology, (Oxford: Oxford University Press, 2012); and de Gaál, *The Theology of Pope Benedict XVI*.

6. Jürgen Mettepenningen, *Nouvelle Théologie—New Theology* (London: T & T Clark International, 2010), 115. I do not discuss Schillebeeckx's position in this chapter, but in his preconciliar phase he too wrote a significant book on Mary: *Mary, Mother of the Redemption*, trans. N. D. Smith (New York: Sheed and Ward, 1964), originally published in Dutch in 1954. Schillebeeckx argues that by dying in perfect love, Mary merited immediate resurrection: "Her utter dedication to God and her dispossession of herself were, therefore, perfectly expressed and embodied in her physical death. Mary's death—her *dormitio*, or 'falling asleep in love'—can thus be seen as the supreme example of every Christian death, and contained the promise of immediate resurrection. This took place at once in Mary's case. Her assumption, on death, became an immediate reality" (ibid., 74–75). He goes on to explain:

> The essential moment of Christ's act of redemption is not restricted to his sacrificial death. The divine acceptance of the sacrifice is complementary and co-essential to that sacrifice. This acceptance by God is in fact Jesus' *resurrection*. . . . Going a stage further, we can, by analogy with Christ's resurrection, conclude from the fact of Mary's *resurrection* that her life-sacrifice was also fully accepted by God. Her assumption into heaven was not merely a privilege bestowed on her without relation to the rest of her life. It formed the summit of her sublime redemption. . . . Dogma informs us that Mary was not obliged to wait, as we are, until the end of time for physical redemption. This is a clear indication of the unique quality of her sublime state of redemption. It also indicates the fact of her redemption by exemption—that at no moment of her existence did sin cast a shadow over the brightness of her life with God. (ibid., 76)

Elizabeth A. Johnson, C.S.J., criticizes Schillebeeckx's position and adds that he "clearly would not treat the subject the same way today, having criticized his own position and wishing, after his monumental work on Jesus, to hew to a more biblical approach." See Johnson, *Truly Our Sister: A Theology of Mary in the Communion of Saints* (New York: Continuum, 2006), 80; and cf. Edward Schillebeeckx, O.P., *Christ: The Experience of Jesus as Lord*, trans. John Bowden (New York: Seabury Press, 1980). Schillebeeckx outlines his new, much reduced understanding of Mary in his "Mariology: Yesterday, Today, Tomorrow," in *Mary: Yesterday, Today, Tomorrow*, ed. Edward Schillebeeckx, O.P., and Catharina Halkes, trans. John Bowden (New York: Crossroad, 1993), 12–42. For incisive criticism of this work see John Breck, *Scripture in Tradition: The Bible and Its Interpretation in the Orthodox Church* (Crestwood, NY: St Vladimir's Seminary Press, 2001), 229–38.

7. This book finally appeared in volume 9 of Rahner's complete works. See Karl Rahner, S.J., *Maria, Mutter des Herrn: Mariologische Studien*, ed. Regina

Pacis Meyer (Freiburg im Breisgau: Herder, 2004), 3–392. For discussion see Meyer's "Editionsbericht," xi–lvi.

8. Karl Rahner, S.J., "The Interpretation of the Dogma of the Assumption," in *Theological Investigations*, vol. 1, *God, Christ, Mary and Grace*, trans. Cornelius Ernst, O.P. (Baltimore, MD: Helicon Press, 1961), 215–27, at 215. See also *Mary, Mother of the Lord*, the short, much more speculatively modest book on Mary that Rahner published in German in 1956, especially 89–90. On Rahner's Mariology see, e.g., Karl Neufeld, "Zur Mariologie Karl Rahners— Materialien und Grundlinien," *Zeitschrift für katholische Theologie* 109 (1987): 431–39; Karl Neufeld, "Mariologie in der Sicht K. Rahners," *Ephemerides Mariologicae* 50 (2000): 285–97; Daley, "Woman of Many Names," 846–69, at 863–66; and Philip Endean, S.J., "How to Think about Mary's Privileges: A Post-Conciliar Exposition," in Boss, *Mary: The Complete Resource*, 284–91, at 288–90. For discussion of Rahner's eschatology see especially Peter Phan, "Eschatology," in *The Cambridge Companion to Karl Rahner*, ed. Declan Marmion and Mary E. Hines (Cambridge: Cambridge University Press, 2005), 174–92; and Peter Phan, *Eternity in Time: A Study of Karl Rahner's Eschatology* (London: Associated University Presses, 1988).

9. Rahner, "The Interpretation of the Dogma of the Assumption," 215.

10. Ibid., 218.

11. For further discussion see Rahner, *Mary, Mother of the Lord*, 13. On Mary as the type of the Church, see also Semmelroth, *Mary, Archetype of the Church*, 26–57. For Reformed critiques of the view that Mary, as sinless, is the type of the Church, see Duff, "Mary, the Servant of the Lord," in Gaventa and Rigby, *Blessed One*, 59–70, at 66–68; and Migliore, "Woman of Faith," in Gaventa and Rigby, *Blessed One*, 117–30, at 125–27.

12. Rahner, "The Interpretation of the Dogma of the Assumption," 219.

13. Ibid.

14. Ibid. See also Joseph Ratzinger's 1967 essay "II. Resurrection of the Body; B. Theological," in *Sacramentum Mundi*, ed. Karl Rahner (New York: Herder and Herder, 1970), 340–42.

15. Rahner, "The Interpretation of the Dogma of the Assumption," 220. Along these lines see also John Saward, "The Assumption," in Stacpoole, *Mary's Place in Christian Dialogue*, 108–22, at 113–17.

16. Rahner, "The Interpretation of the Dogma of the Assumption," 220.

17. Ibid., 220n2.

18. Ibid., 222.

19. Ibid., 224.

20. Ibid.

21. Ibid.

22. Ibid., 225.

23. Ibid.

24. Ibid.

25. Ibid., 226.

26. Ibid.

27. Ibid.

28. Ibid.

29. See Henry Denzinger, *The Sources of Catholic Dogma*, no. 540, trans. Roy J. Deferrari from the 30th edition (revised by Karl Rahner, S.J.) of Henry Denzinger's *Enchiridion Symbolorum* (Fitzwilliam, NH: Loreto Publications, 2002), 198.

30. Karl Rahner, S.J., "The Intermediate State," in *Theological Investigations*, vol. 17, *Jesus, Man, and the Church*, trans. Margaret Kohl (New York: Crossroad, 1981), 114–24, at 115. For extensive development of the theory of resurrection-in-death see Gisbert Greshake, *Auferstehung der Toten: Ein Beitrag zur gegenwärtigen theologischen Diskussion über die Zukunft der Geschichte* (Essen: Ludgerus, 1969); Gisbert Greshake, "Das Verhältnis 'Unsterblichkeit der Seele' und 'Auferstehung des Leibes' in problemgeschichtlicher Sicht," in *Naherwartung—Auferstehung—Unsterblichkeit*, ed. Gisbert Greshake and Gerhard Lohfink (Freiburg im Breisgau: Herder, 1975), 82–120; and Gisbert Greshake and Jacob Kremer, *Resurrectio Mortuorum. Zum theologischen Verständnis der leiblichen Auferstehung* (Darmstadt: Wissenschaftliche Buchgesellschaft, 1986). For criticism of this view, as well as valuable background, see Paul O'Callaghan, *Christ Our Hope: An Introduction to Eschatology* (Washington, D.C.: Catholic University of America Press, 2011), 318–26; Bryan Kromholtz, O.P., *On the Last Day: The Time of the Resurrection of the Dead according to Thomas Aquinas* (Fribourg: Fribourg University Press, 2010); Leo Scheffczyk, "'Unsterblichkeit' bei Thomas von Aquin auf dem Hintergrund der neueren Diskussion," *Bayerische Akademie der Wissenschaften, Philosophisch-Historische Klasse, Sitzungsberichte* 4 (1989): 14–27; Terrence P. Ehrman, "The Metaphysics of the Resurrection: Exploring Human Embodiedness beyond Richard Swinburne's Dualism and Kevin Corcoran's Christian Materialism" (PhD Dissertation, Catholic University of America, 2012); and Wolfhart Pannenberg, *Systematic Theology*, vol. 3, trans. Geoffrey W. Bromiley (Grand Rapids, MI: Eerdmans, 1998), 577–80. For contrasting responses among specialists in Mariology to the theory of resurrection-in-death, see Donal Flanagan, "Eschatology and the Assumption," *Concilium* 41 (1969): 135–46; and Healy, *The Assumption of Mary*, 118–21.

31. Rahner, "The Intermediate State," 115.

32. Ibid.

33. As Rahner says in his *Mary, Mother of the Lord*, 21–22: "When he [a Catholic] opens the Scriptures, they are always for him the Church's book; he receives them from the Church, and reads them with her interpretation. This being understood, it is true to say that if he wishes to meditate more closely on the blessed Virgin, he first of all opens the Scriptures. For true though it may be that Holy Scripture can only be read correctly under the guidance of the

teaching authority of the Church, yet conversely, Holy Scripture, by its inseparable connection with the Church and her teaching office, is a norm and standard for her faith and magisterium. The Church preaches what she reads in Scripture." In his dogmatic reflections in *Mary, Mother of the Lord*, however, he begins with theological anthropology.

34. For the opposite view see Jon D. Levenson, *Resurrection and the Restoration of Israel: The Ultimate Victory of the God of Life* (New Haven, CT: Yale University Press, 2006), 35–81.

35. Rahner, "The Intermediate State," 117.

36. Ibid.

37. Ibid., 118.

38. Ibid.

39. For a similar position, indebted to Rahner, see Eamon R. Carroll, O.Carm., *Understanding the Mother of Jesus* (Wilmington, DE: Michael Glazier, 1979), 86–89. Carroll is careful to emphasize that the view that "all who have fallen asleep in the Lord are already in union with the Risen Christ" (88) is a hypothesis rather than a certainty. See also the remarks of Laurentin, *A Short Treatise on the Virgin Mary*, 249–50; and Hugh M. McElwain, O.S.M., "Christian Eschatology and the Assumption," *Marian Studies* 18 (1967): 84–102. Even more strongly in favor of Rahner's position is Charles Decelles, "A Fresh Look at the Assumption of Mary or The Idea of Resurrection Immediately Following Death," *American Ecclesiastical Review* 167 (1973): 147–63.

40. Rahner, "The Intermediate State," 120.

41. Ibid.

42. Ibid., 121.

43. Ibid., 123.

44. Ibid.

45. Ibid.

46. For a defense of the intermediate state, see chapter 1 of my *Jesus and the Demise of Death*. See also, on death and the separated soul, Randall S. Rosenberg, "Being-Toward-a-Death-Transformed: Aquinas on the Naturalness and Unnaturalness of Human Death," *Angelicum* 83 (2006): 747–66; and Eleonore Stump, *Aquinas* (London: Routledge, 2003), 191–217.

47. Hans Urs von Balthasar, *The Threefold Garland: The World's Salvation in Mary's Prayer*, trans. Erasmo Leiva-Merikakis (San Francisco: Ignatius Press, 1982), 127. For a similar view see Schillebeeckx, *Mary, Mother of the Redemption*, 76. On Balthasar's Mariology, see Francesca Aran Murphy, "Immaculate Mary: The Ecclesial Mariology of Hans Urs von Balthasar," in Boss, *Mary: The Complete Resource*, 300–313; Rino Fisichella, "Marie dans la théologie d'Hans Urs von Balthasar," *Communio* [French edition] 29 (2004): 87–98; Hilda Steinhauer, *Maria als dramatische Person bei von Balthasar: Zum marianischen Prinzip seines Denkens* (Vienna: Tyrolia Verlag, 2001); Brendan Leahy, *The Marian Profile in the Ecclesiology of Hans Urs von Balthasar* (New York: New City

Press, 2000); Edward T. Oakes, S.J., *Pattern of Redemption: The Theology of Hans Urs von Balthasar* (New York: Continuum, 1994), 253–62; Lucy Gardner, "Balthasar and the Figure of Mary," in *The Cambridge Companion to Hans Urs von Balthasar*, ed. Edward T. Oakes, S.J., and David Moss (Cambridge: Cambridge University Press, 2004), 64–78; Aidan Nichols, O.P., *No Bloodless Myth: A Guide through Balthasar's Dramatics* (Washington, D.C.: T & T Clark, 2000), 114–15; James Heft, S.M., "Marian Themes in the Writing of Hans Urs von Balthasar," *Communio* 7 (1980): 127–39, and W. T. Dickens, *Hans Urs von Balthasar's* Theological Aesthetics: *A Model for Post-Critical Biblical Intepretation* (Notre Dame, IN: University of Notre Dame Press, 2003), 208–33. For criticism of Balthasar's Mariology from a feminist theological perspective, see Johnson, *Truly Our Sister*, 57–60. See also the critical reflections of the Protestant theologian Steffen Lösel, "Conciliar, Not Conciliatory: Hans Urs von Balthasar's Ecclesiological Synthesis of Vatican II," *Modern Theology* 24 (2008): 23–49. Lösel comments: "While Protestants will be uncomfortable with the ecclesiological use of Mary as such, Catholic women might suspect the emphasis on Mary's obedience and docility to be merely a thinly veiled attempt of the all-male hierarchy to preserve its own privilege. Indeed, one might argue that the traditional depiction of Mary, which we find in von Balthasar's theology, provides the best evidence for the need to include sociological analysis and critique in the theological enterprise" (ibid., 41). Lösel also warns against "the danger of superimposing a theological typology on one's reading of scripture. While Mary features prominently in von Balthasar's treatment, she is largely absent in the New Testament, whereas Mary Magdalene seems to have had a very prominent role among Jesus' disciples—yet von Balthasar has no room for her in his christological constellation" (ibid.). Lösel, however, uncritically employs the very account of Christian "privilege" that Balthasar, in his Mariology, is at pains to contest. See also David L. Schindler, "Catholic Theology, Gender, and the Future of Western Civilization," in Schindler, *Heart of the World, Center of the Church: Communio Ecclesiology, Liberalism, and Liberation* (Grand Rapids, MI: Eerdmans, 1996), 237–74; and Schmemann, *The Virgin Mary*, 64–68.

48. Balthasar, *The Threefold Garland*, 128.

49. Ibid. See Rahner, "The Interpretation of the Dogma of the Assumption," 220.

50. Balthasar, *The Threefold Garland*, 128.

51. Ibid.

52. Ibid., 128–29. See Nicholas Healy and David L. Schindler, "For the Life of the World: Hans Urs von Balthasar on the Church as Eucharist," in Oakes and Moss, *The Cambridge Companion to Hans Urs von Balthasar*, 51–63. See also, with regard to Mary, Alyssa Lyra Pitstick, *Light in Darkness: Hans Urs von Balthasar and the Catholic Doctrine of Christ's Descent into Hell* (Grand Rapids, MI: Eerdmans, 2007), 274–76.

53. Balthasar, *The Threefold Garland*, 129. See also Semmelroth, *Mary, Archetype of the Church*, 169. For criticism of this interpretation of Ephesians 5, see Dickens, *Hans Urs von Balthasar's* Theological Aesthetics, 211–20.

54. Balthasar, *The Threefold Garland*, 129.

55. Ibid., 131.

56. Ibid., 129–30.

57. Ibid., 130.

58. Ibid., 132. See especially Andrew Hofer, O.P., "Balthasar's Eschatology on the Intermediate State: The Question of Knowability," *Logos* 12 (2009): 148–72.

59. Hans Urs von Balthasar, *Mary for Today*, trans. Robert Nowell (San Francisco: Ignatius Press, 1987), 29.

60. Ibid.

61. Ibid., 30. A similar perspective is found in Ratzinger, "The Assumption of Mary," 357–61, at 360. In this homily from 1968, Ratzinger leaves open the question of whether Mary's Assumption signals what will happen to all of us when we die.

62. Balthasar, *Mary for Today*, 30.

63. Ibid., 31.

64. Ibid.

65. Ibid.

66. Hans Urs von Balthasar, *Theo-Drama: Theological Dramatic Theory*, vol. 5, *The Last Act*, trans. Graham Harrison (San Francisco: Ignatius Press, 1998), 346.

67. Ibid., 348.

68. Ibid., 352.

69. Ibid., 353. See Rahner, "The Interpretation of the Dogma of the Assumption," 220.

70. Balthasar, *The Last Act*, 353. Balthasar here refers the reader to his *Theo-Drama: Theological Dramatic Theory*, vol. 3, *The Dramatis Personae: The Person in Christ*, trans. Graham Harrison (San Francisco: Ignatius Press, 1992 [orig. German ed. 1978]), 110.

71. Balthasar, *The Last Act*, 353.

72. Cf. ibid., 376–77.

73. Ibid., 357; cf. 360–69.

74. Ibid., 358.

75. Ibid., 358.

76. Ibid., 359.

77. Ibid.

78. Ibid.

79. Ibid., 360.

80. Balthasar goes on to say that Christ "opens the new life to us: those who arose from their graves 'after his Resurrection' and showed themselves in

the 'Holy City' will also have ascended into heaven with him. His Mother followed him in her entire humanity. The same was assumed of John the Evangelist, as we have already mentioned. And what of the 'first resurrection' in Revelation 20:5? Could this not refer to the resurrection of the 'saints and blessed ones' who, together with Christ, 'rule' world history during the time of the Church on the basis of their special missions? We simply do not know how resurrection is implemented along (and across) chronological world-time" (ibid., 377).

81. Balthasar, *The Dramatis Personae: The Person in Christ*, 273. See also Hans Urs von Balthasar, "The Marian Mold of the Church," in Ratzinger and Balthasar, *Mary: The Church at the Source*, 125–44.

82. Balthasar, *The Dramatis Personae: The Person in Christ*, 283.

83. See ibid., 288.

84. Ibid., 302–3. Cf. Steenberg, "The Role of Mary as Co-recapitulator in St. Irenaeus of Lyons," 117–37.

85. See Balthasar, *The Dramatis Personae: The Person in Christ*, 338–39, 351–53.

86. Ibid., 334–35. The early Fathers did not draw out this implication, but their successors did.

87. Ibid., 336.

88. Ibid.

89. See ibid., 337. For discussion see Gardner, "Balthasar and the Figure of Mary," in Oakes and Moss, *The Cambridge Companion to Hans Urs von Balthasar*, 74. Gardner is both appreciative and critical of Balthasar's Mariology. She concludes that we should "[search] out, precisely in the flexibility and instability of his accounts, the eternal truths to which Balthasar, like Mary, points and which he, like every Christian and theologian, at once 'sees' and yet spectacularly misrecognizes" (ibid., 78).

90. Balthasar, *The Dramatis Personae: The Person in Christ*, 337.

91. Louis Bouyer, *The Seat of Wisdom: An Essay on the Place of the Virgin Mary in Christian Theology*, trans. A. V. Littledale (London: Darton, Longman & Todd, 1960), 27.

92. Ibid., 28.

93. Ibid. For a stimulating, if at certain points highly unlikely, historical reconstruction of the development of personified Wisdom in the religious traditions of Israel and the application of these traditions to Mary, see Margaret Barker, "Wisdom, the Queen of Heaven," in *The Great High Priest: The Temple Roots of Christian Liturgy* (London: T & T Clark, 2003), 229–61.

94. Bouyer, *The Seat of Wisdom*, 30–31.

95. Ibid., 35. Compare Richard B. Hays's argument that "[o]f all the evangelists, Luke is the most intentional, and the most skillful, in narrating the story of Jesus in a way that joins it seamlessly to Israel's story." Hays, "The Liberation of Israel in Luke-Acts: Intertextual Narration as Countercultural Practice," in

Reading the Bible Intertextually, ed. Richard B. Hays, Stefan Alkier, and Leroy A. Huizenga (Waco, TX: Baylor University Press, 2009), 101–17, at 103.

96. Bouyer, *The Seat of Wisdom*, 36.

97. Ibid., 40. See also de Satgé, *Down to Earth*, 121–28.

98. See also Semmelroth, *Mary, Archetype of the Church*, 164–66; O'Meara, *Mary in Protestant and Catholic Theology*, 80–81.

99. Bouyer, *The Seat of Wisdom*, 41. The biblical scholars whose discussions resulted in *Mary in the New Testament: A Collaborative Assessment by Protestant and Roman Catholic Scholars*, ed. Raymond E. Brown, Karl P. Donfried, Joseph A. Fitzmyer, and John Reumann (New York: Paulist Press, 1978), arrived at the following conclusion regarding Revelation 12: "A secondary reference, then, to Mary in Revelation 12 remains possible but uncertain, so far as the intention of the seer himself is concerned. What is more certain is that his symbol of the woman who is the mother of the Messiah might well lend itself to Marian interpretation, once Marian interest developed in the later Christian community. And eventually when Revelation was placed in the same canon of Scripture with the Gospel of Luke and the Fourth Gospel, the various images of the virgin, the woman at the cross, and the woman who gave birth to the Messiah would reinforce each other" (239). For a richer discussion see Kurz, "Mary, Woman and Mother in God's Saving New Testament Plan," 801–18, at 809–15; André Feuillet, "The Messiah and His Mother According to Apocalypse XII," in *Johannine Studies*, trans. Thomas E. Crane (Staten Island, NY: Alba House, 1964), 257–92, at 286–91; in the same volume, Feuillet, "The Hour of Jesus and the Sign of Cana," 17–37, at 36–37; and Ignace de la Potterie, S.J., *Mary in the Mystery of the Covenant*, trans. Bertrand Buby, S.M. (Staten Island, NY: Alba House, 1992), 246–63.

100. Bouyer, *The Seat of Wisdom*, 193.

101. Ibid., 196.

102. There are connections here with Sergius Bulgakov's Sophiology: see especially Bulgakov's *The Bride of the Lamb*, trans. Boris Jakim (Grand Rapids, MI: Eerdmans, 2002).

103. Bouyer, *The Seat of Wisdom*, 196–97. See also M.-D. Philippe, O.P., "The Assumption in the Spiritual Life," *The Thomist* 14 (1951): 93–108, at 103–4. Mary's role here flows from the work of the Holy Spirit because the grace of the Holy Spirit enables her to act in accord with God's wisdom.

104. In his *Protestants, Catholics, and Mary*, Stephen Benko proposes "self-emptying or *kenosis*" (141) as an ecumenical principle of Mariology: "In the kenosis theology is the essence of Mariology" (144). He draws quite different conclusions than Bouyer, however.

105. For a similar view see Semmelroth, *Mary, Archetype of the Church*, 166: "The material world's completed redeemed state must also shine forth in Mary as Archetype of the Church. The essential point of view by which Mary is seen as the Type of the Church is as follows: Mary typifies the essence of the

Church, a community of men and the Mystical Body of Christ, in whom the Divine Life of Christ dwells. This life is to be given to everyone who has been incorporated into this Body as a living member. The Church has performed her receptive co-redemption in Mary, her representative. It is in Mary that the Church has fully received her Redemption."

106. Bouyer, *The Seat of Wisdom,* 203.

107. Ibid., 204.

108. Joseph Ratzinger, *Eschatology: Death and Eternal Life,* trans. Michael Waldstein and Aidan Nichols, O.P., 2nd ed. (Washington, D.C.: Catholic University of America Press, 2007), 107. In his essay "Between Death and Resurrection: Some Supplementary Reflections," included as Appendix I in his *Eschatology* (241–60), Ratzinger notes that Ernst Troeltsch and Karl Barth sought to overcome the apparent difficulty regarding Jesus' imminent eschatology by holding to "the complete incommensurability of time and eternity. The person who dies steps outside time. He enters upon the 'end of the world,' which is not the final day of the cosmic calendar but is, rather, something alien to the diurnal round of this world's time. . . . The end of time, as time's boundary, is not only very close but reaches into time's very midst" (251–52). On this topic see also Joseph Ratzinger, "The End of Time," in *The End of Time? The Provocation of Talking about God,* ed. Tiemo Rainer Peters and Claus Urban, trans. and ed. J. Matthew Ashley (New York: Paulist Press, 2004), 4–25. For discussion of Ratzinger's view of time, see Gerhard Nachtwei, *Dialogische Unsterblichkeit* (Leipzig: St. Benno, 1986); and Ferdinand Schumacher, "Ich Glaube an die Auferstehung der Toten: Das Ende der Zeit in der Theologie Joseph Ratzingers," in *Der Theologe Joseph Ratzinger,* ed. Frank Meier-Hamidi and Ferdinand Schumacher (Basel: Herder, 2007), 73–99.

109. Ratzinger, *Eschatology,* 108. For discussion of Rahner and Ratzinger on this point, see Dulles, "The Dogma of the Assumption," in Anderson, Stafford, and Burgess, *The One Mediator, the Saints, and Mary: Lutherans and Catholics in Dialogue VIII,* 279–94, at 292–93.

110. Ratzinger, *Eschatology,* 109. See Christian Tapp, "Joseph Ratzinger on Resurrection Identity," in *Personal Identity and Resurrection: How Do We Survive Our Death?,* ed. George Gasser (Burlington, VT: Ashgate, 2010), 207–24.

111. Ratzinger, *Eschatology,* 109.

112. For exegetical support of this position, see Wright, *Surprised by Hope*; James D. G. Dunn, *The Theology of Paul the Apostle* (Grand Rapids, MI: Eerdmans, 1998), 489; and Andrew T. Lincoln, *Paradise Now and Not Yet: Studies in the Role of the Heavenly Dimension in Paul's Thought with Special Reference to His Eschatology* (Cambridge: Cambridge University Press, 1981), 69.

113. Congregation for the Doctrine of the Faith, "Letter on Certain Questions Regarding Eschatology," *Acta Apostolicae Sedis* 71 (1979): 939–43. This document appeared two years before Ratzinger himself became prefect of the Congregation. Ratzinger comments on the Congregation's Letter in his

"Between Death and Resurrection: Some Supplementary Reflections," included as Appendix I in his *Eschatology*. In the intermediate state, according to both the Congregation's Letter and Ratzinger, the dead live with Christ (cf. Phil 1:23, 2 Cor 5:8, Rev 6:9–11) and await the bodily resurrection and the final judgment that will come at the end of history. As Ratzinger puts it, "a 'resurrection' which concerns neither matter nor the concrete historical world is no resurrection at all" (Ratzinger, "Between Death and Resurrection," in *Eschatology*, 253). See also, for the same point, Ratzinger's "Afterword to the English Edition," written in 1987 and included as Appendix II in his *Eschatology*, 261–74. For further discussion see the International Theological Commission's 1992 document "Some Current Questions in Eschatology," published in *Irish Theological Quarterly* 58 (1992): 209–43.

114. Ratzinger, *Daughter Zion*. The theme of Daughter Zion is also central to the work of de la Potterie, *Mary in the Mystery of the Covenant*, and Deiss, *Mary, Daughter of Sion*.

115. Ratzinger, *Daughter Zion*, 9.

116. Ibid., 12. For discussion of Ratzinger's approach see de Gaál, *The Theology of Pope Benedict XVI*, 288–96; and Aidan Nichols, O.P., *The Thought of Pope Benedict XVI: An Introduction to the Theology of Joseph Ratzinger*, 2nd ed. (London: Continuum, 2007), 143–44.

117. Ratzinger, *Daughter Zion*, 16.

118. Ibid., 18. See also St. Gregory Palamas, *Mary the Mother of God: Sermons by Saint Gregory Palamas*, ed. Christopher Veniamin (South Canaan, PA: Mount Thabor, 2005), 73.

119. Ratzinger, *Daughter Zion*, 23–24.

120. Ibid., 27. See also Joseph Ratzinger, "'Hail, Full of Grace': Elements of Marian Piety According to the Bible," in Ratzinger and Balthasar, *Mary: The Church at the Source*, 61–79, at 69:

> When man's relation to God, the soul's open availability for him, is characterized as "faith", this word expresses the fact that the infinite distance between Creator and creature is not blurred in the relation of the human I to the divine Thou. It means that the model of "partnership", which has become so dear to us, breaks down when it comes to God, because it cannot sufficiently express the majesty of God and the hiddenness of his working. It is precisely the man who has been opened up entirely into God who comes to accept God's otherness and the hiddenness of his will, which can pierce our will like a sword. The parallel between Mary and Abraham begins in the joy of the promised son but continues apace until the dark hour when she must ascend Mount Moriah, that is, until the Crucifixion of Christ. Yet it does not end there; it also extends to the miracle of Isaac's rescue—the Resurrection of Jesus Christ.

121. Ratzinger, *Daughter Zion*, 32.

122. For further comparison of John the Baptist and Mary, see Yves Congar, O.P., *Christ, Our Lady and the Church: A Study in Eirenic Theology*, trans. Henry St. John, O.P. (London: Longmans, Green, 1957), 14.

123. Ratzinger, *Daughter Zion*, 62.

124. See also Joseph Ratzinger, "'Et Incarnatus Est de Spiritu Sancto ex Maria Virgine,'" in Ratzinger and Balthasar, *Mary: The Church at the Source*, 81–95, at 89–90.

125. Ratzinger, *Daughter Zion*, 68.

126. Ibid., 70.

127. Ibid., 72. See Laurentin, *A Short Treatise on the Virgin Mary*, 248. Ratzinger's book frequently draws upon Laurentin's work.

128. Ratzinger, *Daughter Zion*, 78.

129. Ibid., 79.

130. See also Montague, "Eschatology and Our Lady," 65–83. For the Pauline framework that Ratzinger employs here, see also the Anglican-Roman Catholic International Commission's statement *Mary: Grace and Hope in Christ. The Seattle Statement of the Anglican-Roman Catholic International Commission: The Text with Commentaries and Study Guide*, ed. Donald Bolen and Gregory Cameron (New York: Continuum, 2006).

131. Ratzinger, *Daughter Zion*, 81.

132. See also Joseph Ratzinger, "'Hail, Full of Grace,'" in Ratzinger and Balthasar, *Mary: The Church at the Source*, 62–66; in the same volume Ratzinger, "'Et Incarnatus Est de Spiritu Sancto ex Maria Virgine,'" 87–88, 93–94. On Mary as the new ark of the covenant, see also John Saward, *Redeemer in the Womb: Jesus Living in Mary* (San Francisco: Ignatius Press, 1993), 27–31, 125–27.

Chapter 4
The Validity and Scope of Typological Exegesis

1. See Newman, *An Essay on the Development of Christian Doctrine*, 346. On this point see also Frances Young, "Exegetical Method and Scriptural Proof: The Bible in Doctrinal Debate," *Studia Patristica* 19 (1989): 291–304. Jean Daniélou concludes that "typology is an intrinsic element of Christian doctrine. It stems from the apostolic teaching; the New Testament is full of it; it was the basis of all sound scriptural interpretation in Patristic times; and it is freely used in the Christian liturgy" (Daniélou, "Symbolism and History," 130–46, at 141).

2. For a definition of typology as distinct from allegory (cf. Gal 4:21–31), see Griffiths, *Song of Songs*, lvii. For further discussions of biblical typology, see—in addition to works cited in chapter 1, note 29—Kevin J. Vanhoozer, "Ascending the Mountain, Singing the Rock: Biblical Interpretation Earthed, Typed, and Transfigured," *Modern Theology* 28 (2012): 781–803; Benjamin J.

Ribbens, "Typology of Types: Typology in Dialogue," *Journal of Theological Interpretation* 5 (2011): 81–96; Karl-Heinrich Ostmeyer, "Typologie und Typos: Analyse eines schwierigen Verhältnisses," *New Testament Studies* 46 (2000): 112–31; Frances Young, "Typology," in *Crossing the Boundaries: Essays in Biblical Interpretation in Honour of Michael D. Goulder*, ed. Stanley E. Porter, Paul Joyce, and David E. Orton (New York: E. J. Brill, 1994), 29–48; P. Joseph Cahill, "Hermeneutical Implications of Typology," *Catholic Biblical Quarterly* 44 (1982): 266–81; Leonhard Goppelt, *Typos: The Typological Interpretation of the Old Testament in the New*, trans. D. H. Madvig (Grand Rapids, MI: Eerdmans, 1982 [orig. English ed. 1939]); G. W. H. Lampe and K. J. Woollcombe, *Essays on Typology* (Naperville, IL: Alec R. Allenson, 1957); E. Earle Ellis, *Paul's Use of the Old Testament* (Edinburgh: Oliver and Boyd, 1957), 126–35; Erich Auerbach, "'Figura,'" trans. Ralph Manheim, in *Scenes from the Drama of European Literature: Six Essays* (Gloucester, MA: Peter Smith, 1973), 11–76, especially 49–60; and Gerhard von Rad, *Old Testament Theology*, vol. 2, trans. D. M. G. Stalker (New York: Harper & Row, 1965), 319–429. See also the criticisms mounted by James Barr, *Old and New in Interpretation: A Study of the Two Testaments* (New York: Harper & Row, 1966), chap. 4. Richard B. Hays argues that neither typology nor other categories such as midrash or allegory do justice to the scope of Paul's exegesis. In Hays's view, Paul's reading of Scripture generally relies on dialectical intertextuality. See Hays, *Echoes of the Scripture in the Letters of Paul* (New Haven, CT: Yale University Press, 1989), 173–78. For my purposes, the term "typology" can suffice, since there is no need to limit it in the way that Hays (sensitive to the meaning that "typology" had taken on within Protestant scholarship) does.

3. Newman, *An Essay on the Development of Christian Doctrine*, 343.

4. See ibid., 339.

5. Ibid., 342–43.

6. John Henry Newman, *A Letter Addressed to the Rev. E. B. Pusey, DD on Occasion of His Eirenicon: Certain Difficulties Felt by Anglicans in Catholic Teaching* (1866), in *Mary: The Virgin Mary in the Life and Writings of John Henry Newman*, 241–42. On Newman's Mariology see, e.g., Charles Stephen Dessain, "Cardinal Newman's Teaching about the Blessed Virgin Mary," in Stacpoole, *Mary's Place in Christian Dialogue*, 232–47; John T. Ford, C.S.C., "Newman on 'Sensus Fidelium' and Mariology," *Marian Studies* 28 (1977): 120–45; Francis J. Friedel, *The Mariology of Cardinal Newman* (New York: Benziger, 1929); and John J. Wright, "Mariology in the English-Speaking World," in *Mary Our Hope: A Selection from the Sermons, Addresses, and Papers of Cardinal John J. Wright*, ed. R. Stephen Almagno, O.F.M. (San Francisco: Ignatius Press, 1984), 47–64. See also, for the Mariology of the Oxford Movement, A. M. Allchin, *The Joy of All Creation: An Anglican Meditation on the Place of Mary* (London: Darton, Longman & Todd, 1984), 101–15.

7. Newman, *An Essay on the Development of Christian Doctrine*, 416. See also John D. Dadosky's defense of this allegorical meaning in light of René Girard's theory of envy and mimetic rivalry: Dadosky, "Woman without Envy," 15–40, at 39–40.

8. For further discussion, see my *Participatory Biblical Exegesis: A Theology of Biblical Interpretation* (Notre Dame: University of Notre Dame Press, 2008).

9. Richard B. Hays, *First Corinthians* (Louisville, KY: John Knox Press, 1997), 173; cf. Hays's "The Conversion of the Imagination: Scripture and Eschatology in 1 Corinthians," in *The Conversion of the Imagination: Paul as Interpreter of Israel's Scripture* (Grand Rapids, MI: Eerdmans, 2005), 1–24. See also the moving evocation of the power of typological reading to draw readers into the biblical story in G. W. H. Lampe, "The Reasonableness of Typology," in Lampe and Woollcombe, *Essays on Typology*, 9–38, at 9–14.

10. Hays, *First Corinthians*, 160.

11. Ibid.

12. Ibid., 161. Frances Young similarly dissociates typological reasoning from historical claims. She argues that typology "does not simply operate in the linear-eschatological time-frame, nor in defining it should we be tempted to bring back the historicity of the event. . . . Typology belongs to the literary phenomenon of intertextuality, to the genre of liturgy and sacred story. The sacred text is no mere pretext for something else, as in allegory: rather story and symbol carry a surplus of significance" (Young, "Typology," in Porter, Joyce, and Orton, *Crossing the Boundaries*, 48). She concludes that history is not "the appropriate measure for identifying typology" (ibid.). I would agree that typological reasoning is liturgical and evokes "a surplus of significance," but it does not follow that typological reasoning must necessarily, in each case, be opposed to "the historicity of the event" (unless by "history" one means solely what can be reconstructed by modern historiography). In this regard, see for example Thomas Aquinas's insistence that allegory and typology be regulated by Scripture's literal sense, as set forth by Olivier-Thomas Venard, O.P., *Pagina sacra: Le passage de l'Écriture sainte à l'écriture théologique* (Paris: Cerf, 2009), 419–20. For Young's perspective, see also Frances Young, "Allegory and the Ethics of Reading," in *The Open Text: New Directions for Biblical Studies?*, ed. Francis Watson (London: SCM Press, 1993), 103–20; and Frances Young, *The Art of Performance: Towards a Theology of Holy Scripture* (London: Darton, Longman & Todd, 1993).

13. For this connection see also Michael Schneider, "How Does God Act? Intertextual Readings of 1 Corinthians 10," in Hays, Alkier, and Huizenga, *Reading the Bible Intertextually*, 35–52, at 48–49.

14. Hays, *First Corinthians*, 173. See also James W. Aageson's effort to understand Paul's scriptural interpretation (and ours) as "an interaction, similar to

a dialogue, between text and interpreter." Aageson, *Written Also for Our Sake: Paul and the Art of Biblical Interpretation* (Louisville, KY: Westminster/John Knox Press, 1993), 8. For Aageson, however, "This does not mean that modern biblical hermeneutics can or should try to repristinate Pauline methodology. Our context is different. Our sense of appropriate and acceptable interpretation is different. The state of our knowledge and our traditions of interpretation are not those of Paul's day" (ibid., 5). In certain ways, Hays could clearly agree with this: he is involved actively in exegetical conversations whose form and practices are quite different from those of Paul. But Hays seems nonetheless to have less fear of committing a "hermeneutical anachronism." Commenting on Galatians 4:21–31, Aageson observes: "Allegory as a form of conversation with the biblical text has a long tradition in the history of biblical interpretation but, once again, in most contexts in which scripture is used today allegory is thought to be an inadequate form of conversation. It clearly is a method of engaging the text, but a method that in most cases does not fit within modern 'circles of plausibility'" (ibid., 53). He does not seem to consider this unfortunate.

15. Hays, *First Corinthians*, 173.

16. Ibid., 162.

17. Ibid., 151.

18. See Gregory of Nyssa, *The Life of Moses*, trans. Abraham J. Malherbe and Everett Ferguson (New York: Paulist Press, 1978), 82–92.

19. Hays, *First Corinthians*, 160.

20. Ibid., 167.

21. Ibid.

22. Ibid., 168.

23. Hays is much more appreciative of sacramental participation in Christ in his "What Is 'Real Participation in Christ'? A Dialogue with E. P. Sanders on Pauline Soteriology," in *Redefining First-Century Jewish and Christian Identities: Essays in Honor of Ed Parish Sanders*, ed. Fabian E. Udoh et al. (Notre Dame: University of Notre Dame Press, 2008), 336–51. He states, for example:

> An analysis, then, of real participation in Christ in Paul's letters should find anchor points not only in Paul's portrayal of the church as the body of Christ (1 Cor 12:12–31; see Rom 12:4–8) but also in texts such as Rom 6:3–11, where Paul speaks of being "baptized into Christ Jesus," and Gal 3:27–29, where he links baptism with being clothed in Christ, belonging to Christ, and living in a community that anticipates the eschatological transcendence of the fleshly distinctions that divide us. Such an analysis of real participation would probe in depth the meaning of a communal meal in which, as the story of Jesus' death is told again and again, these words are spoken: "This is my body, which is for you," and "This cup is the new covenant in my blood" (1 Cor 11:23–26). By receiving these sacramental elements, members of the community concretely experience participation in Christ. (ibid., 345)

24. Hays, *Echoes of the Scripture in the Letters of Paul*, 91.

25. Ibid.

26. Ibid.

27. Ibid.

28. Ibid.

29. Ibid.

30. Ibid., 95.

31. Ibid., 96.

32. Ibid., 97.

33. Ibid., 100–101.

34. Ibid., 154.

35. Ibid., 155.

36. Ibid.

37. Hays draws on the work of Michael Fishbane. See especially Fishbane, *Biblical Interpretation in Ancient Israel*. For intertextual (and typological) connections in the New Testament, see Rikk E. Watts, *Isaiah's New Exodus in Mark* (Grand Rapids, MI: Baker Academic, 1997); Joel Marcus, *The Way of the Lord: Christological Exegesis of the Old Testament in the Gospel of Mark* (Louisville, KY: Westminster/John Knox Press, 1992); and Mary Ann Beavis, "The Resurrection of Jephthah's Daughter: Judges 11:34–40 and Mark 5:21–24, 35–43," *Catholic Biblical Quarterly* 72 (2010): 46–62.

38. Hays, *Echoes of the Scripture in the Letters of Paul*, 159.

39. Ibid., 160.

40. Ibid., 161.

41. Ibid.

42. Ibid., 164.

43. Ibid., 170.

44. Ibid., 178.

45. Ibid., 181.

46. Ibid., 187. As an example, he reads Romans 9:6–9 in the context of the allegory in Galatians 4:21–31. This reading is not exactly typological, but it does extend Paul's mode of thought through intertextual echoes.

47. Ibid., 191.

48. Ibid., 183; cf. 191–92.

49. Ibid., 183.

50. Ibid., 186. Cf. Patricia Cox, "Origen and the Witch of Endor: Toward an Iconoclastic Typology," *Anglican Theological Review* 66 (1984): 137–47.

51. Hays, *Echoes of the Scripture in the Letters of Paul*, 190.

52. Richard N. Longenecker, "Preface to the Second Edition," in *Biblical Exegesis in the Apostolic Period*, 2nd ed. (Grand Rapids, MI: Eerdmans, 1999), xiii–xli, at xxxiv. From a different perspective, but with a similar result, see Friedrich Baumgärtel, "The Hermeneutical Problem of the Old Testament,"

trans. Murray Newman, in *Essays on Old Testament Hermeneutics*, ed. Claus Westermann (Richmond, VA: John Knox Press, 1964), 134–59, at 143–44:

> The other principle of understanding in the New Testament is *typological re-presentation* of the Old Testament witness. Re-presentation in this sense means that the type has happened *for us* and is written *for us*. The *parakalein* is included in the type: written for us, warning for us, comfort for us. This New Testament manner of realization of the Old Testament Word is therefore no longer possible for us today, because our contemporary historical thinking demands of us—for the sake of truth as it confronts the historical thinker—that the literal meaning of the Old Testament witness be "understood." It must, therefore, be *the literal meaning* which has power for us today and not a meaning interpolated into the witness. . . . For us today the type lacks the power to achieve a re-presentation. The New Testament was able to achieve such a re-presentation in its recital of the type, for it did not see the Old Testament as a historically conditioned witness (today we cannot at all see it otherwise!) but as the inspired Word of God in a formal sense (which it can no longer be for us today). Because they are conditioned historically, the New Testament's methods of understanding cannot be accepted by contemporary theological thinkers.

53. Peter Enns, *Inspiration and Incarnation: Evangelicals and the Problem of the Old Testament* (Grand Rapids, MI: Baker Academic, 2005), 47; cf. 17, 21. See also my "The Inspiration of Scripture: A *Status Quaestionis*," *Letter and Spirit* 6 (2010): 281–314, at 290–91.

54. For concerns about this analogy, see Lewis Ayres and Stephen E. Fowl, "(Mis)reading the Face of God: *The Interpretation of the Bible in the Church*," *Theological Studies* 60 (1999): 513–28.

55. For related discussion of accommodation, including its role in the Fathers, see Kenton L. Sparks, *God's Word in Human Words: An Evangelical Appropriation of Critical Biblical Scholarship* (Grand Rapids, MI: Baker Academic, 2008), 229–59. See also Nicholas Wolterstorff, *Divine Discourse: Philosophical Reflections on the Claim That God Speaks* (Cambridge: Cambridge University Press, 1995), 206–12. G. K. Beale offers an extended critique of Enns's position in Beale, *The Erosion of Inerrancy in Evangelicalism* (Wheaton, IL: Crossway Books, 2008), especially 25–122. For further criticism see D. A. Carson's review essay on John Webster's *Holy Scripture*, N. T. Wright's *The Last Word*, and Peter Enns's *Inspiration and Incarnation*: Carson, "Three More Books on the Bible: A Critical Review," *Trinity Journal* 27 (2006): 1–62.

56. Enns, *Inspiration and Incarnation*, 110.

57. Ibid., 114.

58. Ibid., 116.

59. Ibid. (emphasis his).

60. Ibid., 120. Moving behind the biblical text, Anthony Le Donne explores how "certain typological interpretations were applied to early memories of Jesus and thus give a window into historical memory" (Le Donne, *The Historiographical Jesus*, 92; cf. 267–68). As Le Donne recognizes, "typological localization" can lead to what he calls "distortion by narrativization," that is to say distortion of a particular event by tying it too closely to a standard type (ibid., 77). Yet, as he says, typology functions already within our remembering of events: types often shape our memories rather than being imposed upon nontypological memories. Memory, history, and typology thus cannot be separated. I would add that although types may distort, they may also be true—especially given a providential understanding of history.

61. James L. Kugel gives numerous examples of this mode of interpretation. Discussing the tower of Babel, for instance, he shows how various Jewish and Christian interpreters (including Philo, 3 Baruch, Targum Neophyti, Ephraem, Josephus, Tibat Marqa, Jerome, and Augustine) came to suppose that Nimrod built the tower in open rebellion against God. Paul joins such sources as Pseudo-Philo and Tosefta *Sukkah* 3:11 in describing a traveling rock in 1 Corinthians 10:4. See James L. Kugel, *The Bible As It Was* (Cambridge, MA: Harvard University Press, 1997), 123–27, 363. See also Kugel, *How to Read the Bible*; and Jacob Neusner, *Performing Israel's Faith: Narrative and Law in Rabbinic Theology* (Waco, TX: Baylor University Press, 2005). By contrast, indebted to Harold Bloom's theory of the "anxiety of influence," Herbert Marks claims that "Paul's subordination of the Jewish scriptures to their 'spiritual' understanding is a paradigmatic instance of revisionary power realized in the process of overcoming a tyranny of predecession. In historical terms, this approach leads to conclusions that might be characterized vaguely as Marcionite." Marks, "Pauline Typology and Revisionary Criticism," *Journal of the American Academy of Religion* 52 (1984): 71–92, at 72. Marks goes on to speculate that typological exegesis "played an initiatory or constitutive rather than a merely expository role in the New Testament's evolution," and he considers that Paul's typological exegesis means that "the content of the gospel is never fixed" so long as interpreters imitate Paul (ibid., 74, 88). Marks's argument about Paul's revisionary and quasi-Marcionite (because prophetic) reading of Scripture hinges largely upon his rejection of Paul's eschatological claims. Hays responds to Marks in *Echoes of the Scripture in the Letters of Paul*, 95–102, 156–60.

62. Enns, *Inspiration and Incarnation*, 133.

63. Cf. Steve McKenzie, "Exodus Typology in Hosea," *Restoration Quarterly* 22 (1979): 100–108.

64. Enns, *Inspiration and Incarnation*, 134.

65. Ibid., 136.

66. Ibid., 138.

67. For a careful survey of this interpretive rendering of original texts in Paul and his Greco-Roman contemporaries, see Christopher D. Stanley, *Paul*

and the Language of Scripture: Citation Technique in the Pauline Epistles and Contemporary Literature (Cambridge: Cambridge University Press, 1992).

68. See also the reflections of Aageson, *Written Also for Our Sake*, 121–25; and Ellis, *Paul's Use of the Old Testament*, 66–70.

69. Enns, *Inspiration and Incarnation*, 153.

70. Ibid., 154.

71. For a similar approach to the Old Testament see Walther Eichrodt, "Is Typological Exegesis an Appropriate Method?," trans. James Barr, in Westermann, *Essays on Old Testament Hermeneutics*, 224–45. After discussing various viewpoints on biblical typology, including those of Gerhard von Rad and Friedrich Baumgärtel, Eichrodt concludes: "Probably we need to emphasize still more strongly the decisive significance of the people of God in both Testaments in its vocation to living fellowship with God, and to characterize exegesis as something that proceeds from the analogy of faith or the analogy of communication. However this may be, typology will play only an ancillary part in it, but within this ancillary position will not be unworthy of appropriate exegesis" (ibid., 245).

72. Enns, *Inspiration and Incarnation*, 155.

73. Ibid.

74. Ibid., 158.

75. Ibid., 159.

76. See also Barr, *Old and New in Interpretation*, 139; and Christopher Seitz, *The Character of Christian Scripture: The Significance of a Two-Testament Bible* (Grand Rapids, MI: Baker Academic, 2011), 23–24.

77. Enns, *Inspiration and Incarnation*, 160.

78. Ibid., 161.

79. Ibid., 162.

80. Ibid., 163.

81. Ibid., 157.

82. See Peter J. Leithart, *Deep Exegesis: The Mystery of Reading Scripture* (Waco, TX: Baylor University Press, 2009). As Joseph Cahill says (from a different theological perspective): "The most evident hermeneutical implications of biblical typology are its interpretative assumptions. These center on the nature of history, the human mind, and the capacities of one committed to a biblical tradition to participate in human history" (Cahill, "Hermeneutical Implications of Typology," 275).

83. Leithart, *Deep Exegesis*, 22.

84. See Immanuel Kant, *Religion within the Limits of Reason Alone*, trans. Theodore M. Greene and Hoyt H. Hudson (New York: Harper & Row, 1960).

85. Leithart, *Deep Exegesis*, 29.

86. Joseph Ratzinger holds a view that might seem similar to the husk/kernel approach, but arguably differs (although perhaps not in a way that would satisfy Leithart) because of its Christological realism: "As Christians we read

Holy Scripture with Christ. He is our guide all the way through it. He indicates to us in reliable fashion what an image is and where the real, enduring content of a biblical expression may be found. At the same time he is freedom from a false slavery to literalism and a guarantee of the solid, realistic truth of the Bible, which does not dissipate into a cloud of pious pleasantries but remains the sure ground upon which we can stand." Ratzinger, *'In the Beginning . . .' A Catholic Understanding of the Story of Creation and the Fall*, trans. Boniface Ramsey, O.P. (Huntington, IN: Our Sunday Visitor, 1990), 34. That there has to be some kind of husk/kernel distinction appears in Ratzinger's treatment of Jesus' interpretation of the Mosaic law: "Only God himself could reinterpret the law from the ground up as Jesus did; only God himself could show that the transformation and preservation that opened up the law had been the true intention of the law all along." Ratzinger, "Jesus of Nazareth, Israel and Christianity: Their Relation and Their Mission according to the *Catechism of the Catholic Church*," in *Gospel, Catechesis, Catechism: Sidelights on the* Catechism of the Catholic Church (San Francisco: Ignatius Press, 1997), 73–97, at 90. To speak of "transformation and preservation" is to make some distinction between an enduring reality and a reality that does not endure; but the latter are not mere husks that can be simply discarded, as Kant and Hegel supposed. The historical form of the "real, enduring content of a biblical expression" cannot be simply tossed aside. See also Joseph Ratzinger, "Biblical Interpretation in Conflict: On the Foundations and the Itinerary of Exegesis Today," trans. Adrian Walker, in *Opening Up the Scriptures: Joseph Ratzinger and the Foundations of Biblical Interpretation*, ed. José Granados, Carlos Granados, and Luis Sánchez-Navarro (Grand Rapids, MI: Eerdmans, 2008), 1–29. For further insight see Augustine's *Answer to Faustus, a Manichean*, trans. Roland Teske, S.J. (Hyde Park, NY: New City Press, 2007).

87. Leithart, *Deep Exegesis*, 34.

88. For further discussion see Ben Witherington III, *Grace in Galatia: A Commentary on St Paul's Letter to the Galatians* (Grand Rapids, MI: Eerdmans, 1998), 321–40; and Hays, *Echoes of the Scripture in the Letters of Paul*, 111–21.

89. Leithart, *Deep Exegesis*, 37. See Enns, *Inspiration and Incarnation*, 115.

90. See Steve Moyise, *Paul and Scripture* (Grand Rapids, MI: Baker Academic, 2010), 41–43, 51–52; and Patrick G. Barker, "Allegory and Typology in Galatians 4:21–31," *St Vladimir's Theological Quarterly* 38 (1994): 193–209. Regarding allegory and typology, Barker finds that Paul uses both and that "these two procedures, far from being irreconcilable opposites, are in fact most effective when used jointly" (ibid., 209).

91. Leithart, *Deep Exegesis*, 38.

92. Although Leithart's perspective differs from Gerhard von Rad's, one might compare Leithart's view at this juncture with von Rad's remark in his "Typological Interpretation of the Old Testament," trans. John Bright, in Westermann, *Essays on Old Testament Hermeneutics*, 17–39, at 17: "[T]ypological thinking is an elementary function of all human thought and interpretation."

For von Rad, Old Testament typology has to do with "the eschatological corre-spondence between beginning and end" (ibid., 19), without undermining the linear (rather than cyclic) progression of history. The New Testament continues this typological reasoning, which von Rad distances from allegory. Von Rad adds a plea for the return of typology, which he considers to have been wrongly marginalized by J. D. Michaelis's *Entwurf der typischen Gottesgelahrtheit* (1755), a book that concerned itself not with events but "with 'the religious truths' sym-bolically enshrined in the Old Testament" (ibid., 22). On von Rad's view of ty-pology see Barr, *Old and New in Interpretation*, 111–12, 137.

93. Leithart, *Deep Exegesis*, 65.

94. Ibid. See also John Sailhamer, "Hosea 11:1 and Matthew 2:15," *West-minster Theological Journal* 63 (2001): 87–96. Dan G. McCartney and Peter Enns respond in the same issue of *Westminster Theological Journal*: "Matthew and Hosea: A Response to John Sailhamer," 97–105.

95. Leithart, *Deep Exegesis*, 173.

96. Ibid., 174.

97. For earlier typological readings of John, see Robert Houston Smith, "Exodus Typology in the Fourth Gospel," *Journal of Biblical Literature* 81 (1962): 329–42.

98. Leithart, *Deep Exegesis*, 207. For discussion see especially Henri de Lubac, S.J., *Exégèse médiévale: Les quatre sens de l'écriture*, three volumes of which have appeared in English translation as *Medieval Exegesis: The Four Senses of Scripture*, trans. Mark Sebanc (vol. 1) and E. M. Macierowski (vols. 2–3) (Grand Rapids, MI: Eerdmans, 1998–2009).

99. Leithart, *Deep Exegesis*, 207.

100. For Leithart's ecclesiology, see especially Peter J. Leithart, *The Priest-hood of the Plebs: A Theology of Baptism* (Eugene, OR: Wipf and Stock, 2003); and Peter J. Leithart, *Defending Constantine: The Twilight of an Empire and the Dawn of Christendom* (Downers Grove, IL: IVP Academic, 2010).

101. Michael D. Goulder argues that the biblical authors' typological rea-soning necessarily mired them in mythmaking: "St Matthew believed that things for which he had no evidence and which were in fact untrue, came to pass that it might be fulfilled which was spoken by the prophets. St Luke be-lieved this too, but he was not content to write about them in two or three lines as did his predecessor. And as he wrote, his method made plain to him subcon-sciously that he was selecting, taking a sentence from this type and a phrase from that, writing an account of an ideal incident, the birth, or the ascension of the Saviour, or the coming of his Spirit. And it was in this gift that he excelled. It is the myths of St Luke which dominate the Christian calendar." Goulder, *Type and History in Acts* (London: SPCK, 1964), 205. Goulder grants that "[i]t is when we find the typologies strewn more thickly that we run into difficulties. We can never be certain that type and fact did not coincide for any particular

incident or detail. . . . But, on the other hand, it is not our experience that history does fulfil type in every detail, and we know that the early Christians were prepared to believe that Old Testament types had been fulfilled without adequate evidence" (ibid., 181). Goulder's arguments are reminiscent of the standard arguments against biblical miracles.

102. Le Donne, *The Historiographical Jesus*, 136.

103. Stanley Gundry, "Typology as a Means of Interpretation: Past and Present," *Journal of the Evangelical Theological Society* 12 (1969): 233–40, at 235. For further cautions, see Ellis, *Paul's Use of the Old Testament*, 134; W. Edward Glenny, "Typology: A Summary of the Present Evangelical Discussion," *Journal of the Evangelical Theological Society* 40 (1997): 627–38; and Everett Ferguson, "The Typology of Baptism in the Early Church," *Restoration Quarterly* 8 (1965): 41–52, at 52.

104. For my use of typology and allegory, see my *Ezra and Nehemiah* (Grand Rapids, MI: Brazos Press, 2007).

105. Thus, without entertaining the notion of Mary's Assumption, Enns argues that we share in the apostles' encounter with the risen Christ within "the witness of the church through time"—where the "church" means both "congregation, denomination, or larger tradition" and more broadly "a global reality," dependent in all cases on "the direct involvement of the Spirit of God" (Enns, *Inspiration and Incarnation*, 162). The truth of the Church's typological interpretation of the whole biblical portrait of Mary is not authorized or demonstrated by this or that text. Rather, it is ultimately authorized by the Holy Spirit who guides the Church's (liturgical) proclamation of divine revelation—and thus by the same Holy Spirit who inspired the New Testament authors in their typological interpretations of Israel's Scripture. Attention to typology and to the Holy Spirit's guidance does not introduce an extrinsic or eisegetical element into the interpretation of Scripture.

106. For discussion see, e.g., Flanagan, *The Theology of Mary*, 67.

Chapter 5
The Authority of the Church as Interpreter of Revelation

1. John Henry Newman, "The Glories of Mary for the Sake of Her Son," in Newman, *Mary: The Virgin Mary in the Life and Writings of John Henry Newman*, 129–48, at 145.

2. Thus the Church's authority as an interpreter of Revelation must not be reduced simply to moments in which the exercise of authority is most visible. Writing a century before the formal definition of the dogma of Mary's Assumption, Newman affirms its truth on the grounds of this broad understanding of the Church's "authority." See also Vladimir Lossky's understanding of "tradition" in his "Panagia," in Mascall, *The Mother of God*, 24–36, at 26–27.

3. This question assumes that the realities of salvation can be adequately, even if not fully, expressed in dogmatic formulations. Since dogmatic statements are made in the concepts available at particular historical periods, dogmatic statements can at times be clarified and deepened—though not in a way that negates their original meaning—by means of conceptual resources available to later periods. In his *The Survival of Dogma* (Garden City, NY: Doubleday, 1971), Avery Dulles, S.J., tries to strike a balance by affirming that on the one hand, "the concepts and propositions expressing the Church's faith should be constantly updated to keep pace with the growth of human consciousness under the impact of successive historical experiences," while on the other hand some concepts "enable one to achieve noetic insight into the realities to which they refer" (193). The latter aspect is crucial and should guide Dulles's discussion more than it does, as for example when he claims: "If formulated for the first time today, the definition of [papal] infallibility would probably sound very different. Perhaps even the word 'infallibility' would not be used" (198). This exaggerates the inadequacy of the concept "infallibility" for speaking about the power of teaching without error. For the balance that Dulles's book aims to achieve, see especially Charles Journet, *What Is Dogma?*, trans. Mark Pontifex, O.S.B. (San Francisco: Ignatius Press, 2011 [French ed. 1963]). See also (on the concept *homoousios*) Joseph Ratzinger, "Variations on the Theme of Faith, Religion, and Culture," in *Truth and Tolerance: Christian Belief and World Religions*, trans. Henry Taylor (San Francisco: Ignatius Press, 2004), 80–109, at 90–95. For the balanced approach characteristic of Dulles, see Dulles's "How Real Is the Real Presence?," in *Church and Society*, 455–67.

4. Steinmetz, "Mary Reconsiderzed," 45–51, at 51.

5. I treat this topic more extensively in my *Engaging the Doctrine of Revelation: The Mediation of the Gospel in Church and Scripture* (Grand Rapids, MI: Baker Academic, 2014).

6. David Seccombe, "Luke's Vision for the Church," in *A Vision for the Church: Studies in Early Christian Ecclesiology in Honour of J. P. M. Sweet*, ed. Markus Bockmuehl and Michael B. Thompson (Edinburgh: T & T Clark, 1997), 45–63, at 49. For the eschatological restoration/transformation of Israel brought about by Jesus' death, Resurrection, and sending of his Spirit, as well as for the resulting mission to the nations, see also Max Turner, *Power from on High: The Spirit in Israel's Restoration and Witness in Luke-Acts* (Sheffield: Sheffield Academic Press, 1996), especially chaps. 9–10 and 13; and David W. Pao, *Acts and the Isaianic New Exodus* (Grand Rapids, MI: Baker Academic, 2002). As the eschatological community, the Church does not simply reprise the same teaching authority already possessed by the people of Israel prior to Christ.

7. Seccombe, "Luke's Vision for the Church," 49. Seccombe remarks, "Part of the task of the shepherd-guardian is to resist all attempts to re-centre the faith of the Church anywhere but on Christ himself (Acts 20.28–30)" (ibid.). He

would likely fear that the Catholic and Orthodox teachings about Mary do this. Furthermore, Seccombe seems to suppose that the connection of teaching and priesthood in the patristic Church was the very opposite of what was the case in the earliest Church, where, in Seccombe's view, teaching was something any talented person could do.

8. Ibid., 55. Commenting on Acts 20:28, Seccombe adds, "The divine Son of God shed his blood to purchase a people for God whom he is gathering and assembling in his Father's presence" (ibid., 57). On the relationship between the Church and particular churches, see Rudolf Schnackenburg, *The Church in the New Testament*, trans. W. J. O'Hara (New York: Seabury Press, 1965), 144–47.

9. For Pelikan's later view of Mary, with a focus on her maternal mediation according to the Orthodox liturgy, see Jaroslav Pelikan, "*Most* Generations Shall Call Me Blessed: An Essay in Aid of a Grammar of Liturgy," in Braaten and Jenson, *Mary, Mother of God*, 1–18. See also Pelikan's *Mary Through the Centuries*. A development in Pelikan's viewpoint can be seen already in his introduction to Semmelroth, *Mary, Archetype of the Church*, vii–xiv. On Pelikan's theological journey see Robert Louis Wilken, "Jaroslav Pelikan and the Road to Orthodoxy," *Concordia Theological Quarterly* 74 (2010): 93–103.

10. For a similar perspective, see Heiko A. Oberman, "*Quo Vadis, Petre?* Tradition from Irenaeus to *Humani Generis*," in *The Dawn of the Reformation: Essays in Late Medieval and Early Reformation Thought* (Grand Rapids, MI: Eerdmans, 1992), 269–96. Oberman contrasts two views, which he terms Tradition I ("the single exegetical tradition of interpreted scripture") and Tradition II ("the two-sources theory which allows for an extra-biblical oral tradition") (ibid., 280). He describes the conquest of the latter, formalized in his view at the Council of Trent, as follows: "In theory the material sufficiency of Holy Scripture is upheld long after it has been given up in actuality. The key term of this development is the word 'implicit' and the history of this term is one of increasing loss in content. When then finally the two propositions—'Holy Scripture implicitly says' and 'Holy Scripture silently says'—are equated, the exegetical concept of Tradition I has fully developed into what we called Tradition II" (ibid., 281–82).

11. See Jaroslav Pelikan, *The Riddle of Roman Catholicism* (Nashville, TN: Abingdon Press, 1959), 82. On the relationship of Scripture and Tradition according to the Catholic Church, see the Second Vatican Council's Dogmatic Constitution on Divine Revelation, *Dei Verbum*. See also Congar, *Tradition and Traditions*; Congar, *The Meaning of Tradition*, trans. A. N. Woodrow (San Francisco: Ignatius Press, 2004); Paul Evdokimov, *Orthodoxy*, trans. Jeremy Hummerstone and Callan Slipper (Hyde Park, NY: New City Press, 2011 [orig. French ed. 1979]), 202–4; and Joseph Ratzinger, "The Question of the Concept of Tradition: A Provisional Response," in *God's Word: Scripture, Tradition, Office*, ed. Peter Hünermann and Thomas Söding, trans. Henry Taylor (San

Francisco: Ignatius Press, 2008), 41–89. For a Protestant perspective, requiring that the Bible be allowed to correct errors contained in Tradition, see Richard Bauckham, "Tradition in Relation to Scripture and Reason," in *Scripture, Tradition and Reason: A Study in the Criteria of Christian Doctrine*, ed. Richard Bauckham and Benjamin Drewery (Edinburgh: T & T Clark, 1988), 117–45. Note that Ratzinger grants that

> it is essential that, just as there is an office of watchman for the Church and for her inspired witness, so also there be an office of watchman for exegesis, which investigates the literal sense and thus preserves the connection with the *sarx* of the Logos against every kind of Gnosis. In that sense there is then something like an independence of Scripture, as a self-sufficient and in many respects unambiguous criterion vis-à-vis the teaching office of the Church. There is no doubt that Luther's insight was correct and that not enough space was accorded it in the Catholic Church because of the claims of the teaching office, whose inner limitations were not always perceived clearly enough. (Ratzinger, "The Question of the Concept of Tradition," in *God's Word*, 66)

12. Pelikan, *The Riddle of Roman Catholicism*, 83. The problem is certainly not one invented by Pelikan: see, for example, Ian Christopher Levy, *Holy Scripture and the Quest for Authority at the End of the Middle Ages* (Notre Dame, IN: University of Notre Dame Press, 2012).

13. Pelikan, *The Riddle of Roman Catholicism*, 83. See, for example, the Pastoral Letter of the German Lutheran Bishops, signed by Bishop Hans Meiser of Bavaria, translated in F. E. Mayer, "German Lutheran Bishops Denounce Rome's New Dogma," *Concordia Theological Monthly* 22 (1950): 144–46; and Robert McAfee Brown, *The Ecumenical Revolution* (London: Burns & Oates, 1969), 298. See also the statement composed by five Protestant theologians of the University of Heidelberg in the summer of 1950 in hopes of averting the definition: Edmund Schlink et al., "An Evangelical Opinion on the Proclamation of the Dogma of the Bodily Assumption of Mary," trans. by the journal editor, *Lutheran Quarterly* 3 (1951): 123–41. For a survey of critical Protestant responses, see Arthur Carl Piepkorn, "Mary's Place within the People of God according to Non-Roman-Catholics," *Marian Studies* 18 (1967): 46–83, at 60–66.

14. Pelikan, *The Riddle of Roman Catholicism*, 83.

15. Nonetheless, Pelikan's criticisms of Catholic ecclesiology are less harsh than those which one finds coming from some Catholic theologians, indebted not least to Ernst Troeltsch, in the decades after the Council. See for example Edward Schillebeeckx, O.P., *Church: The Human Story of God*, trans. John Bowden (New York: Crossroad, 1993); Roger Haight, S.J., *Christian Community in History*, vol. 1, *Historical Ecclesiology* (New York: Continuum, 2004); and Paul Lakeland, *The Liberation of the Laity: In Search of an Accountable Church* (New York: Continuum, 2003).

16. Martin Luther, "The Pagan Servitude of the Church," in *Martin Luther: Selections from His Writings*, ed. John Dillenberger (New York: Doubleday, 1962), 249–359, at 250. See also Eric W. Gritsch, "Lutheran Teaching Authority: Past and Present," in *Teaching Authority and Infallibility in the Church*, ed. Paul C. Empie, T. Austin Murphy, and Joseph A. Burgess, Lutherans and Catholics in Dialogue VI (Minneapolis, MN: Augsburg, 1980), 138–48.

17. Luther, "The Pagan Servitude of the Church," 250.

18. Martin Luther, "An Open Letter to Pope Leo X," in *Martin Luther*, 43–52, at 45.

19. Ibid., 50. John Calvin warns as a general principle that "it is unlawful to go beyond the simplicity of the Gospel," because Christ alone is our true teacher and his doctrine is perfect. See Calvin, *Institutes of the Christian Religion*, trans. Henry Beveridge (Grand Rapids, MI: Eerdmans, 1989), vol. 1, book 2, chap. 15, p. 427.

20. Luther, "An Open Letter to Pope Leo X," in *Martin Luther*, 51.

21. See Beth Kreitzer, *Reforming Mary: Changing Images of the Virgin Mary in Lutheran Sermons of the Sixteenth Century* (Oxford: Oxford University Press, 2004), 128; Lois Malcolm, "What Mary Has to Say about God's Bare Goodness," in Gaventa and Rigby, *Blessed One*, 131–44; O'Meara, *Mary in Protestant and Catholic Theology*, 112–25; and William J. Cole, S.M., "Was Luther a Devotee of Mary?," *Marian Studies* 21 (1970): 94–202. See also Eric W. Gritsch, "The Views of Luther and Lutheranism on the Veneration of Mary," in Anderson, Stafford, and Burgess, *The One Mediator, the Saints, and Mary*, 235–48. For late-medieval background to Luther's theology of Mary, see Heiko A. Oberman, *The Harvest of Medieval Theology: Gabriel Biel and Late Medieval Nominalism*, 3rd ed. (Grand Rapids, MI: Baker Academic, 2000), 281–322. Oberman discusses a representative, and embarrassing, sermon of Gabriel Biel on Mary's Assumption: "In one of his most fascinating Marian sermons Biel describes in detail and with great warmth Mary's arrival in heaven and reunion with her Son. In his welcoming speech Christ announces that he will share the kingdom of his father with her; of its two parts Christ will give his mother the responsibility for compassion. He himself will be responsible for justice and truth" (Oberman, *The Harvest of Medieval Theology*, 311). Although for Biel "Mary does not rule by power but by influence" (ibid.), and although this is by God's gift, nonetheless the result is aptly summed up by Oberman: "Christ becomes more and more the severe judge, almost identified with God the Father. The righteous God could not possibly hear the prayer of a sinner; what is needed is therefore a mediator with the mediator. From eternity God has provided one, thus erecting a new trinitarian hierarchy: the Virgin Mary hears the sinner, the Son hears his Mother, and the Father his Son" (ibid., 312).

22. Pelikan, *The Riddle of Roman Catholicism*, 92. Like the young Pelikan, the Reformed theologian Lukas Vischer extends this principle to Scripture as well: "Must we not take this consideration even a step further and ask whether

in certain areas the earliest church made flawed decisions? One thinks, for example, of its attitude toward slavery and toward the role of women in the church. Both themes are addressed directly in the New Testament. It is becoming increasingly clear today that the solutions of that age did not reflect the gospel's deepest spirit." Vischer, "Difficulties in Looking to the New Testament for Guidance," in *Unity of the Church in the New Testament and Today*, ed. Lukas Vischer, Ulrich Luz, and Christian Link, trans. James E. Crouch (Grand Rapids, MI: Eerdmans, 2010), 7–27, at 17. See also George Lindbeck, "The Reformation and the Infallibility Debate," in Empie, Murphy, and Burgess, *Teaching Authority and Infallibility in the Church*, 101–19.

23. Pelikan grants that the doctrine of Mary's Assumption need not be antiscriptural: "[W]hat is the basic difference between the assumption of Mary and the ideas about the ascension of Enoch and of Elijah that formed part of orthodox Protestant theology for centuries and still belong to the faith of many believers? If the latter have room within Protestantism, must a doctrine of the assumption of Mary be ruled out as not only unscriptural but antiscriptural?" (Pelikan, *The Riddle of Roman Catholicism*, 239). Lindbeck, too, considers that the doctrine of Mary's Assumption is not antiscriptural: see Lindbeck, "The Reformation and the Infallibility Debate," in Empie, Murphy, and Burgess, *Teaching Authority and Infallibility in the Church*, 117. For the same view see Alain Blancy, Maurice Jourjon, and the Dombes Group, *Mary in the Plan of God and in the Communion of Saints: Toward a Common Christian Understanding*, trans. Matthew J. O'Connell (New York: Paulist Press, 2002), 125–26. By contrast, Walter Künneth finds Mary's Assumption to be antiscriptural in his *Christus oder Maria? Ein evangelisches Wort zum Mariendogma* (Berlin: Wichern, 1950), 10. See also in this vein F. E. Mayer, "The Dogma of Mary's Assumption: A Symptom of Anti-Christian Theology," *Concordia Theological Monthly* 22 (1950): 181–89.

24. See Pelikan, *The Riddle of Roman Catholicism*, 21–33.

25. Ibid., 93.

26. See ibid., 93. Since Pelikan does not fully accept Luther's view of Scripture's authority, his preeminent models of mature Christians—at this early stage of his career—are Friedrich Schleiermacher and Paul Tillich: see ibid., 229–30.

27. The fundamental issue therefore could not be resolved by the structural changes proposed by the Ukrainian Catholic theologian Adam A. J. DeVille, whose laudable goal is unity between Orthodox and Catholics by means of the establishment of a "permanent ecumenical synod . . . as the means through which all the patriarchs together, under the presidency of the pope, could take responsibility for the unity of the one, holy, Catholic, apostolic, and Orthodox Church of Christ." DeVille, *Orthodoxy and the Roman Papacy: Ut Unum Sint and the Prospects of East-West Unity* (Notre Dame, IN: University of Notre Dame Press, 2011), 160.

28. Like the early Pelikan, Mark E. Powell argues that the problem is the claim to inerrant dogmatic teaching:

> [T]he Christian faith is too often viewed as an all-or-nothing affair where one either has the truth, or one is outside the truth. If we compare this notion, though, with how we view other cases of knowledge, it is apparent how misguided this view is. No one would claim that all of their general beliefs are true and that they hold no false beliefs. In fact, we regularly change our opinion and grow in our knowledge of the world. Such changes do not suggest that beforehand we were completely devoid of knowledge. Rather, growth in knowledge is viewed as a lifelong journey, and there is a confidence that much of what we believe is true. The same is true of the Christian faith. The church can be confident that the Holy Spirit has guided it, and that much of what we believe about the gospel is true. However, this does not mean that there will be no differences of opinion, or changes in our own beliefs. The Christian life too is a journey. God can and does work in spite of some false beliefs on our part to bring about God's primary goal, our spiritual transformation. (Powell, *Papal Infallibility: A Protestant Evaluation of an Ecumenical Issue* [Grand Rapids, MI: Eerdmans, 2009], 209)

In Powell's view, it follows that "papal infallibility wrongly assumes that epistemic certainty is not only required to secure doctrine, but also to maintain unity in the Church" (ibid., 210). I would respond that dogma primarily serves true worship and praise of God, which must be rooted in receptivity. It is the Church's worship, not merely the epistemic state of believers, that is at stake. This would be even clearer if Powell specified which doctrines he includes in his confidence that "much of what we believe about the gospel is true."

29. See John Henry Newman, "The Introduction of Rationalistic Principles into Revealed Religion," in *Essays Critical and Historical*, vol. 1 (London: Longmans, Green, 1895 [orig. ed. 1835]), 30–99; Newman, "Private Judgment," in *Essays Critical and Historical*, vol. 2 (London: Longmans, Green, 1895 [orig. ed. 1841]), 336–74. See also Alasdair MacIntyre's related account of tradition-dependent enquiry: MacIntyre, *Three Rival Versions of Moral Enquiry: Encyclopaedia, Genealogy, Tradition* (Notre Dame, IN: University of Notre Dame Press, 1990).

30. See Ratzinger, "The Question of the Concept of Tradition," in *God's Word*, 65, where he points out that the Church's authoritative proclamation, while rooted in the Scriptures, "is not interpretation in the sense of mere exegetical interpretation, but in the spiritual authority of the Lord that is implemented in the whole of the Church's existence, in her faith, her life, and her worship."

31. Evdokimov, *Orthodoxy*, 204.

32. For an excellent approach to the prophets in communal/canonical context, see Christopher R. Seitz, *Prophecy and Hermeneutics: Toward a New Introduction to the Prophets* (Grand Rapids, MI: Baker Academic, 2007).

33. See Jerome T. Walsh, *1 Kings* (Collegeville, MN: Liturgical Press, 1996), 248–49.

34. For discussion see Peter J. Leithart, *1 & 2 Kings* (Grand Rapids, MI: Brazos Press, 2006), 135–37. Leithart concludes typologically: "Carmel anticipates another mountain, a mountain outside Jerusalem, where the fire of God's judgment falls on a substitute Israel, when Jesus, the altar of God, is crucified to save his people. At Carmel, in the third year, Yahweh sends rain that renews the land; and in Jerusalem, on the third day, he raises Jesus from the dead to renew the world. At Carmel, the judgment of God is followed by rain; and at Jerusalem, the one who baptized by fire on the cross ascends to baptize his disciples with the Holy Spirit, pouring out the Spirit like showers from heaven" (ibid., 137).

35. Leithart, *1 & 2 Kings*, 141. For comparison of Elijah and Moses see also Walsh, *1 Kings*, 271–72.

36. Leithart, *1 & 2 Kings*, 142.

37. See Walsh, *1 Kings*, 274, 277.

38. Leithart, *1 & 2 Kings*, 142.

39. Nicholas Perrin, *Jesus the Temple* (Grand Rapids, MI: Baker Academic, 2010), 183.

40. See Jacob Neusner, *A Rabbi Talks with Jesus: An Intermillennial, Interfaith Exchange* (New York: Doubleday, 1993), especially chap. 2.

41. Neusner emphasizes "the difficulty of making sense, within the framework of the Torah, of a teacher who stands apart from, perhaps above, the Torah. At many points in this protracted account of Jesus' specific teachings [Matthew 5–7], we now recognize that at issue is the figure of Jesus, not the teachings at all" (Neusner, *A Rabbi Talks with Jesus*, 31).

42. For a broad treatment of this theme, see G. K. Beale, *The Temple and the Church's Mission: A Biblical Theology of the Dwelling Place of God* (Downers Grove, IL: InterVarsity Press, 2004), although Beale insists too strictly on Israel's tabernacle and temple being "patterned after the model of Eden" (ibid., 369). Certainly Beale is right to speak of "God's goal of universally expanding the temple of his glorious presence" and to conclude that in the eschaton "[e]verything of which Old Testament temples were typologically symbolic, a recapitulated and escalated Garden of Eden and whole cosmos, will have finally been materialized" (ibid.). For further background in Jewish theology, see Jon D. Levenson, *Sinai and Zion: An Entry into the Jewish Bible* (San Francisco: Harper & Row, 1985).

43. See Schnackenburg, *The Church in the New Testament*, 187–92. See also Schnackenburg's *God's Rule and Kingdom*, trans. John Murray (New York: Herder and Herder, 1963).

44. Joseph Ratzinger/Pope Benedict XVI, *Jesus of Nazareth: From the Baptism in the Jordan to the Transfiguration*, trans. Adrian J. Walker (New York: Doubleday, 2007), 120.

45. See René Laurentin, "Peter as the Foundation Stone in the Present Uncertainty," trans. Sarah Fawcett, in *Truth and Certainty*, ed. Edward Schillebeeckx and Bas van Iersel (New York: Herder and Herder, 1973), 95–113. For further ecumenical discussion see Olivier Clément, *You Are Peter: An Orthodox Theologian's Reflection on the Exercise of Papal Primacy*, trans. M. S. Laird (Hyde Park, NY: New City Press, 2003), especially 25–31; Evdokimov, *Orthodoxy*, 140–42; Joseph Ratzinger, "The Papal Primacy and the Unity of the People of God," in *Church, Ecumenism and Politics*, 29–45, at 39–44; and Joachim Gnilka, "The Ministry of Peter—New Testament Foundations," 24–35 and Theodore Stylianopoulos, "Concerning the Biblical Foundation of Primacy," 37–63, both in *The Petrine Ministry: Catholics and Orthodox in Dialogue*, ed. Walter Kasper, trans. the staff of the Pontifical Council for Promoting Christian Unity (New York: Paulist Press, 2006). From a Protestant perspective, Martin Hengel argues that Peter's (and Paul's and John's) "apostolic witness is in itself unique and their authority cannot be replaced or expanded. There is thus also no 'office of Peter.'" Hengel, *Saint Peter: The Underestimated Apostle*, trans. Thomas H. Trapp (Grand Rapids, MI: Eerdmans, 2010), 99. Although he condemns the Catholic doctrine of papal infallibility, Stylianos Harkianakis argues that "[t]he infallibility of the Church constitutes, both from a subjective as well as an objective viewpoint of religion, the most central postulate and the most essential presupposition, not only for the correct meaning of the religion of revelation *par excellence*, namely Christianity, but also for its purpose, so that, as the visible Church, it may guide the human person to the truth and salvation brought about by the incarnate Logos and Son of God." Harkianakis, *The Infallibility of the Church in Orthodox Theology* (Redfern, Australia: St Andrew's Orthodox Press, 2008), 245.

46. See Schnackenburg, *God's Rule and Kingdom*, 226–34. The quest for the historical Peter admittedly yields rather meager results: see Markus Bockmuehl, *Simon Peter in Scripture and Memory: The New Testament Apostle in the Early Church* (Grand Rapids, MI: Baker Academic, 2012).

47. Perrin, *Jesus the Temple*, 189. For further discussion along these lines, see especially N. T. Wright, *The New Testament and the People of God* (Minneapolis, MN: Fortress Press, 1992); and N. T. Wright, *Jesus and the Victory of God* (Minneapolis, MN: Fortress Press, 1996). It is surprising, then, to find N. T. Wright saying, "The Great Tradition has seriously and demonstrably distorted the gospels. Eager to explain who 'God' really was, the church highlighted Christology; wanting to show that Jesus was divine, it read the Gospels with that as the question; looking for Jesus' divinity, it ignored other central themes such as the kingdom of God. By the fourth century the church was not so eager to discover that God's kingdom had arrived and was to be implemented in Jesus'

way, so it screened out that kingdom inauguration which lies at the heart of the Synoptic tradition." Wright, "Response to Richard Hays," in *Jesus, Paul and the People of God: A Theological Dialogue with N. T. Wright*, ed. Nicholas Perrin and Richard B. Hays (Downers Grove, IL: InterVarsity Press, 2011), 62–65, at 63; cf. Wright's further remarks in the same volume in his "Whence and Whither Historical Jesus Studies in the Life of the Church?," 115–58, at 140–41. This assertion neglects the Fathers' understanding of faith, the sacraments, and almsgiving as uniting believers in Christ's eschatological kingdom.

48. See Joseph A. Fitzmyer, S.J., "The Office of Teaching in the Christian Church According to the New Testament," in Empie, Murphy, and Burgess, *Teaching Authority and Infallibility in the Church*, 186–212.

49. In his (overly ambitious) reconstruction of the politics of the earliest Church, Michael D. Goulder proposes that for Matthew

> [t]here was however a second and greater source of divine law since Jesus came, and he had not only laid down many prescriptions for the Church himself, but had also set up a kind of Christian Sanhedrin, the Apostolic College, to interpret his rulings. Jesus had called Simon Cephas, the Rock; and Matthew took this to mean that he was like a foundation stone to the Church as a building, to which, in another metaphor, he held the keys. . . . Binding and loosing were regular Jewish terms for the authority of Sages to enforce rules or make exceptions (Mishnah, *Ter.* 5.4, Mishnah, *Pes.* 4.5; Josephus, *Bell. Jud.* 11.5.2), and Peter is being given this same authority in the Church. Any enforcements or exceptions he makes, Jesus will ratify. Exactly the same words are used in the plural to the Twelve at 18.18, so Matthew sees the Apostolic College as a Christian equivalent to the Sanhedrin. Caiaphas was the chairman at Jesus' trial in Matt 26, and Peter is similarly thought of as chairman of the Apostles. (Goulder, "Matthew's Vision for the Church," in Bockmuehl and Thompson, *A Vision for the Church*, 19–32, at 22–23)

In Goulder's view, Matthew "takes over the Jewish idea of a continuous chain of authoritative interpreters" (ibid., 22).

50. For discussion, with particular attention to the status of John's Gospel, see Peter Stuhlmacher, "Spiritual Remembering: John 14.26," in *The Holy Spirit and Christian Origins: Essays in Honor of James D. G. Dunn*, ed. Graham N. Stanton, Bruce W. Longenecker, and Stephen C. Barton (Grand Rapids, MI: Eerdmans, 2004), 55–68. See also Joseph Ratzinger's "Luther and the Unity of the Churches," in *Church, Ecumenism and Politics*, 99–134, at 117–19, in response to Ernst Käsemann's *The Testament of Jesus: A Study of the Gospel of John in Light of Chapter 17* (Philadelphia: Fortress Press, 1968). As Ratzinger says, "John wrote his gospel for and in the context of the great Church as a whole and . . . the idea of a unity of Christians in separated Churches is completely alien to him" (119).

51. For theological commentary from an Eastern Orthodox perspective, see Peter C. Bouteneff, *Sweeter than Honey: Orthodox Thinking on Dogma and Truth* (Crestwood, NY: St Vladimir's Seminary Press, 2006), 117–24. Andrew T. Lincoln sees these passages as an effort by the evangelist to validate his own perspective: see Lincoln, *The Gospel According to Saint John* (London: Continuum, 2005), 385–86. For his part, J. C. O'Neill proposes that John's Gospel is composed of disparate "visions" by various Christian prophets: O'Neill, "A Vision for the Church: John's Gospel," in Bockmuehl and Thompson, *A Vision for the Church*, 79–93, at 91. More fruitfully, see Leon Morris, *The Gospel according to John*, rev. ed. (Grand Rapids, MI: Eerdmans, 1995), 583. At issue is whether Jesus prepared his disciples for an apostolic ministry in which the Church would truly be guided by the Holy Spirit so as to faithfully communicate divine revelation to all generations.

52. Hans Küng argues that "[j]ust as there is no a priori infallible teaching office, so there is no a priori infallible teaching book in Christendom. As the community of believers, the Church does not possess any propositional infallibility, but she certainly does have a fundamental indefectibility in the truth." Küng, *Infallible? An Inquiry*, trans. Edward Quinn (Garden City, NY: Doubleday, 1971), 219. For Küng's viewpoint, see also his "A Short Balance-Sheet of the Debate on Infallibility," trans. David Smith, in Schillebeeckx and Iersel, *Truth and Certainty*, 129–36. Non-propositional "indefectibility" turns out to mean simply that Jesus is in some way salvific. For his part, Edward Schillebeeckx, O.P., states: "If the promise of God's help is to be at all meaningful in history, those holding office must therefore have authority to define Christian faith *here and now*. The articulation of this judgment will, however, always be conditioned by history" (Schillebeeckx, "The Problem of the Infallibility of the Church's Office: A Theological Reflection," trans. David Smith, in Schillebeeckx and Iersel, *Truth and Certainty*, 77–94, at 91). Schillebeeckx holds that the truth of each dogma must be "subjected to the criticism of the totality of faith within the whole of history" (ibid.), an eschatological standard of truth. What remains, then, is a historically conditioned proposition backed by the raw power of the bishops and pope.

53. See Jean Giblet, "Aspects of the Truth in the New Testament," trans. Dinah Livingstone, in Schillebeeckx and Iersel, *Truth and Certainty*, 35–42. See also John Paul II, *Ut Unum Sint*, § 9, in *The Encyclicals of John Paul II*, ed. J. Michael Miller, C.S.B. (Huntington, IN: Our Sunday Visitor, 2001), 786.

54. See Timothy S. Laniak, *Shepherds after My Own Heart: Pastoral Traditions and Leadership in the Bible* (Downers Grove, IL: InterVarsity Press, 2006), chap. 13. See also Andrew Lincoln's remark: "Now Peter is charged with being the undershepherd who will protect, nourish and tend the flock of the good shepherd himself. This task is in continuity with the charge to all the disciples in the farewell discourse to love, serve and lay down their lives for another (cf. 13.14–15, 34; 15.12–14, 17). . . . Peter's love will show itself as he keeps Jesus'

word about loving others in the particular form of shepherding the flock" (Lincoln, *The Gospel According to Saint John*, 518). Francis J. Moloney, S.D.B., comments, "The pastoral role that Peter is called to fill associates him with the good shepherd. He is charged to 'shepherd' and 'feed' the 'lambs' and 'sheep' of Jesus. Discussions of the Petrine office in the Roman tradition of Christianity are out of place in any reading of this passage." Moloney, *Love in the Gospel of John: An Exegetical, Theological, and Literary Study* (Grand Rapids, MI: Baker Academic, 2013), 182. The effort to rule out discussions of the Petrine office is mistaken, since the unique role of Peter opens up inevitably to just such discussions, unless one imagines that Christ has no perspective on history.

55. See Schnackenburg, *God's Rule and Kingdom*, 259–65; and Turner, *Power from on High*, 331–47.

56. For further discussion, see Benedict XVI, *Saint Paul*, English translation by *L'Osservatore Romano* (Vatican City: Libreria Editrice Vaticana, 2009), 26–42. Paul's confrontation with Peter in Galatians 2:11–14 is probed by Karlfried Froehlich, "Fallibility Instead of Infallibility? A Brief History of the Interpretation of Galatians 2:11–14," in Empie, Murphy, and Burgess, *Teaching Authority and Infallibility in the Church*, 259–69.

57. See Joseph A. Fitzmyer, S.J., *First Corinthians* (New Haven, CT: Yale University Press, 2008), 225–26. For a survey of the voluminous research on apostolic authority in 1 Corinthians, see John K. Goodrich, *Paul as an Administrator of God in 1 Corinthians* (Cambridge: Cambridge University Press, 2012), 2–12. Goodrich focuses on Paul's use of the double-sided metaphor of administrator/steward (*oikonomos*), which evokes both "social, legal, and structural degradation" and "authority, immunity, and privilege" (ibid., 201). He concludes that "when Paul's rights and authority in some way obstruct the power of the gospel and thus prohibit the expansion and maturation of the church, he subjects that authority to his greater apostolic mandate" (ibid., 204).

58. Raymond F. Collins remarks that "Paul's judicial language is strikingly similar to that used in Roman judicial proceedings and the deliberations of the Sanhedrin. . . . Qumran's community council, comprised of the main body of the community, convened to render judicial decisions (cf. 1QS 6:8–10). It was empowered to find guilty all those who transgressed the covenant. Paul expected the Corinthians to judge the incestuous man and impose an appropriate punishment. It is generally acknowledged that there are some structural similarities between the Qumran community and some of the early Christian communities." Collins, *First Corinthians* (Collegeville, MN: Liturgical Press, 1999), 207. Collins downplays Paul's role and emphasizes the authority of the community, but in so doing he overlooks, I think, the force of Paul's repeated claims to authority. Thus Collins argues that the "rod" (1 Cor 4:21) is merely "a motif associated with paternal correction (cf. 3:1–2, 4:15, 17). It is an instrument of *paideia*, rearing a child (cf. Prov 22:15). Even today 'spare the rod and spoil the child' is an adage expressing the common wisdom of a culture" (ibid., 202). Cf.

the contrasting understandings of Paul the pastor in James W. Thompson, *Pastoral Ministry according to Paul: A Biblical Vision* (Grand Rapids, MI: Baker Academic, 2006), and Hans Urs von Balthasar, *Paul Struggles with His Congregation: The Pastoral Message of the Letters to the Corinthians*, trans. Brigitte L. Bojarska (San Francisco: Ignatius Press, 1992).

59. See Fitzmyer, *First Corinthians*, 223: "In sending Timothy as an emissary, Paul is exercising his apostolic authority and power, because through Timothy he himself will be present to them."

60. See Collins, *First Corinthians*, 196–99, 594–96.

61. See Schnackenburg, *The Church in the New Testament*, 95–100; and George T. Montague, S.M., *First and Second Timothy, and Titus* (Grand Rapids, MI: Baker Academic, 2008), 84–87.

62. See Jerome D. Quinn, "The Terminology for Faith, Truth, Teaching, and the Spirit in the Pastoral Epistles: A Summary," in Empie, Murphy, and Burgess, *Teaching Authority and Infallibility in the Church*, 232–37. Regarding Paul's authorship of the letters attributed to him, Luke Timothy Johnson notes that "a broad consensus has developed. Nearly all critical scholars accept seven letters—Romans, 1 Thessalonians, 1 and 2 Corinthians, Philemon, Galatians, and Philippians as written directly by Paul. There is almost equal unanimity in rejecting 1 and 2 Timothy and Titus. Serious debate can occasionally be found concerning 2 Thessalonians, Colossians, and Ephesians, but the clear and growing scholarly consensus does not accept them as Pauline." Johnson, *The Writings of the New Testament: An Interpretation* (Philadelphia: Fortress Press, 1986), 255. Johnson himself favors Pauline authorship of 2 Thessalonians, Colossians, and Ephesians, and he is open to the possibility of Pauline authorship of 1 and 2 Timothy and Titus.

63. Paul Evdokimov states, "The spiritual attributes of the priesthood do not depend on personal qualities but are functional and objective, opening the way to Jacob's ladder, the sacraments" (Evdokimov, *Orthodoxy*, 48). Likewise, Ratzinger points out that hierarchy "means not holy domination but holy origin. Hierarchical service and ministry is thus guarding an origin that is holy, and not making arbitrary dispositions and decisions" (Ratzinger, "Luther and the Unity of the Churches," 128). Ratzinger adds that "a council is not a parliament which makes laws that 'the congregations' then have to obey. It is a place of witness. Admittedly, to a certain extent it rests on the idea of representation. But this representation rests not on the delegation of people's wills but on the sacrament. To receive the 'sacrament of order' means to represent the faith of the whole Church, the 'holy origin', to be a witness of the faith of the Church" (ibid., 129).

64. Timothy B. Savage argues that Paul purposefully comes to his communities "in a premeditated spirit of meekness and gentleness. That is not to say that he comes without boldness. On the contrary, it is precisely in such 'weakness' that he intends to engage in bold warfare, tearing down strongholds and taking captive the self-exalting attitudes which come into conflict with the

knowledge of God (10:3–6). It is through meekness and gentleness that he seeks to win his converts' obedience to Christ." Savage, *Power through Weakness: Paul's Understanding of the Christian Ministry in 2 Corinthians* (Cambridge: Cambridge University Press, 1996), 69. Yet Savage grants that Paul conceives of his apostolic authority as also justifying a forceful approach: "If it becomes clear to Paul that his reluctance to wield a rod has failed to stem the tide of sin among the Corinthians (cf. 12:21) and has not brought every thought captive for obedience to Christ (10:5), then he will have little choice but, on his next visit, to use great severity (13:2). He is resolved to do just that (13:1), even at the risk of causing his converts to exult in his forcefulness" (ibid.). See also, in Frank J. Matera, *II Corinthians: A Commentary* (Louisville, KY: Westminster John Knox Press, 2003), 299–310, the superb discussion of Paul's conception of his apostolic authority.

65. See Witherington, *Grace in Galatia*, 84–85.

66. Collins finds a contrast here with 1 Corinthians 5: "As is customary in the Pastoral Epistles the text of 1 Tim 1:18–20 focuses uniquely on Paul as the one who has decreed the excommunication. In 1 Corinthians the excommunication is a joint endeavor of Paul and the community and relies on the authority of the Lord Jesus. Another difference is that the procedure to which 1 Timothy makes reference has as its purpose the correction of the sinner (1 Tim 1:20; cf. Mt 18:15–18). What is at issue in the excommunication Paul urges upon the community is the holiness of the community, its own eschatological salvation" (Collins, *First Corinthians*, 208). The difference between the holiness of the community and the correction of the sinner, however, may be somewhat exaggerated by Collins.

67. See Schnackenburg, *The Church in the New Testament*, 156–62, 171–76; and Hans Urs von Balthasar, "*Casta Meretrix*," trans. John Saward, in *Explorations in Theology*, vol. 2, *Spouse of the Word* (San Francisco: Ignatius Press, 1991), 193–288. For differing views of the image of the flock and the shepherd, see Luke Timothy Johnson, *The Acts of the Apostles* (Collegeville, MN: Liturgical Press, 1992), 362–64; and Paul S. Minear, *Images of the Church in the New Testament* (Louisville, KY: Westminster John Knox Press, 2004 [orig. ed. 1960]), 264–65.

68. This perennial question has been recently addressed in Christian Smith, *The Bible Made Impossible: Why Biblicism Is Not a Truly Evangelical Reading of Scripture* (Grand Rapids, MI: Brazos Press, 2011); and Craig Allert, *A High View of Scripture? The Authority of the Bible and the Formation of the New Testament Canon* (Grand Rapids, MI: Baker Academic, 2007). See also Schnackenburg, *The Church in the New Testament*, 9–10.

69. See Guy Mansini, O.S.B., "Ecclesial Mediation of Grace and Truth," *The Thomist* 75 (2011): 555–83.

70. See Cantalamessa, *Mary: Mirror of the Church*, 65.

71. See Schnackenburg, *The Church in the New Testament*, 22–33, 68, 74–77, 126–28. See also the reflections of Jeremy S. Begbie, "The Shape of Things to Come? Wright Amidst Emerging Ecclesiologies," in Perrin and Hays, *Jesus, Paul and the People of God*, 183–208.

72. See Jerome Kodell, O.S.B., *The Eucharist in the New Testament* (Collegeville, MN: Liturgical Press, 1988), 72–74; Schnackenburg, *The Church in the New Testament*, 40–45, 66–67, 192–93; and Schnackenburg, *God's Rule and Kingdom*, 249–58. The Eucharist is what is missing from Paul M. Hoskins's reflections on Jesus as the fulfillment of the Temple:

> Since Jesus is the true Temple and the fulfillment of the Old Testament feasts, it might pay dividends for Christians to reflect upon the logic of these typological relationships. If the Temple and Old Testament feasts anticipate and reach their fullness through the blessings that Jesus brings, one wonders if we are doing an adequate job of celebrating what God has done for us. . . . Reading about celebrating these feasts in various Jewish sources made me wonder if we could learn something from the joy and wonder that celebrating them at the Temple appears to have created. Some Christians are now following the lead of Jewish Christians in celebrating the Old Testament feasts in such a way as to point to Christ. This is a good start. (Hoskins, *Jesus as the Fulfillment of the Temple in the Gospel of John* [Milton Keynes, England: Paternoster, 2006], 203)

73. Thus Ulrich Luz remarks: "It is immediately obvious that church unity did not mean in the Constantinian age what it meant in the New Testament period. Less obvious is what the different understandings of church unity have in common. Even within the New Testament age, the differences are quite substantial, and there were considerable developments and changes precisely in this period" (Luz, "On the Way to Unity: The Community of the Church in the New Testament," in Vischer, Luz, and Link, *Unity of the Church in the New Testament and Today*, 29–161, at 31; cf. 90). Just as Luz can say little historically about the identity of the Church, so also he has little to say about Jesus' identity as Son.

74. Joseph Ratzinger, "Appendix II: Afterword to the English Edition," in *Eschatology*, 261–74, at 270. See also Ratzinger, *The Nature and Mission of Theology: Essays to Orient Theology in Today's Debates*, trans. Adrian Walker (San Francisco: Ignatius Press, 1995), 61–65. In his reflections on the Church as a "subject," Ratzinger echoes the work of Yves Congar, O.P., and John Henry Newman. Elsewhere Ratzinger states: "The Church is not some piece of machinery, is not just an institution, is not even one of the usual sociological entities. It is a person. It is a woman. It is a mother. It is living. The Marian understanding of the Church is the most decisive contrast to a purely organizational or bureaucratic concept of the Church. We cannot make the Church; we have to be it. And it is only to the extent that faith moulds our being beyond any question of

making that we *are* the Church, that the Church is in us. It is only in being Marian that we become the Church" (Ratzinger, "The Ecclesiology of the Second Vatican Council," in *Church, Ecumenism and Politics*, 3–28, at 20). For further discussion of Ratzinger's ecclesiology, see especially Maximilian Heinrich Heim, *Joseph Ratzinger: Life in the Church and Living Theology; Fundamentals of Ecclesiology with Reference to* Lumen Gentium, trans. Michael J. Miller (San Francisco: Ignatius Press, 2007). See also Francis Martin, "Mary in Sacred Scripture: An Ecumenical Reflection," *The Thomist* 72 (2008): 525–69, at 544–45.

75. Ratzinger, *Eschatology*, 270. This is the essential conclusion of Ian Levy's historical study of the disastrous controversy between John Wyclif and Jan Hus, on the one side, and Jean Gerson, William Woodford, and Thomas Netter on the other: see Levy, *Holy Scripture and the Quest for Authority at the End of the Middle Ages*, 222–35.

76. Ratzinger, *Eschatology*, 270.

77. Florovsky, "The Ever-Virgin Mother of God," in Mascall, *The Mother of God*, 62.

78. As Francis Martin says, early Christian biblical interpretation "is 'liturgical' in the sense that much commentary takes place in a liturgical setting, and also because the manner in which the event is treated and made present in the liturgy itself has a bearing on how it is understood" (Martin, "Mary in Sacred Scripture," 554).

79. St. Basil the Great, *On the Holy Spirit*, trans. David Anderson (Crestwood, NY: St Vladimir's Seminary Press, 1997), § 64, p. 97. For discussion see Lewis Ayres, *Nicaea and Its Legacy: An Approach to Fourth-Century Trinitarian Theology* (Oxford: Oxford University Press, 2004), 218. See also Gilles Emery, O.P., *The Trinity: An Introduction to Catholic Doctrine on the Triune God*, trans. Matthew Levering (Washington, D.C.: Catholic University of America Press, 2011), chap. 1; and Khaled Anatolios, *Retrieving Nicaea: The Development and Meaning of Trinitarian Doctrine* (Grand Rapids, MI: Baker Academic, 2011), 173.

80. See, for example, A. Edward Siecienski, "Mariology in Antioch: Mary in the Writings of Chrysostom, Theodoret of Cyrus, and Nestorius," *St Vladimir's Theological Quarterly* 56 (2012): 133–69; and Paul Ladouceur, "Old Testament Prefigurations of the Mother of God," *St Vladimir's Theological Quarterly* 50 (2006): 5–57, at 45–47.

81. See also Yves Congar, O.P., "Norms of Christian Allegiance and Identity in the History of the Church," trans. John Griffiths, in Schillebeeckx and Iersel, *Truth and Certainty*, 11–25.

82. On Psalm 45, in connection with the Song of Solomon and in light of patristic exegesis, see Ladouceur, "Old Testament Prefigurations of the Mother of God," 26–33, 49–57. Regarding Psalm 45:17, "I will cause your name to be celebrated in all generations; therefore the peoples will praise you for ever and ever," Ladouceur states, "The memory of the holy Virgin is guarded as a precious treasure in the Tradition of the Church, and she is honored both as the

Mother of the Savior, and as the first person to have attained perfection and *theosis*, union with God, and who is the first to have entered, body, soul, and spirit, into the Kingdom of God" (ibid., 57). Ladouceur notes, of course, that "the Mother of God cannot be separated from Christ, and her importance in the theology and piety of the Orthodox Church rests essentially on her divine motherhood, as expressed in the dogmatic proclamations on the Theotokos" (ibid., 47).

83. These texts are also read at Vespers on the Orthodox Feasts of the Annunciation (March 25), the Nativity of the Mother of God (September 8), and the Entry into the Temple of the Mother of God (November 21). See Ladouceur, "Old Testament Prefigurations of the Mother of God," 6–14. On Genesis 28 and its patristic interpretation, see ibid., 15–19; on Ezekiel 43–44, see ibid., 41–44. On the Orthodox Feast of the Entry into the Temple of the Mother of God, a feast not celebrated in the Catholic liturgical calendar, see Nonna Verna Harrison, "The Entry of the Mother of God into the Temple," *St Vladimir's Theological Quarterly* 50 (2006): 149–60.

84. See "15 August" on the website of the Ecumenical Patriarchate of Constantinople, New Rome, Archdiocese of Thyateira and Great Britain, translations of Orthodox liturgical and patristic texts, http://anastasis.org.uk/15aug .htm.

85. Alexander Schmemann, *The Historical Road of Eastern Orthodoxy*, trans. Lydia W. Kesich (Crestwood, NY: St Vladimir's Seminary Press, 2003), 193.

86. Alexander Schmemann, *Introduction to Liturgical Theology*, trans. Asheleigh E. Moorehouse (Crestwood, NY: St Vladimir's Seminary Press, 2003), 17–18. See also Wainwright, *Doxology*.

87. Joseph Ratzinger, *God and the World: Believing and Living in Our Time; A Conversation with Peter Seewald*, trans. Henry Taylor (San Francisco: Ignatius Press, 2002), 293.

88. Cf. Bertrand de Margerie, S.J., "Dogmatic Development by Abridgement or by Concentration?," trans. J. B. Carol, O.F.M., *Marian Studies* 27 (1976): 64–98. De Margerie notes that Edward Yarnold and Avery Dulles had raised the possibility that the Marian dogmas, because of their secondary place in the hierarchy of truths (cf. Vatican II's *Redintegratio Unitatis*, § 11), need not be required of Protestants in the case of ecclesial reunion. This understanding of the hierarchy of truths inevitably led to the question of whether Catholics, too, must assent to these truths—and to other less central truths taught by the Church. See Edward J. Yarnold, S.J., "Marian Dogmas and Reunion," *The Month* 131 (June 1971): 177–79; and Avery Dulles, S.J., "A Proposal to Lift Anathemas," *Origins* 4 (1974): 418–21. See also Karl Rahner, S.J., "Pluralism in Theology and the Oneness of the Church's Profession of Faith," in *The Development of Fundamental Theology*, ed. Johannes B. Metz (New York: Paulist Press, 1969), 103–23; George H. Tavard, A.A., "'Hierarchia Veritatem': A Preliminary Investigation,"

Theological Studies 32 (1971): 278–89, at 289; Heinrich Fries and Karl Rahner, *Unity of the Churches: An Actual Possibility*, trans. Ruth C. L. Gritsch and Eric W. Gritsch (Philadelphia: Fortress Press, 1985); as well as, from an Anglican perspective, E. L. Mascall, "The Dogmatic Theology of the Mother of God," in Mascall, *The Mother of God*, 37–50, at 45. James L. Heft, S.M., seeks a middle way on this topic in his "Papal Infallibility and the Marian Dogmas: An Introduction," *Marian Studies* 33 (1982): 47–82, which makes clear that a key underlying issue, in addition to the ecumenism that was Dulles's focus, was the effort by many Catholic theologians to justify dissent from the teaching of *Humanae Vitae*. For Dulles's view of dogma during this period, see Avery Dulles, S.J., "Dogma as an Ecumenical Problem," *Theological Studies* 29 (1968): 397–416; Dulles, *The Survival of Dogma*; and Dulles, "Moderate Infallibilism," in Empie, Murphy, and Burgess, *Teaching Authority and Infallibility in the Church*, 81–100. See also the concerns raised by William H. Marshner, "Criteria for Doctrinal Development in the Marian Dogmas: An Essay in Metatheology," *Marian Studies* 28 (1977): 47–97. For the position opposed by de Margerie, see more recently Walter N. Sisto, "Marian Dogmas and Reunion: What Eastern Catholics Can Teach Us about Catholic Ecumenism," *Journal of Ecumenical Studies* 46 (2011): 150–62; and Leona M. English, "Roman Catholic Solutions to the Marian Question in Anglican–Roman Catholic Dialogue," *Journal of Ecumenical Studies* 37 (2000): 142–51.

89. Newman, *An Essay on the Development of Christian Doctrine*, 89.

90. Ibid. For further discussion of the Church's authority (and the Pope's), in dialogue with Oscar Cullmann, see Jean Daniélou, S.J., *God and the Ways of Knowing*, trans. Walter Roberts (San Francisco: Ignatius Press, 2003), 152–66. Daniélou observes:

> Just as the sacraments are the embodiment of the unique act of salvation, so tradition is the embodiment of the unique act of revelation. . . . It is clear that there is no other act of salvation besides that of the death and Resurrection of Jesus. The sacraments cannot, then, be another act of salvation. They are only that unique act rendered present, but in an effective manner—which effectiveness is divine. It is the same with revelation. There is only one revelation, the one made to the Apostles. It is perfectly clear, then, that the time of the revelation is a uniquely privileged historical time. But this revelation is rendered infallibly present through the action of God in the time of the Church by the Magisterium. (Ibid., 161)

Chapter 6
The Fittingness of Mary's Assumption in God's Economy of Salvation

1. Newman, "The Glories of Mary for the Sake of Her Son," 129–48, at 145. On Mary as "Queen of heaven," see Edward Sri, *Queen Mother: A Biblical*

Theology of Mary's Queenship (Steubenville, OH: Emmaus Road, 2005). See also Paul Hinnebusch, O.P., *Mother of Jesus Present with Us* (Libertyville, IL: Prow Books, 1980), 146–48.

2. Yves Congar, O.P., followed later by the Second Vatican Council's Dogmatic Constitution on Divine Revelation (*Dei Verbum*), describes this doctrinal fittingness as "the analogy of faith." Noting the presence of typological portraits of Mary in Scripture, Congar states that Mary's Assumption is supported by Scripture "[i]n the sense that in the absence of one or more definite and explicit texts, there exist in Scripture texts or statements, closely related to each other, that demand, if their plenary sense is really to be made manifest, another statement which, as such, is not to be found in Scripture. This again is the analogy of faith, which, incidentally, may well not be recognised immediately, but only after the lapse of time, during which, if it is the time of the Church, the guidance of him who is to lead the disciples into all truth (Jn 16:13) will not be lacking." See Congar, "Theological Notes on the Assumption," 3–10, at 6; cf. 10. (This essay was originally published in French in 1951.) By contrast, Sally Cunneen claims "[t]here were many arguments for the Assumption, though none of them were biblical or apostolic." Cunneen, *In Search of Mary: The Woman and the Symbol* (New York: Random House, 1996), 237.

3. Newman, "On the Fitness of the Glories of Mary," 149–66, at 150.

4. Ibid., 152.

5. On this point see Longenecker and Gustafson, *Mary: A Catholic-Evangelical Debate*, 131–32.

6. Newman, "On the Fitness of the Glories of Mary," 163.

7. Ibid., 166.

8. *Catechism of the Catholic Church*, 2nd ed. (Vatican City: Libreria Editrice Vaticana, 1997), § 114; cf. *Dei Verbum*, § 12. Romanus Cessario, O.P., connects perception of faith's coherence (and thus appreciation for reasons of fittingness) with knowledge as a gift of the Holy Spirit. As he states with regard to Mary's Immaculate Conception,

> the gift of knowledge facilitates our judging the implications of this doctrine for other mysteries of the faith. These implications can include both those that are articulated in propositions and those that are not. For example, one can consider Mary's unique privilege as a starting point for additional inquiries about her capacity to commit sin, about what she knew concerning Christ's person and his mission, about how the example of her virtues succors Christian living, and about still other developments of this faith proposition. Knowledge also illumines the relationship of this article of faith to other Marian doctrines, such as the Assumption or Mary's maternal mediation for the Church, as well as to all the other articles of faith. The one who lovingly contemplates the Immaculate Conception does not confront simply a "dogma" about the Mother of God, but the whole drama of salvation as the blessed Virgin personally embodies it. (Cessario,

Christian Faith and the Theological Life [Washington, D.C.: Catholic University of America Press, 1996], 178)

9. John H. Walton, *The Lost World of Genesis One: Ancient Cosmology and the Origins Debate* (Downers Grove, IL: InterVarsity Press, 2009), 87.

10. For background from various perspectives, see Anderson, *The Genesis of Perfection*; James Barr, *The Garden of Eden and the Hope of Immortality* (Minneapolis, MN: Fortress Press, 1992); Peter C. Bouteneff, *Beginnings: Ancient Christian Readings of the Biblical Creation Narratives* (Grand Rapids, MI: Baker Academic, 2008); J. Richard Middleton, *The Liberating Image: The* Imago Dei *in Genesis 1* (Grand Rapids, MI: Brazos Press, 2005); and Matthew Levering, "The *Imago Dei* in David Novak and Thomas Aquinas: A Jewish-Christian Dialogue," *The Thomist* 72 (2008): 259–311.

11. In his commentary on Genesis, Walter Brueggemann states about Enoch: "The mode of his life-ending, 'God took him,' could suggest something other than death, and that is likely the root of much later speculation. But as this phrase stands in isolation, nothing can be made of it. Even in this terse form, it reflects that Enoch represents some role in overcoming the utter discontinuity of God and humankind." Brueggemann, *Genesis* (Louisville, KY: Westminster John Knox Press, 2010), 69.

12. R. W. L. Moberly fruitfully compares Genesis 6–9 to Exodus 32–34 and concludes: "God deals with the world in general in the same way as with Israel in particular. If both Israel and the world show themselves to be faithless at the outset and to be continuingly faithless ('evil in thought' and 'stiff-necked'), then their continued existence is similarly to be understood in terms of the merciful forbearance of God toward those who do not deserve it: Life for both Israel and the world is a gift of grace—recognition of which should elicit a gratitude that renounces faithlessness." Moberly, *The Theology of the Book of Genesis* (Cambridge: Cambridge University Press, 2009), 120. For further discussion of Genesis 6–9, see Brueggemann, *Genesis*, 73–91; and Bill T. Arnold, *Genesis* (Cambridge: Cambridge University Press, 2009), 110–11.

13. For discussion see Mark J. Boda, *A Severe Mercy: Sin and Its Remedy in the Old Testament* (Winona Lake, IN: Eisenbrauns, 2009), 99–111.

14. See Jo Bailey Wells, *God's Holy People: A Theme in Biblical Theology* (Sheffield: Sheffield Academic Press, 2000), 71–97.

15. For historical-critical commentary which treats this verse in terms of *imitatio Dei*, see Jacob Milgrom, *Leviticus 17–22: A New Translation with Introduction and Commentary* (New York: Doubleday, 2000), 1602–8.

16. Hans Urs von Balthasar observes that this glory is not without its warning: even here God "chooses the garment of darkness and hiddenness. The aspect of his glory as light is represented by the sun and the magnificent temple; this will prove a dissociation with heavy consequences. God has occupied the temple, but, as it were, with reservations. In the third theophany (1 Kings 9.1–9) God makes everything (even the promise to David in v. 5) dependent on the

conditional clause: '*if* you live in my sight as your father David lived.' If not, 'I will renounce the temple which I have consecrated in honour of my name, and Israel shall become the byword and the derision of all peoples.' Neither the promise to David nor the temple nor the ark can be used by man as mortgages against God." Balthasar, *The Glory of the Lord: A Theological Aesthetics*, vol. 6, *Theology: The Old Covenant*, trans. Brian McNeil, C.R.V., and Erasmo Leiva-Merikakis, ed. John Riches (San Francisco: Ignatius Press, 1991), 117–18.

17. For a Lutheran perspective on Ezekiel 36, emphasizing (with some admitted difficulty) *simul iustus et peccator*, see Horace D. Hummel, *Ezekiel 21–48* (Saint Louis, MO: Concordia Publishing House, 2007), 1038–62.

18. On the ark of the covenant and the tabernacle, see Carol Meyers, *Exodus* (Cambridge: Cambridge University Press, 2005), 224–31. Describing the "mercy seat" or cover of the ark and the cherubim located on top of the mercy seat, Meyers writes: "Divine immanence and transcendence merge, and are not in tension with each other, in this feature of the ark. This invisible presence of God in specific spatial confines can be called 'empty space aniconism,' for it rejects images of the deity but provides for the highly important sense of divine immanence, usually inherent in cult images, by creating a numinous 'empty space'" (ibid., 228). The ark is both "covenant repository" and "the locus of God's presence" (ibid.).

19. Alexander Schmemann observes in this regard that "Mary, being in the tradition and experience of the Church the very 'epiphany' of spirituality, being herself the first, the highest and most perfect fruit of the Holy Spirit in the entire creation, reveals to us by her very presence the true nature and the true effects of the Descent of the Holy Spirit which is *the* source of the Church's life." See Schmemann, *The Virgin Mary*, 75. From a historical-critical perspective, Joseph Fitzmyer, S.J., states that the meaning is that Mary "is favored by God to be the mother of the descendant of David and the Son of the Most High," rather than filled with the grace of the Holy Spirit (Fitzmyer, *The Gospel According to Luke (I–IX)*, 345). Commenting on the angel's promise that the Holy Spirit will come upon Mary, Fitzmyer states that here "the Spirit is understood in the OT sense of God's creative and active power present to human beings" (ibid., 350). It would be a mistake in his view to see here the Holy Spirit (or the Son) of the later doctrine of the Trinity: "Only the elements of that doctrine are to be found here, not the doctrine itself. It is, moreover, to be noted that there is no evidence here in the Lucan infancy narrative of Jesus' preexistence or incarnation" (ibid., 351). Even if one were to grant the accuracy of Fitzmyer's stripping of this passage of later theological interpretations—which I do not—it remains that case that the divine presence to Mary cannot be a merely extrinsic or merely physical relation.

20. For the view that these living waters are to flow from the believer, see Mary L. Coloe, P.B.V.M., *God Dwells with Us: Temple Symbolism in the Fourth Gospel* (Collegeville, MN: Liturgical Press, 2001), 125–34.

21. For creative biblical development of the Eve-Mary typology (and the Mary/Israel/Church typology), see L. S. Thornton, "The Mother of God in Holy Scripture," in Mascall, *The Mother of God*, 9–23.

22. Fitzmyer observes that "her motherhood will serve the Lucan picture of Christian discipleship. . . . Mary's enthusiastic response to the angel depicts her from the very beginning of the account as one who cooperates with God's plan of salvation. . . . For Luke, Mary is the model believer (see 1:45), pronounced blessed" (Fitzmyer, *The Gospel According to Luke (I–IX)*, 341).

23. For discussion of Jesus' brothers and sisters, see Ben Witherington III, *Women in the Ministry of Jesus* (Cambridge: Cambridge University Press, 1984), 88–90; Ben Witherington III, *What Have They Done with Jesus? Beyond Strange Theories and Bad History—Why We Can Trust the Bible* (New York: HarperCollins, 2006), 111, 124, 174ff.; José M. Pedrozo, "The Brothers of Jesus and His Mother's Virginity," *The Thomist* 63 (1999): 83–104; Richard Bauckham, "The Brothers and Sisters of Jesus: An Epiphanian Response to John P. Meier," *Catholic Biblical Quarterly* 56 (1994): 686–700; Richard Bauckham, *Jude and the Relatives of Jesus in the Early Church* (Edinburgh: T & T Clark, 1990), 19–36; John P. Meier, "The Brothers and Sisters of Jesus in Ecumenical Perspective," *Catholic Biblical Quarterly* 54 (1992): 1–28; John P. Meier, "On Retrojecting Later Questions from Later Texts: A Reply to Richard Bauckham," *Catholic Biblical Quarterly* 59 (1997): 511–27; and Matthew Levering, "The Brothers and Sisters of Jesus," *First Things* online, Nov. 30, 2007. http://www.firstthings.com/onthesquare/2007/11/the-brothers-and-sisters-of-je.

24. This point is made frequently, indeed to the exclusion of any other insight, in the discussion of Mary that we find in Ben Witherington III's *John's Wisdom*.

25. Fitzmyer considers it to be decisive that Luke, unlike John, does not report Mary's presence at the foot of the Cross, thereby showing that the "sword" to which Simeon refers simply pertains to Mary's struggle (like other Israelites) to learn "that obedience to the word of God will transcend even family ties" (Fitzmyer, *The Gospel According to Luke (I–IX)*, 430). Regarding interpretations that connect the "sword" with Mary's suffering at the public rejection and death of her Son, Fitzmyer states that "[a]ll such attempts explain the sword on the basis of material extraneous to the Lucan Gospel and could scarcely have been envisaged by Luke" (ibid.). Surely Fitzmyer exaggerates here. For a more nuanced view see Luke Timothy Johnson, *The Gospel of Luke* (Collegeville, MN: Liturgical Press, 1991), 53–58. See also Gary Culpepper's exposition of Martin Luther's interpretation of this text, in Culpepper, "'A Sword Will Pierce through Your Own Soul Also,'" 28–45, at 37–42.

26. For further discussion see Schmemann, *The Virgin Mary*, 64–65, 91–92, in addition to the writings that we canvassed in the first three chapters above.

27. Joel S. Kaminsky, *Yet I Loved Jacob: Reclaiming the Biblical Concept of Election* (Nashville, TN: Abingdon Press, 2007), 41. See also Joel N. Lohr, *Chosen and Unchosen: Conceptions of Election in the Pentateuch and Jewish-Christian Interpretation* (Winona Lake, IN: Eisenbrauns, 2009).

28. Kaminsky, *Yet I Loved Jacob*, 41.

29. See ibid., 155.

30. Ibid., 170. I agree with his contention that "[t]he argument between Judaism and Christianity is over who held the proper key to repair the fractured relationship between humans and God. Was this accomplished through the giving of the Torah to the Jews at Sinai (and the dynamics of repentance and reconciliation inherent in Torah observance), or through the death and resurrection of Christ at Golgotha (with its alternative schema of divine-human reconciliation)?" (ibid., 171). Yet I would add that the latter event is itself intrinsically related, according to Christians, to the giving of the Torah and its observance by Christ. On this point see my *Christ's Fulfillment of Torah and Temple: Salvation According to St. Thomas Aquinas* (Notre Dame, IN: University of Notre Dame Press, 2002).

31. On Mary's election or predestination, see Florovsky, "The Ever-Virgin Mother of God," in Mascall, *The Mother of God*, 51–63, at 55–59. Fitzmyer does not discuss election in this context (either Israel's election or Mary's), but he does observe: "In the conclusion to the Magnificat (vv. 54–55) Mary recognizes that the salvation that is to come through the birth, life, and career of Jesus is related to the covenant made by God with Abraham of old. The nation of Israel, God's Servant, is recalled, as are the patriarchs. The remnant of Israel is to have a new meaning, for it is to be reconstituted in a way that will extend the promises of old to others not under the Law" (Fitzmyer, *The Gospel According to Luke (I–IX)*, 361). For Fitzmyer, of course, the Magnificat is not Mary's song but rather a composition reflective of Jewish Christianity that Luke inserted here.

32. Florovsky argues that "Mary had the grace of the Incarnation, as the Mother of the Incarnate, but this was not yet the *complete* grace, since the Redemption had not yet been accomplished"; yet nonetheless Mary's "personal purity was preserved by the perpetual assistance of the Spirit," so that in her there is no room for "any sensual and selfish desires or passions, any dissipation of the heart and mind. The bodily integrity or incorruption is but an outward sign of the internal purity" (Florovsky, "The Ever-Virgin Mother of God," in Mascall, *The Mother of God*, 59, 61).

33. Francesca Aran Murphy comments that "Hannah was a maverick in a culture that mixed soliciting the gods of sexual reproduction with pilgrimages to the shrine of Yahweh." Murphy, *1 Samuel* (Grand Rapids, MI: Brazos Press, 2010), 21. Hannah is atypical in her real commitment to YHWH. Historical-critical scholarship would attend at this juncture to rival priesthoods, including that of Shiloh: see Richard Elliott Friedman, *Who Wrote the Bible?* (New York:

Simon & Schuster, 1987). For our purposes, Hannah's (and Mary's) focus on God is clearly the central element.

34. See Levenson, *Resurrection and the Restoration of Israel*, 172–73.

35. See Bill T. Arnold's remark: "By his powerful word, God has broken the grip of death, hopelessness, and barrenness. The joyous laughter is the end of sorrow and weeping (Matt. 5:4; Luke 6:21; John 16:20–24). Laughter is a biblical way of receiving a newness which cannot be explained. The newness is sheer gift—underived, unwarranted" (Arnold, *Genesis*, 182).

36. On this theme see especially N. T. Wright's immensely creative *The New Testament and the People of God*, chap. 10.

37. See also Ignace de la Potterie, S.J., *The Hour of Jesus: The Passion and the Resurrection of Jesus according to John; Text and Spirit*, trans. Gregory Murray, O.S.B. (Middlegreen, England: St. Paul Publications, 1989), 140–44.

38. See Mary L. Coloe, P.B.V.M., *Dwelling in the Household of God: Johannine Ecclesiology and Spirituality* (Collegeville, MN: Liturgical Press, 2007), 55–56.

39. See Thérèse of Lisieux, *Story of a Soul: The Autobiography of St. Thérèse of Lisieux*, 3rd ed., trans. John Clarke, O.C.D. (Washington, D.C.: ICS Publications, 1996).

40. See Sean M. McDonough, *Christ as Creator: Origins of a New Testament Doctrine* (Oxford: Oxford University Press, 2009), chapter 10.

41. See Trevor J. Burke, *Adopted into God's Family: Exploring a Pauline Metaphor* (Downers Grove, IL: InterVarsity Press, 2006), chapter 8.

42. For discussion see Florovsky, "The Ever-Virgin Mother of God," in Mascall, *The Mother of God*, 53–54.

43. On "privilege," a concept that has fallen out of favor, see Aurel Kolnai, *Ethics, Value, and Reality* (New Brunswick, NJ: Transaction, 2008). See also G. J. McAleer's use of "privilege," indebted to Kolnai, in his *Ecstatic Morality and Sexual Politics: A Catholic and Antitotalitarian Theory of the Body* (New York: Fordham University Press, 2005).

44. Commenting on Dante's *Paradiso*, Ralph McInerny remarks that "[t]he uniqueness of Mary's role in the providential plan explains her place in the celestial empyrean and the love and devotion shown to her by the blessed. If Mary had not accepted the angel's message, none of them would be here." McInerny, *Dante and the Blessed Virgin* (Notre Dame, IN: University of Notre Dame Press, 2010), 130.

45. A standard historical-critical reconstruction of Matthew's narrative of the virgin birth is provided by W. D. Davies and Dale C. Allison, Jr. in *A Critical and Exegetical Commentary on the Gospel According to Saint Matthew*, vol. 1, *Introduction and Commentary on Matthew I–VII* (London: T & T Clark, 1988), 190–97. They summarize their position, indebted to Raymond Brown and others, as follows:

[S]tage I in the development of the Matthean infancy narrative, the Mosaic stage, told of a dream in which Jesus' father was commanded to take his wife because her child would deliver Israel. It also told of two other similar dreams in which Joseph was again given commands and explanations— whence the common pattern still preserved in 1.18–25; 2.13–15; and 2.19–21. But when the primitive story line was expanded in the interests of a Davidic Christology (stage II), certain traditions were added, including that of the virgin birth, this last being passed on in the standard angelic annunciation of birth pattern (cf. Lk 1.26–38). The result was the confluence of two once independent structures. To the traditional story taken up into 1.18–25, Matthew (stage III) added a general introductory statement (18a), inserted a formula quotation (22–3), and rewrote 24–5 in accordance with an OT sentence form. (Ibid., 197)

One can here see why the virgin birth is as difficult for many scholars to accept as is Mary's Assumption.

46. Against the view that Luke 8:19–21, for example, indicates a rift between Jesus and his mother (and brothers), see Richard J. Bauckham, "The Family of Jesus," in *Jesus among Friends and Enemies: A Historical and Literary Introduction to Jesus in the Gospels*, ed. Chris Keith and Larry W. Hurtado (Grand Rapids, MI: Baker Academic, 2011), 103–25, at 121. But Bauckham does hold that "during his ministry he did not always enjoy the full support of his mother and siblings" (ibid., 125).

47. See Fitzmyer, *The Gospel According to Luke (I–IX)*, 341.

48. For a survey of historical-critical conjectures regarding the potential background to the story of Jesus' transfiguration, see W. D. Davies and Dale C. Allison, Jr., *A Critical and Exegetical Commentary on the Gospel According to Saint Matthew*, vol. 2, *Commentary on Matthew VIII–XVIII* (London: T & T Clark, 1991), 684–706.

49. For further background to John 2:1–12, see especially Francis Martin, "Mary in Sacred Scripture," 525–69.

50. See Witherington, *John's Wisdom*, 78.

51. Thomas Merton, *New Seeds of Contemplation* (Boston: Shambala, 2003 [orig. ed. 1961]), 176. The opposite view is that "Mary's function was historically complete in the virginal conception and bearing of the Saviour. She had no ongoing function in the *ordo salutis* which is the work of the Holy Spirit alone" (Donald G. Dawe, "From Dysfunction to Disbelief: The Virgin Mary in Reformed Theology," in Stacpoole, *Mary's Place in Christian Dialogue*, 142–50, at 146). For Dawe's own position, which from a Reformed perspective sets forth a highly sympathetic account of the doctrine of Mary's Assumption, see Dawe, "The Assumption of the Blessed Virgin in Ecumenical Perspective," 41–54.

52. See Thomas Joseph White, O.P., "The Virgin Mary and the Church: The Marian Exemplarity of Ecclesial Faith," *Nova et Vetera* 11 (2013): 375–405, at 403. See also Marie-Dominique Philippe, O.P., *The Mysteries of Mary:*

Growing in Faith, Hope, and Love with the Mother of God (Charlotte, NC: Saint Benedict Press, 2011).

53. In the following two paragraphs, I quote from the English translation of Pope Benedict XVI's "Homily for August 15, 2011, the Feast of the Assumption," available at http://www.zenit.org/article-33198?l=english.

54. For the biblical and patristic theologies of communion and their philosophical antecedents, see Nicholas Sagovsky, *Ecumenism, Christian Origins and the Practice of Communion* (Cambridge: Cambridge University Press, 2000).

Conclusion

1. A possible exception might be the small stir caused by Pope John Paul II in his General Audience of June 25, 1997, where he affirmed that Mary truly died. One might also mention the highly unfortunate claim of Leonardo Boff, O.F.M., that Mary's Assumption reveals the "hypostatic union of the Holy Spirit with Mary": see Boff, *The Maternal Face of God: The Feminine and Its Religious Expressions*, trans. Robert R. Barr and John W. Diercksmeier (San Francisco: Harper & Row, 1987 [Spanish ed. 1979]), 174. Boff's theology of God is Hegelian rather than Catholic: "God, as eternal life in the permanent process of self-realization, encounters a new expression of divine reality in the feminine as made humanly concrete in its highest degree in and by Mary" (ibid.).

2. See John Paul II, *Redemptoris Mater* § 22.

3. Benedict XVI, Homily on the Assumption of Mary, August 15, 2005, reprinted in *Maria: Pope Benedict XVI on the Mother of God* (San Francisco: Ignatius Press, 2009), 25.

4. Russell, "The Blessed Virgin Mary in the Bible," in Stacpoole, *Mary's Place in Christian Dialogue*, 45–50, at 45.

5. Benedict XVI, Homily on the Assumption of Mary, August 15, 2006, reprinted in *Maria*, 79.

6. Ibid. Benedict XVI emphasizes that in guiding us to praise the mother of the incarnate Son, God does not thereby guide us away from himself. Rather, praising God's gifts is a central way of praising God.

7. Tim Perry, *Mary for Evangelicals: Toward an Understanding of the Mother of Our Lord* (Downers Grove, IL: IVP Academic, 2006), 263. This distinction between the historical Mary and the symbolic Mary is also made by Catharina Halkes, "Mary and Women," trans. David Smith, in Küng and Moltmann, *Mary in the Churches*, 66–73, at 67.

8. See Perry, *Mary for Evangelicals*, 290. Perry rules out the idea that Mary's suffering at the foot of the Cross "was coredemptive with the suffering of Christ" in the sense of laboring for the birth of the Church rather than simply grieving over her Son's death: see Perry, *Mary for Evangelicals*, 306. For discussion of how Christ's grace enables us to participate in his sacrificial love, see

Michael J. Gorman, *Inhabiting the Cruciform God: Kenosis, Justification, and Theosis in Paul's Narrative Soteriology* (Grand Rapids, MI: Eerdmans, 2009). See also Kyriaki Karidoyanes FitzGerald, "Mary the *Theotokos* and the Call to Holiness," in Braaten and Jenson, *Mary, Mother of God*, 80–99, at 94–97. For his part, the Lutheran theologian David Yeago, in light of his understanding of the "scriptural Christ," accepts that "there is no redemptive relationship to Jesus Christ that does not contain within itself a relationship to Mary, though not, of course, the same relationship" (Yeago, "The Presence of Mary in the Mystery of the Church," in Braaten and Jenson, *Mary, Mother of God*, 58–79, at 59).

9. Johnson, *Truly Our Sister*, 313; cf. 79, 95.

10. Ibid., 130. For feminist criticism of the relationship of Mary and Eve in *Lumen Gentium*, see also Tina Beattie, *God's Mother, Eve's Advocate: A Marian Narrative of Women's Salvation* (London: Continuum, 2002), 151; and Anne E. Carr, *Transforming Grace: Christian Tradition and Women's Experience* (San Francisco: Harper & Row, 1990), 191. Beattie's book, like Johnson's, does not attend to Mary's Assumption, although Beattie does mention Mary's Assumption in claiming that "there is no symbolic recognition of the redemption of the female body in Catholic Christianity, even though the doctrine of the Assumption entails the belief that at least one woman, the Virgin Mary, has been bodily assumed into heaven" (Beattie, *God's Mother, Eve's Advocate*, 54). Similarly, the contributors to *A Feminist Companion to Mariology*, ed. Amy-Jill Levine with Maria Mayo Robbins (London: T & T Clark International, 2005), do not treat Mary's Assumption. In her *Rediscovering Mary: Insights from the Gospels* (London: Burns & Oates, 1995), Beattie presents the Eve-Mary parallel more positively in a brief commentary on the wedding at Cana (Jn 2). For further studies of Mary from broadly feminist perspectives, see Rubin, *Mother of God*; Bonnie J. Miller, "'Pondering All These Things': Mary and Motherhood," in Gaventa and Rigby, *Blessed One*, 97–114; Sarah Coakley, "Mariology and 'Romantic Feminism': A Critique," in *Women's Voices: Essays in Contemporary Feminist Theory*, ed. Teresa Elwes (London: Marshall Pickering, 1992), 97–110; Kyriaki Karidoyanes FitzGerald, "The Eve-Mary Typology and Women in the Orthodox Church: Reconsidering Rhodes," *Anglican Theological Review* 84 (2002): 627–44; and Maja Weyermann, "The Typologies of Adam-Christ and Eve-Mary, and Their Relationship to One Another," *Anglican Theological Review* 84 (2002): 609–26. See also the concerns raised by Kilian McDonnell, O.S.B., "Feminist Mariologies: Heteronomy/ Subordination and the Scandal of Christology," *Theological Studies* 66 (2005): 527–67. For a view of traditional Marian devotion as invariably a tool of power-hungry clergy and oppressive despots, see Nicholas Perry and Loreto Echeverría, *Under the Heel of Mary* (London: Routledge, 1988).

11. See also Elizabeth A. Johnson's "The Symbolic Character of Theological Statements about Mary," *Journal of Ecumenical Studies* 22 (1985): 312–35.

12. See Larry W. Hurtado, *At the Origins of Christian Worship: The Context and Character of Earliest Christian Devotion* (Grand Rapids, MI: Eerdmans, 1999); and James D. G. Dunn, *Did the First Christians Worship Jesus?* (Louisville, KY: Westminster John Knox Press, 2010). See also, Larry W. Hurtado, *How on Earth Did Jesus Become a God? Historical Questions about Earliest Devotion to Jesus* (Grand Rapids, MI: Eerdmans, 2005); Larry W. Hurtado, *Lord Jesus Christ: Devotion to Jesus in Earliest Christianity* (Grand Rapids, MI: Eerdmans, 2003); and Daniel Liderbach, S.J., *Christ in the Early Christian Hymns* (New York: Paulist Press, 1998).

13. John Macquarrie, *Mary for All Christians* (Grand Rapids, MI: Eerdmans, 1990), 95–96. For a similar Anglican perspective, see Mascall, "The Dogmatic Theology of the Mother of God," in Mascall, *The Mother of God*, 37–51. See also the work of the Lutheran theologian Ulrich Wickert, *Ein evangelischer Theologe schreibt über Maria* (Berlin: Morus-Verlag, 1979).

14. Along these lines, the Anglican theologian John de Satgé argues that Mary's Assumption should be understood "as the end of the great Pauline series [Romans 8:29–30]; Mary the woman whose predestination has been advanced to its full term of conformation to the image of God's son and hers; Mary who was called and who responded totally; Mary who was justified and rejoiced in her salvation; Mary who has been glorified" (de Satgé, *Down to Earth*, 79). De Satgé considers that although Scripture is silent about Mary's Assumption, the doctrine is nonetheless "congruent with Scripture" (ibid.) and can be held to be true even if not necessary for salvific faith.

15. Vanhoozer, *The Drama of Doctrine*, 268.

Bibliography

Aageson, James W. *Written Also for Our Sake: Paul and the Art of Biblical Interpretation*. Louisville, KY: Westminster/John Knox Press, 1993.

Allchin, A. M. *The Joy of All Creation: An Anglican Meditation on the Place of Mary*. London: Darton, Longman & Todd, 1984.

Allert, Craig. *A High View of Scripture? The Authority of the Bible and the Formation of the New Testament Canon*. Grand Rapids, MI: Baker Academic, 2007.

Altaner, Berthold. "Zur Frage der Definibilität der Assumptio B. V. M." *Theologische Revue* 44 (1948): 129–40.

———. "Zur Frage der Definibilität der Assumptio B. V. M." *Theologische Revue* 45 (1949): 129–42.

———. "Zur Frage der Definibilität der Assumptio B. V. M." *Theologische Revue* 46 (1950): 5–20.

Anatolios, Khaled. *Retrieving Nicaea: The Development and Meaning of Trinitarian Doctrine*. Grand Rapids, MI: Baker Academic, 2011.

Anderson, Gary A. *The Genesis of Perfection: Adam and Eve in Jewish and Christian Imagination*. Louisville, KY: Westminster John Knox Press, 2001.

Anderson, H. George, J. Francis Stafford, and Joseph A. Burgess, eds. *The One Mediator, the Saints, and Mary: Lutherans and Catholics in Dialogue VIII*. Minneapolis, MN: Augsburg Fortress, 1992.

Anglican-Roman Catholic Commission in Canada. "A Response to 'Mary: Grace and Hope in Christ.'" *One in Christ* 43 (2009): 167–82.

Arnold, Bill T. *Genesis*. Cambridge: Cambridge University Press, 2009.

Auerbach, Erich. "'Figura.'" Translated by Ralph Manheim. In *Scenes from the Drama of European Literature: Six Essays*. Gloucester, MA: Peter Smith, 1973: 11–76.

Augustine. *Answer to Faustus, a Manichean*. Translated by Roland Teske, S.J. Hyde Park, NY: New City Press, 2007.

Ayres, Lewis. *Nicaea and Its Legacy: An Approach to Fourth-Century Trinitarian Theology*. Oxford: Oxford University Press, 2004.

———. "'There's Fire in That Rain': On Reading the Letter and Reading Allegorically." *Modern Theology* 28 (2012): 616–34.

Ayres, Lewis, and Stephen E. Fowl. "(Mis)reading the Face of God: *The Interpretation of the Bible in the Church*." *Theological Studies* 60 (1999): 513–28.

Bagatti, Bellarmino, O.F.M., M. Piccirillo, and A. Prodomo, O.F.M. *New Discoveries at the Tomb of Virgin Mary in Gethsemane*. Jerusalem: Franciscan Printing Press, 1975.

Balić, Carolus, O.F.M. *Testimonia de Assumptione Beatae Virginis Mariae ex omnibus saeculis. Pars prior: ex aetate ante concilium tridentine*. Rome: Academia Mariana, 1948.

Balthasar, Hans Urs von. "*Casta Meretrix*." Translated by John Saward. In *Explorations in Theology*. Vol. 2, *Spouse of the Word*. San Francisco: Ignatius Press, 1991: 193–288.

———. *The Glory of the Lord: A Theological Aesthetics*. Vol. 6, *Theology: The Old Covenant*. Translated by Brian McNeil, C.R.V., and Erasmo Leiva-Merikakis. Edited by John Riches. San Francisco: Ignatius Press, 1991.

———. "The Marian Mold of the Church." In *Mary: The Church at the Source*. By Joseph Ratzinger and Hans Urs von Balthasar. Translated by Adrian Walker. San Francisco: Ignatius Press, 2005: 125–44.

———. *Mary for Today*. Translated by Robert Nowell. San Francisco: Ignatius Press, 1987.

———. *Paul Struggles with His Congregation: The Pastoral Message of the Letters to the Corinthians*. Translated by Brigitte L. Bojarska. San Francisco: Ignatius Press, 1992.

———. *Theo-Drama: Theological Dramatic Theory*. Vol. 3, *The Dramatis Personae: The Person in Christ*. Translated by Graham Harrison. San Francisco: Ignatius Press, 1992.

———. *Theo-Drama: Theological Dramatic Theory*. Vol. 5, *The Last Act*. Translated by Graham Harrison. San Francisco: Ignatius Press, 1998.

———. *The Threefold Garland: The World's Salvation in Mary's Prayer*. Translated by Erasmo Leiva-Merikakis. San Francisco: Ignatius Press, 1982.

Barker, Margaret. *The Great High Priest: The Temple Roots of Christian Liturgy*. London: T & T Clark, 2003.

Barker, Patrick G. "Allegory and Typology in Galatians 4:21–31." *St Vladimir's Theological Quarterly* 38 (1994): 193–209.

Barr, James. *The Garden of Eden and the Hope of Immortality*. Minneapolis, MN: Fortress Press, 1993.

———. *Old and New in Interpretation: A Study of the Two Testaments*. New York: Harper & Row, 1966.

Barth, Karl. *Church Dogmatics*. Vol. I, part 2, *The Doctrine of the Word of God*. Translated by G. T. Thomason and Harold Knight. Edinburgh: T & T Clark, 1956.

———. *The Great Promise: Luke I*. Translated by Hans Freund. Eugene, OR: Wipf and Stock, 2004.

———. "A Letter about Mariology." In *Ad Limina Apostolorum: An Appraisal of Vatican II*. Translated by Keith R. Crim. Richmond, VA: John Knox Press, 1968: 57–62.

Basil the Great. *On the Holy Spirit*. Translated by David Anderson. Crestwood, NY: St Vladimir's Seminary Press, 1997.

Bastero, Juan Luis. "El Espíritu Sancto y María en *Lumen Gentium* y en el Magisterio de Pablo VI." *Scripta Theologica* 38 (2006): 701–35.

Bauckham, Richard. "The Brothers and Sisters of Jesus: An Epiphanian Response to John P. Meier." *Catholic Biblical Quarterly* 56 (1994): 686–700.

———. "The Family of Jesus." In *Jesus among Friends and Enemies: A Historical and Literary Introduction to Jesus in the Gospels*. Edited by Chris Keith and Larry W. Hurtado. Grand Rapids, MI: Baker Academic, 2011: 103–25.

———. *The Fate of the Dead: Studies on Jewish and Christian Apocalypses*. Leiden: Brill, 1998.

———. *Jesus and the God of Israel: God Crucified and Other Studies on the New Testament's Christology of Divine Identity*. Grand Rapids, MI: Eerdmans, 2008.

———. *Jude and the Relatives of Jesus in the Early Church*. Edinburgh: T & T Clark, 1990.

———. "Tradition in Relation to Scripture and Reason." In *Scripture, Tradition and Reason: A Study in the Criteria of Christian Doctrine*. Edited by Richard Bauckham and Benjamin Drewery. Edinburgh: T & T Clark, 1988: 117–45.

Bauckham, Richard, and Benjamin Drewery, eds. *Scripture, Tradition and Reason: A Study in the Criteria of Christian Doctrine*. Edinburgh: T & T Clark, 1988.

Baumgärtel, Friedrich. "The Hermeneutical Problem of the Old Testament." Translated by Murray Newman. In *Essays on Old Testament Hermeneutics*. Edited by Claus Westermann. Richmond, VA: John Knox Press, 1964: 134–59.

Beale, G. K. *The Erosion of Inerrancy in Evangelicalism*. Wheaton, IL: Crossway Books, 2008.

———. *The Temple and the Church's Mission: A Biblical Theology of the Dwelling Place of God*. Downers Grove, IL: InterVarsity Press, 2004.

Beattie, Tina. *God's Mother, Eve's Advocate: A Marian Narrative of Women's Salvation*. London: Continuum, 2002.

———. *Rediscovering Mary: Insights from the Gospels*. London: Burns & Oates, 1995.

Beavis, Mary Ann. "The Resurrection of Jephthah's Daughter: Judges 11:34–40 and Mark 5:21–24, 35–43." *Catholic Biblical Quarterly* 72 (2010): 46–62.

Begbie, Jeremy S. "The Shape of Things to Come? Wright Amidst Emerging Ecclesiologies." In *Jesus, Paul and the People of God: A Theological Dialogue with N. T. Wright.* Edited by Nicholas Perrin and Richard B. Hays. Downers Grove, IL: InterVarsity Press, 2011: 183–208.

Benedict XVI. "Homily for August 15, 2011, the Feast of the Assumption." http://www.zenit.org/article-33198?l=english.

———. *Maria: Pope Benedict XVI on the Mother of God.* San Francisco: Ignatius Press, 2009.

———. *Saint Paul.* Translated by *L'Osservatore Romano.* Vatican City: Libreria Editrice Vaticana, 2009.

———. *Saved in Hope – Spe Salvi.* San Francisco: Ignatius Press, 2008.

Benko, Stephen. *Protestants, Catholics, and Mary.* Valley Forge, PA: Judson Press, 1968.

———. *The Virgin Goddess: Studies in the Pagan and Christian Roots of Mariology.* Leiden: E. J. Brill, 1993.

Bissonnette, George, A.A. "The Twelfth Chapter of the Apocalypse and Our Lady's Assumption." *Marian Studies* 2 (1951): 170–77.

Blancy, Alain, Maurice Jourjon, and the Dombes Group. *Mary in the Plan of God and in the Communion of Saints: Toward a Common Christian Understanding.* Translated by Matthew J. O'Connell. New York: Paulist Press, 2002.

Bockmuehl, Markus. *Simon Peter in Scripture and Memory: The New Testament Apostle in the Early Church.* Grand Rapids, MI: Baker Academic, 2012.

Bockmuehl, Markus, and Michael B. Thompson, eds. *A Vision for the Church: Studies in Early Christian Ecclesiology in Honour of J. P. M. Sweet.* Edinburgh: T & T Clark, 1997.

Boda, Mark J. *A Severe Mercy: Sin and Its Remedy in the Old Testament.* Winona Lake, IN: Eisenbrauns, 2009.

Boersma, Hans. *Heavenly Participation: The Weaving of a Sacramental Tapestry.* Grand Rapids, MI: Eerdmans, 2011.

———. *Nouvelle Théologie and Sacramental Ontology: A Return to Mystery.* Oxford: Oxford University Press, 2009.

Boff, Leonardo. *The Maternal Face of God: The Feminine and Its Religious Expressions.* Translated by Robert R. Barr and John W. Diercksmeier. San Francisco: Harper & Row, 1987.

Bolen, Donald, and Gregory Cameron, eds. *Mary: Grace and Hope in Christ. The Seattle Statement of the Anglican-Roman Catholic International Commission: The Text with Commentaries and Study Guide.* New York: Continuum, 2006.

Bonino, Serge-Thomas, O.P., ed. *Surnaturel: A Controversy at the Heart of Twentieth-Century Thomistic Thought.* Translated by Robert Williams. Ave Maria, FL: Sapientia Press, 2009.

Bonnefoy, Jean-François. "L'Assomption de la T. S. Vierge et sa predestination." In *Vers le dogme de l'Assomption. Journées d'études mariales, Montréal 12–15 Août 1948*. Edited by Adrien-M. Malo, O.F.M. South Bend, IN: Fides, 1948: 293–335.

Børresen, Kari. "Mary in Catholic Theology." In *Mary in the Churches*. Edited by Hans Küng and Jürgen Moltmann. New York: Seabury Press, 1983: 48–56.

Borsch, Frederick H. "Mary and Scripture: A Response to *Mary: Grace and Hope in Christ*." *Anglican Theological Review* 89 (2007): 375–99.

Boss, Sarah Jane, ed. *Mary: The Complete Resource*. Oxford: Oxford University Press, 2007.

Bourque, Emmanuel. "Le sens de l'Assomption dans la liturgie." In *Vers le dogme de l'Assomption. Journées d'études mariales, Montréal 12–15 Août 1948*. Edited by Adrien-M. Malo, O.F.M. South Bend, IN: Fides, 1948: 151–202.

Bouteneff, Peter C. *Beginnings: Ancient Christian Readings of the Biblical Creation Narratives*. Grand Rapids, MI: Baker Academic, 2008.

———. *Sweeter than Honey: Orthodox Thinking on Dogma and Truth*. Crestwood, NY: St Vladimir's Seminary Press, 2006.

Bouyer, Louis. *The Seat of Wisdom: An Essay on the Place of the Virgin Mary in Christian Theology*. Translated by A. V. Littledale. London: Darton, Longman & Todd, 1960.

Box, H. S. "The Assumption." In *The Blessed Virgin Mary: Essays by Anglican Writers*. Edited by E. L. Mascall and H. S. Box. London: Darton, Longman & Todd, 1963: 89–102.

Braaten, Carl E., and Robert W. Jenson, eds. *Mary, Mother of God*. Grand Rapids, MI: Eerdmans, 2004.

Bradshaw, Timothy. "The Anglican Commentary." In *Mary: Grace and Hope in Christ. The Seattle Statement of the Anglican-Roman Catholic International Commission: The Text with Commentaries and Study Guide*. Edited by Donald Bolen and Gregory Cameron. New York: Continuum, 2006: 133–65.

Breck, John. *Scripture in Tradition: The Bible and Its Interpretation in the Orthodox Church*. Crestwood, NY: St Vladimir's Seminary Press, 2001.

Brock, Sebastian. "Mary in Syriac Tradition." In *Mary's Place in Christian Dialogue: Occasional Papers of the Ecumenical Society of the Blessed Virgin Mary, 1970–1980*. Edited by Alberic Stacpoole, O.S.B. Middlegreen, England: St. Paul Publications, 1982: 182–91.

Brown, Raymond E., S.S. *The Death of the Messiah: From Gethsemane to the Grave*. 2 vols. New York: Doubleday, 1994.

———. *The Gospel according to John (I–XII)*. Garden City, NY: Doubleday, 1966.

Brown, Raymond E., Karl P. Donfried, Joseph A. Fitzmyer, and John Reumann, eds. *Mary in the New Testament: A Collaborative Assessment by Protestant and Roman Catholic Scholars*. New York: Paulist Press, 1978.

Brown, Robert McAfee. *The Ecumenical Revolution*. London: Burns & Oates, 1969.

Brueggemann, Walter. *Genesis*. Louisville, KY: Westminster John Knox Press, 2010.

Buggert, Donald W., Louis P. Rogge, and Michael J. Wastag, eds. *Mother, Behold Your Son: Essays in Honor of Eamon R. Carroll, O.Carm*. Washington, D.C.: Carmelite Institute, 2001.

Bulgakov, Sergius. *The Bride of the Lamb*. Translated by Boris Jakim. Grand Rapids, MI: Eerdmans, 2002.

Burghardt, Walter J., S.J. "On Early Christian Exegesis." *Theological Studies* 11 (1950): 78–116.

———. "The Testimony of the Patristic Age Concerning Mary's Death." *Marian Studies* 8 (1957): 58–99.

Burke, Trevor J. *Adopted into God's Family: Exploring a Pauline Metaphor*. Downers Grove, IL: InterVarsity Press, 2006.

Cahill, P. Joseph. "Hermeneutical Implications of Typology." *Catholic Biblical Quarterly* 44 (1982): 266–81.

Calvin, John. *Institutes of the Christian Religion*. Translated by Henry Beveridge. Grand Rapids, MI: Eerdmans, 1989.

Campenhausen, Hans von. *The Virgin Birth in the Theology of the Ancient Church*. Translated by Frank Clarke. London: SCM Press, 1964.

Cantalamessa, Raniero. *Mary: Mirror of the Church*. Translated by Frances Lonergan Villa. Collegeville, MN: Liturgical Press, 1992.

Capelle, Bernard. "Les Homélies liturgique de prétendu Timothée de Jérusalem." *Ephemerides liturgicae* 63 (1949): 5–26.

Cardinale, H. E. "Pope Pius XII and the Blessed Virgin Mary." In *Mary's Place in Christian Dialogue: Occasional Papers of the Ecumenical Society of the Blessed Virgin Mary, 1970–1980*. Edited by Alberic Stacpoole, O.S.B. Middlegreen, England: St. Paul Publications, 1982: 248–60.

Caro, Roberto, S.J. *La Homiletica Mariana Griega en el Siglo V*. 3 vols. Dayton, OH: University of Dayton Press, 1971–73.

Carol, Juniper B., O.F.M. "A Bibliography of the Assumption." *The Thomist* 14 (1951): 133–60.

———. "The Definability of Mary's Assumption." *American Ecclesiastical Review* 118 (1948): 161–77.

Carr, Anne E. *Transforming Grace: Christian Tradition and Women's Experience*. San Francisco: Harper & Row, 1990.

Carroll, Eamon R., O.Carm. *Understanding the Mother of Jesus*. Wilmington, DE: Michael Glazier, 1979.

Carson, D. A. "Three More Books on the Bible: A Critical Review." *Trinity Journal* 27 (2006): 1–62.

Carter, David. "Mary in Ecumenical Dialogue and Exchange." In *Mary: The Complete Resource*. Edited by Sarah Jane Boss. Oxford: Oxford University Press, 2007: 89–102.

Catechism of the Catholic Church. 2nd ed. Vatican City: Libreria Editrice Vaticana, 1997.

Cessario, Romanus, O.P. Christian Faith and the Theological Life. Washington, D.C.: Catholic University of America Press, 1996.

Clark, Alan. "The Holy Spirit and Mary." In Mary's Place in Christian Dialogue: Occasional Papers of the Ecumenical Society of the Blessed Virgin Mary, 1970–1980. Edited by Alberic Stacpoole, O.S.B. Middlegreen, England: St. Paul Publications, 1982: 79–88.

Clément, Olivier. You Are Peter: An Orthodox Theologian's Reflection on the Exercise of Papal Primacy. Translated by M. S. Laird. Hyde Park, NY: New City Press, 2003.

Clooney, Francis X., S.J. Divine Mother, Blessed Mother: Hindu Goddesses and the Virgin Mary. Oxford: Oxford University Press, 2005.

Coakley, Sarah. "Mariology and 'Romantic Feminism': A Critique." In Women's Voices: Essays in Contemporary Feminist Theory. Edited by Teresa Elwes. London: Marshall Pickering, 1992: 97–110.

Cole, William J., S.M. "Was Luther a Devotee of Mary?" Marian Studies 21 (1970): 94–202.

Collins, Raymond F. First Corinthians. Collegeville, MN: Liturgical Press, 1999.

Coloe, Mary L., P.B.V.M. Dwelling in the Household of God: Johannine Ecclesiology and Spirituality. Collegeville, MN: Liturgical Press, 2007.

———. God Dwells with Us: Temple Symbolism in the Fourth Gospel. Collegeville, MN: Liturgical Press, 2001.

Congar, Yves, O.P. Christ, Our Lady and the Church: A Study in Eirenic Theology. Translated by Henry St. John, O.P. London: Longmans, Green, 1957.

———. Faith and Spiritual Life. Translated by A. Manson and L. C. Sheppard. New York: Herder and Herder, 1968.

———. The Meaning of Tradition. Translated by A. N. Woodrow. San Francisco: Ignatius Press, 2004.

———. "Norms of Christian Allegiance and Identity in the History of the Church." Translated by John Griffiths. In Truth and Certainty. Edited by Edward Schillebeeckx and Bas van Iersel. New York: Herder and Herder, 1973: 11–25.

———. "Theological Notes on the Assumption." In Faith and Spiritual Life. Translated by A. Manson and L. C. Sheppard. New York: Herder and Herder, 1968: 3–10.

———. Tradition and Traditions: An Historical and Theological Essay. Translated by Michael Naseby and Thomas Rainborough. New York: Macmillan, 1967.

———. True and False Reform in the Church. Translated by Paul Philibert, O.P. Collegeville, MN: Liturgical Press, 2011.

Congregation for the Doctrine of the Faith. "Letter on Certain Questions Regarding Eschatology." Acta Apostolicae Sedis 71 (1979): 939–43.

Coppens, Joseph. "La définibilité de l'Assomption." *Ephemerides theologicae Lovanienses* 23 (1947): 5–35.

Cox, Patricia. "Origen and the Witch of Endor: Toward an Iconoclastic Typology." *Anglican Theological Review* 66 (1984): 137–47.

Crichton, J. D. *Our Lady in the Liturgy*. Collegeville, MN: Liturgical Press, 1997.

Culpepper, Gary. "'A Sword Will Pierce through Your Own Soul Also': The Sanctification, Conversion, and Exemplary Witness of the Blessed Mary." *Pro Ecclesia* 19 (2010): 28–45.

Cunneen, Sally. *In Search of Mary: The Woman and the Symbol*. New York: Random House, 1996.

Cunningham, Lawrence S. "Born of a Woman (Gal. 4:4): A Theological Meditation." In *Mary, Mother of God*. Edited by Carl E. Braaten and Robert W. Jenson. Grand Rapids, MI: Eerdmans, 2004: 36–48.

Dadosky, John D. "Woman without Envy: Toward Reconceiving the Immaculate Conception." *Theological Studies* 72 (2011): 15–40.

Daley, Brian E., S.J. "Woman of Many Names: Mary in Orthodox and Catholic Theology." *Theological Studies* 71 (2010): 846–69.

Daniélou, Jean, S.J. *From Shadows to Reality: Studies in the Biblical Typology of the Fathers*. Translated by Dom Wulstan Hibberd, O.S.B. London: Burns & Oates, 1960.

———. *God and the Ways of Knowing*. Translated by Walter Roberts. San Francisco: Ignatius Press, 2003.

———. "Le culte marial et le paganisme." In *Maria: Etudes sur la Sainte Vierge*. Edited by D'Hubert du Manoir. Paris: Beauchesne, 1949: 159–81.

———. "Les Orientations présentes de la pensée religieuse." *Études* 249 (1946): 5–21.

———. *The Lord of History: Reflections on the Inner Meaning of History*. Translated by Nigel Abercrombie. Chicago: Henry Regnery, 1958.

———. "Symbolism and History." In *The Lord of History: Reflections on the Inner Meaning of History*. Translated by Nigel Abercrombie. Chicago: Henry Regnery, 1958: 130–46.

———. *The Theology of Jewish Christianity*. Translated by John A. Baker. London: Darton, Longman & Todd, 1964.

Davies, W. D., and Dale C. Allison, Jr. *A Critical and Exegetical Commentary on the Gospel According to Saint Matthew*. Vol. 1, *Introduction and Commentary on Matthew I–VII*. London: T & T Clark, 1988.

———. *A Critical and Exegetical Commentary on the Gospel According to Saint Matthew*. Vol. 2, *Commentary on Matthew VIII–XVIII*. London: T & T Clark, 1991.

Dawe, Donald G. "The Assumption of the Blessed Virgin in Ecumenical Perspective." *The Way*, Supplement 45 (1982): 41–54.

———. "From Dysfunction to Disbelief: The Virgin Mary in Reformed Theology." In *Mary's Place in Christian Dialogue: Occasional Papers of the Ecu-*

menical Society of the Blessed Virgin Mary, 1970–1980. Edited by Alberic Stacpoole, O.S.B. Middlegreen, England: St. Paul Publications, 1982: 142–50.

Decelles, Charles. "A Fresh Look at the Assumption of Mary or The Idea of Resurrection Immediately Following Death." American Ecclesiastical Review 167 (1973): 147–63.

de Gaál, Emery. The Theology of Pope Benedict XVI: The Christocentric Shift. New York: Palgrave Macmillan, 2010.

Deiss, Lucien, C.S.Sp. Mary, Daughter of Sion. Translated by Barbara T. Blair. Collegeville, MN: Liturgical Press, 1972.

De Koninck, Charles. The Writings of Charles De Koninck. Vol. 2. Edited and translated by Ralph McInerny. Notre Dame, IN: University of Notre Dame Press, 2009.

de la Potterie, Ignace, S.J. The Hour of Jesus: The Passion and the Resurrection of Jesus according to John; Text and Spirit. Translated by Gregory Murray, O.S.B. Middlegreen, England: St. Paul Publications, 1989.

———. Mary in the Mystery of the Covenant. Translated by Bertrand Buby, S.M. Staten Island, NY: Alba House, 1992.

de Lubac, Henri, S.J. Medieval Exegesis: The Four Senses of Scripture. 3 vols. Translated by Mark Sebanc (vol. 1) and E. M. Macierowski (vols. 2–3). Grand Rapids, MI: Eerdmans, 1998–2009.

———. Scripture in the Tradition. Translated by Luke O'Neill. New York: Crossroad, 2000.

———. "'Typologie' et 'allégorisme.'" Recherches de science religieuse 34 (1947): 180–226.

de Margerie, Bertrand, S.J. "Dogmatic Development by Abridgement or by Concentration?" Translated by J. B. Carol, O.F.M. Marian Studies 27 (1976): 64–98.

———. "Ecumenical Problems in Mariology." Translated by Aloysius J. Owen, S.J. Marian Studies 26 (1975): 180–203.

Denzinger, Henry. The Sources of Catholic Dogma. Translated by Roy J. Deferrari from the 30th edition of Henry Denzinger's Enchiridion Symbolorum. Fitzwilliam, NH: Loreto Publications, 2002.

de Satgé, John. Down to Earth: A Protestant Vision of the Virgin Mary. Wilmington, NC: Consortium Books, 1976.

de Satgé, John, and John McHugh. "Bible and Tradition in regard to the Blessed Virgin Mary." In Mary's Place in Christian Dialogue: Occasional Papers of the Ecumenical Society of the Blessed Virgin Mary, 1970–1980. Edited by Alberic Stacpoole, O.S.B. Middlegreen, England: St. Paul Publications, 1982: 51–58.

Dessain, Charles Stephen. "Cardinal Newman's Teaching about the Blessed Virgin Mary." In Mary's Place in Christian Dialogue: Occasional Papers of the Ecumenical Society of the Blessed Virgin Mary, 1970–1980. Edited by

Alberic Stacpoole, O.S.B. Middlegreen, England: St. Paul Publications, 1982: 232–47.

Dever, William G. *Did God Have a Wife? Archaeology and Folk Religion in Ancient Israel.* Grand Rapids, MI: Eerdmans, 2005.

DeVille, Adam A. J. *Orthodoxy and the Roman Papacy: Ut Unum Sint and the Prospects of East-West Unity.* Notre Dame, IN: University of Notre Dame Press, 2011.

Dickens, W. T. *Hans Urs von Balthasar's* Theological Aesthetics: *A Model for Post-Critical Biblical Intepretation.* Notre Dame, IN: University of Notre Dame Press, 2003.

Donnelly, Doris, ed. *Mary, Woman of Nazareth: Biblical and Theological Perspectives.* New York: Paulist Press, 1990.

Duff, Nancy J. "Mary, the Servant of the Lord: Christian Vocation at the Manger and the Cross." In *Blessed One: Protestant Perspectives on Mary.* Edited by Beverly Roberts Gaventa and Cynthia L. Rigby. Louisville, KY: Westminster John Knox Press, 2002: 59–70.

Duhr, Joseph, S.J. *The Glorious Assumption of the Mother of God.* Translated by John Manning Fraunces, S.J. New York: P. J. Kenedy & Sons, 1950.

Dulles, Avery, S.J. "Dogma as an Ecumenical Problem." *Theological Studies* 29 (1968): 397–416.

———. "The Dogma of the Assumption." In *The One Mediator, the Saints, and Mary: Lutherans and Catholics in Dialogue VIII.* Edited by H. George Anderson, J. Francis Stafford, and Joseph A. Burgess. Minneapolis, MN: Augsburg Fortress, 1992: 279–94.

———. "How Real Is the Real Presence?" In *Church and Society: The Laurence J. McGinley Lectures, 1988–2007.* New York: Fordham University Press, 2008: 455–67.

———. *Magisterium: Teacher and Guardian of the Faith.* Naples, FL: Sapientia Press, 2007.

———. "Mary at the Dawn of the New Millennium." In *Church and Society: The Laurence J. McGinley Lectures, 1988–2007.* New York: Fordham University Press, 2008: 248–61.

———. "Moderate Infallibilism." In *Teaching Authority and Infallibility in the Church.* Edited by Paul C. Empie, T. Austin Murphy, and Joseph A. Burgess. Lutherans and Catholics in Dialogue VI. Minneapolis, MN: Augsburg, 1980: 81–100.

———. "A Proposal to Lift Anathemas." *Origins* 4 (1974): 418–21.

———. *The Survival of Dogma.* Garden City, NY: Doubleday, 1971.

Dunn, James D. G. *Did the First Christians Worship Jesus?* Louisville, KY: Westminster John Knox Press, 2010.

———. *The Theology of Paul the Apostle.* Grand Rapids, MI: Eerdmans, 1998.

Ebeling, Gerhard. "Zur Frage nach dem Sinn des mariologischen Dogmas." *Zeitschrift für Theologie und Kirche* 47 (1950): 383–91.

Ehrman, Terrence P. "The Metaphysics of the Resurrection: Exploring Human Embodiedness beyond Richard Swinburne's Dualism and Kevin Corcoran's Christian Materialism." PhD Dissertation, Catholic University of America, 2012.

Eichrodt, Walther. "Is Typological Exegesis an Appropriate Method?" Translated by James Barr. In *Essays on Old Testament Hermeneutics*. Edited by Claus Westermann. Richmond, VA: John Knox Press, 1964: 224–45.

Eire, Carlos. *A Very Brief History of Eternity*. Princeton, NJ: Princeton University Press, 2010.

Ellis, E. Earle. *Paul's Use of the Old Testament*. Edinburgh: Oliver and Boyd, 1957.

Elwes, Teresa, ed. *Women's Voices: Essays in Contemporary Feminist Theory*. London: Marshall Pickering, 1992.

Emery, Gilles, O.P. *The Trinity: An Introduction to Catholic Doctrine on the Triune God*. Translated by Matthew Levering. Washington, D.C.: Catholic University of America Press, 2011.

Empie, Paul C., T. Austin Murphy, and Joseph A. Burgess, eds. *Teaching Authority and Infallibility in the Church*. Lutherans and Catholics in Dialogue VI. Minneapolis, MN: Augsburg, 1980.

Endean, Philip. "How to Think about Mary's Privileges: A Post-Conciliar Exposition." In *Mary: The Complete Resource*. Edited by Sarah Jane Boss. Oxford: Oxford University Press, 2007: 284–91.

English, Leona M. "Roman Catholic Solutions to the Marian Question in Anglican–Roman Catholic Dialogue." *Journal of Ecumenical Studies* 37 (2000): 142–51.

Enns, Peter. *Inspiration and Incarnation: Evangelicals and the Problem of the Old Testament*. Grand Rapids, MI: Baker Academic, 2005.

Ernst, Johann. *Die leibliche Himmelfahrt Mariä: Historisch-dogmatisch nach ihrer Definierbarkeit beleuchtet*. Regensburg: Manz, 1921.

———. "Neues zur Knotroverse über die Definierbarkeit der Himmelfahrt Mariä." *Bonner Zeitschrift* 6 (1929): 289–304; 7 (1930): 16–31.

Evdokimov, Paul. *Orthodoxy*. Translated by Jeremy Hummerstone and Callan Slipper. Hyde Park, NY: New City Press, 2011.

Farkasfalvy, Denis, O.Cist. "Reconstructing Mariology: Mary's Virginity and the Future of Mariology." *Communio* 37 (2010): 47–68.

Farrer, Austin. "Mary, Scripture, and Tradition." In *The Blessed Virgin Mary: Essays by Anglican Writers*. Edited by E. L. Mascall and H. S. Box. London: Darton, Longman & Todd, 1963: 27–52.

Feingold, Lawrence. *The Natural Desire to See God according to St. Thomas Aquinas and His Interpreters*. 2nd ed. Ave Maria, FL: Sapientia Press, 2010.

Ferguson, Everett. "The Typology of Baptism in the Early Church." *Restoration Quarterly* 8 (1965): 41–52.

Feuillet, André. *Johannine Studies*. Translated by Thomas E. Crane. Staten Island, NY: Alba House, 1964.

————. "Les adieux du Christ à sa mère (Jn 19, 25–27) et la maternité spirituelle de Marie." *Nouvelle revue théologique* 86 (1964): 469–89.

Filograssi, J., S.J. "Theologia catholica et Assumptio B. V. M." *Gregorianum* 31 (1950): 323–60.

Fishbane, Michael. *Biblical Interpretation in Ancient Israel*. Oxford: Oxford University Press, 1985.

Fisichella, Rino. "Marie dans la théologie d'Hans Urs von Balthasar." *Communio* [French edition] 29 (2004): 87–98.

FitzGerald, Kyriaki Karidoyanes. "The Eve-Mary Typology and Women in the Orthodox Church: Reconsidering Rhodes." *Anglican Theological Review* 84 (2002): 627–44.

————. "Mary the *Theotokos* and the Call to Holiness." In *Mary, Mother of God*. Edited by Carl E. Braaten and Robert W. Jenson. Grand Rapids, MI: Eerdmans, 2004: 80–99.

Fitzmyer, Joseph A., S.J. *First Corinthians*. New Haven, CT: Yale University Press, 2008.

————. *The Gospel According to Luke (I–IX)*. Garden City, NY: Doubleday, 1981.

————. "The Office of Teaching in the Christian Church According to the New Testament." In *Teaching Authority and Infallibility in the Church*. Edited by Paul C. Empie, T. Austin Murphy, and Joseph A. Burgess. Lutherans and Catholics in Dialogue VI. Minneapolis, MN: Augsburg, 1980: 186–212.

Flanagan, Donal. "An Ecumenical Future for Roman Catholic Theology of Mary." In *Mary's Place in Christian Dialogue: Occasional Papers of the Ecumenical Society of the Blessed Virgin Mary, 1970–1980*. Edited by Alberic Stacpoole, O.S.B. Middlegreen, England: St. Paul Publications, 1982: 3–24.

————. "Eschatology and the Assumption." *Concilium* 41 (1969): 135–46.

————. *The Theology of Mary*. Hales Corners, WI: Clergy Book Service, 1976.

Florovsky, Georges. "The Ever-Virgin Mother of God." In *The Mother of God: A Symposium*. Edited by E. L. Mascall. London: Dacre Press, 1949: 51–63.

Flynn, Gabriel, and Paul D. Murray, eds. *Ressourcement: A Movement for Renewal in Twentieth-Century Catholic Theology*. Oxford: Oxford University Press, 2012.

Ford, John T., C.S.C. "Newman on 'Sensus Fidelium' and Mariology." *Marian Studies* 28 (1977): 120–45.

Foucauld, Charles de. *Charles de Foucauld: Writings*. Maryknoll, NY: Orbis Books, 1999.

France, R. T. *Jesus and the Old Testament: His Application of Old Testament Passages to Himself and His Mission*. Vancouver, B.C.: Regent College Publishing, 1998.

Freithoff, Caspar, O.P. "The Dogmatic Definition of the Assumption." *The Thomist* 14 (1951): 41–58.

Friedel, Francis J. *The Mariology of Cardinal Newman*. New York: Benziger, 1929.

Friedman, Richard Elliott. *Who Wrote the Bible?* New York: Simon & Schuster, 1987.

Fries, Heinrich, and Karl Rahner. *Unity of the Churches: An Actual Possibility*. Translated by Ruth C. L. Gritsch and Eric W. Gritsch. Philadelphia: Fortress Press, 1985.

Froehlich, Karlfried. "Fallibility Instead of Infallibility? A Brief History of the Interpretation of Galatians 2:11–14." In *Teaching Authority and Infallibility in the Church*. Edited by Paul C. Empie, T. Austin Murphy, and Joseph A. Burgess. Lutherans and Catholics in Dialogue VI. Minneapolis, MN: Augsburg, 1980: 259–69.

Gambero, Luigi, S.M. *Mary and the Fathers of the Church: The Blessed Virgin Mary in Patristic Thought*. Translated by Thomas Buffer. San Francisco: Ignatius Press, 1999.

——. *Mary in the Middle Ages: The Blessed Virgin Mary in the Thought of Medieval Latin Theologians*. Translated by Thomas Buffer. San Francisco: Ignatius Press, 2005.

Gardner, Lucy. "Balthasar and the Figure of Mary." In *The Cambridge Companion to Hans Urs von Balthasar*. Edited by Edward T. Oakes, S.J., and David Moss. Cambridge: Cambridge University Press, 2004: 64–78.

Garrigou-Lagrange, Réginald, O.P. *Grace: Commentary on the* Summa theologica *of St. Thomas, Ia IIae, q. 109–14*. Translated by the Dominican Nuns of Corpus Christi Monastery. St. Louis, MO: B. Herder, 1952.

——. "La Théologie nouvelle, où va-t-elle?" *Angelicum* 23 (1946): 126–45.

——. *The Mother of the Saviour and Our Interior Life*. Translated by Bernard J. Kelly, C.S.Sp. Charlotte, NC: TAN Books, 1993.

——. *Predestination*. Translated by Dom Bede Rose, O.S.B. Rockford, IL: TAN Books, 1998.

Garrigues, Jean-Miguel. "The 'Natural Grace' of Christ in St. Thomas." In *Surnaturel: A Controversy at the Heart of Twentieth-Century Thomistic Thought*. Edited by Serge-Thomas Bonino, O.P. Translated by Robert Williams. Ave Maria, FL: Sapientia Press, 2009: 103–15.

Gaventa, Beverly Roberts. *Mary: Glimpses of the Mother of Jesus*. Minneapolis, MN: Fortress Press, 1999.

——. "'Nothing Will Be Impossible with God': Mary as the Mother of Believers." In *Mary, Mother of God*. Edited by Carl E. Braaten and Robert W. Jenson. Grand Rapids, MI: Eerdmans, 2004: 19–35.

——. "'Standing Near the Cross': Mary and the Crucifixion of Jesus." In *Blessed One: Protestant Perspectives on Mary*. Edited by Beverly Roberts Gaventa and Cynthia L. Rigby. Louisville, KY: Westminster John Knox Press, 2002: 47–56.

Gaventa, Beverly Roberts, and Cynthia L. Rigby, eds. *Blessed One: Protestant Perspectives on Mary*. Louisville, KY: Westminster John Knox Press, 2002.

George, Timothy. "The Blessed Virgin Mary in Evangelical Perspective." In *Mary, Mother of God*. Edited by Carl E. Braaten and Robert W. Jenson. Grand Rapids, MI: Eerdmans, 2004: 100–122.

Giblet, Jean. "Aspects of the Truth in the New Testament." Translated by Dinah Livingstone. In *Truth and Certainty*. Edited by Edward Schillebeeckx and Bas van Iersel. New York: Herder and Herder, 1973: 35–42.

Glenny, W. Edward. "Typology: A Summary of the Present Evangelical Discussion." *Journal of the Evangelical Theological Society* 40 (1997): 627–38.

Gnilka, Joachim. "The Ministry of Peter—New Testament Foundations." In *The Petrine Ministry: Catholics and Orthodox in Dialogue*. Edited by Walter Kasper. Translated by the staff of the Pontifical Council for Promoting Christian Unity. New York: Paulist Press, 2006: 24–35.

Goodrich, John K. *Paul as an Administrator of God in 1 Corinthians*. Cambridge: Cambridge University Press, 2012.

Goppelt, Leonhard. *Typos: The Typological Interpretation of the Old Testament in the New*. Translated by D. H. Madvig. Grand Rapids, MI: Eerdmans, 1982.

Gorman, Michael J. *Inhabiting the Cruciform God: Kenosis, Justification, and Theosis in Paul's Narrative Soteriology*. Grand Rapids, MI: Eerdmans, 2009.

Goulder, Michael D. "Matthew's Vision for the Church." In *A Vision for the Church: Studies in Early Christian Ecclesiology in Honour of J. P. M. Sweet*. Edited by Markus Bockmuehl and Michael B. Thompson. Edinburgh: T & T Clark, 1997: 19–32.

———. *Type and History in Acts*. London: SPCK, 1964.

Graef, Hilda. *Mary: A History of Doctrine and Devotion*. With a new chapter "Vatican II and Beyond" by Thomas M. Thompson, S.M. Notre Dame, IN: Ave Maria Press, 2009.

Granados, José, D.C.J.M. "Through Mary's Memory to Jesus' Mystery." *Communio* 33 (2006): 11–42.

Granados, José, Carlos Granados, and Luis Sánchez-Navarro, eds. *Opening Up the Scriptures: Joseph Ratzinger and the Foundations of Biblical Interpretation*. Grand Rapids, MI: Eerdmans, 2008.

Grassi, Joseph A. "The Role of Jesus' Mother in John's Gospel: A Reappraisal." *Catholic Biblical Quarterly* 48 (1986): 67–80.

Greeley, Andrew. *The Mary Myth: On the Femininity of God*. New York: Seabury Press, 1977.

Green, Joel B. "Blessed Is She Who Believed: Mary, Curious Exemplar in Luke's Narrative." In *Blessed One: Protestant Perspectives on Mary*. Edited by Beverly Roberts Gaventa and Cynthia L. Rigby. Louisville, KY: Westminster John Knox Press, 2002: 9–20.

———. *The Gospel of Luke*. Grand Rapids, MI: Eerdmans, 1997.

Gregory of Nyssa. *The Life of Moses*. Translated by Abraham J. Malherbe and Everett Ferguson. New York: Paulist Press, 1978.

Gregory Palamas. *Mary the Mother of God: Sermons by Saint Gregory Palamas*. Edited by Christopher Veniamin. South Canaan, PA: Mount Thabor, 2005.

Greshake, Gisbert. *Auferstehung der Toten: Ein Beitrag zur gegenwärtigen theologischen Diskussion über die Zukunft der Geschichte*. Essen: Ludgerus, 1969.

———. "Das Verhältnis 'Unsterblichkeit der Seele' und 'Auferstehung des Leibes' in problemgeschichtlicher Sicht." In *Naherwartung—Auferstehung—Unsterblichkeit*. Edited by Gisbert Greshake and Gerhard Lohfink. Freiburg im Breisgau: Herder, 1975: 82–120.

Greshake, Gisbert, and Jacob Kremer. *Resurrectio Mortuorum: Zum theologischen Verständnis der leiblichen Auferstehung*. Darmstadt: Wissenschaftliche Buchgesellschaft, 1986.

Griffiths, Paul J. *Song of Songs*. Grand Rapids, MI: Brazos Press, 2011.

Gritsch, Eric W. "Lutheran Teaching Authority: Past and Present." In *Teaching Authority and Infallibility in the Church*. Edited by Paul C. Empie, T. Austin Murphy, and Joseph A. Burgess. Lutherans and Catholics in Dialogue VI. Minneapolis, MN: Augsburg, 1980: 138–48.

———. "The Views of Luther and Lutheranism on the Veneration of Mary." In *The One Mediator, the Saints, and Mary: Lutherans and Catholics in Dialogue VIII*. Edited by H. George Anderson, J. Francis Stafford, and Joseph A. Burgess. Minneapolis, MN: Augsburg Fortress, 1992: 138–48.

Gundry, Stanley. "Typology as a Means of Interpretation: Past and Present." *Journal of the Evangelical Theological Society* 12 (1969): 233–40.

Hahn, Scott. *Hail, Holy Queen: The Mother of God in the Word of God*. New York: Doubleday, 2001.

Haight, Roger, S.J. *Christian Community in History*. Vol. 1, *Historical Ecclesiology*. New York: Continuum, 2004.

Haldane, John. "Examining the Assumption." *Heythrop Journal* 43 (2002): 411–29.

Halkes, Catharina. "Mary and Women." Translated by David Smith. In *Mary in the Churches*. Edited by Hans Küng and Jürgen Moltmann. New York: Seabury Press, 1983: 66–73.

Harkianakis, Stylianos. *The Infallibility of the Church in Orthodox Theology*. Redfern, Australia: St Andrew's Orthodox Press, 2008.

Harrison, Nonna Verna. "The Entry of the Mother of God into the Temple." *St Vladimir's Theological Quarterly* 50 (2006): 149–60.

Hauke, Manfred. "The Immaculate Conception of Mary in the Greek Fathers and in an Ecumenical Context." *Chicago Studies* 45 (2006): 327–46.

Hays, Richard B. *The Conversion of the Imagination: Paul as Interpreter of Israel's Scripture*. Grand Rapids, MI: Eerdmans, 2005.

———. *Echoes of the Scripture in the Letters of Paul*. New Haven, CT: Yale University Press, 1989.

———. *First Corinthians*. Louisville, KY: John Knox Press, 1997.

———. "The Liberation of Israel in Luke-Acts: Intertextual Narration as Countercultural Practice." In *Reading the Bible Intertextually*. Edited by Richard B. Hays, Stefan Alkier, and Leroy A. Huizenga. Waco, TX: Baylor University Press, 2009: 101–17.

———. "What Is 'Real Participation in Christ'? A Dialogue with E. P. Sanders on Pauline Soteriology." In *Redefining First-Century Jewish and Christian Identities: Essays in Honor of Ed Parish Sanders*. Edited by Fabian E. Udoh et al. Notre Dame, IN: University of Notre Dame Press, 2008: 336–51.

Hays, Richard B., Stefan Alkier, and Leroy A. Huizenga, eds. *Reading the Bible Intertextually*. Waco, TX: Baylor University Press, 2009.

Healy, Kilian J., O.Carm. "The Assumption among Mary's Privileges." *The Thomist* 14 (1951): 72–92.

———. *The Assumption of Mary*. Edited by William J. Harry, O.Carm., and Michael M. Gorman. Darien, IL: Carmelite Media, 2011.

Healy, Nicholas, and David L. Schindler. "For the Life of the World: Hans Urs von Balthasar on the Church as Eucharist." In *The Cambridge Companion to Hans Urs von Balthasar*. Edited by Edward T. Oakes, S.J., and David Moss. Cambridge: Cambridge University Press, 2004.

Heft, James L., S.M. "Marian Themes in the Writing of Hans Urs von Balthasar." *Communio* 7 (1980): 127–39.

———. "Papal Infallibility and the Marian Dogmas: An Introduction." *Marian Studies* 33 (1982): 47–82.

Heiler, Friedrich. "Assumptio." *Theologische Literaturzeitung* 79 (1954): 1–51.

Heim, Maximilian Heinrich. *Joseph Ratzinger: Life in the Church and Living Theology; Fundamentals of Ecclesiology with Reference to* Lumen Gentium. Translated by Michael J. Miller. San Francisco: Ignatius Press, 2007.

Hengel, Martin. *Saint Peter: The Underestimated Apostle*. Translated by Thomas H. Trapp. Grand Rapids, MI: Eerdmans, 2010.

Hinnebusch, Paul, O.P. *Mother of Jesus Present with Us*. Libertyville, IL: Prow Books, 1980.

Hofer, Andrew, O.P. "Balthasar's Eschatology on the Intermediate State: The Question of Knowability." *Logos* 12 (2009): 148–72.

Holsinger-Friesen, Thomas. *Irenaeus and Genesis: A Study of Competition in Early Christian Hermeneutics*. Winona Lake, IN: Eisenbrauns, 2009.

Hoskins, Paul M. *Jesus as the Fulfillment of the Temple in the Gospel of John*. Milton Keynes, England: Paternoster, 2006.

———. *That Scripture Might Be Fulfilled: Typology and the Death of Christ*. Maitland, FL: Xulon Press, 2009.

Hummel, Horace D. *Ezekiel 21–48*. Saint Louis, MO: Concordia Publishing House, 2007.

Hurtado, Larry W. *At the Origins of Christian Worship: The Context and Character of Earliest Christian Devotion.* Grand Rapids, MI: Eerdmans, 1999.

——. *How on Earth Did Jesus Become a God? Historical Questions about Earliest Devotion to Jesus.* Grand Rapids, MI: Eerdmans, 2005.

——. *Lord Jesus Christ: Devotion to Jesus in Earliest Christianity.* Grand Rapids, MI: Eerdmans, 2003.

Hütter, Reinhard. "Catholic Theology in America: Quo Vadis?" *Nova et Vetera* 9 (2011): 539–47.

——. "Theological Faith Enlightening Sacred Theology: Renewing Theology by Recovering Its Unity as *sacra doctrina*." *The Thomist* 74 (2010): 369–405.

International Theological Commission. "Some Current Questions in Eschatology." *Irish Theological Quarterly* 58 (1992): 209–43.

Janssens, Aloïs. *The Assumption of Our Lady.* Fresno, CA: Academy Library Guild, 1954.

Jasianek, Jarislaw. "La Presencia del Espíritu Santo en la Maternidad de María." *Scripta Theologica* 38 (2006): 671–700.

Jenson, Robert W. "An Attempt to Think about Mary." *Dialog* 31 (1992): 259–64.

——. "A Space for God." In *Mary, Mother of God.* Edited by Carl E. Braaten and Robert W. Jenson. Grand Rapids, MI: Eerdmans, 2004: 49–57.

John Duns Scotus. *Four Questions on Mary.* Translated by Allan B. Wolter, O.F.M. Saint Bonaventure, NY: Franciscan Institute, 2000.

John Paul II. *Redemptoris Mater.* In *The Encyclicals of John Paul II.* Edited by J. Michael Miller, C.S.B. Huntington, IN: Our Sunday Visitor, 2001: 318–63.

——. *Ut Unum Sint.* In *The Encyclicals of John Paul II.* Edited by J. Michael Miller, C.S.B. Huntington, IN: Our Sunday Visitor, 2001: 782–831.

Johnson, Elizabeth A., C.S.J. "The Incomprehensibility of God and the Image of God Male and Female." *Theological Studies* 45 (1984): 441–65.

——. "Mary and the Female Face of God." *Theological Studies* 50 (1989): 500–526.

——. "The Symbolic Character of Theological Statements about Mary." *Journal of Ecumenical Studies* 22 (1985): 312–35.

——. *Truly Our Sister: A Theology of Mary in the Communion of Saints.* New York: Continuum, 2006.

Johnson, Luke Timothy. *The Acts of the Apostles.* Collegeville, MN: Liturgical Press, 1992.

——. *The Gospel of Luke.* Collegeville, MN: Liturgical Press, 1991.

——. *The Writings of the New Testament: An Interpretation.* Philadelphia: Fortress Press, 1986.

Journet, Charles. *What Is Dogma?* Translated by Mark Pontifex, O.S.B. San Francisco: Ignatius Press, 2011.

Kaminsky, Joel S. *Yet I Loved Jacob: Reclaiming the Biblical Concept of Election*. Nashville, TN: Abingdon Press, 2007.

Kant, Immanuel. *Religion within the Limits of Reason Alone*. Translated by Theodore M. Greene and Hoyt H. Hudson. New York: Harper & Row, 1960.

Käsemann, Ernst. *The Testament of Jesus: A Study of the Gospel of John in Light of Chapter 17*. Philadelphia: Fortress Press, 1968.

Kasper, Walter, ed. *The Petrine Ministry: Catholics and Orthodox in Dialogue*. Translated by the staff of the Pontifical Council for Promoting Christian Unity. New York: Paulist Press, 2006.

Keefe, Donald J., S.J. "Mary as Created Wisdom, the Splendor of the New Creation." *The Thomist* 47 (1983): 395–420.

Kereszty, Roch, O.Cist. "Toward the Renewal of Mariology." *Nova et Vetera* 11 (2013): 779–99.

Kodell, Jerome, O.S.B. *The Eucharist in the New Testament*. Collegeville, MN: Liturgical Press, 1988.

Kolnai, Aurel. *Ethics, Value, and Reality*. New Brunswick, NJ: Transaction, 2008.

Kreitzer, Beth. *Reforming Mary: Changing Images of the Virgin Mary in Lutheran Sermons of the Sixteenth Century*. Oxford: Oxford University Press, 2004.

Kromholtz, Bryan, O.P. *On the Last Day: The Time of the Resurrection of the Dead according to Thomas Aquinas*. Fribourg: Fribourg University Press, 2010.

Kugel, James L. *The Bible As It Was*. Cambridge, MA: Harvard University Press, 1997.

———. *How to Read the Bible: A Guide to Scripture, Then and Now*. New York: Free Press, 2007.

Küng, Hans. *Christ Sein*. Munich: Piper, 1974.

———. *Infallible? An Inquiry*. Translated by Edward Quinn. Garden City, NY: Doubleday, 1971.

———. "Mary in the Churches." In *Mary in the Churches*. Edited by Hans Küng and Jürgen Moltmann. New York: Seabury Press, 1983.

———. "A Short Balance-Sheet of the Debate on Infallibility." Translated by David Smith. In *Truth and Certainty*. Edited by Edward Schillebeeckx and Bas van Iersel. New York: Herder and Herder, 1973: 129–36.

Küng, Hans, and Jürgen Moltmann, eds. *Mary in the Churches*. New York: Seabury Press, 1983.

Künneth, Walter. *Christus oder Maria? Ein evangelisches Wort zum Mariendogma*. Berlin: Wichern, 1950.

Kurz, William S., S.J. "Mary, Woman and Mother in God's Saving New Testament Plan." *Nova et Vetera* 11 (2013): 801–18.

Labourdette, Marie-Michel, O.P. "La Théologie et ses sources." *Revue thomiste* 46 (1946): 353–71.

Ladouceur, Paul. "Old Testament Prefigurations of the Mother of God." *St Vladimir's Theological Quarterly* 50 (2006): 5–57.

Lakeland, Paul. *The Liberation of the Laity: In Search of an Accountable Church.* New York: Continuum, 2003.

Lampe, G. W. H. "The Reasonableness of Typology." In *Essays on Typology*, by G. W. H. Lampe and K. J. Woollcombe. Naperville, IL: Alec R. Allenson, 1957: 9–38.

Lampe, G. W. H., and K. J. Woollcombe *Essays on Typology.* Naperville, IL: Alec R. Allenson, 1957.

Laniak, Timothy S. *Shepherds after My Own Heart: Pastoral Traditions and Leadership in the Bible.* Downers Grove, IL: InterVarsity Press, 2006.

Laurentin, René. "Peter as the Foundation Stone in the Present Uncertainty." Translated by Sarah Fawcett. In *Truth and Certainty*. Edited by Edward Schillebeeckx and Bas van Iersel. New York: Herder and Herder, 1973: 95–113.

———. "Pluralism about Mary: Biblical and Contemporary." *The Way*, Supplement 45 (1982): 78–92.

———. *A Short Treatise on the Virgin Mary.* Translated by Charles Neumann, S.M. Washington, NJ: AMI Press, 1991.

Leahy, Brendan. *The Marian Profile in the Ecclesiology of Hans Urs von Balthasar.* New York: New City Press, 2000.

Le Donne, Anthony. *The Historiographical Jesus: Memory, Typology, and the Son of David.* Waco, TX: Baylor University Press, 2009.

Leeming, Bernard, S.J. "The Assumption and the Christian Pattern." *The Month* 19 (1951): 142–50.

Leithart, Peter J. *1 & 2 Kings.* Grand Rapids, MI: Brazos Press, 2006.

———. *Deep Exegesis: The Mystery of Reading Scripture.* Waco, TX: Baylor University Press, 2009.

———. *Defending Constantine: The Twilight of an Empire and the Dawn of Christendom.* Downers Grove, IL: IVP Academic, 2010.

———. *The Priesthood of the Plebs: A Theology of Baptism.* Eugene, OR: Wipf and Stock, 2003.

Levenson, Jon D. *Resurrection and the Restoration of Israel: The Ultimate Victory of the God of Life.* New Haven, CT: Yale University Press, 2006.

———. *Sinai and Zion: An Entry into the Jewish Bible.* San Francisco: Harper & Row, 1985.

Levering, Matthew. "The Brothers and Sisters of Jesus." *First Things* online. Nov. 30, 2007. http://www.firstthings.com/onthesquare/2007/11/the-brothers-and-sisters-of-je.

———. *Christ's Fulfillment of Torah and Temple: Salvation According to St. Thomas Aquinas.* Notre Dame, IN: University of Notre Dame Press, 2002.

———. *Engaging the Doctrine of Revelation: The Mediation of the Gospel in Church and Scripture.* Grand Rapids, MI: Baker Academic, 2014.

———. *Ezra and Nehemiah*. Grand Rapids, MI: Brazos Press, 2007.

———. "The *Imago Dei* in David Novak and Thomas Aquinas: A Jewish-Christian Dialogue." *The Thomist* 72 (2008): 259–311.

———. "The Inspiration of Scripture: A *Status Quaestionis*." *Letter and Spirit* 6 (2010): 281–314.

———. *Jesus and the Demise of Death: Resurrection, Afterlife, and the Fate of the Christian*. Waco, TX: Baylor University Press, 2012.

———. *Participatory Biblical Exegesis: A Theology of Biblical Interpretation*. Notre Dame, IN: University of Notre Dame Press, 2008.

———. *Predestination: Biblical and Theological Paths*. Oxford: Oxford University Press, 2011.

Levine, Amy-Jill, and Maria Mayo Robbins, eds. *A Feminist Companion to Mariology*. London: T & T Clark International, 2005.

Levy, Ian Christopher. *Holy Scripture and the Quest for Authority at the End of the Middle Ages*. Notre Dame, IN: University of Notre Dame Press, 2012.

Liderbach, Daniel, S.J. *Christ in the Early Christian Hymns*. New York: Paulist Press, 1998.

Lincoln, Andrew T. *The Gospel According to Saint John*. London: Continuum, 2005.

———. *Paradise Now and Not Yet: Studies in the Role of the Heavenly Dimension in Paul's Thought with Special Reference to His Eschatology*. Cambridge: Cambridge University Press, 1981.

Lindbeck, George. "The Reformation and the Infallibility Debate." In *Teaching Authority and Infallibility in the Church*. Edited by Paul C. Empie, T. Austin Murphy, and Joseph A. Burgess. Lutherans and Catholics in Dialogue VI. Minneapolis, MN: Augsburg, 1980: 101–19.

Lohr, Joel N. *Chosen and Unchosen: Conceptions of Election in the Pentateuch and Jewish-Christian Interpretation*. Winona Lake, IN: Eisenbrauns, 2009.

Lonergan, Bernard, S.J. "The Assumption and Theology." In *Vers le dogme de l'Assomption. Journées d'études mariales, Montréal 12–15 Août 1948*. Edited by Adrien-M. Malo, O.F.M. South Bend, IN: Fides, 1948.

Long, Steven A. *Natura Pura: On the Recovery of Nature in the Doctrine of Grace*. New York: Fordham University Press, 2010.

Longenecker, Dwight, and David Gustafson. *Mary: A Catholic-Evangelical Debate*. Grand Rapids, MI: Brazos Press, 2003.

Longenecker, Richard N. "Preface to the Second Edition." In *Biblical Exegesis in the Apostolic Period*. 2nd ed. Grand Rapids, MI: Eerdmans, 1999.

López, Antonio. "Mary, Certainty of Our Hope." *Communio* 35 (2008): 174–99.

Lösel, Steffen. "Conciliar, Not Conciliatory: Hans Urs von Balthasar's Ecclesiological Synthesis of Vatican II." *Modern Theology* 24 (2008): 23–49.

Lossky, Vladimir. "Panagia." In *The Mother of God: A Symposium*. Edited by E. L. Mascall. London: Dacre Press, 1949: 24–36.

Louth, Andrew. *Mary and the Mystery of the Incarnation: An Essay on the Mother of God in the Theology of Karl Barth.* Oxford: SLG Press, 1977.

Luther, Martin. *Martin Luther: Selections from His Writings.* Edited by John Dillenberger. New York: Doubleday, 1962.

Luz, Ulrich. "On the Way to Unity: The Community of the Church in the New Testament." In *Unity of the Church in the New Testament and Today.* Edited by Lukas Vischer, Ulrich Luz, and Christian Link. Translated by James E. Crouch. Grand Rapids, MI: Eerdmans, 2010: 29–161.

MacIntyre, Alasdair. *Three Rival Versions of Moral Enquiry: Encyclopaedia, Genealogy, Tradition.* Notre Dame, IN: University of Notre Dame Press, 1990.

MacKenzie, J. A. Ross. "The Patristic Witness to the Virgin Mary as the New Eve." *Marian Studies* 29 (1978): 67–78.

Macquarrie, John. *Mary for All Christians.* Grand Rapids, MI: Eerdmans, 1990.

Malcolm, Lois. "What Mary Has to Say about God's Bare Goodness." In *Blessed One: Protestant Perspectives on Mary.* Edited by Beverly Roberts Gaventa and Cynthia L. Rigby. Louisville, KY: Westminster John Knox Press, 2002: 131–44.

Malo, Adrien-M., O.F.M. "La Bible et l'Assomption." In *Vers le dogme de l'Assomption. Journées d'études mariales, Montréal 12–15 Août 1948.* Edited by Adrien-M. Malo, O.F.M. South Bend, IN: Fides, 1948: 103–22.

———, ed. *Vers le dogme de l'Assomption. Journées d'études mariales, Montréal 12–15 Août 1948.* South Bend, IN: Fides, 1948.

Manns, Frédéric, O.F.M. *Le Récit de la dormition de Marie (Vatican grec 1982): Contribution à l'étude de origins de l'exégèse chrétienne.* Jerusalem: Franciscan Printing Press, 1989.

Mansini, Guy, O.S.B. "Ecclesial Mediation of Grace and Truth." *The Thomist* 75 (2011): 555–83.

Marcus, Joel. *The Way of the Lord: Christological Exegesis of the Old Testament in the Gospel of Mark.* Louisville, KY: Westminster/John Knox Press, 1992.

Marks, Herbert. "Pauline Typology and Revisionary Criticism." *Journal of the American Academy of Religion* 52 (1984): 71–92.

Marmion, Declan, and Mary E. Hines, eds. *The Cambridge Companion to Karl Rahner.* Cambridge: Cambridge University Press, 2005.

Marshner, William H. "Criteria for Doctrinal Development in the Marian Dogmas: An Essay in Metatheology." *Marian Studies* 28 (1977): 47–97.

Martens, Peter W. "Revisiting the Allegory/Typology Distinction: The Case of Origen." *Journal of Early Christian Studies* 16 (2008): 283–317.

Martin, Francis. "Mary in Sacred Scripture: An Ecumenical Reflection." *The Thomist* 72 (2008): 525–69.

Mascall, E. L. "The Dogmatic Theology of the Mother of God." In *The Mother of God: A Symposium.* Edited by E. L. Mascall. London: Dacre Press, 1949: 37–50.

———. *The Mother of God: A Symposium.* London: Dacre Press, 1949.

Mascall, E. L., and H. S. Box, eds. *The Blessed Virgin Mary: Essays by Anglican Writers*. London: Darton, Longman & Todd, 1963.

Matera, Frank J. *II Corinthians: A Commentary*. Louisville, KY: Westminster John Knox Press, 2003.

Mayer, F. E. "The Dogma of Mary's Assumption: A Symptom of Anti-Christian Theology." *Concordia Theological Monthly* 22 (1950): 181–89.

———. "German Lutheran Bishops Denounce Rome's New Dogma." *Concordia Theological Monthly* 22 (1950): 144–46.

McAleer, G. J. *Ecstatic Morality and Sexual Politics: A Catholic and Antitotalitarian Theory of the Body*. New York: Fordham University Press, 2005.

McCartney, Dan G., and Peter Enns. "Matthew and Hosea: A Response to John Sailhamer." *Westminster Theological Journal* 63 (2001): 97–105.

McDonnell, Kilian, O.S.B. "Feminist Mariologies: Heteronomy/Subordination and the Scandal of Christology." *Theological Studies* 66 (2005): 527–67.

McDonough, Sean M. *Christ as Creator: Origins of a New Testament Doctrine*. Oxford: Oxford University Press, 2009.

McElwain, Hugh M. "Christian Eschatology and the Assumption." *Marian Studies* 18 (1967): 84–102.

McHugh, John. *The Mother of Jesus in the New Testament*. Garden City, NY: Doubleday, 1975.

———. "The Second Eve: Newman and Irenaeus." *The Way*, Supplement 45 (1982): 13–21.

McInerny, Ralph. *Dante and the Blessed Virgin*. Notre Dame, IN: University of Notre Dame Press, 2010.

McKenzie, John, S.J. "The Mother of Jesus in the New Testament." In *Mary in the Churches*. Edited by Hans Küng and Jürgen Moltmann. New York: Seabury Press, 1983: 3–11.

McKenzie, Steve. "Exodus Typology in Hosea." *Restoration Quarterly* 22 (1979): 100–108.

McKnight, Scot. *The Real Mary: Why Evangelical Christians Can Embrace the Mother of Jesus*. Brewster, MA: Paraclete Press, 2007.

Meier, John P. "The Brothers and Sisters of Jesus in Ecumenical Perspective." *Catholic Biblical Quarterly* 54 (1992): 1–28.

———. "On Retrojecting Later Questions from Later Texts: A Reply to Richard Bauckham." *Catholic Biblical Quarterly* 59 (1997): 511–27.

Merton, Thomas. *New Seeds of Contemplation*. Boston: Shambala, 2003.

Mettepenningen, Jürgen. *Nouvelle Théologie—New Theology*. London: T & T Clark International, 2010.

Metz, Johannes B., ed. *The Development of Fundamental Theology*. New York: Paulist Press, 1969.

Meyendorff, John. *Byzantine Theology: Historical Trends and Doctrinal Themes*. 2nd ed. New York: Fordham University Press, 1979.

Meyers, Carol. *Exodus*. Cambridge: Cambridge University Press, 2005.

Middleton, J. Richard. *The Liberating Image: The* Imago Dei *in Genesis 1.* Grand Rapids, MI: Brazos Press, 2005.

Migliore, Daniel L. "Woman of Faith: Toward a Reformed Understanding of Mary." In *Blessed One: Protestant Perspectives on Mary.* Edited by Beverly Roberts Gaventa and Cynthia L. Rigby. Louisville, KY: Westminster John Knox Press, 2002: 117–30.

Milbank, John. *The Suspended Middle: Henri de Lubac and the Debate concerning the Supernatural.* Grand Rapids, MI: Eerdmans, 2005.

Milgrom, Jacob. *Leviticus 17–22: A New Translation with Introduction and Commentary.* New York: Doubleday, 2000.

Miller, Bonnie J. "'Pondering All These Things': Mary and Motherhood." In *Blessed One: Protestant Perspectives on Mary.* Edited by Beverly Roberts Gaventa and Cynthia L. Rigby. Louisville, KY: Westminster John Knox Press, 2002: 97–114.

Mimouni, Simon Claude. *Dormition et assumption de Marie: Histoire des traditions anciennes.* Paris: Beauchesne, 1995.

———. *Les traditions anciennes sur la Dormition et l'Assomption de Marie: Études littéraires, historiques et doctrinales.* Leiden: Brill, 2011.

Minear, Paul S. *Images of the Church in the New Testament.* Louisville, KY: Westminster John Knox Press, 2004.

Moberly, R. W. L. *The Theology of the Book of Genesis.* Cambridge: Cambridge University Press, 2009.

Moloney, Francis, S.D.B. *The Gospel of John.* Collegeville, MN: Liturgical Press, 1998.

———. *Love in the Gospel of John: An Exegetical, Theological, and Literary Study.* Grand Rapids, MI: Baker Academic, 2013.

Montague, George T., S.M. "Eschatology and Our Lady." *Marian Studies* 17 (1966): 65–83.

———. *First and Second Timothy, and Titus.* Grand Rapids, MI: Baker Academic, 2008.

Moralejo, Gaspar Calvo, and Stefano Cecchin, eds. *L'Assunzione di Maria Madre di Dio: Significato storico-salvifico a 50 anni dalla definizione dogmatica.* Vatican City: Pontificia Academia Mariana Internationalis, 2001.

Morin, Clément. "The Assumption and the Liturgy." In *Vers le dogme de l'Assomption. Journées d'études mariales, Montréal 12–15 Août 1948.* Edited by Adrien-M. Malo, O.F.M. South Bend, IN: Fides, 1948: 391–97.

Morris, Leon. *The Gospel according to John.* Rev. ed. Grand Rapids, MI: Eerdmans, 1995.

Moyise, Steve. *Paul and Scripture.* Grand Rapids, MI: Baker Academic, 2010.

Murphy, Francesca Aran. "Immaculate Mary: The Ecclesial Mariology of Hans Urs von Balthasar." In *Mary: The Complete Resource.* Edited by Sarah Jane Boss. Oxford: Oxford University Press, 2007: 300–313.

———. *1 Samuel*. Grand Rapids, MI: Brazos Press, 2010.

Musurillo, Herbert, S.J. "Shadow and Reality: Thoughts on the Problem of Typology." *Theological Studies* 22 (1961): 455–60.

Nachtwei, Gerhard. *Dialogische Unsterblichkeit*. Leipzig: St. Benno, 1986.

Neufeld, Karl. "Mariologie in der Sicht K. Rahners." *Ephemerides Mariologicae* 50 (2000): 285–97.

———. "Zur Mariologie Karl Rahners—Materialien und Grundlinien." *Zeitschrift für katholische Theologie* 109 (1987): 431–39.

Neusner, Jacob. *Performing Israel's Faith: Narrative and Law in Rabbinic Theology*. Waco, TX: Baylor University Press, 2005.

———. *A Rabbi Talks with Jesus: An Intermillennial, Interfaith Exchange*. New York: Doubleday, 1993.

Newman, John Henry. *An Essay in Aid of a Grammar of Assent*. Westminster, MD: Christian Classics, 1973.

———. *An Essay on the Development of Christian Doctrine*. 6th ed. Notre Dame, IN: University of Notre Dame Press, 1989.

———. *Essays Critical and Historical*. 2 vols. London: Longmans, Green, 1895.

———. "The Glories of Mary for the Sake of Her Son." In *Mary: The Virgin Mary in the Life and Writings of John Henry Newman*. Edited by Philip Boyce. Grand Rapids, MI: Eerdmans, 2001: 129–48.

———. *Mary: The Virgin Mary in the Life and Writings of John Henry Newman*. Edited by Philip Boyce. Grand Rapids, MI: Eerdmans, 2001.

———. "On the Fitness of the Glories of Mary." In *Mary: The Virgin Mary in the Life and Writings of John Henry Newman*. Edited by Philip Boyce. Grand Rapids, MI: Eerdmans, 2001: 149–66.

Nichols, Aidan, O.P. *No Bloodless Myth: A Guide through Balthasar's Dramatics*. Washington, D.C.: T & T Clark, 2000.

———. *Reason with Piety: Garrigou-Lagrange in the Service of Catholic Thought*. Ave Maria, FL: Sapientia Press, 2008.

———. "Thomism and the *Nouvelle Théologie*." *The Thomist* 64 (2000): 1–19.

———. *The Thought of Pope Benedict XVI: An Introduction to the Theology of Joseph Ratzinger*. 2nd ed. London: Continuum, 2007.

Nissiotis, Nikos. "Mary in Orthodox Theology." In *Mary in the Churches*. Edited by Hans Küng and Jürgen Moltmann. New York: Seabury Press, 1983: 25–39.

Oakes, Edward T., S.J. *Pattern of Redemption: The Theology of Hans Urs von Balthasar*. New York: Continuum, 1994.

Oakes, Edward T., S.J., and David Moss, eds. *The Cambridge Companion to Hans Urs von Balthasar*. Cambridge: Cambridge University Press, 2004.

Oberman, Heiko A. *The Dawn of the Reformation: Essays in Late Medieval and Early Reformation Thought*. Grand Rapids, MI: Eerdmans, 1992.

———. *The Harvest of Medieval Theology: Gabriel Biel and Late Medieval Nominalism*. 3rd ed. Grand Rapids, MI: Baker Academic, 2000.

———. "The Virgin Mary in Evangelical Perspective." *Journal of Ecumenical Studies* 1 (1964): 271–98.

O'Callaghan, Paul. *Christ Our Hope: An Introduction to Eschatology.* Washington, D.C.: Catholic University of America Press, 2011.

O'Connell, John P. "The Testimony of the Sacred Liturgy Relative to Mary's Death." *Marian Studies* 8 (1957): 125–42.

O'Keefe, John J., and R. R. Reno. *Sanctified Vision: An Introduction to Early Christian Interpretation of the Bible.* Baltimore, MD: Johns Hopkins University Press, 2005.

O'Malley, John W., S.J. "Vatican II: Historical Perspectives on Its Uniqueness and Interpretation." In *Vatican II: The Unfinished Agenda; A Look to the Future.* Edited by Lucien Richard, Daniel T. Harrington, and John W. O'Malley. New York: Paulist Press, 1987: 22–32.

———. *What Happened at Vatican II.* Cambridge, MA: Harvard University Press, 2008.

O'Meara, Thomas A., O.P. *Mary in Protestant and Catholic Theology.* New York: Sheed and Ward, 1966.

O'Neill, J. C. "A Vision for the Church: John's Gospel." In *A Vision for the Church: Studies in Early Christian Ecclesiology in Honour of J. P. M. Sweet.* Edited by Markus Bockmuehl and Michael B. Thompson. Edinburgh: T & T Clark, 1997: 79–93.

Ostmeyer, Karl-Heinrich. "Typologie und Typos: Analyse eines schwierigen Verhältnisses." *New Testament Studies* 46 (2000): 112–31.

Pannenberg, Wolfhart. *Systematic Theology.* Vol. 3. Translated by Geoffrey W. Bromiley. Grand Rapids, MI: Eerdmans, 1998.

Pao, David W. *Acts and the Isaianic New Exodus.* Grand Rapids, MI: Baker Academic, 2002.

Parker, David. "Evangelicals and Mary: Recent Theological Evaluations." *Evangelical Review of Theology* 30 (2006): 121–40.

Paul VI. *Marialis Cultus.* www.vatican.va.

———. *Signum Magnum.* www.vatican.va.

Pedrozo, José M. "The Brothers of Jesus and His Mother's Virginity." *The Thomist* 63 (1999): 83–104.

Pelikan, Jaroslav. *Mary Through the Centuries: Her Place in the History of Culture.* New Haven, CT: Yale University Press, 1996.

———. "*Most* Generations Shall Call Me Blessed: An Essay in Aid of a Grammar of Liturgy." In *Mary, Mother of God.* Edited by Carl E. Braaten and Robert W. Jenson. Grand Rapids, MI: Eerdmans, 2004: 1–18.

———. *The Riddle of Roman Catholicism.* Nashville, TN: Abingdon Press, 1959.

Perkins, Pheme. "Mary in Johannine Traditions." In *Mary, Woman of Nazareth: Biblical and Theological Perspectives.* Edited by Doris Donnelly. New York: Paulist Press, 1990: 109–22.

Perrin, Nicholas. *Jesus the Temple.* Grand Rapids, MI: Baker Academic, 2010.

Perrin, Nicholas, and Richard B. Hays, eds. *Jesus, Paul and the People of God: A Theological Dialogue with N. T. Wright*. Downers Grove, IL: InterVarsity Press, 2011.

Perry, Nicholas, and Loreto Echeverría. *Under the Heel of Mary*. London: Routledge, 1988.

Perry, Tim. *Mary for Evangelicals: Toward an Understanding of the Mother of Our Lord*. Downers Grove, IL: IVP Academic, 2006.

————. "'What Is Little Mary Here For?' Barth, Mary, and Election." *Pro Ecclesia* 19 (2010): 46–68.

Phan, Peter. "Eschatology." In *The Cambridge Companion to Karl Rahner*. Edited by Declan Marmion and Mary E. Hines. Cambridge: Cambridge University Press, 2005: 174–92.

————. *Eternity in Time: A Study of Karl Rahner's Eschatology*. London: Associated University Presses, 1988.

Philippe, Marie-Dominique, O.P. "The Assumption in the Spiritual Life." *The Thomist* 14 (1951): 93–108.

————. *The Mysteries of Mary: Growing in Faith, Hope, and Love with the Mother of God*. Charlotte, NC: Saint Benedict Press, 2011.

Piepkorn, Arthur Carl. "Mary's Place within the People of God according to Non-Roman-Catholics." *Marian Studies* 18 (1967): 46–83.

Pitstick, Alyssa Lyra. *Light in Darkness: Hans Urs von Balthasar and the Catholic Doctrine of Christ's Descent into Hell*. Grand Rapids, MI: Eerdmans, 2007.

Pius XII. *Mediator Dei*. www.vatican.va.

————. *Munificentissimus Deus*. www.vatican.va.

Poirier, Léandre. "Le chapitre XII de l'Apocalypse fait-il allusion à l'Assomption?" In *Vers le dogme de l'Assomption. Journées d'études mariales, Montréal 12–15 Août 1948*. Edited by Adrien-M. Malo, O.F.M. South Bend, IN: Fides, 1948: 93–102.

Pomplun, Trent. "Mary." In *The Blackwell Companion to Catholicism*. Edited by James J. Buckley, Frederick Christian Bauerschmidt, and Trent Pomplun. Oxford: Blackwell, 2007: 312–25.

Porter, Stanley E., Paul Joyce, and David E. Orton, eds. *Crossing the Boundaries: Essays in Biblical Interpretation in Honour of Michael D. Goulder*. New York: E. J. Brill, 1994.

Portier, William L. "Twentieth-Century Catholic Theology and the Triumph of Maurice Blondel." *Communio* 38 (2011): 103–37.

Powell, Mark E. *Papal Infallibility: A Protestant Evaluation of an Ecumenical Issue*. Grand Rapids, MI: Eerdmans, 2009.

Puech, Léonard-M., O.F.M. "Une preuve scotiste: la mediation parfaite due Christ." In *Vers le dogme de l'Assomption. Journées d'études mariales, Montréal 12–15 Août 1948*. Edited by Adrien-M. Malo, O.F.M. South Bend, IN: Fides, 1948: 337–58.

Quinn, Jerome D. "The Terminology for Faith, Truth, Teaching, and the Spirit in the Pastoral Epistles: A Summary." In *Teaching Authority and Infallibility in the Church*. Edited by Paul C. Empie, T. Austin Murphy, and Joseph A. Burgess. Lutherans and Catholics in Dialogue VI. Minneapolis, MN: Augsburg, 1980: 232–37.

Rahner, Hugo. *Our Lady and the Church*. Translated by Sebastian Bullough, O.P. Bethesda, MD: Zacchens Press, 2004.

Rahner, Karl, S.J. "The Intermediate State." In *Theological Investigations*. Vol. 17, *Jesus, Man, and the Church*. Translated by Margaret Kohl. New York: Crossroad, 1981: 114–24.

———. "The Interpretation of the Dogma of the Assumption." In *Theological Investigations*. Vol. 1, *God, Christ, Mary and Grace*. Translated by Cornelius Ernst, O.P. Baltimore, MD: Helicon Press, 1961: 215–27.

———. *Maria, Mutter des Herrn: Mariologische Studien*. Edited by Regina Pacis Meyer. Freiburg im Breisgau: Herder, 2004.

———. *Mary, Mother of the Lord: Theological Meditations*. Translated by W. J. O'Hara. New York: Herder and Herder, 1963.

———. "Pluralism in Theology and the Oneness of the Church's Profession of Faith." In *The Development of Fundamental Theology*. Edited by Johannes B. Metz. New York: Paulist Press, 1969: 103–23.

Ratzinger, Joseph. "Anglican-Catholic Dialogue: Its Problems and Hopes." In *Church, Ecumenism and Politics: New Essays in Ecclesiology*. Translated by Robert Nowell. New York: Crossroad, 1988: 65–98.

———. "The Assumption of Mary." In *Dogma and Preaching: Applying Christian Doctrine to Daily Life*. Translated by Michael J. Miller and Matthew J. O'Connell. San Francisco: Ignatius Press, 2011: 357–61.

———. "Biblical Interpretation in Conflict: On the Foundations and the Itinerary of Exegesis Today." Translated by Adrian Walker. In *Opening Up the Scriptures: Joseph Ratzinger and the Foundations of Biblical Interpretation*. Edited by José Granados, Carlos Granados, and Luis Sánchez-Navarro. Grand Rapids, MI: Eerdmans, 2008: 1–29.

———. *Church, Ecumenism and Politics: New Essays in Ecclesiology*. Translated by Robert Nowell. New York: Crossroad, 1988.

———. *Daughter Zion: Meditations on the Church's Marian Belief*. Translated by John M. McDermott, S.J. San Francisco: Ignatius Press, 1983.

———. *Dogma and Preaching: Applying Christian Doctrine to Daily Life*. Translated by Michael J. Miller and Matthew J. O'Connell. San Francisco: Ignatius Press, 2011.

———. "The Ecclesiology of the Second Vatican Council." In *Church, Ecumenism and Politics: New Essays in Ecclesiology*. Translated by Robert Nowell. New York: Crossroad, 1988: 3–28.

———. "The End of Time." In *The End of Time? The Provocation of Talking about God*. Edited by Tiemo Rainer Peters and Claus Urban. Translated and edited by J. Matthew Ashley. New York: Paulist Press, 2004: 4–25.

———. *Eschatology: Death and Eternal Life*. Translated by Michael Waldstein and Aidan Nichols, O.P. 2nd ed. Washington, D.C.: Catholic University of America Press, 2007.

———. "'Et Incarnatus Est de Spiritu Sancto ex Maria Virgine.'" In *Mary: The Church at the Source*. By Joseph Ratzinger and Hans Urs von Balthasar. Translated by Adrian Walker. San Francisco: Ignatius Press, 2005: 81–95.

———. *God and the World: Believing and Living in Our Time; A Conversation with Peter Seewald*. Translated by Henry Taylor. San Francisco: Ignatius Press, 2002.

———. *God's Word: Scripture, Tradition, Office*. Edited by Peter Hünermann and Thomas Söding. Translated by Henry Taylor. San Francisco: Ignatius Press, 2008.

———. *Gospel, Catechesis, Catechism: Sidelights on the* Catechism of the Catholic Church. San Francisco: Ignatius Press, 1997.

———. "'Hail, Full of Grace': Elements of Marian Piety According to the Bible." In *Mary: The Church at the Source*. By Joseph Ratzinger and Hans Urs von Balthasar. Translated by Adrian Walker. San Francisco: Ignatius Press, 2005: 61–79.

———. *'In the Beginning . . .' A Catholic Understanding of the Story of Creation and the Fall*. Translated by Boniface Ramsey, O.P. Huntington, IN: Our Sunday Visitor, 1990.

———. *Jesus of Nazareth: From the Baptism in the Jordan to the Transfiguration*. Translated by Adrian J. Walker. New York: Doubleday, 2007.

———. "Luther and the Unity of the Churches." In *Church, Ecumenism and Politics: New Essays in Ecclesiology*. Translated by Robert Nowell. New York: Crossroad, 1988: 99–134.

———. *The Nature and Mission of Theology: Essays to Orient Theology in Today's Debates*. Translated by Adrian Walker. San Francisco: Ignatius Press, 1995.

———. "On the Position of Mariology and Marian Spirituality within the Totality of Faith and Theology." In *The Church and Women: A Compendium*. Translated by Maria Shrady and Lothar Krauth. San Francisco: Ignatius Press, 1988: 67–81.

———. "The Papal Primacy and the Unity of the People of God." In *Church, Ecumenism and Politics: New Essays in Ecclesiology*. Translated by Robert Nowell. New York: Crossroad, 1988: 29–45.

———. "II. Resurrection of the Body; B. Theological." In *Sacramentum Mundi*. Edited by Karl Rahner. New York: Herder and Herder, 1970: 340–42.

———. "The Sign of the Woman: An Introduction to the Encyclical 'Redemptoris Mater.'" In *Mary: God's Yes to Man; John Paul's Encyclical* Redemptoris Mater. San Francisco: Ignatius Press, 1988: 9–40.

———. "The Sign of the Woman: An Introductory Essay on the Encyclical *Redemptoris Mater.*" In *Mary: The Church at the Source.* By Joseph Ratzinger and Hans Urs von Balthasar. Translated by Adrian Walker. San Francisco: Ignatius Press, 2005: 37–60.

———. "Thoughts on the Place of Marian Doctrine and Piety in Faith and Theology as a Whole." In *Mary: The Church at the Source.* By Joseph Ratzinger and Hans Urs von Balthasar. Translated by Adrian Walker. San Francisco: Ignatius Press, 2005: 19 36.

———. *Truth and Tolerance: Christian Belief and World Religions.* Translated by Henry Taylor. San Francisco: Ignatius Press, 2004.

Ratzinger, Joseph, and Hans Urs von Balthasar. *Mary: The Church at the Source.* Translated by Adrian Walker. San Francisco: Ignatius Press, 2005.

Ribbens, Benjamin J. "Typology of Types: Typology in Dialogue." *Journal of Theological Interpretation* 5 (2011): 81–96.

Robertson, A. T. *The Mother of Jesus: Her Problems and Her Glory.* New York: George H. Doran, 1925.

Roschini, Gabriel M., O.S.M. "The Assumption and the Immaculate Conception." *The Thomist* 14 (1951): 59–71.

Rosenberg, Randall S. "Being-Toward-a-Death-Transformed: Aquinas on the Naturalness and Unnaturalness of Human Death." *Angelicum* 83 (2006): 747–66.

Rowland, Tracey. *Ratzinger's Faith: The Theology of Pope Benedict XVI.* Oxford: Oxford University Press, 2008.

Rubin, Miri. *Mother of God: A History of the Virgin Mary.* New Haven, CT: Yale University Press, 2009.

Russell, Ralph, O.S.B. "The Blessed Virgin Mary in the Bible: The Scriptural Basis of Ecumenical Dialogue." In *Mary's Place in Christian Dialogue: Occasional Papers of the Ecumenical Society of the Blessed Virgin Mary, 1970–1980.* Edited by Alberic Stacpoole, O.S.B. Middlegreen, England: St. Paul Publications, 1982: 42–50.

Sagovsky, Nicholas. *Ecumenism, Christian Origins and the Practice of Communion.* Cambridge: Cambridge University Press, 2000.

Sailhamer, John. "Hosea 11:1 and Matthew 2:15." *Westminster Theological Journal* 63 (2001): 87–96.

Savage, Timothy B. *Power through Weakness: Paul's Understanding of the Christian Ministry in 2 Corinthians.* Cambridge: Cambridge University Press, 1996.

Saward, John. "The Assumption." In *Mary's Place in Christian Dialogue: Occasional Papers of the Ecumenical Society of the Blessed Virgin Mary, 1970–1980.* Edited by Alberic Stacpoole, O.S.B. Middlegreen, England: St. Paul Publications, 1982: 108–22.

———. *Redeemer in the Womb: Jesus Living in Mary.* San Francisco: Ignatius Press, 1993.

Scheeben, Matthias Joseph. *Mariology*. 2 vols. Translated by T. L. M. J. Geukers. St. Louis, MO: B. Herder, 1946–48.

Scheffczyk, Leo. *Maria: Mutter und Gefährtin Christi*. Augsburg: Sankt Ulrich Verlag, 2003.

———. "'Unsterblichkeit' bei Thomas von Aquin auf dem Hintergrund der neueren Diskussion." *Bayerische Akademie der Wissenschaften, Philosophisch-Historische Klasse, Sitzungsberichte* 4 (1989): 14–27.

Schillebeeckx, Edward, O.P. *Christ: The Experience of Jesus as Lord*. Translated by John Bowden. New York: Seabury Press, 1980.

———. *Church: The Human Story of God*. Translated by John Bowden. New York: Crossroad, 1993.

———. "Mariology: Yesterday, Today, Tomorrow." In *Mary: Yesterday, Today, Tomorrow*. Edited by Edward Schillebeeckx, O.P., and Catharina Halkes. Translated by John Bowden. New York: Crossroad, 1993: 12–42.

———. *Mary, Mother of the Redemption*. Translated by N. D. Smith. New York: Sheed and Ward, 1964.

———. "The Problem of the Infallibility of the Church's Office: A Theological Reflection." Translated by David Smith. In *Truth and Certainty*. Edited by Edward Schillebeeckx and Bas van Iersel. New York: Herder and Herder, 1973: 77–94.

Schillebeeckx, Edward, and Bas van Iersel, eds. *Truth and Certainty*. New York: Herder and Herder, 1973.

Schillebeeckx, Edward, O.P., and Catharina Halkes, eds. *Mary: Yesterday, Today, Tomorrow*. Translated by John Bowden. New York: Crossroad, 1993.

Schindler, David L. *Heart of the World, Center of the Church: Communio Ecclesiology, Liberalism, and Liberation*. Grand Rapids, MI: Eerdmans, 1996.

Schlink, Edmund et al. "An Evangelical Opinion on the Proclamation of the Dogma of the Bodily Assumption of Mary." Translated by the journal editor. *Lutheran Quarterly* 3 (1951): 123–41.

Schmemann, Alexander. *The Historical Road of Eastern Orthodoxy*. Translated by Lydia W. Kesich. Crestwood, NY: St Vladimir's Seminary Press, 2003.

———. *Introduction to Liturgical Theology*. Translated by Asheleigh E. Moorehouse. Crestwood, NY: St Vladimir's Seminary Press, 2003.

———. *The Virgin Mary*. With selections translated from the Russian by John A. Jillions. Crestwood, NY: St Vladimir's Seminary Press, 1995.

Schnackenburg, Rudolf. *The Church in the New Testament*. Translated by W. J. O'Hara. New York: Seabury Press, 1965.

———. *The Epistle to the Ephesians: A Commentary*. Translated by Helen Heron. Edinburgh: T & T Clark, 1991.

———. *God's Rule and Kingdom*. Translated by John Murray. New York: Herder and Herder, 1963.

Schneider, Michael. "How Does God Act? Intertextual Readings of 1 Corinthians 10." In *Reading the Bible Intertextually*. Edited by Richard B. Hays,

Stefan Alkier, and Leroy A. Huizenga. Waco, TX: Baylor University Press, 2009: 35–52.

Schreiner, Klaus. *Maria: Jungfrau, Mutter, Herrscherin*. Munich: Carl Hanser Verlag, 1994.

Schumacher, Ferdinand. "Ich Glaube an die Auferstehung der Toten: Das Ende der Zeit in der Theologie Joseph Ratzingers." In *Der Theologe Joseph Ratzinger*. Edited by Frank Meier-Hamidi and Ferdinand Schumacher. Basel: Herder, 2007: 73–99.

Seccombe, David. "Luke's Vision for the Church." In *A Vision for the Church: Studies in Early Christian Ecclesiology in Honour of J. P. M. Sweet*, Edited by Markus Bockmuehl and Michael B. Thompson. Edinburgh: T & T Clark, 1997: 45–63.

Seitz, Christopher R. *The Character of Christian Scripture: The Significance of a Two-Testament Bible*. Grand Rapids, MI: Baker Academic, 2011.

———. *Prophecy and Hermeneutics: Toward a New Introduction to the Prophets*. Grand Rapids, MI: Baker Academic, 2007.

Semmelroth, Otto, S.J. *Mary, Archetype of the Church*. Translated by Maria von Eroes and John Devlin. New York: Sheed and Ward, 1963.

Senior, Donald, C.P. "Gospel Portraits of Mary: Images and Symbols from the Synoptic Tradition." In *Mary, Woman of Nazareth: Biblical and Theological Perspectives*. Edited by Doris Donnelly. New York: Paulist Press, 1990: 92–108.

Servais, Jacques, S.J. "Mary's Role in the Incarnation." *Communio* 30 (2003): 5–25.

Shoemaker, Stephen J. *Ancient Traditions of the Virgin Mary's Dormition and Assumption*. Oxford: Oxford University Press, 2002.

Siecienski, A. Edward. "Mariology in Antioch: Mary in the Writings of Chrysostom, Theodoret of Cyrus, and Nestorius." *St Vladimir's Theological Quarterly* 56 (2012): 133–69.

Sisto, Walter N. "Marian Dogmas and Reunion: What Eastern Catholics Can Teach Us about Catholic Ecumenism." *Journal of Ecumenical Studies* 46 (2011): 150–62.

Smith, Christian. *The Bible Made Impossible: Why Biblicism Is Not a Truly Evangelical Reading of Scripture*. Grand Rapids, MI: Brazos Press, 2011.

Smith, Mark S. *The Early History of God: Yahweh and the Other Deities in Ancient Israel*. 2nd ed. Grand Rapids, MI: Eerdmans, 2002.

Smith, Robert Houston. "Exodus Typology in the Fourth Gospel." *Journal of Biblical Literature* 81 (1962): 329–42.

Sommer, Benjamin D. *The Bodies of God and the World of Ancient Israel*. Cambridge: Cambridge University Press, 2009.

Sparks, Kenton L. *God's Word in Human Words: An Evangelical Appropriation of Critical Biblical Scholarship*. Grand Rapids, MI: Baker Academic, 2008.

Speyr, Adrienne von. *Mary in the Redemption.* Translated from the third edition by Helena M. Tomko. San Francisco: Ignatius Press, 2003.

Sri, Edward. *Queen Mother: A Biblical Theology of Mary's Queenship.* Steubenville, OH: Emmaus Road, 2005.

Stacpoole, Alberic, O.S.B., ed. *Mary's Place in Christian Dialogue: Occasional Papers of the Ecumenical Society of the Blessed Virgin Mary, 1970–1980.* Middlegreen, England: St. Paul Publications, 1982.

Stanley, Christopher D. *Paul and the Language of Scripture: Citation Technique in the Pauline Epistles and Contemporary Literature.* Cambridge: Cambridge University Press, 1992.

Steenberg, M. C. "The Mother of God as Mediatrix in Orthodox and Roman Catholic Thought." *Sobornost* 26 (2004): 6–26.

———. "The Role of Mary as Co-recapitulator in St. Irenaeus of Lyons." *Vigiliae Christianae* 58 (2004): 117–37.

Steinhauer, Hilda. *Maria als dramatische Person bei von Balthasar: Zum marianischen Prinzip seines Denkens.* Vienna: Tyrolia Verlag, 2001.

Steinmetz, David C. "Mary Reconsidered." In *Taking the Long View: Christian Theology in Historical Perspective.* Oxford: Oxford University Press, 2011: 45–51.

Stookey, Laurence Hull. "Marcion, Typology, and Lectionary Preaching." *Worship* 66 (1992): 251–62.

Stuhlmacher, Peter. "Spiritual Remembering: John 14.26." In *The Holy Spirit and Christian Origins: Essays in Honor of James D. G. Dunn.* Edited by Graham N. Stanton, Bruce W. Longenecker, and Stephen C. Barton. Grand Rapids, MI: Eerdmans, 2004: 55–68.

Stump, Eleonore. *Aquinas.* London: Routledge, 2003.

Stylianopoulos, Theodore. "Concerning the Biblical Foundation of Primacy." In *The Petrine Ministry: Catholics and Orthodox in Dialogue.* Edited by Walter Kasper. Translated by the staff of the Pontifical Council for Promoting Christian Unity. New York: Paulist Press, 2006: 37–63.

Suenens, Léon Josef. "The Relation that Exists Between the Holy Spirit and Mary." In *Mary's Place in Christian Dialogue: Occasional Papers of the Ecumenical Society of the Blessed Virgin Mary, 1970–1980.* Edited by Alberic Stacpoole, O.S.B. Middlegreen, England: St. Paul Publications, 1982: 67–78.

Tambasco, Anthony J. *What Are They Saying about Mary?* New York: Paulist Press, 1984.

Tanner, Norman P., S.J., ed. *Decrees of the Ecumenical Councils.* Vol. 2, *Trent to Vatican II.* Washington, D.C.: Georgetown University Press, 1990.

Tapp, Christian. "Joseph Ratzinger on Resurrection Identity." In *Personal Identity and Resurrection: How Do We Survive Our Death?* Edited by George Gasser. Burlington, VT: Ashgate, 2010: 207–24.

Tavard, George H., A.A. "'Hierarchia Veritatem': A Preliminary Investigation." *Theological Studies* 32 (1971): 278–89.

———. "John Duns Scotus and the Immaculate Conception." In *The One Mediator, the Saints, and Mary: Lutherans and Catholics in Dialogue VIII*. Edited by H. George Anderson, J. Francis Stafford, and Joseph A. Burgess. Minneapolis, MN: Augsburg Fortress, 1992: 209–17.

———. *The Thousand Faces of the Virgin Mary*. Collegeville, MN: Liturgical Press, 1996.

Taylor, Joan E. *Christians and the Holy Places: The Myth of Christian Origins*. Oxford: Clarendon Press, 1993.

Testa, Emmanuele, O.F.M. "Lo sviluppo della 'Dormitio Mariae' nella letteratura, nella teologìa e nella archeologìa." *Marianum* 44 (1982): 316–89.

Thérèse of Lisieux. *Story of a Soul: The Autobiography of St. Thérèse of Lisieux*. 3rd ed. Translated by John Clarke, O.C.D. Washington, D.C.: ICS Publications, 1996.

Thompson, James W. *Pastoral Ministry according to Paul: A Biblical Vision*. Grand Rapids, MI: Baker Academic, 2006.

Thompson, Thomas M., S.M. "A Changed Context for Marian Doctrine." In *Mother, Behold Your Son: Essays in Honor of Eamon R. Carroll, O.Carm*. Edited by Donald W. Buggert, O.Carm., Louis P. Rogge, O.Carm., and Michael J. Wastag, O.Carm. Washington, D.C.: Carmelite Institute, 2001: 195–213.

Thornton, L. S. "The Mother of God in Holy Scripture." In *The Mother of God: A Symposium*. Edited by E. L. Mascall. London: Dacre Press, 1949: 9–23.

Thurian, Max. *Mary, Mother of the Lord, Figure of the Church*. Translated by Neville B. Cryer. London: Mowbray, 1985.

Tillard, J. M. R., O.P. "Sensus Fidelium." *One in Christ* 11 (1975): 2–29.

Torrell, Jean-Pierre, O.P. *La Vierge Marie dans la foi catholique*. Paris: Cerf, 2010.

Turner, Denys. "Allegory in Christian Late Antiquity." In *The Cambridge Companion to Allegory*. Edited by Rita Copeland and Peter Struck. Cambridge: Cambridge University Press, 2010: 71–82.

Turner, Max. *Power from on High: The Spirit in Israel's Restoration and Witness in Luke-Acts*. Sheffield: Sheffield Academic Press, 1996.

Unger, Dominic J. "Did Saint John See the Virgin Mary in Glory?" *Catholic Biblical Quarterly* 11 (1949): 249–62, 392–405.

———. "Did Saint John See the Virgin Mary in Glory?" *Catholic Biblical Quarterly* 12 (1950): 75–83, 155–61, 292–300, 405–15.

van Esbroeck, Michel. *Aux origines de la Dormition de la Vierge: Études historique sur les traditions orientales*. London: Variorum, 1995.

Vanhoozer, Kevin J. "Ascending the Mountain, Singing the Rock: Biblical Interpretation Earthed, Typed, and Transfigured." *Modern Theology* 28 (2012): 781–803.

————. *The Drama of Doctrine: A Canonical-Linguistic Approach to Christian Theology.* Louisville, KY: Westminster John Knox Press, 2005.

Vanhoye, Albert, S.J. "Interrogation johannique et éxègese de Cana (Jn 2:4)." *Biblica* 55 (1974): 157–67.

Venard, Olivier-Thomas, O.P. *Pagina sacra: Le passage de l'Écriture sainte à l'écriture théologique.* Paris: Cerf, 2009.

Vischer, Lukas. "Difficulties in Looking to the New Testament for Guidance." In *Unity of the Church in the New Testament and Today.* Edited by Lukas Vischer, Ulrich Luz, and Christian Link. Translated by James E. Crouch. Grand Rapids, MI: Eerdmans, 2010: 7–27.

Vischer, Lukas, Ulrich Luz, and Christian Link, eds. *Unity of the Church in the New Testament and Today.* Translated by James E. Crouch. Grand Rapids, MI: Eerdmans, 2010.

Voderholzer, Rudolf. *Meet Henri de Lubac: His Life and Work.* Translated by Michael J. Miller. San Francisco: Ignatius Press, 2008.

Vollert, Cyril, S.J. *A Theology of Mary.* New York: Herder and Herder, 1965.

von Rad, Gerhard. *Old Testament Theology.* Vol. 2. Translated by D. M. G. Stalker. New York: Harper & Row, 1965.

————. "Typological Interpretation of the Old Testament." Translated by John Bright. In *Essays on Old Testament Hermeneutics.* Edited by Claus Westermann. Richmond, VA: John Knox Press, 1964: 17–39.

Wainwright, Geoffrey. *Doxology: The Praise of God in Worship, Doctrine, and Life.* New York: Oxford University Press, 1980.

Walgrave, Jan Hendrik, O.P. *Unfolding Revelation: The Nature of Doctrinal Development.* Philadelphia: Westminster, 1972.

Walsh, Jerome T. *1 Kings.* Collegeville, MN: Liturgical Press, 1996.

Walton, John H. *The Lost World of Genesis One: Ancient Cosmology and the Origins Debate.* Downers Grove, IL: InterVarsity Press, 2009.

Ware, Kallistos. "The Mother of God in Orthodox Theology and Devotion." In *Mary's Place in Christian Dialogue: Occasional Papers of the Ecumenical Society of the Blessed Virgin Mary, 1970–1980.* Edited by Alberic Stacpoole, O.S.B. Middlegreen, England: St. Paul Publications, 1982: 169–81.

————. *The Orthodox Way,* rev. ed. Crestwood, NY: St Vladimir's Seminary Press, 2002.

Warner, Marina. *Alone of All Her Sex: The Myth and Cult of the Virgin Mary.* New York: Vintage Books, 1983.

Warner, Martin. "*Mary, Grace and Hope in Christ*: A New Understanding of Scripture and Tradition?" *International Journal for the Study of the Christian Church* 5 (2005): 265–71.

Watson, Francis, ed. *The Open Text: New Directions for Biblical Studies?* London: SCM Press, 1993.

Watts, Rikk E. *Isaiah's New Exodus in Mark.* Grand Rapids, MI: Baker Academic, 1997.

Webster, John. *Holy Scripture*. Cambridge: Cambridge University Press, 2003.

Weinandy, Thomas, O.F.M.Cap. "The Annunciation and Nativity: Undoing the Sinful Act of Eve." *International Journal of Systematic Theology* 14 (2012): 217–32.

Wells, David F. *Revolution in Rome*. London: Tyndale, 1973.

Wells, Jo Bailey. *God's Holy People: A Theme in Biblical Theology*. Sheffield: Sheffield Academic Press, 2000.

Wenger, Antoine, A.A. *L'Assomption de la T. S. Vierge dans la tradition Byzantine du VIe au Xe siècle*. Paris: Institut Français d'Études Byzantines, 1955.

Westermann, Claus, ed. *Essays on Old Testament Hermeneutics*. Richmond, VA: John Knox Press, 1964.

Weston, Keith. "Mary: An Evangelical Viewpoint." In *Mary's Place in Christian Dialogue: Occasional Papers of the Ecumenical Society of the Blessed Virgin Mary, 1970–1980*. Edited by Alberic Stacpoole, O.S.B. Middlegreen, England: St. Paul Publications, 1982: 158–66.

Weyermann, Maja. "The Typologies of Adam-Christ and Eve-Mary, and Their Relationship to One Another." *Anglican Theological Review* 84 (2002): 609–26.

White, Thomas Joseph, O.P. "The Virgin Mary and the Church: The Marian Exemplarity of Ecclesial Faith." *Nova et Vetera* 11 (2013): 375–405.

Wickert, Ulrich. *Ein evangelischer Theologe schreibt über Maria*. Berlin: Morus-Verlag, 1979.

Wilken, Robert Louis. "Jaroslav Pelikan and the Road to Orthodoxy." *Concordia Theological Quarterly* 74 (2010): 93–103.

Williams, Paul. "The Virgin Mary in Anglican Tradition." In *Mary: The Complete Resource*. Edited by Sarah Jane Boss. Oxford: Oxford University Press, 2007: 314–39.

Williams, Rowan. "The Literal Sense of Scripture." *Modern Theology* 7 (1991): 121–34.

Witherington, Ben, III. *Grace in Galatia: A Commentary on St Paul's Letter to the Galatians*. Grand Rapids, MI: Eerdmans, 1998.

———. *John's Wisdom: A Commentary on the Fourth Gospel*. Louisville, KY: Westminster John Knox Press, 1995.

———. *What Have They Done with Jesus? Beyond Strange Theories and Bad History—Why We Can Trust the Bible*. New York: HarperCollins, 2006.

———. *Women in the Ministry of Jesus*. Cambridge: Cambridge University Press, 1984.

Wolterstorff, Nicholas. *Divine Discourse: Philosophical Reflections on the Claim That God Speaks*. Cambridge: Cambridge University Press, 1995.

Woollcombe, K. J. "The Biblical Origins and Patristic Development of Typology." In *Essays on Typology*, by G. W. H. Lampe and K. J. Woollcombe. Naperville, IL: Alec R. Allenson, 1957: 39–75.

Wright, John J. *Mary Our Hope: A Selection from the Sermons, Addresses, and Papers of Cardinal John J. Wright.* Edited by R. Stephen Almagno, O.F.M. San Francisco: Ignatius Press, 1984.

Wright, N. T. *Jesus and the Victory of God.* Minneapolis, MN: Fortress Press, 1996.

———. *The New Testament and the People of God.* Minneapolis, MN: Fortress Press, 1992.

———. "Response to Richard Hays." In *Jesus, Paul and the People of God: A Theological Dialogue with N. T. Wright.* Edited by Nicholas Perrin and Richard B. Hays. Downers Grove, IL: InterVarsity Press, 2011: 62–65.

———. *Surprised by Hope: Rethinking Heaven, the Resurrection, and the Mission of the Church.* New York: HarperCollins, 2008.

———. "Whence and Whither Historical Jesus Studies in the Life of the Church?" In *Jesus, Paul and the People of God: A Theological Dialogue with N. T. Wright.* Edited by Nicholas Perrin and Richard B. Hays. Downers Grove, IL: InterVarsity Press, 2011: 115–58.

Yarnold, Edward J., S.J. "Marian Dogmas and Reunion." *The Month* 131 (June 1971): 177–79.

Yeago, David. "The Presence of Mary in the Mystery of the Church." In *Mary, Mother of God.* Edited by Carl E. Braaten and Robert W. Jenson. Grand Rapids, MI: Eerdmans, 2004: 58–79.

Young, Frances M. "Allegory and the Ethics of Reading." In *The Open Text: New Directions for Biblical Studies?* Edited by Francis Watson. London: SCM Press, 1993: 103–20.

———. *The Art of Performance: Towards a Theology of Holy Scripture.* London: Darton, Longman & Todd, 1993.

———. *Biblical Exegesis and the Formation of Christian Culture.* Cambridge: Cambridge University Press, 1997.

———. "Exegetical Method and Scriptural Proof: The Bible in Doctrinal Debate." *Studia Patristica* 19 (1989): 291–304.

———. "Typology." In *Crossing the Boundaries: Essays in Biblical Interpretation in Honour of Michael D. Goulder.* Edited by Stanley E. Porter, Paul Joyce, and David E. Orton. New York: E. J. Brill, 1994: 29–48.

Index

Beattie, Tina, 223n10
Bellarmine, Robert, 19
Benedict XII, 55, 57
Benedict XVI. *See* Ratzinger, Joseph
Benedictus Deus (1336), 55
Benko, Stephen, 159n25, 175n55,
    184n104
Bernadino of Siena, 19
Biel, Gabriel, 201n21
Boersma, Hans, 9
Bonaventure, 19
Book of Biblical Antiquities, 98, 100
Bouyer, Louis, 10, 51–52, 67–71,
    73–74, 79, 184nn103–4
Brown, Raymond E., 220n45
Brueggemann, Walter, 216n11
Bulgakov, Sergius, 184n102
Bultmann, Rudolf, 91
burning bush, 117
Byzantine liturgy, 18

Cain, 97, 107, 133, 137
Calvary, 164n7
Calvin, John, 201n19
Cana, wedding at, 23, 27, 31, 69, 144,
    164n7
Cessario, Romanus, 215n8
circumcision, 106
Claudel, Paul, 41
Collins, Raymond F., 208n58, 210n66
Clooney, Francis X., 175n55
Communio (journal), 51, 59
communio sanctorum. See communion
    of the saints
communion of the saints, 21, 64,
    166n17
Concilium (journal), 51
concupiscence, 42
Congar, Yves, 162n46, 211n74, 215n2
Congregation for the Doctrine of the
    Faith, 25, 73, 148, 185n113
Council of Constantinople, 126

Council of Ephesus, 2, 25
Council of Nicaea, 155n6
Council of Trent, 42, 83, 155n6,
    199n10
Cross. *See* Jesus Christ: Cross
Cullmann, Oscar, 214n90
Culpepper, Gary, 162n43
Cunneen, Sally, 215n2

Daley, Brian, 3, 157n15
Daniel (prophet), 97
Daniélou, Jean, 50–51, 53, 168n33,
    187n1, 214n90
Daughter Zion: Israel as, 74; Mary as
    (*see* Mary: Daughter Zion)
David (king), 78, 134–35, 145, 216n16
Dawe, Donald G., 221n51
de Gaál, Emery, 165n12
de Lubac, Henri, 50–51, 168n33
de Margerie, Bertrand, 213n88
de Satgé, John, 224n14
Dei Verbum (Dogmatic Constitution
    on Divine Revelation), 215n2
Deiparae Virginis Mariae (encyclical),
    18
deposit of faith, 15, 17, 34, 43, 45,
    150–51
devil. *See* Satan
DeVille, Adam A. J., 202n27
Duhr, Joseph, 33–36, 38, 47, 154n2,
    171n5
Dulles, Avery, 4–5, 198n3, 213n88
Dunn, James D. G., 151

ecclesiology, 16, 22, 161n35, 200n15,
    211n74
Eichrodt, Walther, 194n71
Elijah, 8, 35, 37, 116–19, 128, 202n23
Elisha, 118–19
Elizabeth (mother of John the Baptist),
    19, 23, 26, 39, 68, 79, 129, 135,
    138, 145, 169n34

Enns, Peter, 10, 84–85, 95–105,
109–10, 197n105
Enoch, 8, 37, 99, 133, 202n23, 216n11
Ephrem the Syrian, 44
Epiphanius of Salamis, 35
Ernst, Johann, 34, 36
Esau, 98
eschatology, 10, 57, 92, 94
Esther, 74
Eucharist, 10, 29, 44, 59–60, 83, 88–89,
108, 112, 124, 155n6, 211n72
Evdokimov, Paul, 115, 209n63
Eve, 7–8, 11, 26, 36–38, 43–44, 65,
67–68, 71, 74, 84, 133, 135, 141,
149, 152, 160n32, 167n22; new
Eve (*see* Mary: new or second Eve)
exodus, the, 85–87, 90, 95, 98, 100,
106–8, 117, 134
Ezekiel, 134
Ezra, 140

Fall, the, 10, 36–37, 42–43, 46, 74, 132,
137–38, 149
Father. *See* God the Father
First Vatican Council, 5, 113–15
Fitzmyer, Joseph A., 184n99, 209n59,
217n19, 218n22, 218n25, 219n31
Florovsky, Georges, 125, 219n32
Francis de Sales, 19
Frings, Joseph Cardinal, 22

Gabriel, 19, 39, 42, 68, 76, 97, 134
Garrigou-Lagrange, Réginald, 10, 33,
38–48, 50, 175n55
George, Timothy, 160n32
Germanus of Constantinople, 18
God the Father, 11, 22, 25, 40–42, 48,
53, 60–61, 67, 70, 112, 120–21,
123, 125, 141, 144, 148, 151,
199n8, 201n21
Goodrich, John K., 208n57
Goulder, Michael D., 196n101, 206n49

grace, 6, 17, 22, 24–29, 31, 33, 39–45,
52–53, 71, 74, 77–78, 86, 90,
92–93, 99, 126, 131–32, 134–35,
137, 149, 152, 159n25, 160n32,
184n103, 216n12, 217n19,
219n32
Greek Orthodox liturgy, 126
Green, Joel, 169n34
Griffiths, Paul J., 8, 168n33
Gundry, Stanley, 109

Hagar, 105–6, 139
Hannah (mother of Samuel), 74, 139,
219n33
Harnack, Adolf von, 91
Hays, Richard B., 10, 84–95, 102–4,
109, 183n95, 187n2, 189n14,
190n23, 191n46
Hazael, 118
Healy, Kilian J., 154n4
Hegel, G. W. F., 194n86, 222n1
Hengel, Martin, 205n45
historical criticism, 94–95
Holy Spirit, 1–2, 7–8, 10–11, 17, 22,
24–26, 28, 32, 35–36, 38, 40–41,
44, 47, 60, 62, 68, 70, 75–76,
79–80, 84, 86–88, 91, 94–96, 103,
105, 109–10, 112, 115, 120–21,
123–26, 128–29, 134–35, 140–42,
148–49, 151–52, 162n46, 163n1,
171n5, 175n55, 184n103,
197n105, 203n28, 204n34,
207n51, 215n8, 217n19, 221n51,
222n1; divinity of, 125
Horeb. *See* Sinai (Horeb)
Hoskins, Paul M., 211n72
Humanae Vitae (encyclical), 213n88
Humani Generis (encyclical), 51
Hurtado, Larry, 151

iconography, 4, 18, 69, 134, 157n15
Illative Sense, 156n11

tradition (*cont.*)
  154n4, 175nn54–55, 189n14,
  199nn10–11, 207n54, 212n82,
  214n90, 220n45
Transfiguration, 61, 120, 143
transubstantiation, 112, 155n6
Trinity, 22, 125, 136, 217n19
Troeltsch, Ernst, 185n108, 200n15
tropology, 108
typology (or, typological exegesis),
  2–3, 5, 7–10, 16–17, 19–21,
  24–25, 30–32, 36–38, 40, 43,
  47–50, 52, 61, 65, 67, 71, 73–95,
  101–10, 112, 126, 129, 132, 136,
  145, 147, 149–51, 157n15,
  158n24, 160n32, 167n22, 168n33,
  169n34, 170n35, 180n47,
  187nn1–2, 189n12, 191n46,
  191n52, 193nn60–61, 194n71,
  194n82, 195n90, 195n92,
  196n101, 197n105, 204n34,
  204n42, 211n72, 215n2

Vanhoozer, Kevin, 9, 152
Vatican I. *See* First Vatican Council
Vatican II. *See* Second Vatican Council
Vischer, Lukas, 201n22
Visitation, 31
Vollert, Cyril, 172n24

Walton, John, 132
Ware, Kallistos, 2–3, 9
Warner, Marina, 162n37
water from the rock, 86, 88–89,
  100–101, 105–6, 108, 117
Witherington III, Ben, 218n24
Wright, N. T., 166n17, 205n47

Yarnold, Edward, 213n88
Yeago, David, 222n8
Young, Frances M., 189n12

Zechariah (father of John the Baptist),
  39, 169n34

Matthew Levering

is the Perry Family Foundation Professor of Theology at Mundelein Seminary.

He is the author of a number of books, including

*Participatory Biblical Exegesis: A Theology of Biblical Interpretation
and Christ's Fulfillment of Torah* and *Temple: Salvation according
to Thomas Aquinas*, both also published by

the University of Notre Dame Press.